THE LIMITS OF LOYALTY

AUSTRIAN AND HABSBURG STUDIES
General Editor: Gary B. Cohen, Center for Austrian Studies,
University of Minnesota

Volume 1
*Austrian Women in the Nineteenth and Twentieth Centuries:
Cross-Disciplinary Perspectives*
Edited by David F. Good, Margarete Grandner, and Mary Jo Maynes

Volume 2
*From World War to Waldheim: Culture and Politics in Austria and
the United States*
Edited by David F. Good and Ruth Wodak

Volume 3
Rethinking Vienna 1900
Edited by Steven Beller

Volume 4
*The Great Tradition and Its Legacy: The Evolution of Dramatic and Musical
Theater in Austria and Central Europe*
Edited by Michael Cherlin, Halina Filipowicz, and Richard L. Rudolph

Volume 5
*Creating the "Other": Ethnic Conflict and Nationalism in Habsburg
Central Europe*
Edited by Nancy M. Wingfield

Volume 6
Constructing Nationalities in East Central Europe
Edited by Pieter M. Judson and Marsha L. Rozenblit

Volume 7
The Environment and Sustainable Development in the New Central Europe
Edited by Zbigniew Bochniarz and Gary B. Cohen

Volume 8
Crime, Jews and News
Edited by Daniel Mark Vyleta

Volume 9
*The Limits of Loyalty: Imperial Symbolism, Popular Allegiances, and State
Patriotism in the Late Habsburg Monarchy*
Edited by Laurence Cole and Daniel L. Unowsky

THE LIMITS OF LOYALTY
*Imperial symbolism, popular allegiances,
and state patriotism in
the late Habsburg Monarchy*

Edited by
Laurence Cole
and
Daniel L. Unowsky

Berghahn Books
NEW YORK • OXFORD

First published in 2007 by
Berghahn Books

www.berghahnbooks.com

© 2007, 2009 Laurence Cole and Daniel L. Unowsky
First paperback edition published in 2009

All rights reserved.
Except for the quotation of short passages
for the purposes of criticism and review, no part of this book
may be reproduced in any form or by any means, electronic or
mechanical, including photocopying, recording, or any information
storage and retrieval system now known or to be invented,
without written permission of the publisher.

Library of Congress Cataloging-in-Publication Data

The limits of loyalty : imperial symbolism, popular allegiances, and state patriotism in the late Habsburg monarchy / edited by Laurence Cole and Daniel L. Unowsky.
 p. cm. — (Austrian and Habsburg studies ; v. 9)
Includes bibliographical references and index.
ISBN 978-1-84545-202-5 (hbk) -- ISBN 978-1-84545-717-4 (pbk)
 1. Habsburg, House of. 2. Austria—Politics and government—1848–1918. 3. Europe, Central—Politics and government. 4. Nationalism—Austria. 5. Group identity—Austria. I. Cole, Laurence. II. Unowsky, Daniel L., 1966– .

DB47.L56 2007
943.6'04—dc22

2007034705

British Library Cataloguing in Publication Data

A catalogue record for this book is available from the British Library

Printed in the United States on acid-free paper

ISBN: 978-1-84545-202-5   hardback
ISBN: 978-1-84545-717-4   paperback

Contents

Contributors — vii

List of Illustrations — ix

Introduction — 1
    Laurence Cole and Daniel L. Unowsky

1. Patriotic and National Myths: National Consciousness and Elementary School Education in Imperial Austria — 11
    Ernst Bruckmüller

2. Military Veterans and Popular Patriotism in Imperial Austria, 1870–1914 — 36
    Laurence Cole

3. Emperor Joseph II in the Austrian Imagination up to 1914 — 62
    Nancy M. Wingfield

4. The Flyspecks on Palivec's Portrait: Francis Joseph, the Symbols of Monarchy, and Czech Popular Loyalty — 86
    Hugh LeCaine Agnew

5. Celebrating Two Emperors and a Revolution: The Public Contest to Represent the Polish and Ruthenian Nations in 1880 — 113
    Daniel L. Unowsky

6. Empress Elisabeth as Hungarian Queen: The Uses of Celebrity Monarchism — 138
    Alice Freifeld

7. State Ritual and Ritual Parody: Croatian Student Protest and
   the Limits of Loyalty at the End of the Nineteenth Century   162
   Sarah Kent

8. Collective Identifications and Austro-Hungarian Jews (1914–1918):
   The Contradictions and Travails of Avigdor Hameiri   178
   Alon Rachamimov

9. Representing Constitutional Monarchy in Late Nineteenth and
   Early Twentieth-century Britain, Germany, and Austria   199
   Christiane Wolf

Afterword   223
   R.J.W. Evans

Select Bibliography   233

Index   236

CONTRIBUTORS

Hugh LeCaine Agnew is Professor of History and International Affairs and Associate Dean of Faculty and Student Affairs at George Washington University. He is the author of *Origins of the Czech National Renascence* (1993), and most recently, *The Czechs and the Lands of the Bohemian Crown* (2004).

Ernst Bruckmüller is Professor of Economic and Social History at the University of Vienna. He was joint coordinator of a major project on the history of the bourgeoisie in the Habsburg Monarchy. His most important works include *Sozialgeschichte Österreichs* (2nd edition, 2001) and *Nation Österreich: kulturelles Bewußtsein und gesellschaftlich-politische Prozesse* (2nd, expanded edition, 1996), which has also appeared in translation as *The Austrian Nation: Cultural Consciousness and Socio-Political Processes* (2003).

Laurence Cole is Lecturer in Modern European History at the University of East Anglia. He is the author of *Für Gott, Kaiser und Vaterland: Nationale Identität der deutschsprachigen Bevölkerung Tirols 1860–1914* (2000), and has recently edited *Different Paths to the Nation: National and Regional Identities in Central Europe and Italy, 1830–1870* (2007). Currently, he is co-editor of *European History Quarterly*.

R.J.W. Evans is Regius Professor of History at the University of Oxford. His most well-known work is *The Making of the Habsburg Monarchy, 1550–1770: an Interpretation* (1979), and he has edited several collections, including (both with H. Pogge von Strandmann) *The Coming of the First World War* (1990) and *The Revolutions in Europe, 1848–9: From Reform to Reaction* (2000). Most recently, he has published a volume of his essays, *Austria, Hungary, and the Habsburgs: Central Europe, c. 1683–1867* (2006).

Alice Freifeld is Associate Professor of History at the University of Florida. Her book, *Nationalism and the Crowd in Liberal Hungary, 1848–1914* (2000), was awarded the 2001 Barbara Jelavich Book Prize of the American Association for the Advancement of Slavic Studies. She is also co-editor (with Peter Bergmann and Bernice Glatzer Rosenthal) of *East Europe Reads Nietzsche* (1998). She is currently working on a study of displaced persons in Hungary after World War II.

Sarah Kent is Professor of History at the University of Wisconsin-Stevens Point. She has published articles on Croatia and Bosnia and is completing a monograph on Franz Joseph's visit to Zagreb in 1895.

Alon Rachamimov is a Senior Lecturer in Modern European History at Tel Aviv University. He is the author of *POWs and the Great War: Captivity on the Eastern Front* (2002), which was awarded the Fraenkel Prize for Contemporary History for a first major work. He is currently working on a comparative study of POW theaters during World War I.

Daniel L. Unowsky is Professor of History at the University of Memphis. He is the author of *The Pomp and Politics of Patriotism: Imperial Celebrations in Habsburg Austria, 1848–1916* (2005), and is working on a study of the 1898 anti-Jewish riots in the Habsburg province of Galicia.

Nancy Wingfield is Professor of History at Northern Illinois University. Among her published works are: *Staging the Past: The Politics of Commemorations in Habsburg Central Europe, 1848 to the Present* (2001) and *Gender and War in Twentieth-Century Eastern Europe* (2006), both edited with Maria Bucur. Her most recent book, *Flag Wars and Stone Saints: How the Bohemian Lands Became Czech* was published by Harvard University Press in 2007.

Christiane Wolf is completing her PhD at the University of Tübingen, and has published articles on Imperial Germany and the comparative history of monarchical cults in late nineteenth-century Europe.

Illustrations

Map 1	Austria-Hungary, 1910	x
Figure 3.1	Statue of Joseph II in Josefsplatz, Vienna.	65
Figure 4.1	Radetzky monument in Prague's Malostranské náměstí/Kleinseitner Ring.	90
Figure 4.2	The May 1868 laying of the foundation stones for the Czech National Theater in Prague.	94
Figure 4.3	The 1868 ceremony at the Czech National Theater construction site in Prague.	95
Figure 4.4	Idealized coronation portrait of Francis Joseph as King of Bohemia.	100
Figure 4.5	The Crown Jewels of the Kingdom of Bohemia.	107
Figure 5.1	Wojciech Kossak, *His Majesty accepts a petition*, 1881.	117
Figure 5.2	Market Square in modern Lviv.	121
Figure 5.3	St. George Cathedral in modern Lviv.	126
Figure 5.4	Ruthenian National Institute in modern Lviv.	127
Figure 6.1	Elisabeth and Franz Joseph as the hands of a pair of scissors.	140
Figure 6.2	Elisabeth in Hungarian folk dress.	144
Figure 6.3	In loving remembrance of our Queen, 1837–1896.	156
Figure 6.4	Embroidered World War I Hungarian wall hanging.	157

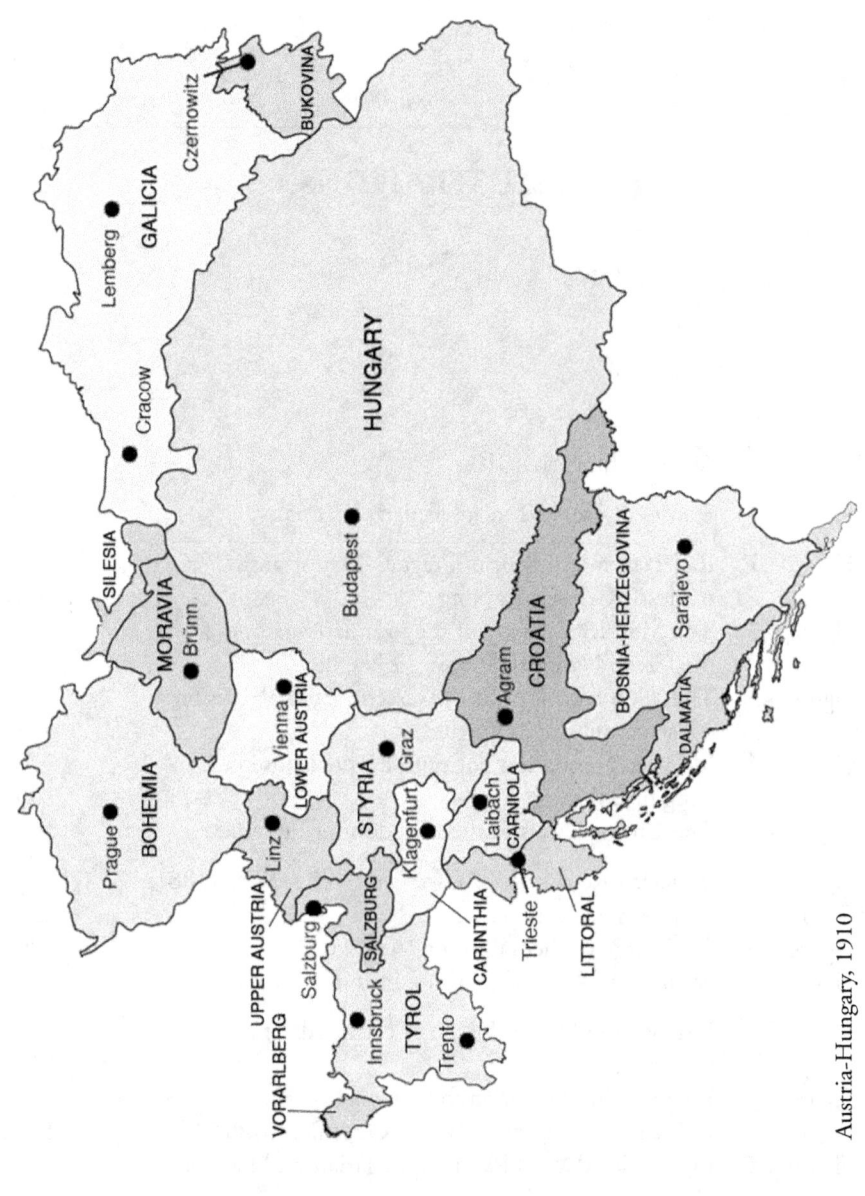

Austria-Hungary, 1910

INTRODUCTION

Imperial Loyalty and Popular Allegiances
in the Late Habsburg Monarchy

Historians and other social scientists have always been concerned with issues of nationalism and national identity, but scholarly interest has expanded rapidly since the publication of a number of influential general works in the 1980s.[1] The research wave intensified during the 1990s in the aftermath of the collapse of the Soviet Empire, as war and ethnic conflicts tragically unfolded in the former USSR and Yugoslavia (while the Czechoslovak state was also dissolved, although in peaceful fashion). At the same time, the passing of the Warsaw pact witnessed a renewed surge of interest—both on the part of the general public and that of scholars—in the history of the region, including that of the Habsburg Monarchy.

These developments have helped produce two notable trends in research on East Central Europe. On the one hand, the collapse of the Soviet bloc has given rise to more comparative discussions of multiethnic empires and imperial collapse.[2] On the other hand, historians investigating the history of the nationalities problem in the multiethnic Habsburg state have begun to revise previous views of the challenges it faced, particularly for the western half of Austria-Hungary. Where general assessments of late nineteenth and early twentieth-century Austria-Hungary once routinely described a situation of terminal crisis, current verdicts are less condemnatory. Alongside the major difficulties caused by national conflicts, historians recognize a more complex and nuanced picture, which includes a better understanding of the constitutional frameworks provided in 1867, the development of political parties and civil society, and the social and economic transformation of Central and East Central Europe.[3] As Gary Cohen has put it, the late Habsburg Monarchy was characterized neither by "absolutism, nor anarchy."[4] Yet, if these developments have opened up new vistas and have encouraged a more refined image of the Habsburg Monarchy, it is still the case that there are some surprising gaps in current scholarship, not least to do with the institution that gave the state its name—the Habsburg dynasty itself.[5]

At least implicitly, the starting point for many investigations of the dynamics of the Habsburg state continues to be Oscar Jászi's famous paradigm of opposing "centrifugal" and "centripetal" forces in Austria-Hungary.[6] Among the former, Jászi placed nationalism first and foremost, together with the awkward "dual-state" character of Austria-Hungary, and the "exploitative" economic relationship between its two halves. Jászi juxtaposed these factors undermining the unity of the state with centripetal forces such as the dynasty, the church, the army, and bureaucracy, as well as specific social groups (Jewish communities) and political forces (socialism). Scholars of the Habsburg Monarchy have largely accepted Jászi's centrifugal/centripetal opposition and focused their attention on those forces militating against state cohesion. Overviews of Habsburg history, as well as numerous articles and monographic studies, highlight particular moments in the Habsburg past when the state failed to overcome these centripetal pressures, detoured from the path leading to healthy modernization, and turned toward inevitable decline and dissolution. For some scholars, the decline begins as early as 1790, with the death of Joseph II and the demise of his centralizing project. Others point to 1815 and the failure to build on the momentum gained by victory in the Napoleonic wars, or to a more familiar catalogue of defeated liberal revolutions in 1848–49, military losses to Piedmont and Prussia, the tensions inherent in the 1867 Compromise creating Austria-Hungary, and so on. Whichever "missed opportunity" is selected, scholars have generally tended to view nationalism as the most significant factor propelling the state toward its ultimate collapse.[7]

By contrast, comparatively little attention has been devoted to the centripetal forces identified by Jászi. More importantly, perhaps, even less scholarship has explicitly questioned the assumption of inherent opposition between national consciousness and imperial loyalty, which is at the heart of Jászi's approach.[8] As recent work shows, the history of the late Habsburg Monarchy cannot just be reduced to a narrative of rising nationalism and diminishing state unity, for the spread of national movements was accompanied by an expansion in forms of monarchical self-representation and dynastic political rituals that aimed to promote a "supranational" patriotism.[9] In short, there is a matter of balance to be achieved: while historians must examine why the Habsburg Monarchy collapsed when it did, they should also ask what held it together for so long. Indeed, only by answering the last question effectively can one expect to provide a satisfactory response to the former.

Particularly apposite here is the brilliant vignette on the year 1898 in Hungary written by the late Hungarian scholar Péter Hanák, who described the "parallel action" by Hungarian nationalists celebrating the 50th anniversary of the 1848 revolution and rebellion against Habsburg rule in the same year—1898—as the festivities for Emperor Franz Joseph's 50th jubilee.[10] In effect, Hanák posited the existence of "parallel realities" in the Habsburg Monarchy: a national reality, where the primary bonds were determined by language and ethnic identity; and a supranational, Habsburg-patriotic reality, defined by loyalty to the dynasty and positive acceptance of the multinational state. Hanák acknowledged the potential power of the latter, but suggested that it was only a sham reality by 1898, one with a spectacular appearance whose once vivid colors were fading fast. In practice, however, it remains to be discovered in detail how these parallel realities worked, not just within Habsburg society as a whole, but within provinces, social classes, ethnic groups, and even individuals. And just as pertinent, it is further open to question as to whether these realities were indeed simply "parallel" and therefore "separate," as Hanák seems to imply, or whether there was not in fact overlap between the national and dynastic or "supranational" spheres.

In order to investigate such issues, a widening of perspective is required. If historians now recognize the different layers of national, regional, and local identities present in Austro-Hungarian society, it follows that the imperial level must be incorporated properly into the analysis of popular allegiances.[11] Eric Hobsbawm once wrote that "it would be desirable to see a study of the attempts by more authentically legitimist dynasties, such as those of the Habsburg and the Romanov, not merely to command the obedience of their peoples as subjects, but to rally their loyalty as potential citizens."[12] Yet, although the role of the dynasty as a binding force for the Habsburg state is mentioned in general works, historians have not seriously engaged with such issues for the period from the mid-nineteenth century onward. To a great extent, the region's subsequent history explains the lack of scholarly attention to the functioning of the "kingship mechanism" in the case of the penultimate Habsburg ruler, Emperor Franz Joseph (1848–1916). In the successor states that rejected "the Habsburg yoke," historians concentrated on investigating the history of their "oppressed" national pasts. And in an Austria characterized by partisan politics in the twentieth century, the subject has been either ignored or viewed uncritically through a semi-nostalgic lens.[13] The handful of serious studies of Franz Joseph and dynastic loyalty in the late Habsburg Monarchy contrasts sharply with the growing body of work on the political and symbolic roles of medieval, renaissance, and baroque courts in Europe, including those of the early modern Habsburgs.[14] There is also considerable scholarly literature on other European countries examining the social and cultural process now conventionally described as "the invention of tradition," namely, the efforts by states and dynasties to create new festivities, establish symbols, and organize ritualized public celebrations in order to bolster state patriotism and/or reaffirm the importance of royalty in the era of mass political mobilization.[15]

By comparison, almost ninety years after it collapsed, we still know far too little about how the modern Habsburg Monarchy worked as a state and social system in which the dynasty provided a symbolic center and formed a deep-rooted element in the "mental structure" of central/east central European society. Certainly, historians such as Robert Kann and Stephen Fischer-Galati pointed some time ago to the role of "loyalty to the Emperor" (*Kaisertreue*) in contemporary political discourse.[16] Friedrich Heer's classic study on Austrian identity also considered the importance of the once sacral image of the emperor, while simultaneously observing that there has not been any attempt at an "anthropological, ethnographical or psychological investigation into belief in the Emperor."[17] Heer was especially concerned with the long-term picture, but his remark can also be applied to the question of popular allegiances in the nineteenth century, because the majority of treatments of Emperor Franz Joseph, his court, members of the imperial family, and imperial celebrations are, with some significant exceptions, limited to popular accounts of family scandals, Elisabeth's beauty secrets, and coffee table books readily available in souvenir shops in Vienna and elsewhere.[18] It is only in the last five to ten years that historians have seriously started to examine the renewal of imperial ritual and celebration as a tool for bolstering state unity and imperial loyalty, and to analyze the adaptation of dynastic imagery by rival political movements in the Habsburg lands in the final decades of the state's existence.[19]

The essays in this volume expand on this emerging body of work and seek to broaden the research agenda by integrating the institution of the dynasty into the study of the Habsburg state and the lives of its inhabitants. The authors examine institutional mechanisms such as schools and the military, which were utilized by the multinational state in its efforts to mobilize the loyalty of its citizens in an age of widening political participation. At the same time, by exploring issues of state patriotism, imperial loyalty, and popular allegiances in various provincial contexts and from differing perspectives, the articles collected here seek to understand how national identities and dynastic loyalties stood in relation to each other, whether in perpetual conflict or complementing one another. Taken together, these essays consider the degree to which the Habsburg dynasty retained meaning and relevance in an emerging modern, mass society, and they assess how successful such efforts at "supranational" integration were. As Hobsbawm noted, we know that the Habsburg state eventually failed in this regard since, after all, the monarchy collapsed in 1918. But was this ultimate failure a "foregone conclusion"?[20] How did the Habsburgs fight against what Francis Oakley has recently described as "the fading nimbus" of modern kingship in a "disenchanted world"?[21]

A first stage in the analysis of this overall problem is provided by an examination of some of the institutional mechanisms used to inspire state loyalty, an area which has been the subject of only a handful of studies hitherto, mainly with regard to the bureaucracy.[22] In his essay, Ernst Bruckmüller explores a crucial area highlighted by Oskar Jászi, namely what the latter alleged to be the Habsburg state's failure to develop a systematic patriotic education designed to ensure the loyalty of future generations to the dynasty and the common fatherland.[23] In analyzing classroom materials used in the Austrian half of the monarchy, Bruckmüller shows that, despite the heavy emphasis placed on the Habsburg family and efforts made to avoid offending ethnic sensibilities, the textbooks used for the study of history in the monarchy's schools did in fact present a coherent message of unity and loyalty, while simultaneously incorporating a range of national myths and local traditions.

Next to the dynasty, the Habsburg army is often seen as one of the key bulwarks of the state, not least because the common army was one of the few institutions active in both halves of the monarchy. The common army was the chief guarantor of the physical unity of the state and was, as István Deák's acclaimed study of the Habsburg Officer Corps illustrated, a potential school of patriotism.[24] Equally, the organization of military veterans associations throughout the monarchy created an institutional basis for widespread patriotic activities. Laurence Cole offers here the first extensive scholarly treatment of these groups. His case study focuses on the south-western periphery of the monarchy, the Italian-speaking Tirol/Trentino, and examines the complex reasons behind the growing popularity of this Habsburg-patriotic movement among considerable—but not all—sections of the population.

Moving from an analysis of institutional mechanisms, the next group of essays focuses more closely on the dynasty. These essays indicate two important aspects of how the dynasty functioned in relation to society. First, the monarch may be said to have possessed a multiple persona in legal and symbolic terms, as embodied in the famous list recited when the mortal remains of deceased Habsburg rulers sought entry to the Capuchin crypt in Vienna for burial. As well as being Emperor of Austria and King of Hungary, Franz Joseph was of course also the—uncrowned—King of Bohemia, alongside his numerous other titles. Habsburg historiography, with its emphasis on individual nationalities within specific crownlands, has largely ignored this dimension to Bohemian history. Hugh Agnew addresses this subject by describing Franz Joseph's visits to Bohemia and the unfulfilled popular expectations that he be crowned Bohemian king. By looking at the series of imperial visits as well as symbolic representations of the Bohemian crown, Agnew suggests how, over time, the image of the crown became less a reminder of Bohemia's link to the Habsburg state than a popular symbol of potential, and later actual, Czech statehood.

Second, the dynasty was multifaceted, by virtue of the range of personalities—both living and historical—that it could offer as points of reference for the peoples under its rule. Put most simply, if one member of the Habsburg dynasty did not attract popular support, there was always another who might be chosen as a channel for maintaining a link with the monarchy and expressing loyalty (and, perhaps also, thereby implicitly presenting an idealized vision of how the current monarch should be). Such a picture, for much of his reign at least, seems to fit with Franz Joseph's role as Hungarian King. His wife Elisabeth, Empress of Austria and Queen of Hungary, remains a popular presence in the souvenir shops of central European cities, but serious scholarly considerations of her personal popularity in Hungary and the political significance of her role as Hungarian queen are far rarer than popular treatments of her fitness regime and eating disorders. Alice Freifeld explores this gap in the scholarly literature through an exploration of Elisabeth's role as an actor on the Hungarian political stage, placing her contribution to the reconciliation of Hungary to Dualism at the center of her analysis. By way of contrast, Nancy Wingfield's piece turns to the complex and contested memorialization of Emperor Joseph II, the only member of the Habsburg clan who bequeathed to posterity a personalized neologism ("Josephinism"). She demonstrates how different social and ethnic groups imbued Joseph II's image with contrasting interpretations during the nineteenth century: he was celebrated as protector of the peasantry, advocate of Jewish freedoms, promoter of progress, creator of the centralized modern bureaucratic state, and opponent of baroque religious practice. Wingfield argues that, in the context of the ethnically defined political battles of the late nineteenth century, the image of Joseph II became increasingly associated with German nationality within the Austrian state, such that his memory no longer served as a unifying symbol of the common fatherland.

In addition to studying dynastic self-representation and perceptions of the dynasty in various parts of the Habsburg Monarchy, other essays underline the important point that explorations of the "invention of tradition" must consider how a variety of social groups and provincial and municipal institutions participated in the process of cultural construction and appropriated dynastic traditions for their own purposes.[25] Given that many studies of "invented tradition" or "imagined communities" pay insufficient attention to the impact in society at large of cultural images or forms of public representation, particular emphasis is placed here on the "reception of tradition" in the various Habsburg lands. One further route into this terrain is offered by discussion of the changes occurring at the political center after the defeat of the 1848–49 revolutions, when Franz Joseph's court sought to restore Habsburg prestige through the revival of formal imperial celebrations, including imperial inspection tours of the provinces.[26] Daniel Unowsky's article shifts the focus to Galicia, the northeastern border province today divided between Poland and Ukraine, and examines three public events from 1880—Franz Joseph's inspection tour, the commemorations of the fiftieth anniversary of the 1830 uprising in Russian Poland, and the centenary celebration of Joseph II's accession to the throne. Analyzing the interplay between ethnic groups, regional institutions, and the Habsburg state, Unowsky argues that national movements within the monarchy must be understood within the context of ongoing interaction with existing and expanding imperial loyalties. If imperial visits could thus bolster the popularity of the political center, the presence of the emperor-king in the provinces also offered opportunities for competing political factions to interpret the monarchical celebration in local political terms, as Sarah Kent likewise shows in her contribution about Croatia in the year 1895. Kent's piece is at once a narrative of a seemingly traditional Habsburg imperial progress and an acute analysis of the challenges to the existing state structures arising in the era of modern political mobilization.

A focus on specific events and particular regions of the monarchy reveals the range of shifting, intricate responses to the imperial message. It is also clear that complex processes of identification and self-definition could take place on an individual level. Alon Rachamimov draws on recent theoretical discussions surrounding the meaning of "identity" and "nationhood" in his exploration of Avigdor Hameiri, most widely remembered today as a major Hebrew writer. Hameiri identified himself at various times and in different contexts as, among other things, a Zionist, a Hungarian patriot, and a Habsburg loyalist. Through his discussion of Hameiri, Rachamimov offers a critique of the historiography of nationalism and of Habsburg Jewry, introducing a new framework for understanding the relationship between Jews and the Habsburg polity.

In the final essay, Christiane Wolf demonstrates that the Habsburg dynasty sought to adapt to the demands of constitutional politics and the modern world in similar ways to those of its European counterparts. Wolf looks at the Habsburg, Hohenzollern, and Saxe-Coburg (later, Windsor) monarchs as active political agents, comparing their respective constitutional roles as well as contemporary discussions concerning the success of these monarchs in fulfilling their subjects' expectations. Utilizing this comparative approach, Wolf evaluates the degree to which Franz Joseph provided a meaningful counterbalance to nationalism. Franz Joseph may have portrayed himself as the "last monarch of the old school," but Wolf's essay, together with the others in this volume, indicate that the Habsburg dynasty adapted to the changing constitutional and mass political environment in a number of ways.

A powerful monarchical cult surrounding the figure of Franz Joseph emerged simultaneously with the development of vibrant national movements in the Habsburg Monarchy. This cult and the related efforts at promoting a "supranational" form of identification proved effective to differing degrees, and the authors in this volume recognize both the extent and the limits to its success. Clearly, the Habsburg polity was not the harmonious "European Union ahead of its time" claimed by some of the more fanciful nostalgists who have emerged with greater voice since 1989.[27] But neither was it completely unloved, nor left helplessly marooned by the challenges of modernity. Contrary to the picture painted in Robert Musil's oft-cited work, *The Man without Qualities,* where the famous "parallel action" for the monarch's projected seventieth jubilee seems to exist in a form of never-never land, the Habsburg dynasty did undertake a series of concrete measures to provide a sense of unity above and alongside national identities. The essays presented here switch the focus of historical discussion toward those elements in society that accepted and positively supported the multinational state. Collectively, these essays suggest that the growth of national consciousness and the development of a dynastic-based patriotism was not necessarily a zero-sum game. What emerges is a more complex picture of the Habsburg Monarchy, one which recognizes more readily its contradictions and ambivalences.

Notes

1. For a good overview of the history of research into nationalism, see Paul Lawrence, *Nationalism. History and Theory* (Harlow, 2005). Of the key theoretical works, see above all John Breuilly, *Nationalism and the State* (Manchester, 1982); Ernest Gellner, *Nations and Nationalism* (Ithaca and London, 1983); Benedict Anderson, *Imagined Communities. Reflec-*

tions *on the Origin and Spread of Nationalism* (London, 1983); Peter Alter, *Nationalismus* (Frankfurt a.M., 1985); Miroslav Hroch, *Social Preconditions for National Revival in Europe* (Cambridge, 1985); Anthony D. Smith, *The Ethnic Origins of Nations* (Oxford, 1986); Eric Hobsbawm, *Nations and Nationalism Since 1780. Programme, Myth, Reality* (Cambridge, 1990).
2. Uri Ra'anan et al, eds., *State and Nation in Multi-Ethnic Societies. The Break-Up of Multinational States* (Manchester, 1991); Richard Rudolph and David Good, eds., *Nationalism and Empire. The Habsburg Empire and the Soviet Union* (New York, 1992); Karen Dawisha and Bruce Parrott, eds., *The End of Empire? The Transformation of the USSR in Comparative Perspective* (Amonk, NY and London, 1997); Karen Barkey and Mark von Hagen, eds., *After Empire. Multiethnic Societies and Nation-Building. The Soviet Union and the Russian, Ottoman, and Habsburg Empires* (New York, 1997); Emil Brix et al., eds., *The End of Empires* (Vienna-Munich, 2001); Aviel Roshwald, *Ethnic Nationalism and the Fall of Empires: Central Europe, Russia and the Middle East* (London, 2001); Dominic Lieven, *Empire. The Russian Empire and its Rivals* (New Haven and London, 2002).
3. For overviews of recent discussion, compare Gerald Stourzh, "The Multi-National Empire Revisited: Reflections on Late Imperial Austria," *Austrian History Yearbook* 23 (1992): 1–22, and Denis Rusinow, "The 'National Question' Revisited: Reflections on the State of the Art," *Austrian History Yearbook* 31 (2000): 1–13.
4. Gary B. Cohen, "Neither Absolutism Nor Anarchy: New Narratives on Society and Government in Late Imperial Austria," *Austrian History Yearbook* 29/Pt.1 (1998): 37–61.
5. Regarding terminology, it should of course be remembered that the term the Habsburg Monarchy (or Habsburg Empire) has been used most prevalently after its demise. When used at the time, this tended to be a form of reference from outside the state itself, which unofficially became known as the Austrian Empire after 1804 and then Austria-Hungary after 1867.
6. Oscar Jászi, *The Dissolution of the Habsburg Monarchy* (Chicago, 1929).
7. For discussions of how historians have treated nationalism in the Habsburg Monarchy, see Paula S. Fichtner, "Americans and the Disintegration of the Habsburg Monarchy: The Shaping of an Historiographical Model," in *The Habsburg Empire in World War I*, ed. Robert A. Kann et al. (New York, 1977), 221–234; Alan Sked, "Historians, the Nationality Question and the Downfall of the Habsburg Empire," *Transactions of the Royal Historical Society* 31 (1981): 175–193.
8. For a discussion of this point, see the introduction to Pieter M. Judson and Marsha L. Rozenblit, *Constructing Nationalities in East Central Europe* (New York and Oxford, 2005).
9. Daniel Unowsky, *The Pomp and Politics of Patriotism: Imperial Celebrations in Habsburg Austria, 1848–1916* (West Lafayette, 2005).
10. Péter Hanák, "Die Parallelaktion von 1898. Fünfzig Jahre ungarische Revolution und fünfzig Jahre Regierungsjubiläum Franz Josephs," in id., *Der Garten und die Werkstatt. Ein kulturgeschichtlicher Vergleich Wien und Budapest um 1900* (Vienna, 1992), 101–115.
11. For an example of such an approach, see Laurence Cole, *Für Gott, Kaiser und Vaterland. Nationale Identität der deutschsprachigen Bevölkerung Tirols 1860–1914* (Frankfurt a.M.-New York, 2000).
12. Eric. J. Hobsbawm, "Mass-Producing Traditions in Europe 1870–1914," in *The Invention of Tradition*, ed. Hobsbawm and Terence Ranger (Cambridge, 1983), 266.
13. Laurence Cole, "Der Habsburger-Mythos," *Memoria Austriae. Bd..I: Menschen – Mythen – Zeiten*, ed. Emil Brix et al. (Vienna-Munich, 2004), 473–504.
14. On the early modern Habsburgs, see Marie Tanner, *The Last Descendant of Aeneas: the Habsburgs and the Mythic Image of the Emperor* (New Haven, 1992); Karl Vocelka, "Habsburg Festivals in the Early Modern Period," in *Festive Culture in Germany and Europe from the Sixteenth to the Twentieth Century*, ed. Karin Friedrich (Lewiston and Lampeter, 2000), 123–135; Jeroen Duindam, *Vienna and Versailles: The Courts of Europe's Dynastic Rivals, 1550–*

1780 (Cambridge, 2003); Karin J. MacHardy, *War, Religion and Court Patronage in Habsburg Austria: The Social and Cultural Dimensions of Political Interaction, 1521–1622* (Basingstoke, 2002). For comparisons, see among others Peter Burke, *The Fabrication of Louis XIV* (New Haven, 1992); John Adamson, ed., *The Princely Courts of Europe. Ritual, Politics and Culture Under the Ancien Regime 1500–1750* (London, 1999).

15. Among many others, see John Gillis, ed., *Commemorations: The Politics of National Identity* (Princeton, 1994); John Plunkett, *Queen Victoria: First Media Monarch* (Oxford, 2003); Elizabeth Fehrenbach, "Images of Kaisertum," in *Kaiser Wilhelm II: New Interpretations,* ed. John C.G. Röhl (Cambridge, England, 1982), 269–285; Werner Blessing, *Staat und Kirche in der Gesellschaft. Institutionelle Autorität und mentaler Wandel in Bayern während des 19. Jahrhunderts* (Göttingen, 1982); Richard Wortman, *Scenarios of Power. Myth and Ceremony in Russian Monarchy* volumes 1 and 2 (Princeton, 1995 & 2000).

16. S. Fischer-Galati, "Nationalism and Kaisertreue," *Slavic Review* 22 (1963): 31–36; R.A. Kann, "The Dynasty and the Imperial Idea," *Austrian History Yearbook* 3/I (1967): 11–31.

17. Friedrich Heer, *Der Kampf um die österreichische Identität* (Vienna, 1981), 258.

18. Brigitte Hamann's work is the most scholarly of such popular publications. *Elisabeth: Kasierin wieder Willen* (Vienna, 1982); *Rudolf: Kronprinz und Rebell* (Vienna, 1978; revised edition 2005). Of considerable use is the essay by Hannes Stekl, "Der Wiener Hof und die Hofgesellschaft in der zweiten Hälfte des 19. Jahrhunderts," in *Hof und Hofgesellschaft in den deutschen Staaten im 19. und beginnenden 20. Jahrhundert,* ed. Karl Möckl (Boppard am Rhein, 1990), 61–78. On Franz Joseph's court, see Ivan Žolger, *Der Hofstaat des Hauses Österreich* (Wien, 1917); Margit Silber, *Obersthofmeister Alfred Fürst von Montenuovo. Höfische Geschichte in den beiden letzten Jahrzehnten der österreichisch-ungarischen Monarchie (1897–1916),* (Diss., University of Vienna, 1987); Unowsky, *Pomp and Politics*. Jean-Paul Bled devotes one chapter of his excellent biography of Franz Joseph to the imperial court, *Franz Joseph,* trans. T. Bridgeman (Oxford, 1987), but other recent works only briefly touch on such issues, if at all. Steven Beller, *Francis Joseph* (London and New York, 1996); Alan Palmer, *Twilight of the Habsburgs. The Life and Times of Emperor Francis Joseph* (London, 1994).

19. For a general discussion, consult Peter Urbanitsch, "Pluralist Myth and Nationalist Realities: The Dynastic Myth of the Habsburg Monarchy—a Futile Exercise in the Creation of Identity?" *Austrian History Yearbook* 35 (2004): 101–141. More specifically, see James Shedel, "Emperor, Church, and People: Religion and Dynastic Loyalty during the Golden Jubilee of Franz Joseph," *Catholic Historical Review* 76 (1990): 71–92; Elisabeth Grossegger, *Der Kaiser-Huldigungs-Festzug Wien 1908* (Wien, 1992); Laurence Cole, "Vom Glanz der Montur. Zum dynastischen Kult der Habsburger und seiner Vermittlung durch militärische Vorbilder im 19. Jh. Ein Bericht über 'work in progress,'" *Österreichische Zeitschrift für Geschichtswissenschaften* 7 (1996): 577–591; Andrea Blöchl, "Die Kaisergedenktage. Die Feste und Feiern zu den Regierungsjubiläen und runden Geburtstagen Kaiser Franz Josephs," in *Der Kampf um das Gedächtnis. Öffentliche Gedenktage in Mitteleuropa,* ed. Emil Brix and Hannes Stekl (Wien, 1997), 117–144; András Gerő, *Francis Joseph, King of the Hungarians* (New York, 2001); Nancy Wingfield and Maria Bucur, eds., *Staging the Past: The Politics of Commemoration in Habsburg Central Europe, 1848 to the Present* (West Lafayette, 2001); Ernst Bruckmüller, "Die österreichische Revolution von 1848 und der Habsburg Mythos des 19. Jahrhunderts," in *Bewegung im Reich der Immobilität,* ed. Hubert Lengauer and Primus Heinz Kucher (Wien, 2001), 1–33; Werner Telesko, "Die Wiener historischen Festzüge von 1879 und 1908. Zum Problem der dynastischen Identitätsfindung des Hauses Österreich," *Wiener Geschichtsblätter* 51/3 (1996): 133–146. In addition, Andrew Wheatcroft, *The Habsburgs: Embodying Empire* (London, 1995), provides an overview of Habsburg self-presentation from its origin until the present day, including brief discussions of imperial celebrations.

20. Hobsbawm, "Mass-Producing Traditions."

21. Francis Oakley, *Kingship* (Oxford, 2006), 132–157.
22. See Karl Megner, *Beamte. Wirtschafts- und sozialgeschichtliche Aspekte des k.k. Beamtentums* (Vienna, 1985); Waltraud Heindl, *Gehorsame Rebellen. Bürokratie und Beamte in Österreich 1780 bis 1848* (Vienna, 1991); E. Lindström, "Ernest von Koerber and the Austrian State Idea: A Re-Interpretation of the Koerber Plan (1900–1904)," *Austrian History Yearbook* 35 (2004): 143–184; Waltraud Heindl, "Bureaucracy, Officials and the State in the Austrian Monarchy: Stages of Change Since the Eighteenth Century," *Austrian History Yearbook* 37 (2006): 35–57.
23. Jászi, *Dissolution of the Habsburg Monarchy*, 433–439.
24. István Deák, *Beyond nationalism. A Social History of the Habsburg Officer Corps* (Oxford, 1990).
25. Hobsbawm, "Introduction," in *Invention of Tradition*, Hobsbawm and Ranger, 1–14.
26. Unowsky, *Pomp and Politics*.
27. For a critical examination of such trends, see Mathias Weber, "Ein Modell für Europa? Die Nationalitätenpolitik in der Habsburgermonarchie – Österreich und Ungarn im Vergleich 1867–1914," *Geschichte in Wissenschaft und Unterricht* 47 (1996): 651–672.

Chapter 1

PATRIOTIC AND NATIONAL MYTHS
National Consciousness and Elementary School Education in Imperial Austria*

Ernst Bruckmüller

The modern nation is unthinkable without a national education system: it transmits to each new generation of schoolchildren the idea of belonging to a greater, nationally delimited community, without which the existence of modern nations cannot be "imagined."[1] States seeking to transform themselves into "nation-states" assigned schools the role of teaching children a standardized national language. At the same time, language was used to disseminate a whole series of ideas, legends, stories and so on, which can be summarized under the heading of "national myths."[2] As studies of other European countries have shown, literature and history were two key disciplines in the process of creating these national mythologies.[3]

For a state such as the Habsburg Monarchy, the relationship between the education system and nation-building was much more complex and potentially problematic. Indeed, following Oscar Jászi's argument, it is often assumed that the Habsburg state failed to produce a common "civic education" for its citizens.[4] Schools in the Habsburg Monarchy certainly had the job of educating pupils "patriotically." However, the fact that the Habsburg polity was not a unitary nation-state meant that a whole series of historical figures, myths, and traditions were potentially in competition with the state's official rhetoric. For example, there already existed histories and legends associated with the old-established territories, such as the Kingdoms of Bohemia and Hungary, or the Duchies of Lower and Upper Austria, but from the first half of the nineteenth century onward, the process of "national awakening" created a new set of symbols, images, and ideas focused around linguistically based national cultures.

While a number of scholars have explored the subject of legislation on schooling,[5] this article will focus on the relationship between schooling and the development of national identity in the Austrian half of the Habsburg Monarchy through an examination of school textbooks. In contrast to the Hungarian half of the Monarchy, this is a topic which has received little attention to date.[6] Certainly, there is other material by which the historian might seek to reconstruct pedagogical practice in Austrian schools, such as the annual reports published by primary and secondary schools, or classroom books, which often recorded from day to day the content imparted to schoolchildren. Likewise, the autobiographical works left by contemporaries who reflected on such issues, such as Stefan Zweig, or the humorously conceived, and at the time, very well-known MEYRIAS by Oskar Kraus, also constitute useful sources.[7] Nevertheless, a full analysis of such material requires a lengthier and more systematic treatment than can be offered here. More importantly, it is essential to establish first of all what the state sought to instruct and what it allowed to be published in this area. Accordingly, two main areas will be discussed here: firstly, the elementary schools (*Volksschulen*) will be investigated by looking at a series of primers or "reading books" in use after 1869. By making a comparison between materials in different languages, it will be possible to ascertain which historical figures and events were utilized in order to mediate a sense of identity beyond the locality and region.[8] Secondly, I will examine which goals the central state set itself for the teaching of history in academic secondary schools (*Gymnasien*),[9] and assess how it sought to control the production of classroom materials in order to guarantee the desired outcome with regard to "patriotic education."[10]

1. Language and teaching in Austrian elementary schools

As Hannelore Burger has shown, the principle of monolingualism started to inform everyday practice in schools in the Austrian half of the Habsburg Monarchy from the mid-nineteenth century onward.[11] Particularly in the lower reaches of the school-system, the method of instruction in just one language came to dominate and replaced almost entirely the former principle of multi- or bilingual teaching. Based on what at the time was considered to be the most up-to-date pedagogical findings, monolingualism was assumed to be the most beneficial and only possible means of teaching children effectively, but this emphasis on the mother-tongue was to have far-reaching consequences.

Following Herder, language was understood to be an expression of a "people's spirit" (*Volksgeist*), whereby a particular language of instruction constituted much more than just a means of communication. Language was considered to be the most pure expression of the culture belonging to a linguistically delineated community—a community that was simultaneously understood as a community of descent. For the majority of contemporaries, this culture consisted not just of language and literature, but also folk music, specific forms of architecture and popular dress (all of which were the object of the new academic discipline of ethnography or *Volkskunde*), a particular mentality, and above all, a shared history. The logic of this understanding of culture meant that one language of instruction was not interchangeable with another and that the values and content of a culture could not be disseminated through other idioms; rather, it was taken for granted that cultural values and traditions were entirely bound up with languages and also varied with them. While Czech and Slovene-speaking children were to learn about the virtues of the "ancient Slavs," German-speaking children were to be acquainted with the equally significant qualities of the "ancient Germans." The central role attributed since the Romantic period to the place of language within the system of culture made this kind of division unavoidable.

For the Habsburg Monarchy, this situation presented a potentially enormous problem, because the multitude of languages of instruction meant that schoolchildren were presented with different sets of images and symbols when learning languages and literature. It was therefore necessary to employ additional tools in order to anchor in children's minds the notion of state unity beyond their own national cultures, such as by drawing on the public image of the "good emperor."[12] The long-standing belief in the "salvation" (*Heil*) offered by the divinely ordained monarch retained a residual effectiveness right down until the collapse of the Habsburg state, albeit in a much changed, weaker form than in earlier times.[13] Indeed, the force of such mechanisms was visible in the way in which Francis Joseph, who at the start of his reign had been very unpopular not just in Hungary and northern Italy, but even in Vienna, eventually became the "old Emperor," a figure beyond criticism.[14] At the same time, the cultivation of a dynastic-based "Austrian idea" placed the traditions of the Habsburg army at center stage.[15] Victorious battles and commanders played an important role alongside the prominently emphasized rulers, though of course—as Ernest Renan long ago pointed out—this process involved as much forgetting as remembering of the past.[16]

Nevertheless, it is important to realize that these attempts at promoting a consciousness of Austria were not placed in opposition to older historical traditions or myths associated with the kingdoms and lands of the Habsburg dynasty. As this article will show, the Habsburg myth was adaptable and responsive to change, despite its basically conservative principles. For example, the "Austrian Plutarch," written by historian, archivist, and publicist Johann von Hormayr (1781–1848) in the early part of the nineteenth century, placed Austrian rulers alongside heroes from Bohemian and Hungarian history (who were always portrayed as loyal to the Habsburgs).[17] In this way, central figures in the newly emerging Czech national mythology such as Libuše and Charles IV (King of Bohemia 1346–78, Holy Roman Emperor 1355–78), who was also the father-in-law of the Habsburg ruler Rudolf IV ("the Founder," 1358–65), could be integrated into the wider Austrian idea. It is interesting to note in this context that Franz Grillparzer, Austria's "patriotic writer" *par excellence,* also wrote a drama *Libussa,* in which the magical princess Libuše and her tragic love for a peasant ploughman appeared on the stage with the figure of Primislaus/Přemysl, the famous founder of a dynasty and the capital of Prague. Similarly, Johann Peter Krafft's monumental painting from the 1820s of Count Miklós Zrínyi's defense of Sziget in the year 1566 depicted the Croatian-Hungarian hero as a loyal soldier of the Emperor, someone who barred the Ottomans' way to Vienna.[18]

In all these instances, the presentation of historical events and figures underlines how important—but also how sensitive—an issue the teaching of history in schools could be. Particularly interesting here is the comparison with Hungary, where history and literature were likewise key subjects for promoting state consciousness (this was reinforced after 1868 by instruction in civil rights and duties, something which was only formally introduced in Austria after 1907).[19] As Joachim von Puttkamer's recent study shows, the Hungarian state concentrated on the idea of the unitary Magyar nation in the teaching of history. While in practice this still allowed room to mention other national cultures, particularly as long as confessional schools retained autonomy, the overall trend was towards a process of "national integration into a Hungarian nation-state," especially after the passing in 1907 of the *Lex Apponyi,* which stipulated that all pupils should be able to read and write in Hungarian after four years of schooling.[20] By contrast, in the Austrian half of the Habsburg Monarchy, the government did not promote the idea of an "Austrian nation" in the same way as the Hungarians did the "Magyar nation," but rather attempted to emphasize the dynasty and by implication, the Habsburg Empire as a whole.

In Cisleithania, the Fundamental Laws of December 1867 set out the right to elementary education in the mother-tongue, provided this was one of the languages in common use in the particular crownland or province. In addition, the constitution held fast to the principle of monolingual schooling (despite the moves towards the enforcement of bilingualism in Bohemia after 1848). As mentioned above, this was in step with a fundamental pedagogical shift which took place around the mid-nineteenth century.[21] It is difficult to overestimate the impact of the subsequent privileging of the mother-tongue as the sole language of instruction in schools on the intensification of nationality conflicts in late imperial Austria. Where bi- or multilingualism had been highly regarded for a long time, and the acquisition of one or more languages was seen as a desirable educational goal, this change in attitude in effect encouraged the nationalist emphasis on achieving complete mastery of the mother-tongue, while tending to devalue other languages (as well as diminishing the possibilities of communication across the monarchy as a whole). The imperial law on elementary schools (*Reichsvolksschulgesetz*) of 1869 respected the principles laid down in the constitution, while specifying that in practice it was now the educational authorities in each province who were responsible for determining which languages of instruction would be employed.[22]

Nevertheless, while undoubtedly important, language of instruction was not on its own decisive. The relationship between national cultures and "official patriotism" in the presentation of history in Austrian schoolbooks proves more complex and more subtle in form than national historiographical traditions have supposed.

2. The representation of history, country, and people in elementary schoolbooks

What did children in imperial Austria learn in elementary school about history, and about their country and people? While it remains difficult to draw hard and fast conclusions about how school life unfolded in reality, a study of contemporary textbooks does offer good insights into the state's intentions, and allows us to infer which pedagogical messages were to be transmitted in the schoolroom itself. Such is also the case because, as a rule, the authors of these books were themselves practicing teachers.

Prior to publication, publishers were obliged to submit textbooks to the Ministry of Religion and Education, where a commission evaluated the content before deciding whether or not to approve the material. The commission issued a report, and ministry officials generally adhered to its verdict when granting permission for the book to be published. Of the history books for primary schoolchildren approved via this process, one good example is the reader produced by Ullrich, Ernst, Vogl, and Branky for use in German language elementary schools.[23] This reader was divided into eight volumes. The first two of these, for children at the start of their school career, are comparatively unrevealing for our purposes. From the third volume, however, it is possible to construct a detailed picture of what was being imparted to pupils from the third year onward. Each volume was split into sections, which followed a certain order: the first section featured tales, fairytales, fables, puzzles, songs, and phrases; the second dealt with natural history and nature; the third contained knowledge about the province or homeland, and subsequently about the Austro-Hungarian Monarchy; the fourth section offered stories from the past.

Samples from the third and fourth sections of this reader indicate how history was presented, with approximately one sixth of the total pages in the third volume of the textbook series consisting of "stories from history."[24] Here, pupils first get a flavor of ancient history, with stories about Croesus and Solon, Croesus and Cyros, and the young Alexander the Great. Contact with "Austrian history" begins with Leopold I ("the Glorious," 976–94), the first Babenberg in the Austrian March, and Leopold III (1095–1136), subsequently Saint Leopold, who founded the monastery at Klosterneuburg, just upriver from Vienna. Stories about castles and knights are followed by three episodes from the life of Rudolf I (1273–91), the first Habsburg to be elected King of the Romans and the founder of the dynasty's claim to imperial status. There is also a further tale about one of his sons, all of which emphasizes the central place Rudolf occupied in the public mythology of the Habsburgs.[25] Other leading personalities from the ruling house are presented via dramatic moments, such as Emperor Maximilian I's (1493–1519) escape from danger on a mountain cliff, or through anecdotes, such as Empress Maria Theresia (1740–80) visiting an institute for officer cadets and conversing there with a cadet from Dalmatia. There are four stories about Emperor Joseph II (1780–90), and patriotic accounts of the Napoleonic Wars, before "the good Emperor" Franz II (I) (1792–1835) is shown accompanying a funeral procession for a pauper. Finally, Emperor Franz Joseph (1848–1916) is presented as the grandson of Emperor Francis. As is the case with all the textbooks described here, the volume closes with the state anthem (Haydn's famous *Volkshymne*).

By the time children were in their fourth year of school, the content of the textbooks became more substantial. At this stage, they received a fairly extensive amount of information about the Austro-Hungarian Monarchy, which among other things is achieved by a descriptive voyage down the Danube, as well as imaginary trips across the Alps, to the Carst, Sudeten and Carpathian mountains, the Moldau/Vlatva and March/Morava rivers, and to towns such as Prague or Brünn/Brno.[26] In particular, the fourth section of the fourth volume brings in "episodes from Austrian history," starting with the medieval period and the likes of Attila (King of the Huns in the fifth century), Severin (the Roman leader of the local population in Bavaria and Austria during the troubles of the fifth century, who was worshipped as a saint), and King Ottokar II Přemysl (1253–78, Margrave of Moravia, Duke of Austria, King of Bohemia, and rival of Rudolf I). Also included is the foundation of the bishopric of Salzburg by St. Rupert (c. 650–716).[27] In short, local and regional legends were incorporated into the master narrative of Austrian history, including that of such a latecomer to the Habsburg dominions as Salzburg, which was only acquired at the end of the Napoleonic Wars.

Moving via Charlemagne and the Avars, a tribe originally from Asia which was present in Central Europe from the sixth century until around the year 800, the textbook constructs a composite picture of the history of the Monarchy as a whole. Symbolically, a poem by Ludwig August Frankl describes the Austrian coat-of-arms, and this is followed by the story of Leopold the Virtuous (1177–94) and the captive English King, Richard the Lionheart. As before, Rudolf I is accorded special attention in the form of three stories, but a number of other figures are introduced as well: Frederick I ("the Handsome," 1314–30), Albrecht II (also known as "the Wise" or "the Lame," 1330–58), Charles IV and his son-in-law Rudolf IV (1358–1365), Frederick IV of Tyrol ("with the empty pocket," 1402–39), and Emperor Maximilian, with his grave in the court church in Innsbruck. Now, too, a sense is given of the Habsburg state's emergence as a European power by recounting the battle of Mohács (1526), the first siege of Vienna by the Turks (1529), the above-mentioned Miklós Zrínyi and his defense of Sziget in 1566, the second Ottoman siege of Vienna (1683), the reconquest of Buda (1687), and the victories of Prince Eugene of Savoy (1663–1736). Bringing the story near to the present time, the reading book brings in Maria Theresia (in two stories), Joseph II, and a series of episodes from the Revolutionary and

Napoleonic Wars, such as the exploits of Archduke Charles (1771–1847), the tale of the priest from Ulrichskirchen who accompanies the disguised Emperor Franz mourning the battlefield dead at Aspern, and Andreas Hofer and the Tyrolean uprising of 1809.

In the fifth school year, the framework becomes more complex still, as the geographical and historical perspective widens. A description of the Habsburg Monarchy again sets the stage, and patriotic poems (*Mein Österreich* and *An mein Vaterland* by Johann Gabriel Seidel) serve as a reminder that instilling love of the homeland remains a primary educational objective, but the fifth volume of the primer places all this within the wider context of Europe, the world, and the earth's geological history. The historical section of the textbook delves into different aspects of antiquity, this time using Troy, Leonidas, Socrates, and Horatius Cocles as examples. The palate becomes more varied through a brief description of the character and customs of the old Germanic tribes, and the story of Hermann, who is placed alongside the medieval Slavs, Libuše, Ottokar II Přemysl, and Prince Svatopluk (lived c. 830–94), ruler of the Greater Moravian Empire, and the Hungarians, with their king, St. Stephen. The history of the Holy Roman Empire also receives greater attention, e.g., in the shape of figures like the Saxon Duke Henry ("the Fowler," East Frankish King 919–36), or the East Frankish King Otto the Great (Holy Roman Emperor 962–73). It goes without saying that there is considerable space for Rudolf I, including the last ride on horseback to his burial place at Speyer. Two central milestones in world history are recognized with the invention of gunpowder and the printing press, while Albrecht Dürer also gets a mention. In returning to Austrian history, the book then recounts what is by now a familiar canon of Emperor Maxilimian, Joseph II, the Napoleonic Wars, Emperor Francis, and Field-Marshall Radetzky, but there is also room here for the Thirty Years War and the victory over the Prussians at the battle of Kolín in 1757.

The seventh volume no longer preserves the strict demarcations between sections characteristic of other books in the series. Instead, this book presents a basic chronological line running from antiquity to the present. Different in this volume is the more obvious presence of a German literary culture. For example, there are numerous poems by writers such as Bürger, Chamisso, Körner, Hoffmann von Fallersleben, Uhland, Rückert, Schiller, Goethe, and Grillparzer. In this respect, it is hard to avoid the impression that this wider German cultural orientation, extending beyond the borders of the Habsburg state, is only offered to pupils once it could be assumed that the Austrian patriotic content of the curriculum had been well embedded. In between the literary texts, there is a variety of historical stories (about Emperor Maximilian, the over-mighty general Albrecht von Wallenstein (1583–1634), and so on) or explanations of economic and technological matters, like the introduction of the potato to Austrian agriculture or the development of the Carinthian mining industry. In short, older primary schoolchildren are familiarized with key works of German literature, especially Weimar classicism, alongside extensive instruction in Austrian history, cultural life, and music (e.g., the works of Schubert, and Beethoven's funeral).

Finally, the last and eighth volume of the German language textbook begins with a famous poem called "Mother-Tongue" (*Muttersprache*) by Schenkendorf, which amounts to a very emotional identification with one's own language. However, the broader German cultural sphere always draws in Austrian elements, with texts by Heinrich von Zeißberg, a highly regarded historian of Austria and Vienna, on the Babenberg period, and by Franz von Krones on the social order in early modern Austria. The book begins with a brief account of the Nibelungen saga, and High German versions of two poems by Walther von der Vogelweide, the medieval minstrel who was believed to stem from Southern Tyrol.[28] Other contributions deal with medieval Christian architecture, soldiers in Prince Eugene's army, the Wachau region of the Danube, and the inventor and engineer Josef Ressel.[29] The educational goal here is to convey an "Austrian-German" way of thinking, which is strongly oriented towards the Habsburg Empire, its dynasty, and key personalities and places from the Habsburg Monarchy's German-speaking lands. At the same time, there is a clear effort when teaching literature to offer examples from the wider German cultural sphere and the territory of the Holy Roman Empire, and to indicate the existence of a common cultural heritage that is self-evidently shared with other Germans (although this point is not unduly emphasized).

This key example of an elementary school reader in German allows us to identify the intended literary and historical canon for people who did not go on to any further schooling. These pupils were taught an impressive amount of material, which was in no sense one-sided. Naturally, Austria and the Habsburg dynasty were at the forefront of the educational program, together with German-Austrian culture and the German-speaking territories of the Monarchy. Yet, the overall perspective was widened by going back to antiquity, and there was much material about the non-German lands, especially concerning heroes loyal or connected to the Habsburgs.

Having established, via the German language textbook, the main set of reference points for the official discourse on educating school children in Austria, we can now turn our attention to textbooks in other languages, which were built up in an analogous fashion. Here too, beginning with the materials intended for use in the third year of study, the primers possess a substantial historical and geographical dimension, and echo the patterns found in the German language readers. In a Czech reader written by Jan Štastný and Josef Sokol, for example, the section on "countries, fatherland, nation" (*země, vlast, národ*) starts with the areas most familiar to those being taught, respectively Bohemia, Moravia, Silesia, Austria, and then Hungary.[30] The book cites the well-known phrase, "who(ever) is at home in Bohemia, is called a Czech [kdo v Čechách domovem jest, jemenuje se Čech]."[31] Czech is referred to as "our" spoken and written language, while a people with a common origin, language and so on, is termed a "nation" (*národ*). While it is also made clear that all the lands subject to "our sovereign" are named the Austro-Hungarian Monarchy, the stories and tales taught at this level relate entirely to the lands of the Bohemian crown.[32] Thus, the book narrates the settlement of the territory in the gray mists of time by those people from whom the Czechs took their name. Thereafter come central figures in Czech national mythology, namely Prince Krok and his daughters, of whom Libuše, possessed of magical powers, is presented more fully in a series of three stories, which include the figure of Přemysl and the founding of Prague. The book then covers the Christianization of Bohemia and Moravia; the eighth-century saints Cyril and Methodius are mentioned in this context, along with the Moravian prince Svatopluk and the ninth-century Czech prince Bořivoy.[33] The effectiveness of the evangelization process is demonstrated by the presence of native saints such as Ludmilla (840–916), the wife of Bořivoy, Wenceslas (c. 907–29, grandson of Ludmilla), and Adalbert/Vojtěch of Prague (c. 956–97).[34] The story of the founding of a monastery at Sázava is also told, and three stories about Joseph II appear, albeit without being connected directly to what has been recounted before. As with the German primer, the book closes with Haydn's national anthem (in Czech translation). While it might seem surprising that nothing appears about the role of the Luxemburg dynasty in Bohemia or that of the early Habsburgs, it is important to remember that this particular volume was aimed at children only eight to nine years old.

The fourth volume of the primer begins with an extensive geographical account of the lands of the Bohemian crown, covering rivers, mountains, the famous West Bohemian spa towns, Prague, Moravia, with its major centers of Brünn/Brno and Olmütz/Olomouc, and the small portion of Silesia belonging to Austria.[35] Thereafter is a description of "the Austro-Hungarian Empire" (*Říše Rakousko-uherská*), with sections on Vienna, the Danube, and all the other main geographical features. Again, the Bohemian lands are placed at the center of this narrative; of the other regions of the monarchy, the Slovene-speaking areas receive significantly more space than others (a slightly greater than average degree of attention is also devoted to the Slovakian areas). The historical section of this volume affirms the sense of belonging to the Czech nation before treating the early history of Bohemia in more detail.[36] Together with the Czechs, all the tribes present in the early middle ages in the region are listed, and these are then subsumed under the "Czechs," which also becomes the term to refer to the land. Short descriptions are given of the eleventh-century Dukes of Bohemia Břetislav I, and Soběslav I, and finally the Kingdom of Bohemia (*Království České*). Members of the Luxemburg dynasty are then mentioned too, especially Charles IV, but also Wenceslas IV (1378–1419) and his brother, the King of Bohemia, Sigmund (who was King from 1419–37, Holy Roman Emperor from 1433–37, and also King of Hungary since 1410); Charles' son-in-law, Albrecht II of Habsburg (1438–39), appears briefly, as Bohemian and Hungarian King. After that, however, comes an abrupt break in proceedings. Bohemia now barely comes to the fore; instead, the primer follows the typology set out in the German language textbook (i.e., Emperors Maximilian, Charles V (1519–56), Ferdinand I (1522–64), the battle of Mohács, the wars against the Turks, and on through Maria Theresia and Joseph II to the Napoleonic Wars). In other words, potentially controversial themes such as the history of Rudolf and Ottokar, Jan Hus (c. 1371–1415), or the defenestration in Prague at the start of the Thirty Years War, were deliberately left out in order to smooth the transition from medieval Bohemia to the "common" history under the Habsburgs.[37]

If the Czech textbooks integrate national mythology into the school curriculum, they also demonstrate the constraints that applied when treating politically sensitive historical periods. This picture is confirmed by a brief examination of some Italian primers.[38] Distinguished by their attractive maps and tables on the population of Austria-Hungary, these textbooks produce a slightly strange narrative combination of the Babenbergs, the Habsburgs, the history of Trieste, and descriptions of the Littoral, Aquileia, and other places. In short, the standard "Habsburg myth" is accompanied by historical and geographical descriptions of the Italian-speaking areas, but in a way which is much more closely modelled on the German language primers than their equivalents in other languages.[39] Although the Italian areas, and above all Trieste, form the primary reference point, these textbooks are much more cautious when it comes to the question of national culture. Moreover, the political events of the mid-nineteenth century meant that the books said nothing whatsoever about the Italian *Risorgimento* or the new Kingdom of Italy.

By contrast to the Italian examples, Slovene language textbooks indicate much more strongly the possibilities for symbiosis between "national" and "Austrian" histories. For example, a primer for third year classes initially describes the "motherland" (*materina dežela*), which is the land in which "we" were born.[40] Given the dispersion of Slovene-speakers across different provinces, this would then be understood respectively as Carniola, Carinthia, Styria, and so on. The primers then emphasize that all of these lands are part of the Austrian state, in which there lives a multitude of other peoples, who have their own different languages and customs. All of these peoples are united under the paternal sovereignty of "our" esteemed Emperor, and Austria is thus "our common homeland [Austrija je tedaj naša občna domovina]."[41]

About half a generation later, a new Slovenian reader appeared for the third year of primary school.[42] It contains the local legend of Martin Krpan, a salt smuggler from the Carst region who was allegedly as strong as a bear.[43] Krpan was constantly in conflict with the provincial authorities, but one day he saved the emperor and his carriage from a dangerous overhang of snow. He is later summoned to Vienna to rid the town of a terrible brute, who is knocking off the imperial knights one by one. After his victory over this monster, and his perhaps even more heroic triumph over intrigues at the imperial court, Krpan returns home as the proud owner of an imperial license to trade in salt. Krpan's tale fits the classic mould of the common man winning out over the high and mighty, a victory for the province over the metropolis, but it is interesting in this context that a story told against authority, as it were, is incorporated into the curriculum.

Following Krpan's story, several poems sing the praises of the homeland (e.g., *Domovina*, by A. Praprotnik), reinforcing the national-cultural education children received when learning poems by Vodnik and Prešeren in literature classes; at the same time, "*Austrija*" is described as the larger homeland, the "*domovina Austrija*."[44] In addition, emphasis is placed on Slavic culture generally. When listing the inhabitants of Austria-Hungary, for example, the nineteen million Slavs are put first, followed by the Germans, Romance, and Magyar peoples. The final section of the reader highlights the role of the Slavic extended family (*zadruga*), which is understood to include all kin and involves "each person working for everyone, all working for each."[45] After this comes the usual roster of familiar personalities and events (e.g., Charlemagne, King Stephen of Hungary, the Babenbergs, etc.), but this "patriotic canon" is occasionally modified in order to bring in matters of local relevance, such as the actions of the Counts of Cilli/Celje and the church-fortresses (*tabori*) that were central to resistance against the Ottomans.[46] Interestingly, this "Austrian" part of the curriculum could also be articulated in the form of a civic education, as a fourth year reader from 1893 suggests. Here, specific reference is made to the rights of Austrian state citizens as expressed in the Fundamental Laws of 1867.[47] The textbook is particularly noteworthy for its glowing Austrian patriotism when comparing antiquity and Austrian history: the author's heart beats for Zrínyi rather than Themistocles, for Archduke Charles ahead of Scipio, and of course for Rudolf of Habsburg in preference to Alexander the Great.[48] Equally, the Catholic dimension to Slovenian patriotism also comes to the fore, with specific attention paid to bishop Martin Slomšek, who in 1859 transferred the seat of the Lavant bishopric from St. Andrä in Carinthia to Marburg/Maribor in southern Styria.[49]

On the whole, therefore, the Slovenian textbooks provide a good illustration of how national culture and state patriotism could be simultaneously inculcated in schoolchildren. However, there was a definite shift in tone around the first decade of the twentieth century.[50] One primer published in 1904, for example, displays a closer concentration on the regions populated by Slovene-speakers, and a stronger sense of national feeling is expressed when describing areas like Bled, Laibach/Ljubljana, Marburg/Maribor, the Savinja valley, and so on.[51] The use of the term "Slovenian homeland" (*domovina Slovencev*) is also revealing, although this is definitely placed within an Austrian-patriotic context: the author describes the 22,000 km^2 in which the pious, faithful Slovene people live and work as a "special pearl" in the crown of the Habsburg rulers. The historical section of the book treats the Babenbergs and Habsburgs in the standard way, while also cultivating myths surrounding the ancient Slavs. The latter are portrayed as likeable, kind hearted, upright, and powerful figures. They love freedom, but so much so that it can lead to disorder and lack of harmony, and this allows aggressive neighbors to extend their rule over the Slavs. In short, this is a depiction of the ancient Slavs entirely along Herderian lines, and the Slavic saints Cyril and Methodius are also integrated into the Slovenian national story. Events from regional and "Inner Austrian" history are of course also depicted, including such events as the establishment of the Carinthian Dukedom, the prominent role of the Counts of Görz/Gorica/Gorizia and Cilli/Celje, the Ottoman incursions, and so on.

This trend towards the absorption of a more pronounced national element in the textbooks is confirmed in the fourth volume of the Slovene reader just mentioned, which appeared in 1909.[52] Particularly striking here is the stronger engagement with the other South Slav peoples. To begin with, an overview of the peoples of Europe emphasizes the Slavic peoples, and a small, separate subsection is devoted to Moscow. Then the author suggest to readers, "Let's go now a little towards our brothers, the Croats!"[53] Alongside all the usual subjects relating to the Habsburg dynasty, some new themes now appear among the historical episodes recounted in the book. Thus, the fight for "traditional rights" embodied by the peasant uprisings in Slovene-speaking areas in the sixteenth century is linked to the person of Matija Gubec, the Croatian peasant leader in 1573. The heroes of battles during the Napoleonic Wars at Malborghetto (on the Friulian border) and Predil (at the pass between Carinthia and Carniola) are now "Croatian" heroes, and seemingly for the first time in a book of this kind, reference is made to the Illyrian provinces under Napoleon. Equally, however, the stronger consciousness of Slovenian identity is related back to Austrian patriotism via the army. When discussing the occupation of Bosnia-Herzegovina in 1878, the book stresses the achievements of the 17th Infantry Regiment, the Carniolan home regiment which was more or less entirely composed of Slovenes. As was common with these school primers, the book closed with Emperor Franz Joseph and the state hymn.

In the case of the Slovene textbooks, a trend is therefore observable away from religious-educational subjects toward national-cultural subjects. Thereby, as the leading Slovene historian Sergij Vilfan has observed, "Slovene national patriotism grew not so much with regard to how the subjects were presented, but rather in the choice of themes" (such as the ancient Slavs). Vilfan also detected a gradual change in how Austrian patriotism was presented: "Austrian patriotism had two components, one legalistic (the Austrian state) and one dynastic (the House of Habsburg). In our school books, the legalistic aspect ('our common homeland') was in retreat, while the dynasty became more prominent; and the dynasty was increasingly represented by Franz Joseph."[54]

More generally, this survey of elementary school textbooks shows that school children were to be taught a sense of belonging to their native region (*Landespatriotismus*), a feeling of loyalty to the Austrian state and dynasty (*Gesamtstaatspatriotismus*), but also quite definitely an identification with "their" linguistic group and "their" nation. All the textbooks are based on a firm pattern, which begins with an exploration of the home province. Above all, a "canon" of personalities and events from Austrian history is established, which then undergoes slight variation and embellishment according to language group. The "national" element in the readers is clearly developed in the Czech and Slovene cases, but much less so for the Italian books, where the official template appears to have been more rigid. In the case of both of the Slavic nationalities, the growing admiration for the ancient Slavs, the major figures from early and medieval Czech history, and the role of the saints Cyril and Methodius constitute integral parts of their national mythologies. Also worthy of note is the attention given to local nobles, who are otherwise rather overlooked in Austrian history writing, and the suggestion of links between the South Slav peoples.

The results from this survey of primary school textbooks indicate that the Habsburg state did not suppress the national element in the learning of history at the elementary level. National myths and legends were—in most cases—part of the curriculum and were recognized as a legitimate part of pride in one's native region. Significantly, however, the curriculum only incorporated those elements which were "uncontroversial" and could be meaningfully linked to a wider story about the Habsburg state and dynasty.

3. The development of state policy on history teaching in secondary schools

As in other countries, the aim of secondary school, and especially *Gymnasium*, education in imperial Austria was to educate social, economic, and political elites. Beginning in the 1850s, the state made a concerted drive towards the modernization and expansion of this sector. Gary Cohen has demonstrated how this led to a major increase in secondary educational provision across Cisleithania, with an increase in enrollments across ethnic and social groups.[55] The importance attached to the upper levels of education meant that the state sought to direct policy here more than at the primary level. Arguably, the need to influence the socialization of adolescents in a patriotic direction was more acute among the elite sections of society. A key question for the Austrian government was therefore how the teaching of history could help to shape the development of youth in an Austrian patriotic direction. Accordingly, it is necessary to establish how state policy in this area evolved, before considering how history textbooks were passed for publication.[56]

In general terms, the goal of educating people towards "love of the fatherland" is traceable to the eighteenth century.[57] Where in the early modern period the term "fatherland" referred to a particular crownland (e.g., Styria, Carinthia), eighteenth-century usage increasingly related this concept to the entire monarchy (although it still continued to be used in the older sense as well).[58] Not surprisingly, instruction about the fatherland was always closely related to the teaching of history, and history as a secular discipline in the Habsburg Monarchy appeared in universities for the first time in 1694.[59] As early as 1735, Emperor Charles VI decreed that a *"studium historicum"* was obligatory in all *Gymnasien,* and in 1775, the Piarist father Gratian Marx gave the teaching of history the shape it would take until 1848. *Gymnasium* would teach the history of different peoples and states in synchronic fashion, but the last school year was reserved for the "history of the fatherland" (*Vaterlandsgeschichte*) and the history of the House of Austria.[60] In many respects, this principle continued in effect until the end of the Habsburg Monarchy, undergoing certain changes along the way. History developed a clearer profile once the system of one teacher for each class was replaced by that of one teacher for each subject, but from 1806–07 onward history was always paired with geography. This link was maintained after the fundamental reforms of 1849, although it became less rigid and geography came to occupy a less subordinate position. Nevertheless, it was not until 1910 that the two subjects were fully separated.

A leading role in the process of school reform after 1849 was played by lawyer and parliamentary deputy Joseph Alexander Freiherrr von Helfert (1820–1910), who was under-secretary of state in the Ministry of Religion and Education. Without a doubt, Helfert was one of the most important representatives of a state-supporting, dynastically loyal, and "supranational" brand of conservatism, and he was responsible for the process of school reform in the post-revolutionary period. Helfert was convinced that the creation of an Austrian consciousness pertaining to the entire state could be achieved above all through the teaching of history. For this reason, in 1853 he called for the cultivation of "national history" (*Nationalgeschichte*), by which was understood the history of the Austrian Empire as a whole.[61] Helfert interpreted *Nationalgeschichte* in an exclusively political manner, as the:

> history of a population belonging together territorially and politically, bound together by the same sovereign authority, and being protected by the same laws. Austrian national history is for us the history of the entire Austrian state and the whole people, the organically intertwined parts of which consist of all those tribes, different in origin, culture, and custom, who live across the vast area of the Empire.[62]

For Helfert, the reorganization of the secondary schools had for the first time integrated history systematically into the curriculum, while the teaching and writing of patriotic history also received a new institutional base with the foundation of the Austrian Academy of Sciences in 1847. One year after Helfert's appeal, the Institute of Austrian Historical Research was founded, with the remit of producing source editions and training scholars in archival work and other auxiliary subjects (the fact that, under Theodor Sickel, the Institute concerned itself increasingly with the history of the Holy Roman Empire at the expense of Austrian history did not correspond to Helfert's original ideal).[63]

When Hermann Bonitz and Franz Serafin Exner, both professors and civil servants in the Ministry of Religion and Education, subsequently planned a new organizational structure for the *Gymnasien*, "national history" was not included in the precise form laid out by Helfert. Nevertheless, the "history of the fatherland" received special attention from this point on until 1918. As indicated by a draft plan for the instruction of geography and history from 1849, the educational goal at the lower level of elite secondary school (*Untergymnasium*) was "a knowledgeable overview of the world and its division into political and natural units; an overview of the most important personalities and events from the history of peoples, namely of the history of Austria, and its chronological context." In particular, the teaching of modern history should concentrate primarily on Austrian history, and the teaching schedule for both the third and fourth *Untergymnasium* classes referred to "Austrian history, with emphasis on events affecting the specific fatherland and attention to major events in world history."[64] For the upper level (*Obergymnasium*), the educational aim laid down in 1849 was an overview of the main developments in world history and of the connections between them, and in particular "exact knowledge of the historical development of the Greeks, Romans and of the fatherland." At this level, early modern and modern history was to be comprehended as world or European history; only in the last school year would the specific history of the Austrian state be taught again. This also implied "attention to the history of its parts, especially of the specific fatherland," as well as including statistical information on the Habsburg Monarchy.[65]

The instructions accompanying this organizational plan explained once again why the teaching of modern history had to focus on the history of the Austrian state. Educational officials considered that the general history of the modern period was too difficult and complicated, and it would only create confusion among the pupils. By contrast, the history of a major state could be imparted to pupils between the ages of ten and fourteen; it was self-evident that this should be the history of the Austrian state, and this would also benefit those children leaving school at fourteen to start work. At the upper level, it was not sufficient just to repeat the chronological path followed at the lower level. Hence, the history of the Austrian state was only to be recalled briefly and the majority of attention was to be paid to the general history of peoples and states, and constitutional developments.[66]

A similar, albeit methodologically more elaborate, set of instructions and a renewed curriculum were issued in 1884 by the Ministry of Education. The new instructions demanded that certain figures from Habsburg history, like Maximilian I, Prince Eugene, Maria Theresia and others, must attain among pupils a position of "dogmatic certainty and definitiveness."[67] At the upper level, pupils should be confronted with the main epochs of modern history—the periods of Reformation, Absolutism, and Revolution—and have their historical meaning explained. As before, the last year would see a return of the educational focus towards Habsburg history, and here difficulties were acknowledged with respect to its "many-sided form." The Austrian state and its history began with the permanent union of the lands of the Bohemian and Hungarian crowns with the Austrian hereditary territories; yet, this was not a chance event, and it was therefore necessary to elucidate the background prior to 1526 which had led to these territories coming together. From the time of Rudolf of Habsburg onward, the history of the dynasty was to be placed center stage, because subsequent events could then easily be grouped around this main narrative. For example, the Luxemburg dynasty was presented as "in a certain sense having prepared the ground for the later position of power assumed by the Habsburgs." The explanation of the pre-1526 era implied a brief discussion of the main territories, namely the Bohemian, Hungarian, and core Austrian lands ("Inner Austria"), while all other territories were to be dealt with more briefly. "Overall," resumed the instructions, "the teacher will have to place the main weight on those moments which became significant for the gradual formation of Austrian state-mindedness." The truthful, objective presentation, "without ostentation," of the great events in Habsburg history would in itself contribute towards the awakening of "love for the ruling house and fatherland" among the young. Patriotism should be attained via recognition of the "ethical importance of the fatherland for the whole of humanity." At the same time, the teacher should include the history of the "immediate homeland" in the curriculum, while "always paying attention to the larger whole."[68]

Neither a slightly changed curriculum in 1892 nor another modified version in 1900 produced any substantial change in the established format. For example, the theme of "Austrian history" in the eighth and final year of secondary school witnessed a change in nomenclature from "homeland" (*Heimat*) to "crownland" (*Kronland*), but without any substantial change in content. There is, however, an increased awareness about the politically sensitive nature of teaching history. Thus, when working in crownlands with ethnically mixed populations, teachers were advised that "special care is needed, in order not to hurt national sensibilities while not damaging historical truth." Yet, schools should remain completely untouched by the influence of "partisan views" of a political and national nature.[69] Seemingly, the concentration on the history of the state as a whole was to be the principle means of achieving this aim. As the last history curriculum to be published before 1914 reiterated, pupils should at the end of their school career:

> thoroughly know the more important events in the history of the Austria-Hungarian Monarchy, its creation, expansion, and internal development, as well as its relationship with other countries and states, with emphasis on cultural, historical and economic events, and further, on the constitution and administration of the Monarchy, with special attention to the Austrian half of the Empire.[70]

There are a number of features that are key to understanding how state policy on the teaching of history at the secondary school level in Cisleithania was formulated: first, the teaching of history and geography had, alongside a dominant place reserved for classical antiquity, a major emphasis on the Habsburg state and its territories, which was designed to encourage and reinforce an emotional bond with the state. Second, this patriotism was focused on the Habsburg Monarchy as a whole, not on the Austrian half of the state (Cisleithania), and this did not change after the 1867 Compromise. Third, the term "fatherland" became reserved exclusively for the monarchy in its entirety, while the "specific fatherland" of 1849 was referred to as the "homeland" and then later "crownland." Fourth and last, it appears to be the case that there was an increasing, and dogmatically more rigid, emphasis on particular periods ("heroic epochs") and personalities, through which a Habsburg/Austrian "canon" of historical themes and subjects could be constructed.

History textbooks formed the medium for the implementation of this state policy. Here, it is important to note that the post–1849 period marked the start of a new era in terms of history teaching, as it did for historical research in general.

With the expansion of secondary education and the institutionalization of the discipline of history, new teaching materials also became necessary. In the Austrian *Gymnasien,* this need was fulfilled by "the Gindely reader," which became the classic textbook. Anton Gindely's general history textbook, the *Lehrbuch der allgemeinen Geschichte* appeared in numerous variations for *Gymnasien,* ordinary secondary schools (*Realschulen*), and vocational schools (*Handelsschulen*), and was translated into many of the Monarchy's principal languages.[71] Gindely (1829–92) wrote in a succinct, emotionless style, without great pathos, and was something of a unique personality in a political and social climate where the pressure to identify with one nationality alone was becoming more relentless. The son of a German-Hungarian father and Czech mother, he consciously viewed himself as a multilingual Bohemian and Austrian who stood between Germans and Czechs and did not feel he belonged to any one grouping.[72] Yet, he did not flaunt his Austrian patriotism brazenly, and he felt that history as a discipline had the duty to serve the truth alone; he was convinced that the value and worth of the Austrian state would logically become clear from a study of the subject. For that reason, he forsook patriotic melodrama, and likewise avoided the description of legendary or emotional events.[73] Other, later authors were different: Franz Martin Mayer, for example, was responsible for producing the tenth edition of Gindely's work (published in Vienna in 1900), and he painted events more fully, and in a style designed to inspire patriotic emotions.[74]

While Gindely's was far and away the most widespread text used, the overall number of schoolbooks grew rapidly after mid-century, the growth also helped by a change in the legislation. Up to 1850, the official, state-owned schoolbook publisher possessed the sole right to print books for use in *Gymnasien.* Thereafter, privately owned publishing houses were increasingly able to enter the market and the last restrictions on competition fell in 1869.[75] Initially, university professors or secondary school teachers such as Gindely, Emanuel Hannak, Constantin Höfler, Franz Martin Mayer, or Vaclav Vladivoj Tomek dominated the scene, but *Gymnasium* teachers subsequently came to the fore.[76] Professional historians, including such famous names as Oswald Redlich, Emil von Ottenthal, Alfons Dopsch, and Adolf Bachmann, were also involved in the evaluation process for manuscripts which had to be submitted by publishers to the Ministry for Religion and Education, not just in the case of new publications but also of new editions of books already approved.[77]

These expert reports on the textbook manuscripts indicate very clearly how and where the state sought to maintain control over history teaching in the classroom.[78] One good case in point is the report by the Slovene historian Anton Kaspret on a history schoolbook published in Zagreb and written for the lower secondary level, which came into consideration for potential use in the small number of secondary schools in imperial Austria where instruction was in Serbo-Croatian (in Istria and Dalmatia).[79] Kaspret wrote his report with close reference to the official instructions and guidelines outlined above, and the question of the book's "Austrian-patriotic content" was at the heart of his submission. The verdict was negative. Kaspret based his decision on the presence of national myths and state histories which competed with the required Habsburg-Austrian narrative focus. In other words, the book's sections on early and medieval history concentrated more on the Croats and on the Magyars taking possession of the region, rather than on the history of the Habsburg state or the Habsburg role in the Holy Roman Empire. The latter was evidently of less interest to the book's author than such subjects as Byzantium, the Venetian Republic, the Mongols, and the Russians. Kaspret especially criticized the depiction of an earlier "Greater Croatia," and the exaggerated expression of Slavic sympathies.

Another episode illustrates how schoolbooks could easily provoke political controversy. A certain Johann Veljaća-Andrović, who was employed by the provincial governor of Dalmatia as a clerk in the local administration of Metković and is described in the official correspondence as having "an extremely over-excited mind," protested against a formulation in the Italian edition of Gindely's teaching book.[80] Backing up his case with extensive material, Veljaća-Andrović was unhappy with a sentence which asserted that "Croatia was definitively incorporated into Hungary at the end of the twelfth century [alla fine del secolo XII la Croazia fù incorporata definitivamente all' Ungheria]." This was firstly, an inaccurate representation of Gindely's original text, which had spoken of "permanent union" with Hungary ("am Ende des XII. Jahrhunderts wurde Kroatien dauernd mit Ungarn vereint"). Secondly, this did not correspond to the historical facts, because Croatia was never "incorporated" into Hungary. In the name of the law and the truth, Veljaća-Andrović demanded that this passage be corrected. Ministerial officials noted dismissively that Veljaća-Andrović's submission contained "much superfluous phrasing" and that he seemed to be a very fanatical supporter of the "Party of Rights." Nevertheless, the protest was upheld because it was confirmed that the Italian translation really was inaccurate; the publisher in Prague was duly warned that the Italian edition would no longer be approved in the current form.[81]

Both the above cases illustrate that government officials had problems with how history was represented in Slavic language regions, but these were not confined to such areas alone. In 1909, for example, Dr. Gustav Waniek reported on a new edition of Hannak's history textbook for the lower secondary level. He refused to give his approval, citing among other reasons the fact that the founder of the new German Empire was described as "the great Emperor Wilhelm I." Not only was this inappropriate, but Wilhelm's alleged "greatness was in no way evident from the description of the events." Moreover, the book as a whole did not correspond to the new curriculum and could not therefore be approved.[82] The incident thus illustrates that the state authorities had to be vigilant with regard to books in all languages, not least because, alongside Austrian history, interest in German history of the medieval and later periods was increasingly evident among the Austrian-German cultural elite, and this seems to have been reflected in new textbooks as well.[83]

Conclusions

As Gary Cohen reminds us in his study of secondary and higher education in imperial Austria:

> social and political values are not created by any one agency. It is extremely difficult to isolate what instruction in secondary schools, universities and technical colleges or students' whole experience in these institutions may contribute to developing such values as distinct from the students' early experiences in family, neighborhood and a host of other influences. At the least, one can claim that advanced education in modern societies encourages and strengthens social and political values that are acquired from a range of sources.

Hence, "it is important to try to describe what, in fact, characterized the social experience of [school] students" in Austria.[84] Here, the attention has been on primary and secondary education during the second half of the nineteenth century in order to ascertain how the state tried to influence this socialization process in an Austrian patriotic direction. This investigation of school textbooks used in imperial Austria suggests a number of preliminary conclusions.

To begin with, it has been established that children in elementary schools in the Austrian half of the Habsburg Monarchy were taught history through the narration of episodes and stories ("myths" in the narrowest sense of the word). This occurred in a series of stages, which were intended to build up a sense of identification with the crownland, the Habsburg Monarchy as a whole, the dynasty, and also with the national culture pertaining to each language group. Significantly, the imperial Austrian state appears to have been reasonably, even surprisingly, tolerant with regard to the learning of national myths in primary school (e.g., Libuše, the ancient Slavs), even if it is acknowledged that these could only appear when placed in a positive relationship to the overarching "Habsburg myth." However, it is also clear that there was much less room for maneuver for language groups whose main center of gravity lay outside the borders of the Habsburg state (above all, the Italians). It was certainly not possible to teach a national history which anticipated the founding of a nation-state.

With regard to secondary education, the teaching of history at this level was oriented more directly towards the Habsburg state and an "Austrian patriotism." This included, where relevant, a consideration of the history of individual crownlands, but there was no attempt to strengthen further the national-cultural (or political) consciousness of the different nationalities. Both the official curriculum guidelines and the evaluation process for history textbooks make this clear. In other words, the state placed a watchful eye over the material provided to the future elite, and it is significant that it sought to maintain central control over classroom material in a situation where provincial authorities otherwise had an important role over the everyday running of schools.

Finally, while the focus here has been on the direction of state policy, it goes without saying that further investigation is required into the impact and reception of patriotic education, as well as the implementation of policy at the provincial level (especially in provinces with a wide degree of practical autonomy like Galicia). Oscar Jászi famously dismissed the concentration on the dynasty in schoolbooks as "the spirit of a nauseating Byzantinism."[85] The fact that the younger, more radical members of national movements were often *Gymnasium* pupils or university students may well suggest that the state-led efforts were ultimately unsuccessful. Yet, such a correlation cannot be considered conclusive on its own, given that many passed through the education system without becoming overtly anti-Habsburg, while the impact of imperial festivities as the nineteenth century progressed indicates that the patriotic message was not without its supporters. Ultimately, therefore, there is a clear need for more specific microhistorical research at the level of towns, villages, and schools. In his ground-breaking work on "Yugoslav" textbooks, for example, Charles Jelavich suggested the rich potential of utilizing educational journals, school almanacs, subscriptions to journals and newspapers as sources for recreating the local socio-cultural environments in which education took place.[86]

Such material, combined with the close analysis of individual life histories and memoirs, both of teachers and pupils, will widen the research agenda and offer deeper insights into the dilemmas which education professionals grappled with at the time. In a submission to the Ministry of Religion and Education in 1887, for example, a *Gymnasium* teacher from Lower Styria voiced his objections to the notion of imparting to pupils something other than the "historical truth" and his reflections provide several interesting pointers for the subject under discussion.[87] In this teacher's view, patriotic exaggeration would only cause harm, and one should not belittle or demean the Habsburgs' opponents. Clearly, the author was speaking from the personal experience of daily life in school, for he strongly believed that the use of punishments was an ineffective means of "fighting against national fanaticism." Teachers did indeed encounter this "intellectual illness" in *Gymnasien,* but hard measures would only aggravate, rather than remedy, the situation. Instead, instructors should treat the history of Germans and Slavs "with the same love and in the same detail," such that fanaticism—and not national consciousness—would be suppressed. In this way, the author maintained, the "malicious side-by-side" existence of pupils from both nations (in this case, Germans and Slovenes) would give way to "noble competition."

The teacher certainly does not give the impression that the often exaggerated, repetitious textbook narratives about the greatness of the Habsburgs were particularly effective in this specific instance. No doubt, in many individual cases this will have been true, but anecdotal evidence of this kind will necessarily remain impressionistic until more systematic research is forthcoming. It remains to be investigated how typical such a situation might have been; what role the experience of learning history played in promoting a feeling of attachment to, or rejection of, the Habsburg dynasty and Austro-Hungarian state; and why, as the material studied here suggests, the Austrian school system adapted more readily to pressures for an increase in the national content of textbooks at the primary level rather than at the secondary level.

Notes

* This article was translated from the German by Laurence Cole.
1. Benedict Anderson, *Imagined Communities. Reflections on the Origins and Spread of Nationalism* (revised edition, London, 1991), esp. 67–82.
2. Monika Flacke, ed., *Mythen der Nationen. Ein europäisches Panorama. Begleitband zur Ausstellung 1998 im Deutschen Historischen Museum Berlin*, (2nd ed., Berlin 2000). Particularly relevant to the discussion here is the introductory piece: Etienne François and Hagen Schulze, "Das emotionale Fundament der Nationen," 17–32.
3. See, among others: Eugen Weber, *Peasants into Frenchmen. The Modernization of Rural France 1870–1914* (Stanford, 1976); Antoine Prost, *Éducation, Société et politiques. Une Histoire de l'enseignement en France de 1945 à nos jours* (Paris, 1992); Carolyn P. Boyd, *Historia Patria. Politics, History, and National Identity in Spain, 1875–1975* (Princeton, 1997).
4. Oscar Jászi, *The Dissolution of the Habsburg Monarchy* (2nd edition, Chicago, 1961), esp. 433–439.
5. Helmut Engelbrecht, *Geschichte des österreichischen Bildungswesens Bd.1–6. Erziehung und Unterricht auf dem Boden Österreichs* (Vienna, 1982-95); Hannelore Burger, *Sprachenrecht und Sprachengerechtigkeit im österreichischen Unterrichtswesen 1867–1918* (Vienna, 1995); Klaus Frommelt, *Die Sprachenfrage im österreichischen Unterrichtswesen 1848–1859* (Graz-Cologne, 1963).
6. On Hungary, see Charles Jelavich, *South Slav Nationalisms. Textbooks and Yugoslav Union before 1914* (Columbus, 1990); Joachim von Puttkamer, *Schulalltag und nationale Integration in Ungarn. Slowaken, Rumänen und Siebenbürger Sachsen in der Auseinandersetzung mit der ungarischen Staatsidee 1867–1914* (Munich, 2003). Compare also: Árpád von Klimó, *Nation, Konfession, Geschichte. Zur nationalen Geschichtskultur Ungarns im europäischen Kontext* (Munich and Vienna, 2003).
7. Stefan Zweig, *Die Welt von Gestern. Erinnerungen eines Europäers* (Frankfurt am Main, 1970), 32–40. The sections on his school years are extremely critical in nature. The author of the Meyeriade, Oskar Kraus, came from a German-Jewish family in Prague and used the Greek epic form as a satirical device for describing the reality of school life. See Oskar Kraus, *ΜΕΥΡΙΑΣ. Humoristisches Epos aus dem Gymnasialleben* (Leipzig, 1892).
8. For a preliminary discussion of these issues, see: Ernst Bruckmüller, "Zur Entstehung der kulturellen Differenz. Fragmentarische Überlegungen zum Verhältnis von Nationalbewußtsein und Grundschulbildung im alten Österreich", in *FOCUS AUSTRIA. Vom Vielvölkerreich zum EU-Staat. Festschrift für Alfred Ableitinger*, ed. Siegfried Behr et al. (Graz, 2003), 164–179.
9. In imperial Austria, the *Gymnasium* was the academically most prestigious of the upper secondary schools, and was distinguished by its attention to the teaching of Latin. Set up in the modern form in the 1850s, it was the equivalent to a grammar school in Great Britain, or the years of middle and high school in the USA. See Gary B. Cohen, *Education and Middle-Class Society in Imperial Austria 1848–1918* (West Lafayette, 1996).
10. Compare: Ernst Bruckmüller "Patriotismus und Geschichtsunterricht. Lehrpläne und Lehrbücher als Instrumente eines übernationalen Gesamtstaatsbewußtseins in den Gymnasien der späten Habsburgermonarchie", in *Vilfanov zbornik. Pravo—zgodovina—narod. Recht—Geschichte—Nation. In memoriam Sergij Vilfan*, ed. Vincenc Rajšp and Ernst Bruckmüller (Ljubljana, 1999), 511–530.
11. Burger, *Sprachenrecht und Sprachengerechtigkeit*, 25–31.
12. On creating patriotism via public festivities, see Daniel Unowsky, *The Pomp and Politics of Patriotism: Imperial Celebrations in Habsburg Austria, 1848–1916* (West Lafayette, 2005).
13. Friedrich Heer, *Der Kampf um die österreichische Identität* (Vienna, 1981), 323f.
14. Peter Urbanitsch, "Pluralist Myth and Nationalist Realities: The Dynastic Myth of the Habsburg Monarchy—a Futile Exercise in the Creation of Identity?," *Austrian History Yearbook* 35 (2004): 101–141.

15. School primers and popular works of history are full of praise of and glory for great rulers and commanders. See here Ernst Bruckmüller, "Österreich—'An Ehren und an Siegen reich'" *Mythen der Nationen. Ein europäisches Panorama,* ed. Monika Flacke (Berlin, 1998), 269–294. On the role of the military in creating a patriotic community, compare also Laurence Cole, "Vom Glanz der Montur. Zum dynastischen Kult der Habsburger und seiner Vermittlung durch militärische Vorbilder im 19. Jahrhundert," *Österreichische Zeitschrift für Geschichtswissenschaften* 7 (1996): 577–590.
16. Ernest Renan, "Qu'est-ce qu'une nation?," *Œvres Complètes* (Paris, 1947–61), vol. 1, 887–906.
17. Joseph Freiherr von Hormayr, *Österreichischer Plutarch, oder Leben und Bildnisse aller Regenten und der berühmtesten Feldherren, Staatsmänner, Gelehrten und Künstler* (originally published Vienna, 1807–14, re-printed in: *Austria: Österreichischer Universal-Kalender,* 2 volumes, Vienna, 1854–57).
18. Eckart Vancsa, *Aspekte der Historienmalerei des 19. Jahrhunderts in Wien* (Diss., Vienna, 1973), 147f.
19. Puttkamer, *Schulalltag und nationale Integration in Ungarn,* 255–264.
20. Ibid., 446; full details of the *Lex Apponyi* at 123–138.
21. Burger, *Sprachenrecht,* passim
22. Burger, *Sprachenrecht,* esp. 37ff. Burger points to the central role of the provincial school authorities, whose intervention could lead to adjustments in the right to instruction in the mother-tongue at elementary level (44ff).
23. Georg Ullrich, J. Vogl, and Franz Branky, *Lesebuch für österreichische allgemeine Volksschulen (Ausgabe in acht Theilen), 1. Theil (Fibel)* (Vienna, 1888, unchanged reprint of the 1887 original); Georg Ullrich, W. Ernst, and Franz Branky, *Lesebuch für österreichische allgemeine Volksschulen (Ausgabe in acht Theilen), 2. Theil* (Vienna, 1888); Georg Ullrich, J. Vogl, and Franz Branky, *Lesebuch für Österreichische allgemeine Volksschulen (Ausgabe in acht Theilen), 3. Theil* (Vienna, 1888); Georg Ullrich, W. Ernst, and Franz Branky, *Lesebuch für österreichische allgemeine Volksschulen (Ausgabe in acht Theilen), 4. Theil* (Vienna, 1888); Georg Ullrich, W. Ernst, and Franz Branky, *Lesebuch für österreichische allgemeine Volksschulen (Ausgabe in acht Theilen), 5. Theil* (Vienna, 1888); Georg Ullrich, W. Ernst, and Franz Branky, *Lesebuch für österreichische allgemeine Volksschulen (Ausgabe in acht Theilen), 7. Theil* (Vienna, 1888); Georg Ullrich, W. Ernst, Franz Branky, *Lesebuch für österreichische allgemeine Volksschulen (Ausgabe in acht Theilen), 8. Theil* (Vienna, 1888). I was unable to locate the sixth volume in this publication series. Here, I would like to thank most warmly Wilbirg Stöger and Erich Pehm of the *Österreichischer Bundesverlag* for the opportunity to work in the publishing house's extensive archive.
24. Ullrich, Vogl, and Branky, *Lesebuch 3. Theil,* 111–135.
25. On this point, see Bruckmüller, "Österreich. An Ehren und an Siegen reich", 273ff. For a more general discussion of Habsburg myth making, see Marie Tanner, *The Last Descendant of Aeneas. The Hapsburgs and the Mythic Image of the Emperor* (New Haven and London, 1993); Andrew Wheatcroft, *The Habsburgs. Embodying Empire* (London, 1995).
26. Ullrich, Ernst, and Branky, *Lesebuch,* 4. Theil, 116–142.
27. Ibid., 143ff.
28. Compare Oswald Egger and Hermann Gummerer, *Walther. Dichter und Denkmal* (Vienna and Bozen, 1990).
29. On Ressel, see Ernst Bruckmüller, "Josef Ressel—ein gemeinsamer 'lieu de mémoire' Mitteleuropas?" in *Transnationale Gedächtnisorte in Zentraleuropa,* ed. Jacques Le Rider, Moritz Csáky, and Monika Sommer (Innsbruck-Vienna-Munich, 2002), 99–108.
30. Jan Šťastný and Josef Sokol, *Čítanka pro školy obecné* (Vydání pětidilné), Dil III (Vienna, 1889), 118ff.
31. Ibid., 119.
32. Ibid., 142ff.
33. Ibid., 151ff.

34. Ibid., 158–164.
35. Jan Šastný and Josef Sokol, *Čítanka pro školy obecné* (Vydání pětidilné), Dil IV (Vienna, 1889) 132–192.
36. Ibid., 193ff.
37. An interesting precedent here for the avoidance of possibly unpleasant memories was established by the censor forbidding the performance of Franz Grillparzer's König Ottokar in the 1820s, out of fear of a critical reaction by the Bohemian nobility. Franz Grillparzer, *König Ottokars Glück und Ende* (Vienna 1823).
38. *Letture per la Terza Classe delle Scuole Elementari* (Vienna, 1878); *Letture per la Quarta Classe delle Scuole Elementari* (Vienna, 1878).
39. Francesco Timéus, *Letture per le Scuole popolari austriache* (edizione in otto parti), parte III e IV (Vienna, 1889–90).
40. *Berilo za tretji razred* (Vienna, 1879), 217f.
41. Ibid., 218.
42. *Tretje berilo za občne ljudske šole. Pregledana izdaja* (Vienna, 1895).
43. Ibid., 37–41. Illustrated editions of this story, retold by Fran Levstik for children, are still widely available in Slovenian bookshops today.
44. Ibid., 56, 58, and 96ff.
45. Ibid., 201ff.
46. Ibid., 219ff and 222f.
47. Peter Končnik, *Četrto berilo za občne ljudske in nadaljevalne šole* (Vienna, 1893), 246ff.
48. Ibid., 258.
49. Ibid., 292. Naturally, this assertion (which is still popular in Slovenia today) does not represent the full complexity of the situation, because such an action required the approval of the Holy See, the Austrian government, and the Archbishop of Salzburg. Compare Sergij Vilfan, "Območja okrožij in Lavantinske škofije v Slomškovem času," *130 let visokega šolstva. Zbornik simpozija* (Maribor-Celje, 1991), 44–54.
50. Compare Jelavich, *South Slav nationalisms*, 244–262.
51. Henrik Schreiner and Fr. Hubad, *Čítanka za obče ljudske šole. III. del* (Vienna, 1904).
52. Henrik Schreiner, *Čítanka za obče ljudske šole. IV. del* (Vienna, 1909).
53. Ibid., 121f.
54. Sergij Vilfan, *Die österreichische Identität aus slowenischer Sicht* (1991), unpublished manuscript in the possession of the author.
55. Cohen, *Education and Middle-Class Society*.
56. It goes without saying that speeches and petitions to parliament are also relevant to this matter, but this requires a fuller discussion than can be offered here.
57. This was an important theme in the Enlightenment, and a text by Josef von Sonnenfels on this subject from the 1750s was still reprinted in shortened form in readers published at the end of the nineteenth century. Compare Josef Lehmann, Franz Branky, and Johann Sommert, *Deutsches Lesebuch für die österreichischen Lehrer- und Lehrerinnen-Bildungsanstalten, II. Theil (für den 2. Jahrgang)* (second edition, Vienna, 1894), 187f. On Sonnenfels' patriotism, see Grete Klingenstein, "Sonnenfels als Patriot," in *Judentum im Zeitalter der Aufklärung*, ed. Ingeborg Wiesbach (Wolfenbüttel, 1977), 211–228.
58. See the contributions in Richard G. Plaschka, Gerald Stourzh, and Jan Niederkorn, eds., *Was heisst Österreich? Inhalt und Umfang des Österreichbegriffs vom 10. Jahrhundert bis heute* (Vienna, 1995).
59. Helmut Engelbrecht, "Geschichtswissenschaft und Vermittlung—Geschichtsunterricht in Gymnasien (bis zum Ende der Donaumonarchie)", *Österreich in Geschichte und Literatur* 42 (1998): 70–86, here 72.
60. Engelbrecht, "Geschichtswissenschaft", 73.
61. Joseph Alexander Frh. von Helfert, *Über Nationalgeschichte und den gegenwärtigen Stand ihrer Pflege in Oesterreich* (Prague, 1853). On Helfert, see Franz Pisecky, *Joseph Alexander*

Frh.v. Helfert als Politiker und Historiker (Diss., Vienna, 1949); Helga Koller, *Die Haltung des Frh. Josef Alexander von Helfert zu den Hauptproblemen der Monarchie* (Diss., Vienna, 1962).
62. Helfert, *Über Nationalgeschichte*, 1f.
63. Alphons Lhotsky, *Geschichte des Instituts für österreichische Geschichtsforschung, 1854–1954* (Graz-Cologne, 1954).
64. *Entwurf der Organisation der Gymnasien und Realschulen in Österreich. Unveränderter Abdruck des Textes vom Jahre 1849* (Vienna, 1879), 30f. On the development of "fatherland studies" (*Vaterlandskunde*), compare Gerald Grimm, *Vaterländische Erziehung im Rahmen der Thunschen Bildungsreform und des neoabsolutistischen Systems 1848–1860* (MA Thesis, Klagenfurt, 1980).
65. *Entwurf der Organisation*, 31f.
66. *Entwurf der Organisation*, 152ff.
67. *Instructionen für den Unterricht an den Gymnasien in Österreich* (Vienna, 1884), 149ff.
68. *Instructionen für den Unterricht*, esp. 158ff.
69. *Lehrplan und Instruction für den Unterricht an den Gymnasien in Österreich* (2nd edition, Vienna, 1900), passim.
70. Engelbrecht, Geschichtswissenschaft, here 75 (citing the *Verordnungsblatt für den Dienstbereich des Ministeriums für Cultus und Unterricht* 1908, Nr. 18, page 190).
71. For example: Anton Gindely, *Lehrbuch der allgemeinen Geschichte für die oberen Classen der Real- und Handelsschulen, 1. Bd. Alterthum* (Prague, 1870); Ibid., *Lehrbuch der allgemeinen Geschichte für die unteren Classen der Mittelschulen, Erster Theil: Das Alterthum* (7th edition, Prague, 1881); Ibid., *Lehrbuch der allgemeinen Geschichte für Ober-Gymnasien 1. Bd. Das Alterthum* (Prague, 1861); Ibid., *Lehrbuch der allgemeinen Geschichte für Realschulen, Bd.2* (Prague, 1865); Ibid., *Manuale di Storia Universale per le Classi Inferiori delle Scuole Secondarie, Parte Prima, L'Antichità* (Vienna-Prague, 1889); Ibid., *Manuale di Storia Universale* (Trieste, 1888); *Gindelys Lehrbuch der allgemeinen Geschichte für die oberen Classen der Gymnasien, III. Bd.* (9th edition, Vienna-Prague, 1896).
72. On Gindely, see Brigitte Hamann, "Anton Gindely—ein altösterreichisches Schicksal", *Nationale Vielfalt und gemeinsames Erbe in Mitteleuropa*, ed. Erhard Busek and Gerald Stourzh (Vienna-Munich, 1990), 27–38.
73. For example, one does not find in Gindely's books the otherwise so popular episode of Rudolf of Habsburg and the priest. Compare Bruckmüller, "Österreich—'An Ehren und an Siegen reich,'" 275.
74. Bruckmüller, "Österreich—'An Ehren und an Siegen reich,'" 273ff.
75. *200 Jahre österreichische Unterrichtsverwaltung 1760–1960* (Vienna, 1960), 83; Günter Treffer, *Drei Jahrhunderte für Schule und Wissenschaft. Der Verlag Hölder-Pichler-Tempsky und seine Vorgänger* (Vienna, 1990), 53 and 66.
76. Engelbrecht, "Geschichtwissenschaft", 84.
77. Österreichisches Staatsarchiv, Allgemeines Verwaltungsarchiv (hereafter AVA), Ministerium für Kultus und Unterricht, 24 D (Geschichte - Lehrbücher), Fasz. 4852, 4853, 4854. Note that there are no reports to be found here on Czech books—they seem to have been transferred to Czechoslovakia after 1919. Likewise, there is nothing on Galicia, which reflects the region's virtual autonomy in such matters. Provincial officials simply informed the Ministry as to which books had been approved for publication.
78. For what follows, see Bruckmüller, "Patriotismus und Geschichtsunterricht", 524–526.
79. Ivan Hoić, *Opca Povjesnia za niže razrede srednjih škola* (Zagreb, 1896). The report is located in: AVA, Ministerium für Kultus und Unterricht, 24 D, Fasz. 4852, Zl. 5132/1898. The fact that books were published in the Hungarian half of the state and approved for use in Croatia did not automatically mean that they were permitted for use in Austria.
80. AVA, Ministerium für Kultus und Unterricht, 24 D, Fasz 4852, 4141/1900.
81. Treffer, *Drei Jahrhunderte für Schule und Wissenschaft*, 65ff.

82. AVA, Ministerium für Kultus und Unterricht, 24 D, Fasz. 4853, 1909.
83. On this, see Ernst Bruckmüller, *Nation Österreich. Kulturelles Bewußtsein und gesellschaftlich-politische Prozesse* (Vienna, 1996), esp. 286ff. In German literature classes, for example, the state sought to counter the danger of too strong an identification with German culture and Germany by concluding the eighth and final year of secondary schooling with a presentation of "Austria's emerging literary life from the Josephinian period, with special emphasis on Grillparzer." In one submission to the Education Ministry, German Literature teachers also demanded extensive treatment of Lenau and Anastasius Grün. See AVA, Ministerium für Kultus und Unterricht, Fasz. 1607, 23086/1887
84. Cohen, *Education and Middle-Class Society,* 212–213.
85. Jászi, *Dissolution of the Habsburg Monarchy,* 435.
86. Jelavich, *South Slav Nationalisms,* 273.
87. AVA, Ministerium für Kultus und Unterricht, Fasz. 1607, Konvolut 2692/1887 contains several statements and submissions from Styria and Carniola, including that discussed here; the author of this particular document is named as one Michael Knittel.

Chapter 2

MILITARY VETERANS AND POPULAR PATRIOTISM IN IMPERIAL AUSTRIA, 1870–1914

Laurence Cole

Of all the manifold images conjured up by the Habsburg military, two of the most enduring are those associated with the *Radetzkymarsch* on the one hand and *The Good Soldier Svejk* on the other. The first of these recalls the most famous Austrian military commander of the nineteenth century, Field-Marshall Count Joseph Anton Wenzel Radetzky (1766–1858), whose deeds—above all, his victories in Northern Italy in 1848–49—were immortalized by Johann Strauss the Elder in his celebratory composition, the *Radetzkymarsch* of 1848. The resounding success of Strauss' tune, with its triumphal invocation of victory and loyalty to the cause, subsequently made it a logical choice for the title of Joseph Roth's eponymous novel, published in 1932. The elegiac, wistful nostalgia of Roth's literary masterpiece extended and bolstered the idea of Radetzky and the Habsburg army as the embodiment of the imperial idea. The second image, that of the good soldier Svejk, could hardly be in greater contrast to the first. The character of Svejk was first brought to life in 1911 by Czech writer, Jaroslav Hašek, in a short story. However, Svejk is most often remembered as the central protagonist in *The Good Soldier Svejk*, the story which was begun in 1921 and left uncompleted at the time of Hašek's death in 1923. Svejk's bumbling subversion of the ideals of army and state leaves an impression of a Habsburg military defined by incompetence, inefficiency, and apathy.

If these images comprise differing verdicts as to the military effectiveness and achievements of the Habsburg army, they also posit contrasting notions of how the military—and by extension, the Habsburg state itself—was able to mobilize the loyalty of the multinational population. As studies of other European countries have indicated, the army and martial images—in particular, that of "the people in arms"—played key roles in constructing a sense of national identity and in mobilizing the male population behind national goals during the nineteenth century.[1] Historians of the Habsburg Monarchy have, by contrast, devoted surprisingly little attention to the role of the army in fostering a sense of state- and dynasty-based loyalty. Certainly, general works on the modern Habsburg Monarchy routinely refer to the army as a "bulwark" of the state.[2] Yet, assertions of this kind have rarely been subjected to closer analysis, with the major exception of István Deák's study of the Habsburg officer corps.[3]

This article investigates a subject which has attracted merely sporadic attention hitherto, namely that of military veteran associations in the Austrian half of the Habsburg Monarchy.[4] The history of these groups, which became increasingly popular after 1870, provides important insights into the place of the army in Habsburg society and its ability to foster imperial loyalty, for it highlights a key area where military and civilian spheres intersect. Analysis of the veterans' movement shows that the Habsburg authorities actively intervened in civil society in order to foster a sense of loyalty to the dynasty and state. Indeed, the Habsburg authorities sought to project the military as a model for the behavior of all the state's citizens.

In exploring these issues, the concern here is exclusively with the Austrian half of the imperial state (Hungary representing a different set of dynamics and field of study).[5] More particularly, close attention is paid to the south-western periphery of imperial Austria, namely the Italian-speaking part of Tyrol (Trentino). A detailed case study of this area enables us to observe how a "community of loyalty" was established at the level of local society.[6]

1. The organization of military veterans in Cisleithania

Aside from the fact that European society as a whole was undergoing a process of militarization at this time, the activities of veterans associations in late nineteenth-century Austria are of particular interest given the notably martial tone to representations of imperial power during the long reign of Emperor Franz Joseph I (1848–1916). Recent scholarship has illuminated how, for a complex variety of reasons, a monarchical cult surrounding the Habsburg ruler grew in popularity as Franz Joseph's rule drew on.[7] The military component constituted a vital feature of dynastic self-representation in this era—much more so than under the Emperor's two immediate predecessors. This was not simply because the restoration of Habsburg authority at the start of his reign was the product of a military-led counter-revolution; Franz Joseph's personal understanding of his own position as the "first soldier of the Empire" manifested itself in the form that he rarely presented himself in public in anything other than military uniform (and he predominantly appeared so in official portraiture).

At the same time, there was a deliberate emphasis on the public visibility of the military: the immediate post-1848 years saw the erection of a series of barracks close to Vienna city center, as well as the building of the new Arsenal (1849–56), which later came to house the military historical museum (*Heeresgeschichtliches Museum*). The latter opened in 1891 and was devoted to the glorification of past victories and heroes.[8] Such buildings were complemented by the laying out of the Heroes' Square (*Heldenplatz*) as part of the extension of the imperial palace in Vienna, and by the festive unveiling of a series of statues to military heroes in various locations around the city. Officially sponsored monuments to Archduke Charles (1860), Prince Eugene of Savoy (1865), and Prince Schwarzenberg (1867) were unveiled in prominent locations in the imperial capital. Later, other monuments followed of Field-Marshall Radetzky (1892), Archduke Albrecht (1899)—these two being funded with the help of contributions from the public and the army—and the *Deutschmeister* regiment (1906).[9]

Examination of the veterans' movement allows us to assess the reception of this martialized imperial image at the ground level. Veterans of military campaigns fought by the Habsburg army formed a recognizable social type in the early modern period, but it was not until after the Napoleonic Wars that groups of veterans started to band together in formal organizations. One contemporary chronicler, Louis Fischer, suggests that the first proper veterans' association in the Habsburg Monarchy was founded in the north Bohemian town of Reichenberg/Liberec in 1820.[10] The association's basic aim was to provide help to ill or needy members and to ensure that the members received a decent funeral. This mutual insurance function formed the main rationale for all such associations subsequently founded. After Reichenberg, other associations were founded in Bohemia, as well as in Vienna in 1840, under the protectorate of Prince Karl von Schwarzenberg. Several more were to follow, principally in the provinces of Bohemia, Upper Austria, Lower Austria, and Salzburg—regions which were to remain core territories of the veterans' movement throughout the period until 1914.

Precise statistical information on the spread of veterans' groups is hard to come by for the period before 1870, but it is clear that the popularity of veterans' associations rapidly began to gather pace in the second half of the nineteenth century. The initial impetus came from the various wars of the mid-century—1848–49 (in northern Italy), 1859 (against Piedmont and France), and especially, 1864 (Denmark), and 1866 (Prussia, Italy). No less than 44 of the 48 associations named by Fischer were founded in the 1860s, which was indicative of the inadequacy of the state-run "Invalids Fund" in covering the needs of all but the most desperate former soldiers.[11]

The decisive phase for the development of the veterans' associations came with the introduction of universal conscription in 1868, as part of the far reaching reforms in response to the army's defeat against Prussia in 1866.[12] In place of the old system of recruitment by district, the army law of 5 December 1868 introduced a universal levy, where conscripts had to serve for a term of three years. On an annual basis, a contingent of 95,000 conscripts was to be raised, a figure which was increased to 103,100 in 1889.[13] In practice, implementation of this legislation was far from perfect and not without opposition, while the whole "army question" of course remained a key point of tension in relations between Austria and Hungary under the Dual Monarchy. Whereas, when the reforms were introduced, there was widespread consensus between the military establishment and the leading political classes over the need for change, opinions began to diverge increasingly toward the end of the century, as liberal criticism of the army was matched by that from the social democrats. Moreover, force—or the threat thereof—had sometimes been required to see that the law was respected. A rebellion had to be crushed in the south Dalmatian mountain district of Krisvosije in 1869, and careful negotiations were necessary to gain Tyrol's participation in the new system.[14] The numbers recruited often fell short of that required and the military would often complain about the quality of recruits. As in all armies, there were also attempts at evasion, though the rates declined for the most part up until 1900 (climbing again thereafter in the Hungarian lands, the Littoral, Carniola, Dalmatia, Galicia, and Bukowina, for reasons that are as yet unclear).[15] However, at least some of these difficulties were due to the Habsburg Monarchy's relative economic weakness compared to the leading Great Powers and the perennial financial constraints on the state coffers.[16]

Despite the problems, the principle of military service was successfully established and gained general acceptance, thus testifying to the success since the early modern period of the Habsburg Monarchy in this area of state building.[17] Moreover, even if the social spread of recruits was not as wide as originally envisaged (as elsewhere in Europe, those with property and education were more likely to avoid the obligation), the composition of the conscript army faithfully reflected the ethnic composition of the state (in contrast to the German dominated officer corps).[18] For the millions of young men who fulfilled their military service in the years after 1868, the experience had a lasting impact on their lives for a variety of reasons. Some of these were of a personal nature, in that military service marked for increasing numbers of—though not necessarily all—young men the transition from youth to adult manhood.[19] On a wider level, it seems fair to assume that such aspects of military service as being obliged to wear "the Emperor's uniform", swearing an oath of loyalty to his person, obeying the commands of his officers, traveling through and/or living in different areas of the monarchy, and being confronted with other ethnic groups (often on a daily basis in barracks, as well as on the outside) would all have raised the individual's consciousness about the multinational state and its ruler.

Given the current state of research, it is still a matter of conjecture as to how far the formative experience of military service possessed an integrative function in terms of fostering a sense of loyalty to the Habsburg Monarchy.[20] For some, it was doubtless the case that the imposition of authority, the obligation to respect the army's rules and discipline, and the sheer monotony of barracks life could have an alienating effect, as memoirs, novels, and critical newspaper reports on excessive disciplinary measures imply.[21] Tensions could also arise in towns with army or navy bases, where ethnic politics could assume anti-militaristic dimensions, exacerbated by the arrogant attitude of officers from another nationality.[22] Socialist and nationalist critiques of the army often sought to play up these issues, while the emergence of the pacifist movement around Bertha von Suttner makes it clear that the army and question of military service could be politically and socially divisive.[23]

On balance, however, it does seem that military service produced a sense of attachment to the Habsburg state among the majority who passed through the army's ranks, certainly if one considers that it was only at a late stage in World War I when a majority of soldiers seriously began to question the existence of the Habsburg state.[24] Above all, the enormous proliferation of military veterans associations across Cisleithania in the last third of the nineteenth century suggests that, for more soldiers than not, military service was not just accepted, but helped produce a loyalist constituency within Austria.

After the gradual growth of veterans' associations through the 1860s, the number of ex-soldiers' groups expanded greatly after 1870 to become one of the most numerous types of civil association in imperial Austria, superseded only by voluntary fire brigades, savings associations, and mutual insurance societies of an essentially economic nature. By 1890, there were already approximately 1,700 veterans' associations in Cisleithania.[25] Further expansion up until 1912 resulted in an official figure of around 2,250 veterans' associations, comprising a membership of several hundred thousand veterans—though these later, centrally collated figures probably underestimate the true picture.[26] Undoubtedly, this massive growth cannot be reduced to patriotic sentiments alone. Aside from the practical, mutual insurance function that provided their initial *raison d'être,* these associations constituted an important forum for male sociability in town and village alike.[27] Yet, the veterans' public, patriotic role was a vital, and increasingly prominent, part of their activities, while the values and ideals they propagated implied a strong, positive identification with the Habsburg state.

This is evident from two main developments. First, the charitable aspect of the associations as a means of mutual insurance against ill health and to defray funeral costs was less dominant as economic development spread and state welfare schemes were introduced. Hermann Hinterstoisser indicates that measures such as the health insurance scheme for tenured laborers (*Dienstboten*) in 1886 helped slow down what had been a phenomenally rapid expansion hitherto.[28] While the original, insurance-based functions were still important for many members, especially in the poorer, more agricultural regions, they were no longer always the primary motivation for forming an association. This allowed greater emphasis to be placed on the wider aims of these veterans groups, whose statutes always placed great value on the maintenance of the "military spirit," the "loyal devotion to the illustrious, hereditary dynasty," and the "conduct of an exemplary life in a moral sense."[29]

Second, state institutions—in particular, the Ministry for Local Defense *(Ministerium für Landesverteidigung)*—sought to become more involved in, and to direct, the activities of military veterans, with the aim of reinforcing their patriotic role in society. After 1868, the Local Defense Ministry embarked upon a campaign to publicize the military and to subsidize the activities of veterans' associations and reservist formations. It reserved pages in leading papers such as the *Österreichische Illustrierte Zeitung*, in order to raise sympathy and awareness for the job carried out by the standing army.[30] From 1880 onward, the Ministry was responsible for the organization of Austrian federal shooting competitions, which brought together veterans, militia, and sharp-shooting groups on a regular basis. Most significantly, around the turn of the century the Ministry made strenuous efforts to establish a unified organization for military veterans in Austria. This proved to be a lengthy process, for the Austrian Imperial Federation of Military Veterans (*Österreichischer Militär-Veteranen-Reichsbund*), founded in Vienna in 1895, was only in 1914 converted into a new organization, the Imperial-Royal Austrian Veterans Association (*k. k. österreichischer Kriegerkorps-Verein*). As part of this process, the limited obligations established in 1889 for member associations to provide militia *(Landsturm)* back-up in case of war were confirmed and given greater weight.[31] Both the *Reichsbund* and *Kriegerkorps* were organized into territorial districts which mirrored the military administrative division of the Habsburg Monarchy.

Working closely with the Interior Ministry and its officials, the Local Defense Ministry sought to regulate and coordinate the veterans' movement, by such measures as sending out standardized copies of association statutes, the exclusion of "criminal elements" from association membership, and the formulation of guidelines for the carrying of uniforms, weapons, and flags. For example, the clothing and equipment for veterans' associations moved away from more informal, local costumes to an army-style uniform, with clearly marked rankings.[32] In all of these respects, the original civil associations assumed an increasingly military character and were subject to greater influence from the state.

Overall, the official attempts to direct the veterans' movement were reasonably successful. Closer regulation by state institutions helped remove doubts and suspicions on the part of the army, which until the 1870s–80s had been concerned about such matters as the carrying of arms by civil associations and the exclusivity of its uniforms and service badges.[33] Greater state involvement, together with the provision of guidance and financial support, helped the veterans' movement burgeon into a patriotic institution which was ever present on official state occasions and public ceremonies.

At the same time, three important qualifications can be made in terms of how far state control over the veterans association spread, although none of these aspects necessarily conflicted with the patriotic momentum. First, official influence was not always as extensive as was aimed for. The sheer number of circulars and reminders issued on the bearing of uniforms, flags, etc., is an indication that the apparently strict rules and norms were often flouted in practice, even if only in a minor way. Second, the greater state influence was not such that it could stultify the autonomous initiatives of a movement which formed a vociferous lobbying group. Not unlike imperial Germany, the degree of patriotic mobilization could outpace the resources and policies of the government of the day.[34] Veterans' publications produced, for example, constant reminders of Austria-Hungary's comparatively weak per capita military strength and argued for more active policies in this area. Third, and more significantly, the veterans' associations did not form an entirely united movement, one that was coherent throughout imperial Austria. Large numbers of individual associations did not join the umbrella federal organization, although the fact that they remained outside it by no means implied dissent from its patriotic aims. Some simply feared a loss of independent control over their activities, or they wanted to concentrate on the primary purpose of mutual assistance. Others did not want, or (more likely) could not afford, to pay the extra contribution that membership of the official organization involved.[35]

In other respects, there were competing interests at stake. There were several publications aimed at veterans and the Czech veterans actually established their own newspaper, *Vysloužilec*, in 1887. This was a clear move away from what Czech veterans saw as German dominance of the upper echelons of the Austrian veterans' movement, which imitated that of the army officer corps. It is noticeable, for example, that the veterans associations in Bohemia cited by Fischer tended to be established first in German-speaking districts, which might imply that loyalty to the Habsburg state was in such instances closely bound up with assertions of German identity, and implicitly, German hegemony in imperial Austria.[36] However, this is an area that still requires closer investigation, because Pokorny points out that Czech veterans were actually also starting to organize around this time, so Fischer may simply not have noticed it. Either way, the fact that Czech veterans often sought to organize their own affairs—albeit without successfully coming together in a unified Czech association—indicates that the military sphere was not immune from the ethnic rivalries characteristic of Bohemian society as a whole.[37]

In short, while the overall development of the veterans' movement in imperial Austria was a success, there were nevertheless clear limits as to what the state could achieve in terms of exercising full control over it. Even in an area so potentially accepting of state authority, therefore, the autonomy of this semi-militarized sphere of civil society must be acknowledged.[38]

2. The growth of veterans' associations in Trentino (Italian-Tyrol) after 1870

The case of Trentino, the Italian-speaking part of the province of Tyrol, offers a useful illustration for the spread of veterans' associations in Cisleithania at the local level. The question of popular patriotism in this region is particularly interesting from several points of view, not least the fact that the place of Italians in the Habsburg armed forces has attracted growing attention recently.[39] Italian-

Tyrol comprised territories that had mostly come into the possession of the Habsburgs in the early sixteenth century, together with the lands of the formerly sovereign Prince-Bishopric of Trento, which—while long associated with Tyrol—had not been fully integrated into the province until the dissolution of the Holy Roman Empire. Becoming a frontier after the losses of Lombardy (1859) and Venetia (1866), this part of the Habsburg Empire bordered on the newly-formed Kingdom of Italy, whose very emergence had come at Austria's expense. Although Italy was gradually to adopt a more cautious policy towards Austria-Hungary, and even entered into the Triple Alliance with it and Germany in 1882, it still posed a latent threat to the Habsburg state thanks to the dream, propagated by nationalists, of reclaiming the *"terre irredente"* of Trentino, Trieste and Gorizia.

All of this made of Trentino a contested area: the state was particularly sensitive to expressions of Italian national sentiment in the region; Tyrol's German majority (approximately 53 percent of the population) sought to maintain its hegemony over the southern part of the region and to maintain the province's territorial integrity; and the Italian population strove for autonomy from the provincial capital of Innsbruck, though the implications of their demands differed across the political spectrum.[40] As in other crownlands, the competing national and political claims of the respective groups made the issue of "loyalty" into a key term in public discourse, but the events of the mid-nineteenth century had highlighted this in a unique way. This was not just due to the secessionist rebellions in Milan and Venice in 1848–49 (which were not imitated in Trentino), but also due to the repeated attempts by Garibaldian volunteers, then and subsequently, to invade the territory and rouse the population against its "oppressors".[41] A few Trentines, mainly members of the local bourgeoisie, did indulge in moderate collaboration, but the Garibaldian campaigns did not strike a chord with most local people, notably in 1866 (even if members of the province's German majority and state officials still voiced anxieties as to the reliability of the Italian-speaking population).[42] Thus, the spread of military veterans' associations in Trentino from the last quarter of the nineteenth century onward must be viewed within an overall context of growing national conflict, in which the National-Liberal wing of the Italian national movement readily denounced close cooperation with the Austrian state as a betrayal of "Italianness" *(Italianità)*.

By 1914, 46 military veterans associations had been established in Trentino, to which could be added the interesting case of a veterans' group formed by Italian migrant laborers in Bludenz (Vorarlberg). Chronologically, it is possible to divide the growth of the veterans' movement in the region into two main phases: the 1870s–80s, and post-1900. The first associations were founded in the mid-1870s, above all in the main towns—Trento (1876) and Rovereto (1877)—but taking in smaller centers too, such as Condino (1877). Further foundations continued in the 1880s, comprising market-towns and valley centers such as Ala (1881), Arco (1886), and Borgo (1884), as well as the trading port of Riva (1886), at the head of Lake Garda. After these first initiatives, the movement lost momentum somewhat during the 1890s, but then reemerged in much greater force after 1900. In summary, by the turn of the century, there were only 13 veterans' associations in existence, meaning that the vast majority of foundations came in the decade and a half prior to 1914. At that point, the rate of expansion grew ever quicker, as the veterans movement spread into villages and communities in the alpine valleys.

What is noticeable here is the relative time lag when compared to other parts of Cisleithania; the density of associations was also less than in the German-speaking part of the province.[43] This resulted from a number of factors, which made the rate of development slower in Trentino. In the first place, it was generally the case that civil associations in imperial Austria developed earliest and most strongly in German and Czech-speaking areas. On the one hand, this was due to stronger socio-economic development and the presence of a more substantial bourgeoisie, the social group which led the way in establishing an extensive civil society. On the other hand, mass politicization in imperial Austria also tended to occur earlier in places like Bohemia, where the national conflict was most prominent, and in German-speaking parts of Alpine Austria, where the *Kulturkampf* of the 1860s–70s had been hardest fought. More peripheral and less economically developed areas, such as Galicia, only witnessed expansion of civil associations on a similar scale after a delay of one or two decades (though they then "caught up" rather quickly). Such was true of Trentino, a predominantly agricultural region, which had suffered a prolonged economic crisis after the loss of Lombardy-Venetia (and had not been so affected by the political battles of the *Kulturkampf*).[44] In addition, veterans tended to come from poorer sections of the population, those most likely to be drafted for service, and those less likely to dispose of the means (either financial or organizational) to found and support a civil association.

This general impression is reinforced by the evidence from the establishment of the first wave of veterans' associations in Trentino. During the 1870s–80s, the initiative in forming these groups came primarily from state officials or from loyalist sections of the local nobility. In the case of the Prince Rudolph Military Veterans' Association in Trento, for instance, the leading role was played by Count Sizzo de Noris, a cavalry officer. At Borgo, in the Valsugana, it was a civil servant, the local head of the financial guard, Carl Wolf, apparently of German mother-tongue, who set the ball rolling.[45] Perhaps the best example, though, is provided by Count Piero Consolati, who served for many years as District Captain *(Bezirkshauptmann)* for the political district of Riva. Consolati played a decisive role in helping set up veterans' associations in Riva, Arco, and the Ledro valley. Here, the genuine concerns of a traditional paternalist for the welfare of the mainly peasant ex-soldiers were important. There was also, however, a clearly political motivation, given that Piero Consolati, with his brother Filippo, was also active in the formation of political Catholicism in the area, as well as writing for semi-official, pro-government newspapers such as the *Gazzetta di Trento* or *La Patria*.[46]

Once the veterans' movement had gained a footing in this way, it gradually took on a momentum of its own, as the association committees became more diverse from the 1880s onward. While state officials and ex-army officers continued to be influential, village-level elites (e.g., parish council leaders), traders, artisans, and also peasants increasingly came to take charge of such groups and often continued to do so for lengthy periods of time. The only conspicuous absence in terms of the leadership in these groups is that of the free professions—the educated bourgeoisie (*Bildungsbürgertum*) was only present in the form of those in state employment. Information on the rank-and-file membership is hard to recover in detail, but the evidence from the group founded at Rovereto in 1877 points to a broad spectrum from the lower and lower middle classes (see Table 2.1.).[47]

As with most civil associations, membership numbers could fluctuate considerably and a group's vitality might often depend on the drive of the association president. If, as at Pieve di Ledro, to the west of Rovereto, the society president was tied up with private business, then comparatively little was done aside from taking part in important public ceremonies, in contrast to the flourishing groups at neighboring Riva and Arco, where lively programs were in evidence.[48] Personal rivalries and local factionalism might of course also interfere with the expansion of the movement. Such was the case at Spormaggiore, where the association had made itself "unpopular" because of its "constant party intrigues," with the result that it saw a drastic fall in numbers.[49] Problems of this kind befell any civil association, however, and need not have equated to rejection of the patriotic values espoused by the veterans movement (had that been the case the local political administration would surely have remarked upon it without fail, given that the state was so sensitive to indications of disloyalty in this part of the monarchy). Membership numbers might drop for other reasons, too, as happened when a new association was founded at Lizzana on the outskirts of Rovereto; a considerable number from Rovereto itself, including original members from the association founded in 1877, left to join the new group.[50] In addition, as the authorities sought to exercise greater control over the movement, they took a stricter line on membership criteria. A lot of associations contained "honorary" and "extraordinary" members, alongside the "ordinary" members. Reading between the lines of some reports, it appears that several groups tolerated the presence of villagers who

Table 2.1. Social Composition of the "Archduke Albert Military Veterans' Association" in Rovereto

State employment: army (incl. 1 military chaplain)	5
State employment: clerical and custodial	17
State employment: tobacco factory workers in Rovereto-Sacco	24
Municipal or communal employees	7
Commercial (shopkeepers/traders/hoteliers)	14
Artisan (carpenters, coopers, tailors, etc.)	21
Workers (rail workers, day laborers)	5
Peasants	17

had not necessarily served in the army, but wished to participate in the group's ceremonial activities (a further indication of their popularity). Increasingly, though, the administration strove to ensure that the membership rules were strictly enforced and such anomalies stopped occurring.

Whatever such short-term fluctuations, the general impression is nevertheless clear. Overall, there was a strong upward trend in the size of the veterans' movement in Trentino: in most instances, membership numbers were stable or rising. While a precise figure for total veteran membership in Trentino cannot be arrived at, it can be stated that associations gained anything from 25 to 60 members on average, with over 150 to 200 possible in the largest towns of Trento and Rovereto. More significantly, the number of associations was increasing very rapidly.

The vitality of veterans' activities in Trentino became clearly visible from around 1900 onward, with the patriotic and ceremonial role of the associations coming ever more to the fore. Generally speaking, it is possible to distinguish three main types of activity that these groups undertook, in addition to their staple function of providing mutual insurance. First, there were a series of events which marked the association's internal calendar year. Given its size and location in the regional center, the association in Trento organized a more elaborate social program than its counterparts in the valleys, but the kinds of activities it organized were typical of what might take place elsewhere. In January, the social year kicked off with the Trento society's annual general assembly; a carnival ball was also regularly held, usually in February. Spring would see an excursion outside the city, such as a short hiking tour, or a reunion with veterans from another town or village. Noteworthy here is the fact that such meetings could include get-togethers with associations from the German-speaking part of Tyrol, though significantly, reports of such activities became less frequent in the 1890s, albeit without diminishing entirely. When the veterans' association in Riva inaugurated the society's banner in 1895, for example, a delegation of fellow ex-soldiers from Bozen was present, and handed over a special ribbon to be attached to the new standard.[51] In the summer, the association at Trento would always organize at least one concert at a local hostelry, where a military band and flowing beer encouraged general merriment.

Second, the activities of military veterans were determined by the fixed dates in the official patriotic calendar, when the associations constituted a key presence alongside state officials and military officers in public ceremonies. In other words, throughout the region—as throughout Cisleithania—the major rituals enacted in the imperial capital would be played out in miniature at the local level: the feast of Corpus Christi (*Fronleichnam*) in late spring; the imperial birthday (18th August); and Franz Joseph's name-day feast (4th October). On such occasions, particularly in smaller localities where the association might fulfill tasks carried out by the army in barracks-towns, veterans would sound the *réveille* or let off a round of mortars at daybreak, before joining in the obligatory church mass. Before and after the mass, they would be involved in the procession to and from the place of worship, wearing their veterans' uniforms, carrying the association flag, and proudly sporting their medals. In the larger towns, the association president might then take part in the official imperial birthday or name-day luncheon, alongside the local mayor, district captain, state officials, army officers, school head-teachers and other worthies. Either at lunchtime or in the evening, the association would hold a festive reunion, often accompanied by a military band.[52] Although—unlike state officials—veterans were under no formal obligation to attend such events, it seems clear that there was an increasingly strong expectation they would do so, and most associations wrote into their statutes that one of their aims was the embellishment of events of this kind and members were obliged to attend.[53] Through their engagement in such festivities, the veterans groups thus sought to enhance state-organized dynastic events and to generate enthusiasm amongst the local population, thereby acting as a conduit for the dissemination of Habsburg-patriotic sentiments in society at large.

Third, veterans associations also played a prominent role in infrequently recurring celebrations, above all, those connected to the imperial house. Franz Joseph's fiftieth (1898) and sixtieth (1908) jubilees stand out in this respect, but the enthusiasm displayed on these occasions was to be found in similar fashion for Franz Joseph and Empress Elisabeth's silver wedding anniversary celebrations (1879) and Crown Prince Rudolph's wedding (1881). Solemn events would of course be marked too, notably the funeral mass held for the murdered Empress Elisabeth in 1898. Different in kind, but revolving around the same expression of dynastic loyalty, public commemorations of significant historic events or individuals also attracted the veterans' participation. These included occasions involving statewide attendance, such as the unveiling of the monument to Field-Marshall Radetzky in Vienna in 1892. A small delegation of 16 local veterans, eight of whom had fought under Radetzky in northern Italy in 1848–49, made the long rail journey to the capital, having been sent off from Trento station to the sound of the *Radetzkymarsch* played by the band of the 18th infantry regiment.[54] In addition, Italian-speaking veterans helped commemorate events of particular local significance, such as the 25th anniversary of the battle of Bezzeca (1866), when Austrian troops had successfully prevented a numerically superior force of Garibaldi's volunteers from invading further into Habsburg territory. They were also present at the centenary celebration of the Tyrolean uprising against Bavarian rule in 1809.

Annual rituals or public festivities of these kinds provided the chief opportunity for the demonstration of imperial loyalty. Indeed, imperial jubilee celebrations directly inspired the foundation of a number of associations. Carlo Giuliani and his comrades wrote to the authorities in February 1900 that they wished to form a veterans' association at Telve, in the Valsugana, in memory of the Emperor's 50th anniversary.[55] Two other good cases in point are the groups in Rabbi, whose plans to form an association on the back of the 1908 jubilee reached fruition in 1910, and Vermiglio, whose founding meeting specifically made mention of the impetus given by the same event.[56] Equally, the regular annual celebrations could have an inspirational effect. The veterans at Terzolas, for example, seem to have sent regular homage telegrams to the Emperor repeating their loyalty on the occasion of the imperial birthday (for which they were duly thanked).[57] At Torcegno in 1900, the veterans' association tried to hurry the authorities into approving its statutes because they wanted to hold their first parade on the occasion of the annual birthday celebration of "our most beloved" (*il Nostro Amatissimo*) emperor.[58]

Attachment to the imperial house was further evidenced by requests for minor Archdukes—of which, fortunately enough, the Habsburg family disposed over a large number—to assume the honorary protectorate of associations. Thus, the group at Scurelle, formed in 1910, managed to get Archduke Franz Karl to take on the role. Malé, in the Val di Sole to the north-west of Trento, named itself in honor of Archduke Ferdinand Karl in 1903. Not to be outdone, the company at Cles, the district center and slightly farther down the valley, went one better in winning the protectorate of the heir to the throne, Archduke Franz Ferdinand in 1904.[59] Particularly in the case of the lower ranking members of the imperial family, some form of direct contact—even if only in the form of correspondence—would enable patriots to focus attention on "their" archduke and establish a "personalized" dialogue of loyalty with them. The veterans' association in Trento, named after Crown Prince Rudolph, provides one such instance. The group expressed its immense joy at Rudolph's nuptial celebrations to Princess Stephanie by sending a congratulatory homage address, including a black-and-white group photo (which led the civil servant forwarding the material to enquire discreetly whether this might really be appropriate to the occasion).[60] Often, the reciprocal relationship set up by the expression of fidelity would then be acknowledged by donations from the association's protector or the emperor himself for extraordinary expenditures, such as the purchase of an association flag or uniforms.

From all of these points of view, therefore, military veterans acted as mediators of the "Austrian idea" in Trentine society. Taking an increasingly prominent role in official celebrations and state holidays, ex-soldiers' groups were expanding rapidly and enjoyed unprecedented popularity in the region before 1914.

3. Military veterans and local society in Trentino

In seeking to understand how and why the veterans' movement came to be successful in the region, three strands of explanation can be pursued, relating respectively to the practical, local, and political functions of the groups.

To begin with, it is clear that the charitable purpose of the associations remained important to the ordinary membership, as highlighted by several examples. The association at Riva, for instance, held a general meeting on the imperial birthday in 1908 and decided to follow Franz Joseph's desire to see his 60th jubilee commemorated by charitable deeds or acts of public benefit. They duly resolved to formalize their mutual aid arrangements, and set up a proper long-term fund to assist members in case of illness.[61] Indeed, there could be no better demonstration of the sense of solidarity among old comrades than the story of one particular veteran from Riva, Domenico Boaria, who had participated in the Austrian interventions in Italy in 1820–21. Boaria had been the first to register as an active member when a veterans' association was founded in the town. Dying in 1893 at the age of 93, he left his entire fortune of 1,000 florins to the good of the association; fittingly, he received a grand send-off, with the band of the 6th *Kaiserjäger* battalion, officers, and his association comrades all present.[62] In terms of their internal cohesion, therefore, the veterans' aim "to maintain their fraternal union, to help each other reciprocally in case of need," as expressed by the group at Castelfondo, continued to have primary significance.[63] The fact that veterans' associations provided an exclusive forum for male sociability further facilitated this desire to build on the companionship and mutual reliance learnt during military service. The veterans' wish to keep alive the spirit of "union among the old comrades-in-arms" testified to the formative experience they had undergone in their younger days and provided a means for them to make sense of their own life stories as their bodies aged.[64]

Besides maintaining soldierly solidarity, the veterans' associations gained appeal through their ability to enhance social integration in the community and to connect with local traditions. The former role was particularly evident in the villages, where the presence of the veterans on ceremonial occasions—whether of local importance or state holidays—was simply a way of adding greater dignity and pomp to the event. In effect, veterans could assert their importance, as well as a position of seniority, within the local order. Just as significant, however, was the fact that the veterans' associations could impart a sense of belonging to the locality (the "lived community") as well as to the wider imperial state (a community that was either "imagined" or had only been experienced temporarily, during a particular phase of the individual's life).

This symbiosis between local and imperial levels might take a very simple form, as at Riva, where the association flag bore the imperial eagle on one side and the municipal coat-of-arms on the other.[65] Elsewhere, like at Cavalese in the Val di Fiemme, the veterans' association fitted in neatly into a local historical tradition, whereby the valley—in the form of the semi-autonomous "Magnificent Community of Fiemme"—had long enjoyed a measure of independence from its overlords, the prince-bishops of Trento, which included the right to bear arms.[66] This sense of identity as a "valley-community" was explicitly reflected in the fact that the association established at Cavalese in 1898 (also, incidentally, in honor of Franz Joseph's fiftieth jubilee) called itself the *Società Veterani Fiemmesi,* and was formed into a series of four groups, comprising eighteen villages that were part of the *Magnifica Communità*.[67] In this respect, the veterans symbolized the centrality of carrying weapons to the identity of this mountain peasant community, invoking the historical narrative of an entity whose concrete powers had—with very minor exceptions—long been assumed by the Habsburg state. At the same time, the fostering of the Habsburg army's traditions by veterans' associations recalled common experiences in the patriotic defense of the land. Chief among these were the Napoleonic Wars (at a time when the commemoration of those wars was at a highpoint in Tyrol as a whole) and the campaigns of 1848, 1859, and 1866, in all of which the Fiemmese militia had played an important role and had responded promptly to the call to arms.[68]

Stories such as these might be repeated in different ways across the region, but the case of Arco provides an excellent example of how local destiny might be tied to a patriotic agenda. In Arco, this was unusually prominent, because of the close association between the town and the Austrian Field-Marshall, Archduke Albrecht (1817–95), who—attracted by the mild climate—chose to retire there after leaving active service.[69] Albrecht had a villa built, which helped to place Arco on the tourist map, and substantially assisted in its transformation from a poor agricultural village into a spa resort of international renown, attracting a clientele from across central Europe.[70] The prestige accorded by the archduke's presence brought in new investment, and Albrecht contributed substantial sums from his personal fortune towards the construction of spa facilities and a promenade— a role that was to be honored by the erection of a monument to his memory, eventually unveiled in the town in 1913.[71] As might be expected, this close personal link to the Field-Marshall created a special atmosphere for the operation of the local veterans' association. Named inevitably after Albrecht, the association benefited from donations by the archduke, enjoyed personal contacts with him, and consequently distinguished itself by the zeal with which it went about its activities.

If both social-charitable and local considerations thus played a part in sustaining the growth of veterans' activities, just as important toward this aim—and perhaps decisive—was the process of mass politicization emerging from the 1890s onward.[72] In other words, veterans' activities constituted a definitely politicized form of sociability within the context of Trentine politics. After the previously broad national movement had started to fracture in the 1860s and 1870s, due to church-state conflicts in Austria and the formation of the new Kingdom of Italy, politics in Italian-Tyrol was dominated by the national liberal party, which long monopolized Trentine representation in the Tyrolean Diet and the Austrian parliament.[73] From the 1890s onward, however, their conservative opponents started to organize more effectively, and adopted a more popular social program. Through cooperative organizations and the promotion of agricultural improvements, the new party's primary aim was to work toward economic autonomy, which was seen as a precondition for the political autonomy of the small "Trentine Fatherland" (*patria trentina*).[74] While defending Italian culture from the incursions of pan-German associations, the new Popular Party (*Partitio Popolare*) rejected the overtly national programs of the liberal and socialist parties, and sympathized with the conservative direction of the Austrian state and its support for the Roman Catholic Church. Above all, the Popular Party argued for a pragmatic strategy, which—in contrast to the liberals, who had frequently boycotted the Tyrolean Diet—involved working with the Austrian state to promote economic improvement and to obtain concessions regarding greater Italian influence in the administration of the province. This policy won the Popular Party sufficient support in the Diet and parliamentary elections to overthrow the previous Liberal dominance and win a comfortable majority among the population in the first decade of the twentieth century.

If the political majority thus sought accommodation with the Austrian state, then the veterans' movement represented the most Austrophile section of Trentine society. Or, as Jiří Pokorny has remarked in the Bohemian context, where the majority supported the Austrian state for a variety of reasons based on rational calculation, the veterans brought strong emotional attachment into the equation.[75] One senior administrative official in Trento expressed exactly this idea when arguing in support of an official subsidy towards the costs of a flag for the military veterans in Rovereto: "in the towns of South Tyrol [N.B., in this context, the Italian Trentino] the veterans' associations constitute an important rallying point for those elements from the lower classes loyal to the empire (*reichstreu*); and just as, on the one hand, they contribute to the raising, promotion and maintenance of patriotic sentiment and loyal devotion to the most high imperial house, so on the other hand, they become, as it were, a mark of identification for the Austrian-minded population as a result of their corporate public appearances."[76] In other words, by assiduously promoting Austrian-patriotic activities and demonstrating a strong sense of identity with the imperial dynasty, the veterans' groups helped consolidate a conservative, Catholic milieu in Trentino, and above all, in the countryside.

The popularity of the veterans' movement coalesced with the emergence of a forceful political Catholicism at two main levels, the "ideological-universal," and the "party political-national". First, in terms of what Quinto Antonelli has called the "universal symbology" of political Catholicism, the patriotic activities promoted by the veterans confirmed the centrality of the dynasty at the apex of the political and social order.[77] Antonelli suggests that political Catholics viewed the world along religious lines of "good" and "evil," whereby they represented the forces of good: upright Christians, loyal subjects, and good patriots (in both the Trentine and Austrian senses). Given that this was a patriarchal and monarchical world-view, Franz Joseph was a credible and necessary secular reference point for a political movement of this kind. The veterans' public celebration of a monarch who was considered a staunch defender of the Catholic Church, a good Christian, and a "father of his peoples" complemented the beliefs of an ideological movement that placed great value on obedience to the existing order.

Where, in terms of their internal cohesion, veterans' groups drew on horizontal models of fraternal solidarity, their public role embodied a verticalized system of male patriarchy, in which higher authority was respected and soldiers (and citizens) did their duty. Association statutes routinely emphasized this sense of duty and the public example that was expected of members, such as when stating that veterans would receive a funeral with all the "honors owed to the good soldier."[78] It was also specified that an "exemplary" moral lifestyle was a precondition for membership and that loyalty to the existing order was part and parcel of the movement's ethos. After agreeing to join the Imperial Federation of Military Veterans, for example, the authorities reminded the association in Romeno to clarify in its statutes that anyone who did not observe its "dynastic-patriotic" purpose would be excluded from membership.[79] From this standpoint, it is clear that political Catholicism and the veterans' movement both saw respect for authority and religion as fundamental values, and these provided common ideological ground between them. The propagation of these values by veterans implied that such values would be maintained and strengthened in their own communities, while demonstrations of loyalty would enable Trentine Catholics to argue that they were good and reliable citizens, who could therefore be trusted with greater political autonomy.

Second, the veterans' movement and political Catholicsm closely overlapped in terms of practical politics, even if the former comprised a more up-front, emotionalized attachment to the Austrian state. To begin with, it is clear that both drew on the same social strata for support, and in some instances, there might even be direct links in terms of personnel. One good example of this was Giovanni Zulian, founding president of the veterans' association in Soraga in the Fassa valley in 1902, who was also director of the main local cooperative organization, the Catholic-run *Famiglia Cooperativa*.[80] In the neighboring Fiemme valley, two leading members of the veterans' association were closely involved in the District Agrarian Consortium (*Consorzio Agrario Distrettuale*), a local section of the provincial agricultural council which was not part of the Catholic associational network but which had close personal links with, and the same aims as, the Trentine cooperative movement.[81] Many of the formal celebrations in which veterans participated involved a holy mass, and this cooperation could clearly lead to support for other activities as well. For example, the association of Trentine veterans in Bludenz (Vorarlberg) benefited from the practical assistance of their local sacristan when asking for their new uniform to be approved by the authorities in time to celebrate the imperial birthday in 1902.[82] While sections of the Trentine Church were not uncritical of Austria, the majority took a pro-Austrian position, and the political dividing lines that had emerged since the 1860s in effect meant that veterans and political Catholics were working in the same direction.[83] A village such as Torcegno in the Valsugana, for example, had expressed its political sympathies very clearly in 1871, sending a petition to Vienna to register its protest against the occupation of Rome by Italian troops and holding public celebrations in honor of the "prisoner in the Vatican."[84] In this respect, the parish could be considered fertile ground for the Austrian-patriotic ideals of the veterans' movement, and an association was founded there in 1900 by the long-serving schoolmaster, Chiliano Parolaro.

As well as this common ground, the veterans associations and political Catholicism shared common opponents, in that both were hostile to socialism and liberalism, and rejected the explicitly national program the respective parties put forward. As in imperial Germany, the veterans' movement at the Austrian level was marked by a clear opposition to social democracy.[85] The official veterans' organization repeatedly disparaged the socialist party, and the distance between the two in Trentino was evident in the fact that the socialist press frequently criticized militarism or mocked displays of Austrian patriotism, while socialist deputies such as Cesare Battisti criticized the military in parliament.[86]

In practical terms, however, it was the national liberal party which represented the more immediate threat, given that support for the socialist party in Trentino was comparatively small (if growing). The sector of society comprising the national liberals was not represented among the veterans, and it seems clear that the two movements were exclusive of one another. Middle-class professionals were more likely to avoid military service altogether through educational or economic dispensations, but they consciously distanced themselves from overtly "Austrian-patriotic" activities, on the basis that this would imply support for the status quo, which meant a lack of political autonomy.[87] The liberal press completely ignored the activities of the veterans' movement, and would only comment on Austrian-patriotic events where these could not be overlooked. In this respect, Trentine society was deeply divided between "Austrophile" and "Italophile" sections (though the latter did not equate to "irredentist" save at the fringe), which mirrored the struggle for political hegemony. Italian national associations, such as the "National League" (*Lega Nazionale*) or "Society of Tridentine Alpinists" (*Società dei Alpinisti Tridentini—SAT*), were present across the region, and enjoyed much greater proliferation in terms of numbers of groups. Yet, this numerical preponderance did not necessarily imply that the national movement represented the majority opinion. Davide Zaffi has indicated that, despite being able to point to a larger number of local groups, national associations in practice often had closely overlapping memberships and executive personnel.[88] In other words, such groups often looked stronger on paper than they were in practice, so the numerical supremacy of the "opponents" of the "Austrianism" (*austriacantismo*) propagated by military veterans was not as clear cut as might first appear. Moreover, national associations found it increasingly hard to recruit outside the liberal, middle-class elite that constituted their core support.[89]

At the same time, military veterans were just one strand in a wider Austrian-patriotic network, which included other organizations with patriotic aims, such as the charitable Provincial Society of the Red Cross. With as many as 52 associations in Italian-Tyrol in 1885, these groups were important in widening the social support for the Austrophile community in Trentino, as they drew on higher social classes than the veterans for their membership (the profile was more educated; again the loyalist nobility was present, as were clergymen, members of the Catholic bourgeoisie, and civil servants).[90] Just as importantly, in contrast to the overtly masculine association formed by the veterans, the Red Cross societies also brought women into the patriotic network.[91] More akin to the activities of the veterans was the growth in sharp-shooters' (*Bersaglieri*, or colloquially, "*scizzeri*") associations in Italian-Tyrol, as part of a province-wide surge in the reorganization and promotion of the tradition of local defense. By 1906, for example, there were 59 shooting-ranges in active use in Trentino (as against 23 in 1847).[92] Activities (and personnel) were often closely connected in the towns and larger villages where both a sharp-shooting and veterans' association existed, and this was also the case in the small parish of Serravalle, where the veterans' group in 1913 took the initiative in trying to build a new shooting-range for military exercises.[93] Elsewhere, towns or villages without a veterans' associations might well have a shooting-range and sharp-shooting group, and hence, an "Austrian-patriotic" institution in their community.

Conclusion

By 1914, military veterans and other Austrian-patriotic groups represented an increasing challenge to the Italian national associations that had more or less monopolized the public scene in Trentino prior to 1900. As the political conflict became more heated with the growing success of the Catholic Popular Party, so too would the animosity between the two sides. Direct contestations might even take place, such as when national associations went into the valley to promote their cause. On one occasion in 1909, the veterans in Ragoli happened to be holding their annual general meeting when they noticed a disturbance outside. The members promptly broke off during the new president's acceptance speech, as the protocol recorded, "to protest against a gang of irredentists who have dared to molest our peaceful village."[94]

At other times, veterans and their supporters stood out as upright Austrian patriots in a three-way contest in mixed language zones, such as the Val di Fassa with its Ladin dialect, or in the German language islands in the Val Fersina. In areas like these, Italian and German national associations sought to win over the (often indifferent or hostile) local population to their program, and as a result clashed in a number of incidents.[95] Where Trentine Catholics vigorously opposed the incursions of pan-German groups (for both religious and national reasons), but rejected the "fanaticism" of the *Lega Nazionale* or *SAT*, so too did the veterans disdain extremist manifestations and looked on both groups as disloyal. The Ladin Val di Fassa is particularly interesting in this respect, because here the veterans, despite historical and economic ties to parts of German-Tyrol (and in an atmosphere of pan-German activity) maintained their affiliation to Italian culture, with all of its written correspondence and statutes appearing in the Italian language. Although in one sense untypical, because of the local Romance dialect, this instance nevertheless shows how the Austrian-patriotic agenda did not require, or imply, a rejection of Italian culture. At issue was the political program and conception of the state. After members of the *Società dei Alpinisti Tridentini* arrived in Vigo di Fassa on a "propaganda mission" on 7 August 1904, two printed posters were pasted during that night on to house walls. They bore the slogans: "Evviva al Tirol! ... Evviva i valerous difensores del pais! Evviva l'Austria! Evviva nos Imperador! [Long live Tyrol! ... Long live the valorous defenders of our country! Long live Austria! Long live our Emperor!]." [96] While the authorities did not find out who put these up, the message was exactly that propagated by the local veterans, and it is not hard to imagine one of their number being involved.

Until 1914, the veterans' movement in Trentino was on a sharp upward curve in a way that reflected what was happening across Cisleithania. While there were specific local reasons and motivations for the growth of this phenomenon, there is evidence to indicate—contrary to what has sometimes been assumed—that the Austrian state was relatively successful in creating vertical ties of loyalty to the imperial center. Put another way, it was able to construct a "language of loyalty," which had a coherent semantic structure in terms of meaning and symbolism, but which was phonetically diverse: the same common message could be accessed and interpreted in different idioms.

At the same time, however, it is clear that there were limits to this success, in that it left a highly influential section of society—the liberal bourgeoisie—unmoved. Over the longer term, it is also open to question whether the degree of success achieved did not carry its own dangers, in that it encouraged the state to think in narrow and inflexible terms of the "loyalty" or "disloyalty" of its subjects, such that it alienated potential sympathizers by its own inflexibility.[97] And, ultimately, the upsurge in Austrian patriotism before 1914 was of course not enough for the monarchy to survive the traumas of the first World War, as the majority of the Trentine population turned decisively against the Habsburg state's failing war campaign.[98]

Nevertheless, there is firm evidence for the period before 1914 of a parallel, Habsburg-patriotic milieu in imperial Austria, alongside the national societies to which historians have devoted more attention. There is, too, a reminder of the comment made some time ago by István Deák, to the effect that the real fault-lines in Central European society were more—or as much—ideological and social in nature than national.[99]

Notes

1. See, among others, Linda Colley, *Britons. Forging the Nation 1707–1837* (New Haven, 1992); Jakob Vogel, *Nationen im Gleichschritt. Der Kult der "Nation in Waffen" in Deutschland und Frankreich, 1871–1914* (Göttingen, 1997); Ute Fevert, *A Nation in Barracks. Modern Germany, Military Conscription and Civil Society* (Oxford and New York, 2004); Eugen Weber, *Peasants into Frenchmen. The Modernization of Rural France 1870–1914* (Stanford, 1976); Joshua Sanborn, *Drafting the Russian Nation. Military Conscription, Total War and Mass Politics, 1905–1925* (DeKalb, Il., 2003).
2. For example: C.A. Macartney, *The Habsburg Empire 1790–1918* (London, 1968), 624–625; Jean Bérenger, *L'Autriche-Hongrie 1815–1918* (Paris, 1994), 17; Ernst Hanisch, *Österreichische Geschichte 1890–1990. Der lange Schatten des Staates: österreichische Gesellschaftsgeschichte im 20. Jahrhundert* (Vienna, 1994), 218.
3. István Deák, *Beyond Nationalism: A Social and Political History of the Habsburg Officer Corps 1848–1918* (Oxford, 1990). See also Peter Melichar, "Metamorphosen eines treuen Dieners. Zum bürgerlichen Offizier der k.(u.)k. Armee im 18. und 19. Jahrhundert," in *Bürger zwischen Tradition und Modernität. Bürgertum in der Habsburgermonarchie VI*, ed. Robert Hoffmann, (Vienna, 1997), 105–141.

4. An important exception is the work of Jiří Pokorny, "Die Tschechen für oder gegen Österreich-Ungarn?," *Der Donauraum* 35/3 (1995): 28–36.
5. For further discussion of Hungary's military position in the Monarchy, see the contributions in: Adam Wandruszka and Peter Urbanitsch, eds., *Die Habsburgermonarchie 1848–1918. Bd. V, Die bewaffnete Macht* (Vienna, 1987).
6. This case study is part of a long term project, as outlined in Laurence Cole, "Vom Glanz der Montur. Zum dynastischen Kult der Habsburger und seiner Vermittlung durch militärische Vorbilder im 19. Jh. Ein Bericht über 'work in progress,'" *Österreichische Zeitschrift für Geschichtswissenschaften* 7 (1996): 577–91.
7. On this subject, see especially Daniel Unowsky, *The Pomp and Politics of Patriotism: Imperial Celebrations in Habsburg Austria, 1848–1916* (West Lafayette, 2005); James Shedel, "Emperor, Church and People: Religion and Dynastic Loyalty During the Golden Jubilee of Franz Joseph," *The Catholic Historical Review* 76 (1990): 71–92; Andrea G. Blöchl, "Die Kaisergedenktage," in *Der Kampf um das Gedächtnis. Öffentliche Gedenktage in Mitteleuropa*, ed. Emil Brix and Hannes Stekl, (Vienna, 1997), 117–144; Peter Urbanitsch, "Pluralist Myth and Nationalist Realities: The Dynastic Myth of the Habsburg Monarchy—a Futile Exercise in the Creation of Identity?" *Austrian History Yearbook* 35 (2004): 101–141.
8. Stefan Riesenfellner, "Steinernes Bewußtsein II. Die 'Ruhmeshalle' und die 'Feldherrnhalle'—das k.(u.)k. 'Nationaldenkmal' im Wiener Arsenal," in *Steinernes Bewußtsein I. Die öffentliche Repräsentation staatlicher und nationaler Identität Österreichs in seinen Denkmälern*, ed. Stefan Riesenfellner (Vienna, 1998), 63–75.
9. Markus Kristian, "Denkmäler der Gründerzeit in Wien," in Riesenfellner, *Steinernes Bewußtsein*, 77–165.
10. Louis Fischer, *Geschichte der Militär-Veteranen-Vereine des österreichischen Kaiserstaates* (Troppau, 1870), 7, 35. Though more of a catalogue than comprehensive history, Fischer's work appears to be the only attempt published in the nineteenth century at an historical overview of the veterans' movement.
11. Fischer, *Geschichte der Militär-Veteranen-Vereine*.
12. Johann C. Allmayer-Beck, "Die bewaffnete Macht in Staat und Gesellschaft," in Wandruszka and Urbanitsch, *Die Habsburger Monarchie 1848–1918 Bd. V,* 1–141; Gunther E. Rothenberg, *The Army of Francis Joseph* (West Lafayette, 1976), 74–89.
13. Christa Hämmerle, "Die k. (u.) k. Armee als 'Schule des Volkes'? Zur Geschichte der Allgemeinen Wehrpflicht in der multinationalen Habsburgermonarchie (1866–1914/18)," in *Der Bürger als Soldat. Die Militarisierung europäischer Gesellschaften im langen 19. Jahrhundert: ein internationaler Vergleich*, ed. Christian Jansen (Essen, 2004), 175–198.
14. Deák, *Beyond Nationalism*, 61; Laurence Cole, *Für Gott, Kaiser und Vaterland. Nationale Identität der deutschsprachigen Bevölkerung Tirols, 1860–1914* (Frankfurt a.M., 2000), 428–433.
15. Hämmerle, "Die k. (u.) k. Armee als 'Schule des Volkes'?"
16. Holger Herwig, *The First World War. Germany and Austria-Hungary 1914–1918* (London, 1997), 12–13; Günther Kronenbitter, "Armeerüstung und wirtschaftliche Entwicklung in Österreich(-Ungarn) 1860 bis 1890," in *Das Militär und der Aufbruch in die Moderne 1860 bis 1890. Armeen, Marinen und der Wandel von Politik, Gesellschaft und Wirtschaft in Europa, den USA sowie Japan*, ed. Michael Epkenhans and Gerhard P. Groß (Munich, 2003), 231–241.
17. Michael Hochedlinger, "Militarisierung und Staatsverdichtung. Das Beispiel der Habsburgermonarchie in der frühen Neuzeit," in *Krieg und Akkulturation*, ed. Thomas Kolnberger et al., (Vienna, 2004), 106–129.
18. Deák, *Beyond Nationalism*.
19. Sabina Loriga, "Die Militärerfahrung," in *Geschichte der Jugend. Bd. II. Von der Aufklärung bis zur Gegenwart*, ed. Giovanni Levi and Jean-Claude Schmidt (Frankfurt a.M., 1997), 20–55; Thomas Kühne, "Der Soldat," in *Der Mensch des 20. Jahrhunderts*, ed. Ute Frevert

and Heinz-Gerhard Haupt (Frankfurt a.M., 2000), 344–371; Ernst Hanisch, *Männlichkeiten. Eine andere Geschichte des 20. Jahrhunderts* (Vienna, 2005), 17–24.
20. Erwin A. Schmidl, "Die k.u.k. Armee: integrierendes Element eines zerfallendes Staates?" in *Das Militär und der Aufbruch der Moderne*, 143–150.
21. There has been almost no serious research on the impact of military service on the ordinary population, aside from a project under completion by Christa Hämmerle at the University of Vienna. See: Hämmerle, "Die k. (u.) k. Armee als 'Schule des Volkes'?"
22. For a detailed study of such a situation in Pula/Pola, see Frank Wiggermann, *K.u.k. Kriegsmarine und Politik. Ein Beitrag zur Geschichte der italienischen Nationalbewegung in Istrien* (Vienna, 2004). On the presence of the military in a barracks-town, see also: Peter Melcihar, "Ästhetik und Disziplin. Das Militär in Wiener Neustadt 1740–1914," in *Die Wienerische Neustadt. Handwerk, Handel und Militär*, ed. Sylvia Hahn et al. (Vienna, 1994), 283–336.
23. On the pacifist movement and social democratic criticism of the military, see respectively Albert Fuchs, *Geistige Strömungen in Österreich 1867–1918* (reprinted edition, Vienna, 1984), 251–275; Harald Troch, *Rebellensonntag. Der 1. Mai zwischen Politik, Arbeiterkultur und Volksfest in Österreich (1890–1918)* (Vienna-Zürich, 1991), 77–80.
24. As argued in the case of Austro-Hungarian POWs by Alon Rachamimov, *POWs and the Great War. Captivity on the Eastern Front* (Oxford - New York, 2001). In this context, see also Péter Hanák, "Volksbriefe aus dem Ersten Weltkrieg," in Hanák, *Der Garten und die Werkstatt. Ein kulturgeschichtlicher Vergleich Wien und Budapest um 1900* (Vienna, 1992), 203–241; Mark Cornwall, *The Undermining of Austria-Hungary 1914–18. The Battle for Hearts and Minds* (Basingstoke, 2001).
25. *Handbuch der Vereine für die im Reichsrathe vertretenen Königreiche und Länder nach dem Stand am Schlusse des Jahres 1890* (Vienna, 1892).
26. *Patrioten-Kalendar für das Jahr 1913. Offizielles Jahrbuch des k.k. österr. Militär-Veteranen-Reichsbundes. XIII Jg.* (Vienna, 1913), 32–83. This publication lists 1,656 associations within the official federation of Austrian military veterans, with a membership of 209,761. It also details a further 589 military veterans associations outside the federation, but does not supply membership numbers for all these cases. However, this last figure is clearly an underestimation, given that it does not include much more than a third of the associations in existence in Italian-Tyrol/Trentino, and is also inaccurate with respect to the figure for German-Tyrol. Thus, the *Patrioten-Kalendar* suggests that there were eighty-seven veterans associations in German-Tyrol in 1912, whereas local administrative figures indicate that there were already 124 in 1907 (Tiroler Landesarchiv, Rep. 625, Vereinskataster für Deutschtirol und Vorarlberg, 1907). If it appears to be somewhere around seventy short of the true 1912 figure for the whole of Tyrol (both German and Italian speaking areas), then the repetition of a similar margin of error across Cisleithania would imply that the overall totals were perhaps 10 percent higher and potentially up to 20 percent higher.
27. Compare: Thomas Rohkrämer, *"Der Militarismus der kleinen Leute". Die Kriegervereine im Deutschen Kaiserreich 1871–1914* (Munich, 1990).
28. Hermann Hinterstoisser, "Die Uniformierung der k.k. österreichischen Militär-Veteranen- und Kriegervereine in Salzburg," *Mitteilungen der Gesellschaft für Salzburger Landeskunde* 136 (1996), 225–254.
29. Österreichisches Staatsarchiv (ÖSA), Kriegsarchiv (KA): K.k. Ministerium für Landesverteidigung, Sonderreihe Kn. 306, Statuten für den Österreichisch-Schlesischen Verein gedienter Soldaten in Wien, 3.9.1904; Statuten des Militär-Veteranen-Vereines für Schwadorf, 17 October 1907.
30. ÖSA, KA: K.k. Ministerium für Landesverteidigung, Sonderreihe Kn. 306, K.k. Min. für Landesverteidigung, Pr. No. 42, 21.3.1912.
31. ÖSA, Allgemeines Verwaltungsarchiv (AVA): K.k. Ministerium des Inneren, Präs. (15/5) Veteranen-, Turn-, Feuerwehr-, Schützenvereine Fasz. 1652–55 (1900–18).
32. Hinterstoisser, "Uniformierung."

33. Hinterstoisser, "Uniformierung."
34. Geoff Eley, *Reshaping the German Right. Radical Nationalism and Political Change after Bismarck* (New Haven, 1980); Roger Chickering, *We Men Who Feel Most German. A Cultural Study of the Pan-German League, 1886–1914* (London, 1984); Marilyn Coetzee, *The German Army League. Popular Nationalism in Wilhelmine Germany* (New York, 1990).
35. Points along these lines were made, for example, by veterans groups in the district of Bozen (German speaking Tyrol) in response to questions whether they would join the *Reichsbund*. Tiroler Landesarchiv (TLA), Statthalterei für Tirol und Vorarlberg (Statth.) 1904 Vereine Allgemein: Nr. 17630 Acten betr. Führung des Reichsadlers und der Bezeichnung kais. königl. seitens der dem Militär-Veteranen-Reichsbund angehörigen Körperschaften, ad Nr. 23018 / 14.05.1904 Bezirkshauptmann Bozen an die Statthalterei.
36. Fischer, *Geschichte der Militär-Veteranen-Vereine.*
37. Pokorny, "Tschechen für oder gegen Österreich-Ungarn?"
38. Compare here the discussion by Gary B. Cohen, "Neither Absolutism nor Anarchy: New Narratives on Society and Government in Late Imperial Austria," in *Austrian History Yearbook* 29/Pt. 1 (1998): 37–61.
39. Lawrence Sondhaus, *In the Service of the Emperor. Italians in the Austrian Armed Forces 1815–1918* (New York, 1990); Claudio Donati, "L'organizzazione militare della monarchia austriaca nel secolo XVIII e i suoi rapporti con i territori e le popolazioni italiane. Prime ricerche," in *Österreichisches Italien—Italienisches Österreich? Interkulturelle gemeinsamkeiten und nationale Differenzen vom 18. Jahrhundert bis zum Ende des Ersten Weltkrieges*, ed. Brigitte Mazohl-Wallnig and Marco Meriggi (Vienna, 1999), 297–329. See also the popular history by Alberto Constantini, *Soldati dell'imperatore. I Lombardi-Veneti nell'esercito austriaco (1814–1866)* (Collegno, 2004).
40. Maria Garbari, "Aspetti politico-istituzionale di una regione di frontiera," in *Storia del Trentino. V. L'età contemporanea 1803–1918*, ed. M. Garbari and A. Leonardi (Bologna, 2003), 13–164.
41. On 1848–49 in Tyrol, see: Hans Heiss and Thomas Götz, *Am Rande der Revolution. Tirol 1848/49* (Wien-Bozen, 1998).
42. Mauro Grazioli, et al., *Garibaldiner. Realtà e immagini della campagna garibaldina del 1866* (Tione, 1987).
43. *Patrioten-Kalender für das Jahr 1913. XIII Jg. Offizielles Jahrbuch des k.k. österreichischen Militär-Veteranen-Reichsbundes* (Vienna, 1913).
44. Andrea Leonardi, *L'economia di una regione alpina* (Trento, 1996).
45. *Neue Tiroler Stimmen*, Nr. 97 Jg. XXVI, 30.04.1886.
46. Archivio dei Conti Consolati, Seregnano.
47. Archivio Storico Comunale Rovereto, 1876 Fasc. C.II.21, No. 5766/25.08.1876 Elenco dei vecchi soldati congedati che aderirono a far parte ad una patriottica Società di Veterani di Rovereto e dintorni della Valle Lagarina.
48. TLA, Statth. 1904 Vereine Allgemein: Nr. 17630 Acten betr. Führung des Reichsadlers, ad Nr. 23018/14.05.1904 Bezirkshauptmann Riva an die Statthalterei.
49. TLA, Statth. 1904 Vereine Allgemein: Nr. 17630 Acten betr. Führung des Reichsadlers, Nr.23018/14.05.1904 Bezirkshauptmann Trient an die Statthalterei.
50. TLA, Statth. 1906 Vereine Rovereto, ad Nr. 9215 ex 1906: ad Nr. 52035 ex 1902, Protocollo di costituzione della Società dei militari veterani di Pieve di Lizzana.
51. Società Veterani Militari Principe Ereditario "Arciduca Rodolfo" in Riva, *Cenni commemorativi sulla Festa della Solenne Benedizione del Vessillo Sociale che ebbe luogo in Riva il 16 Giugno 1895* (Riva, 1895), 14.
52. AST, Sezione di Luogotenenza Trento, Busta 107 1883 Pres. E. 130: Nr. 3649/22.08.1883 Bezirkshauptmann Rovereto an die Statthalterei-Sektion; Busta 117 1886 Pres. E. 74 Nr. 1983/19.08.1886 Polizei-Kommissariat Ala an die Statthalterei-Sektion; Busta 144 1893 Pres. E. 44 Sr. k. u. k. ap. Majestät ah. Geburtstag, Nr. 1353/20.08.1893 Bericht des k. k.

Polizei-Kommissariats Trient; AST, CD Borgo Busta 43 (1908), C.D. Borgo 310-08 K.k. Landesgendarmeriekommando Nr. 3 Abt. Nr. 2 K. k. Bezirksposten Borgo an die k. k. Bezirkshauptmannschaft Borgo, 5. Oktober 1908 betr. Namensfest des Kaisers; CD Cavalese Busta 325 Vorfallenheitsbuch angefangen im Jahre 1902, Berichten betr. Feier des Ah. Geburtsfestes Sr. k.u.k. Apost. Majestät bzw. des Namensfestes.
53. For example: AST, Sezione di Luogotenenza Trento, Busta 108, Vereine 1884 (B. 1-37), Busta 15: Statuto della Società Militare dei Veterani in Borgo di Valsuagana (Borgo, 1898), §7: "Each member resident in Borgo will be obliged, on the Emperor's birthday, to take part in the mass that will be celebrated in the parish church, or in another church"; AST, CD Cavalese Busta 250 (1912, X–XXXI), C.D. Cavalese ad Nr. 4689-1/10.10.1912: Statuto della Società Veterani del distretto di Fassa Comune di Canazei (Bozen, 1908), §11: "All the active members will be obliged, on the birthday of His Majesty the Emperor, to take part *in corpore* at the solemn Holy Mass that will be celebrated in the church of Alba, in the commune of Canazei."
54. AST, Sezione di Luogotenenza Trento, Busta 133 1891 Pres. B. 23 Nr. 732/22.04.1892 K.k. Polizei Kommissariat Trient, Vorfallenheitsbericht vom 22. April 1892.
55. TLA, Statth. 1900 Vereine im Bezirke Borgo: Nr. 5448/7.2.1900 Domanda di Carlo Giuliani, all'eccelsa I.R. Luogotenenza.
56. Archivio di Stato Trento (AST), Capitanato Distrettuale (CD) Cles Busta 214, Fasc. Rabbi: C.D.Cles 19294/08-08-1910, Protocollo dell'assemblea generale tenuta dalla società militari veterani del Commune di Rabbi addi 27. Giugno 1909; Fasc. Vermiglio: C.D.Cles 22482/17-09-1909, Protocollo della fondazione della società veterani militari di Vermiglio.
57. AST, CD Cles Busta 213, Fasc. Terzolas: C.D.Cles 23388/12-12-1906, Antonio Borga, Presidente della Società veterani miliari di Terzolas an Seine k.u.k. Ap. Maj. Franz Joseph I, 15 November 1906.
58. TLA, Statth. 1900 Vereine im Bezirke Borgo, Nr. 27471/17.7.1900 Chiliano Parolaro all' I.R. Luogotenenza pel Tirolo e Vorarlberg.
59. AST, CD Borgo Busta 181, Fasc. 101; CD Cles Busta 214, Fasc. Cles; Fasc. Malè.
60. TLA, Statth. 1881 Nr. 81 Präs. Verhandlungsacten in Bezug auf die Vermählung des Kronprinzen Rudolf: Nr. 1696/12.05.1881 Statthalterei-Rat in Trient an das Statthalterei-Präsidium.
61. TLA, Statth. 1909 Vereine im Bezirke Riva: ad Nr.64330 ex 1909 Presidente della SMV Riva alla Luogotenenza in Innsbruck, 22. Ottobre 1908.
62. AST, Sezione di Luogotenenza Trento, Busta 143 1893 Pres. E. 2: Nr. 278/19.02.1893 Vorfallenheitsbericht Leichenbegängnis eines Veterans.
63. TLA, Statth. Abteilung I 1912, I-4b Zl. 26: Società Militari Veterani e Riservisti Castelfondo alla Sua Sacra Maestà, 28.03.1911.
64. TLA, Statth. 1909 Vereine im Bezirke Tione: ad Nr. 48387 Pietro Bolza alla Luogotenenza, 02.08.1909.
65. AST, Sezione di Luogotenenza Trento, Busta 144 1893 Pres. E. 47 Riva Veteranen-Verein Fahne. Allerhöchste Spende.
66. Marcello Bonazza and Rodolfo Taiani, eds., *Magnifica Communità di Fiemme. Inventario dell'archivio (1234–1945)* (Trento, 1999), xvii–xxxv.
67. TLA, Statth. 1899 Vereine im Bezirke Cavalese: ad Nr. 2275, Nr. 10916/15.03.1899, Statuto della Società Veterani Fiemmesi.
68. Candido Degiampietro, *Le milizie locali fiemmesi dalle guerre naoleopniche alla fine della I^A guerra mondiale (1796–1918)* (Villa Lagarina, 1981).
69. Christoph Allmayer-Beck, *Der stumme Reiter. Erzherzog Albrecht, der Feldherr "Gesamtösterreichs"* (Graz-Vienna, 1997).
70. Mauro Grazioli, *Arco felix. Da borgo rurale a città di cura mitteleuropea* (Arco, 1993); Paolo Prodi, ed., *Il luogo di cura nel tramonto della monarchia d'Asburgo. Arco nell'ottocento* (Bologna, 1996).
71. AST, CD Riva Busta 181 (1913): Erezione Monumento Arciduca Alberto in Arco.

72. On this point, compare: Benjamin Ziemann, "Sozialmilitarismus und militärische Sozialisation im deutschen Kaiserreich 1870–1914," in *Geschichte in Wissenschaft und Unterricht* (2002), 148–64.
73. Ilaria Ganz, *La rappresentanza del Tirolo italiano alla Camera dei Deputatit di Vienna 1861–1914* (Trento, 2001).
74. Fabio Giacomoni, *Potere clericale e movimenti popolari nel Trentino 1906–15* (Trento, 1985), esp. 212–216.
75. Pokorny, "Tschechen für oder gegen Österreich-Ungarn?"
76. TLA, Statth. 1881 Nr. 4 Präs. Begutachtungen über Majestätsgesuche und Gesuche an Erzherzoge: Nr. 2030/03.06.1881 Statthalterei-Rat in Trient an die Statthalterei.
77. Quinto Antonelli, *Fede e Lavoro, ideologia e linguaggio di un universo simbolico. Stampa cattolica trentina tra '800 e '900* (Trento, 1981).
78. AST, CD Riva Busta 215 Società statuti Fasc. 71: Statuto della Società Veterani, Militari e Bersaglieri Provinciali Arciduca Rodolfo nel Circondario Giudiziario di Riva (Riva, 1886).
79. TLA, Statth. 1906 Vereine im Bezirke Cles: Nr. 38821/20.07.1906 Ministerium des Inneren an die Statthalterei. Most association statutes came to contain explicit stipulations of this kind.
80. TLA, Statth. 1897 Vereine im Bezirke Cavalese: Nr. 13705/18.04.1897 Statuto della Famiglia Cooperativa di Soraga; Statth. 1902 Vereine im Bezirke Cavalese: Nr. 45582/28.10.1902 Bezirkshauptmann Cavalese btr. Statuten eines M-V-Vs in Soraga.
81. AST CD Cavalese Busta 222 (1904), B.VIII-19, Prospetto dimostrante le presidenze di tutte le associazioni esistenti nel Comune di Cavalese. See here: Leonardi, *Economia*, 161; Giacomoni, *Potere clericale*, passim.
82. TLA, Statth. 1902 Vereine im Bezirke Bludenz, Nr. 31440/19.07.1902 Società dei Veterani Italiani alla Luogotenenza, 18 Luglio 1902.
83. However, this did not preclude Popular Party deputies from expressing concern about military expenditures or the impact of building fortresses on peasant landholdings.
84. Giulio Candotti, *Torcegno, ieri e oggi. Cenni storici, religiosi, socio-economici, anagrafici e culturali di una picola communità Montana dal 1184 al 1996* (Feltre, 1997), 585–586.
85. Hinterstoisser, "Uniformierung." For Germany, see: Harm-Peer Zimmermann, *"Das feste Wall gegen die rote Flut." Kriegervereine in Schleswig Holstein 1864–1914* (Neumünster, 1989).
86. Ganz, *La rappresentanza del Tirolo italiano*, 241.
87. Laurence Cole, "Patriotic Celebrations in Late Nineteenth and Early Twentieth Century Tirol," in *Staging the Past. The Politics of Commemoration in Habsburg Central Europe, 1848 to the Present*, ed. Maria Bucur and Nancy M. Wingfield (West Lafayette, 2001), 75–111.
88. Davide Zaffi, "L'associazionismo nazionale in Trentino (1849–1919)," in Garbari and Leonardi, *Storia del Trentino*, 225–63. Compare also: Michael Wedekind, "La politicizzazione della montagna. Borghesia, alpinismo e nazionalismo tra Otto e Novecento," in *L'invenzine di un cosmo borghese. Valori sociali e simboli culturali dell'alpinismo nei secoli XIX e XX*, ed. Cluadio Ambrosi and Michael Wedekind (Trento, 2000), 19–52.
89. On this point more generally, see now: Pieter M. Judson, *Guardians of the Nation. Activists on the Language Frontiers of Imperial Austria* (Cambridge/Mass., 2007).
90. *Relazione della Società patriottica provinciale di soccorso della Croca Rossa pel Tirolo sulla sua gestione nell'anno 1885* (Innsbruck, 1886).
91. Compare Jakob Vogel, "Samariter und Schwestern, Geschlechterbilder und -beziehungen im 'Deutschen Roten Kreuz' vor dem Ersten Weltkrieg," in *Landsknechte, Soldatenfrauen und Nationalkrieger. Militär, Krieg und Geschlechterordnung im historischen Wandel*, ed. Karen Hagemann and Ralf Pröve (Frankfurt a.M., 1998), 322–344.
92. On the spread of the sharp-shooters in Trentino, see Cole, *Für Gott, Kaiser und Vaterland*, 494–501.
93. TLA, Statth. Abteilung I 1913, I-4b Zl. 190: Società Militari Veterani di Serravalle all'Eccelso i.r. Comando Supremo, 12.08.1912.

94. TLA, Statth. 1909 Vereine im Bezirke Tione, ad Nr. 48387 ex 1909: ad. Nr. 73850 Protocollo dell'adunanza generale della società veterani militari di Ragoli, 21.11.1909. Compare here Pieter M. Judson, "The Bohemian Oberammergau. Nationalist Tourism in the Austrian Empire," in *Constructing nationalities in East Central Europe,* ed. Pieter M. Judson and Marsha L. Rozenblit (New York, 2005), 89–106.
95. Christoph Perathoner, *Die Dolomitenladiner 1848–1918. Ethnisches Bewußtsein und politische Partizipation* (Vienna-Bozen, 1998).
96. AST, CD Cavalese Busta 222 B.VIII-19, C.D. Cavalese No. 8965/09.08.1904.
97. Rachamimov, *POWs and the Great War.*
98. See, among others, Diego Leoni and Camillo Zadra, eds., *La città di legno. Profughi trentini in Austria 1915–18* (Trento, 1985); Luciana Palla, *Il Trentino Orientale e la Grande Guerra. Combattenti, internati, profughi di Valsugana, Primiero e Tesino (1914–1920)* (Trento, 1994); Gianluigi Fait, ed., *Sui campi di Galizia (1914–1917). Gli italiani d'Austria e il fronte occidentale: uomini, popoli, culture nella guerra europea* (Rovereto, 1997).
99. István Deák, Comments, *Austrian History Yearbook* 3/Pt. I (1967): 303–308. Deàk remarks: "I would argue that there were no dominant nationalities in the Austro-Hungarian Monarchy. There were only dominant classes, institutions, interest groups, and professions," at 303.

Chapter 3

EMPEROR JOSEPH II IN THE AUSTRIAN IMAGINATION UP TO 1914[*]

Nancy M. Wingfield

Sole ruler of Austria for only the decade from 1780 to 1790, the reforming Habsburg Emperor Joseph II left a complicated legacy. From the time of his death through the outbreak of the First World War, the meaning of Joseph II was popularly reinterpreted in connection with contemporary political events. By the centenary of Joseph II's rule in 1880, varied, changing, and sometimes opposing groups had claimed different elements of the emperor's diverse legacy. Their claims were liberal and national; Jewish and Protestant; dynastically loyal (*Habsburgtreu*) and revolutionary. Increasingly, they would be German.

The Habsburg Empress Maria Theresia (1740–1780) and her son, Joseph II, who ruled jointly with her from 1765 to 1780, had sought to replace traditional feudal privileges with centralized administration. In so doing, they laid much of the groundwork for future capitalist expansion and industrial revolution in Austria.[1] As sole regent from 1780 to 1790, Joseph II improved upon and systematically expanded the measures Maria Theresia had initiated.[2] His reforming absolutism crystallized into a philosophy of state and society and into a means of regulating church/state relations—what would later be termed Josephinism.[3] The Austrian form of a general European-wide social, political, and intellectual movement, Josephinism combined modern bureaucratization—Joseph II sought to organize his domains more rationally by creating a centralized and unified bureaucracy serving a well-organized state with obedient subjects—with "Reform Catholicism." There was no area of public or social life that the reforming emperor left untouched during his ten years of sole rule. Although his successor, Leopold II, rescinded some of the numerous measures the indefatigable emperor issued, elements of Joseph II's reforms survived well into the nineteenth century, permeating Austrian culture, government, and society.

Joseph II addressed the question of religion in some of his first official acts as sole ruler with the promulgation of the Edicts of Toleration (*Toleranzpatente*), beginning on 13 October 1781. The emperor introduced some of his most decisive changes in church/state relations, including the removal of privileges and the closing of numerous monasteries, in order to bring the Roman Catholic Church under closer state authority. The first Edict of Toleration mandated the tolerance of Joseph II's Greek Orthodox, Calvinist, and Lutheran subjects. Edicts on the toleration of the Jews in different provinces of the Monarchy followed. Although these edicts faced fierce opposition, as a number of bishops obstructed their implementation, they laid the basis for full legal equality, which Emperor Franz Joseph would eventually grant the Protestants in 1861 and the Jews in 1867.

Joseph II himself was no particular friend of the Jews, but the First Partition of Poland and the concomitant increase in the number of Jews in the monarchy encouraged his endeavors to make them useful citizens, reflected in the Edicts of Toleration, and his institution in 1784 of the use of German first and family names by Jews. These changes played an important role in Jewish assimilation and acculturation. Although the provisions of the various Edicts of Toleration varied, in general, they permitted Jews to live outside the ghettos to which they had heretofore been limited, removed the sumptuary laws to which they had previously been subject, and provided them access to the army, most professions, and the university. The proclamations were interpreted as direct attacks on the traditional Jewish way of life, and were thus opposed by some Orthodox Jews, but they did not provide the Jews with "near equality" either, given the strictures they upheld.[4] Joseph II would, however, come to be regarded as a hero by many in the Jewish communities of Cisleithania. They believed that, with his reign, "the dawn broke for the Jews in the Austrian hereditary lands."[5] Indeed, as a seventeen-year-old, the Austrian-Jewish author Benedikt David Arnstein (1761–1841) of the famous banking family, was so inspired by this "freedom," that in 1782, he wrote *Einige jüdische Familienszenen bey Erblickung des Patentes über die Freyheiten, welche die Juden in den kaiserlichen Staaten erhalten haben* (A few Jewish family scenes when they beheld the edicts of freedom that the Jews in the imperial lands have received), which was long included in German language Jewish literature anthologies in Austria.[6] Moreover, when the Prague ghetto, Judenstadt, was incorporated into the city in 1850, it was renamed Josefstadt/Josefov to honor the Emperor for issuing the Edict of Toleration.[7]

Joseph II promulgated two other key measures upon which collective memories of the Emperor would subsequently be built. One long remembered edict, which lifted *Leibeigenschaft* (personal servitude) in Bohemia, Moravia, and Silesia, followed shortly after the first Edict of Toleration, on 1 November 1781. In addition, perhaps Joseph II's least successful measure as ruler was his proclamation in 1784 of German as the universal language of administration for the core lands of the empire, most notably, Hungary. Indeed, it incited so much opposition that his successor, Emperor Leopold II, had to rescind it.[8] However, it was this proclamation which was to guarantee his being kept alive in the imagination of many nationalists, especially Czechs and Germans, long after the demise of the monarchy.

By 1880, the centenary of his sole rule, the bureaucracy that Maria Theresia and Joseph II created infiltrated every corner of the monarchy. Emblems of uniformity—Austrian uniformity—could be found throughout the realm: in courthouses, post offices, and the stations along the ever-expanding railway network, whose officials wore identical dark blue uniforms and rang identical bells, as well as bore a yellow shield embellished with the increasingly ubiquitous double-headed black eagle.[9] As this article will show, Joseph's place in the Austrian imagination derived from elements of the pre-national emperor's actions being reinterpreted in ways which reflected the vast social changes of the long nineteenth century. This memorialization process resulted in multiple, often conflicting, images of Joseph II, with the contestation of his legacy for Austrian history being especially confrontational in Bohemia.

1. The early after-life of Joseph II

Upon his early death in 1790, Joseph II quickly became the subject of legend. By the middle of the nineteenth century, he had been memorialized in numerous popular ballads, books, poems, statues, etchings, and paintings. These objects primarily reflected two interpretations of his legacy. One was the "official" iconographic version of Joseph II as imperial ruler. This interpretation was embodied in the massive bronze equestrian statue of the emperor with his arm outstretched to protect his people, which his nephew, Emperor Franz II (I), commissioned in 1795. It was unveiled on what became Josephsplatz at the Imperial Palace in Vienna in 1807. This monument incorporated on its base medallions representing Joseph II's many deeds, including the lifting of *Leibeigenschaft* and the promotion of trade. Those actions of Joseph II which did not correspond with the governing principles of Emperor Franz, however, did not appear in the history inscribed on the monument. Thus, Joseph II's relaxation of censorship, for which he would be celebrated during the revolutionary days of March 1848, was not represented. The inscription on the monument, "Josepho II. Aug., qui saluti publicae vixit non diu sed totus" (To Emperor Joseph II, who lived not long, but completely, for the public's well being), links this official image with that of the *Volkskaiser* (People's Emperor).[10] When the equestrian statue of Joseph II was unveiled in Vienna, a seventeen-stanza poem commemorating the event and honoring the Emperor as a *Menschenfreund* (humanitarian) and *Vater des Volk's* [sic] (father of the people) also connected the two interpretations (see figure 3.1).[11]

In the countryside, especially in Moravia, peasants commemorated Joseph II as their friend, as the *Bauernkaiser* (Peasants' Emperor), who abolished *Leibeigen-*

Figure 3.1. Statue of Joseph II in Josephsplatz, Vienna. Photograph by author.

schaft. So, too, did contemporary lithographs and paintings.[12] Joseph II's popularity among "the people" was mirrored in the simple folksong:

> Ich denke hin und denke her,
> 's gibt keinen Kaiser Josef mehr.
> Wenn der Einem in's Auge sah,
> Es war mein' Seel ein Gloria!
> (My thoughts run away with me,
> Emperor Joseph is no more
> When he looked one in the eye,
> It was a blessing for one's soul.)[13]

The peasants quickly constructed legends about the emperor they so esteemed, not only from known characteristics and facts, but also by adding embellishments that came from their own reverent imagination. Tales of Joseph II's deeds were published, became part of oral tradition, and elaborated upon during events connected with him: anniversaries of his accession to the throne, of some of his most important edicts, and of his death.[14] While Bohemian peasants reputedly placed his portrait on the altars of village churches, well into the nineteenth century, many peasants in Styria simply refused to believe that "their" emperor was dead. Numerous anecdotes recounting his visits to small towns and villages and his meetings with common people, be it the butcher, the cattle handler, or the weaver, were passed down from one generation to the next and reflected Joseph II's enduring reputation as the benevolent emperor who behaved, in encounters with his people, as "like among like." Indeed, in the spirit of "George Washington slept here," a village parsonage might have a room named the "Emperor's" in pious honor of the imperial visitor, who stayed in inns rather than noble lodgings or town halls on his travels. More generally, an emperor's avenue down which Joseph II was said to have walked, or portal through which he had entered, might bear his name. There were also emperor's hills from which he had gazed out upon his far-flung domains. Joseph II 's construction of fortresses in the Bohemian lands in the wake of Austria's loss of most of Silesia to Prussia in the Seven Years' War, including one named for him, Josefstadt, between 1780 and 1787, ensured he would live on in popular memory. The village Josefswille/Mlatce in Northern Bohemia had come into being during his rule and local tradition connected its name to his.[15]

Joseph II's reputation as an imperial humanitarian endured and even expanded, and he was popularly celebrated for his paternalistic beneficence in the early nineteenth century. Fluid and open to multiple readings, the increasingly legendary image of the *Volkskaiser* would play an important role in the politicization of the memory of the emperor in the last decades of the monarchy. Embodied in metal and stone throughout Cisleithania, the interpretation of Joseph II as *Volkskaiser* was one which many German speakers in particular would claim for themselves and then reinterpret in the second half of the nineteenth century, first toward liberal ends, then increasingly toward national ones. Although monuments to Joseph II soon appeared throughout the monarchy, including Transylvania, many of the early ones were to be found in the Bohemian lands.[16] Dating from the late eighteenth century, these monuments incorporated accounts of the emperor putting his hand to the plow during his many inspection tours of the Monarchy. The most famous such instance took place in August 1769 near the village of Slawikowitz bei Brünn/Slavíkovice in rural southern Moravia. A lesser-known example of Joseph II putting his hand to the plow in Reichenberg/Liberec took monumental form in the statue that Count Christian Philipp Clam-Gallas unveiled in his palace park, close to where the event occurred.[17]

2. The Image of Joseph II during Vienna's March Days and in the Constitutional Era

While many of Joseph II's reforms were downplayed, and even revoked during the authoritarian *Vormärz* (pre-March) era of Chancellor Klemens von Metternich, his reputation as an imperial reformer—one who sought to limit both feudal privilege and the power of the church—survived. His example served to encourage the liberalizing aspirations of the nascent bourgeois intelligentsia, and Joseph II's reforms were enthusiastically commemorated during the Revolutions of 1848, when there was a virtual "Josephinian renaissance," especially in Vienna, Bohemia, and Moravia, but elsewhere as well.[18] The revolutionaries of 1848, who opposed not only the absolute rule of the emperor and Metternichian policy, but also the Roman Catholic Church, claimed the emperor as a revolutionary, or at least, someone who would have been a revolutionary, had he but lived longer. The attitudes reflected in the rhetoric of 1848 and in the 1860s, following the decade of neoabsolutism, mirrored the varied ways in which both the producers and the consumers of his legacy interpreted Joseph II's actions. At the same time, these interpretations demonstrated that this legacy could also polarize opinions, thus highlighting his lack of efficacy as an integrating figure.

Joseph II loomed large in the Austrian imagination during the March Days of the Viennese Revolution in 1848. Revolutionaries extolled him as an exemplary ruler and stressed the value of his reforms, which complemented the developments of the day, chief among them the granting of freedom of the press. This reflected the constitutional nature of the early part of the revolution, but it also comprised a useful political strategy: by making positive reference to Joseph II, opponents of the government could make their criticism within the framework of loyalty to the dynasty. On Monday, March 13th, the anniversary of the emperor's birth, the Lower Austrian estates assembled on Herrengasse in the center of Vienna for a meeting of the opposition. The significance of this date was not lost on the crowds of burghers, students, and workers who gathered later that day at the equestrian statue of Joseph II on nearby Josephsplatz, invoking the emperor's name in their anti-government protests. While "thundering cries in honor of his memory filled the air," members of the crowd crowned the statue with a wreath, and placed a flag with the inscription, "Freedom of the Press," in its hand.[19] J.P. Lyser's *Ein Frühlingstag vor dem Denkmale des Kaisers Joseph des Zweiten* (A spring day at the statue of Emperor Joseph II) was the first uncensored poem to be published in revolutionary Vienna. Coming from "the people he loved and esteemed," its eight stanzas addressed the emperor's "trust" in his people and their loyalty to him. The poet asserted that Joseph's "people" did not commit treason when they spoke freely, when they took the rights he had long ago offered, but which tyranny had too long denied them. Lyser locates the representation of Joseph II—the statue—within the contemporary revolutionary activity: "the colorful retinue stops to give three cheers" and "put the flag in his hand"—explicitly separating the emperor and "his [now-free] people," who had trusted him and whom he had "imperially protected," from the [imperial] power that had been recently destroyed, power that had "too long been falsely endowed."[20]

Another of Joseph II's reforms was linked to the achievements of the revolution by the youngest deputy to the revolutionary Parliament in Vienna, Hans Kudlich, the Austrian Silesian-born "liberator of the peasants." Himself the son of a peasant, Kudlich proposed to complete the job Joseph II had begun over a half century earlier by emancipating the peasants of Austria from all remaining vestiges of the *robot*. Kudlich consciously honored that element of Joseph II's memory which represented the emperor as the friend of the peasants. Like many Austrian liberals, he would long invoke the emperor's legacy in his politics.[21] Another way in which the memory of Joseph II maintained a permanent place in the Austrian imagination was of course through the adoption of his name by a long-lived successor, Franz Joseph, when he ascended to the throne at Olmütz/Olomouc, in northeastern Moravia in December 1848. The young Archduke Franz's decision to add "Joseph" to his official title as emperor clearly signified his desire to be a reform ruler like his illustrious predecessor. In practice, the unrelenting bureaucratic centralization in the decade of neoabsolutism following the Revolution of 1848 proved to be the major Josephinist element in Franz Joseph's early years of rule.[22]

Beginning in the constitutional era of the 1860s, the legacy of Joseph II in the form of Josephinism played an important role in the *Kulturkampf* (clash of cultures), the ongoing ideological battle between liberals and conservatives in Cisleithania over church/state relations and the place of religion in modern society. This conflict affected Austria's German-speaking regions above all, especially the Tyrol, where it lasted until 1892, with politicians and clergy as the main antagonists. The otherwise politically heterogeneous liberal movement attempted to constrain its common enemy—the Roman Catholic Church—with a series of confessional laws. At least some conservatives accepted liberals' claims to the emperor's legacy, since they, too, considered Joseph II to have laid the foundations for liberalism.[23] For its part, the church assailed liberal reforms and sought to maintain its privileged position following the Concordat of 1855, opposing the threat it perceived from the 1861 reform, the *Protestantenpatent*, which permitted the unrestricted practice of Protestantism in Austria.[24]

The liberals, stressing the Josephinist heritage of the December 1867 constitution, sought to monopolize the memory of Joseph II and attempted to recreate him in their image. At the local level, liberal clubs and organizations kept the memory of Joseph II alive in a myriad of ways, including many that implicitly recognized the emperor's contributions to educational reform. They founded numerous *Lesehalle* (reading rooms), whose goal was continuing intellectual development "in the good German" sense. Some, like the *Verein der deutschen Lesehalle zur deutschen Eiche* of Hohenelbe/Vrchlabí, a small town in the Giant Mountains (Riesengebirge/Krknoše) in northeastern Bohemia, held regular Emperor Joseph festivals on the date of his birth, March 13, or other dates which connected the emperor to the region. The organization donated money earned from these fêtes to liberal, humanitarian causes, ranging from funding education to aid for the families of reservists serving in Bosnia. Later in the century, some of the growing number of branches of the *Deutscher Schulverein* (German School Association), an organization founded during Joseph II's centenary year to defend German school interests in nationally mixed areas of Cisleithania, sponsored Emperor Joseph II celebrations. In an era of increasing Czech-German tension over educational policies in the Bohemian Lands, the emperor's name was raised in terms of his Germanizing actions on the one hand, and his role in school reform, which the church continued to oppose, on the other.[25]

The German liberals, who dominated the Austrian state apparatus since 1867 except for a brief interlude in 1870–71, lost power in 1879. Liberal reluctance for Austria-Hungary to occupy Bosnia-Herzegovina resulted in their removal from the imperial government. Feudal conservatives, who primarily represented the conservative, Roman Catholic Alpine provinces, Slavs, and Clericals comprised the interests that formed Count Eduard Taaffe's "Iron Ring" government, which excluded the German liberals. The Young Czechs (formally the National Liberal Party, founded in 1874), who had recently abandoned their strategy of boycotting the Imperial Parliament, agreed to join the government. Among its first order of business, Taaffe's new coalition published the so-called Stremayr ordinances in April 1880. Named after Minister of Justice Karl von Stremayr, these ordinances ceased favoring the use of the German language in official dealings in the Bohemian Lands and made Czech an official *Landessprache* (administrative language) alongside German in linguistically mixed areas of the Bohemian Lands. In what they considered to be the spirit of Joseph II, the German liberals opposed the ordinances, and struggled for the maintenance of imperial unity and of *Deutschtum* (Germandom) in Austria.[26] Representatives of German cities, towns, and organizations throughout the Bohemian Lands and elsewhere protested the ordinances, which they recognized would benefit Czech speakers in the provincial civil service, who were more likely to be bilingual than were German speakers.[27] This opposition signaled the beginning of a battle that German liberals would wage at the imperial, provincial, and local level. What they interpreted as the defense of *Deutschtum* was in reality the attempt to maintain the privileged position of the Germans in Cisleithania. It was against this background that the centenary celebrations of Joseph II's accession to sole rule of the Habsburg Monarchy took place in November 1880.

3. The Joseph II Centennial in 1880

The formerly dominant German liberals interpreted the Emperor Joseph centenary celebrations as magnificent demonstrations of Austrian liberalism for the unity of the empire and against the recently formed government coalition. They orchestrated the centennial commemorations, which while popular in much of German-speaking Cisleithania, met with little enthusiasm from the imperial government. Some conservative and clerical elements in the population, which characterized the reign of Joseph II as one of the saddest eras in the history of the Habsburg Monarchy, opposed them outright. For example, Conservatives in Tyrol rejected the notion that Joseph II was a "man of freedom," claiming rather that he epitomized absolutism at its zenith.[28] The celebrations reflected the liberal interpretation of the emperor's centralizing reforms as precursors to a modern, liberal, German-dominated Austrian state. They emphasized Joseph II's numerous efforts to bring progress—economic, educational, and political—to Austria throughout the German-speaking hereditary lands. In addition to crediting him with the foundation of the modern unitary state, German liberals in the Monarchy continued to stress what they viewed as the anti-clerical elements of Joseph II's reforms. As long as the memory of the emperor survived, argued the liberals, Austria would remain unified, German, and religiously tolerant, rather than federal, Slavic, and Roman Catholic.

The centenary celebrations planned for the last week in November 1880 highlighted the ongoing domestic political struggle among the clericals, national parties, feudalists, and liberals. Certainly, the liberal appropriation of the emperor was a clever tactical move: liberals utilized Joseph II to lay claim to the state, making it difficult for the government or the Conservative opponents to criticize them. Some German liberals complained about clerical and national party opposition to the planned centenary festivals, which celebrated state unity and German culture. They claimed it was nothing more than a battle by the opponents of Josephinist ideas against honoring the "immortal" emperor, the founder of the unitary Austrian state. These opponents of Josephinist ideas remained reserved vis-à-vis the patriotic commemorations, sometimes even actively opposing them. As Ernst von Plener, a leading German liberal from Bohemia noted in a parliamentary speech in December 1880, "the memory of Emperor Joseph was celebrated with nervous restraint in official circles ..."[29]

The Young Czechs' Prague-based daily, *Národní listy*, elaborated on Czech national opposition to Josephinist ideas, especially to centralization and Germanization. The newspaper savagely criticized the centenary celebrations, as the "newest centralist machinations," and accused the *Páni centralisté* (Centralist Gentlemen) of stopping at nothing to abuse the great historic name of Joseph II. Indeed, in the same way German liberals praised Joseph II for his centralizing policies, the Young Czechs attacked him: for removing the seat of self-government from Hungary, for deliberately not having himself crowned in Hungary or Bohemia (indeed, for moving the Czech and Hungarian crowns to Vienna), and for failing to summon the provincial Diets. The newspaper concluded that the liberals (centralists) had two main articles in their program: the Germanization of the Slavic nations in Austria and the centralization of all the realms and lands of the empire.[30]

Members of the Roman Catholic Church hierarchy of Austria certainly recognized—and opposed—the anti-clerical, liberal centenary festivities. Bishops in Upper Austria and Styria, together with the Cardinal of Vienna, refused to permit Joseph II commemorative services in the churches of their dioceses for a variety of reasons, including the idea that it would be impossible to prevent anti-government protests. Some school administrators in the Viennese suburbs, whose programs for the celebration of the centenary had planned to include an early morning mass, were informed in writing by their local parishes that the Cardinal of Vienna had deemed celebratory masses to be unacceptable. More generally, members of the church hierarchy argued that the festivities commemorating Joseph II would not be in keeping with the spirit of the Holy Mass. Bishop Franz Joseph Rudigier of Linz (the capital of Upper Austria), whose diocese had been founded during Joseph II's reign, and who had earlier come into conflict with Liberals over church/state relations, was even rumored to have considered closing his church, locking out "the jubilant masses, the loyal and true people who were celebrating their best Emperor." In fact, he rejected a request from the Upper Austrian town of Braunau to hold a festive mass in connection with its Emperor Joseph celebration.[31] Rudigier tendentiously asserted that in the governmental realm, Emperor Joseph had put an end to provincial autonomy through the suspension of the provincial diets (when Joseph II's successor, Leopold II, convened the Tyrolean Diet in 1790, it had not been convoked since 1720, well before Joseph's time). In the ecclesiastical realm, the Bishop claimed that Josephinism had completely dominated the church, and he cited a pronouncement by the Austrian Episcopate from 20 March 1874, which allegedly forbade the holding of a religious service on the grounds that it would amount to sanctioning the Josephinist measures.[32]

Some staunch Roman Catholics claimed that where the church did participate in the centenary festivities it was less in the sense of celebrating Joseph II and more in the sense of commemorating the House of Habsburg-Lorraine. Moreover, they wondered why people—liberals—who seldom, if at all, darkened the doors of a church, seemed to think that a solemn Mass was such a necessity for the centenary celebrations, especially when "friend and foe alike knew that Joseph II had gravely damaged the Roman Catholic Church in Austria."[33]

The clergy of the Bohemian lands and elsewhere in Cisleithania were less unified in their response to the planned commemorations than those in Upper Austria and Styria. Bishop Johann Valerian Jirsik/Jan Valerian Jirsík of nationally mixed Budweis/Budějovice in the Bohemian Forest forbade celebratory centenary masses throughout his diocese. Indeed, his own church was entirely dark on the day of the celebrations. The bishop's decision became known during a meeting of the town council, causing much annoyance among the German liberal majority. In reaction, town council members unanimously passed a decision calling on various Czech and German organizations, led by the municipal representatives, to meet in the cathedral on November 30. Although no priest would be standing at the altar, the choir would sing a chorus inside the building. At the subsequent Joseph II celebration, both Czech and German speakers expressed their loyalty to the Habsburg dynasty. Although classes were held that day at the local Czech language schools, the teachers held assemblies to teach their students— if briefly—about the importance of Joseph II's government.[34] In contrast to southern Bohemia, the clergy of several cities in predominantly German-speaking northern Bohemia and nationally mixed northern Moravia celebrated festive High Masses, attended by local dignitaries and imperial officials.[35] Certainly, there was an overt anti-clerical element in some of the centennial speeches. In response to clerical opposition to the centenary celebrations, liberal voices reminded others how farsighted Joseph II had been in his dealings with the Roman Catholic Church. They noted that a century earlier, he had achieved what the French Republic was now attempting, namely the reform of church/state relations: "he had closed the cloisters of the barefoot, begging monks and firmly placed the Roman Catholic Church under the legal authority of the state."[36]

Elsewhere in the empire, the Greek Catholic (Uniate) churches in Galicia, from St. George Cathedral in Lemberg/L'viv/Lwów to the smallest rural parishes, held special services to honor the "Emperor-Liberator," whose legacy of both religious tolerance and moderating serfdom had played an important role in the development of Ruthenian national, anti-Polish politics. Indeed, an All-Party Ruthenian meeting was held on November 30, in conjunction with the centenary celebrations.[37]

The center of the centenary festivities was Vienna. Celebrations of the self-styled *Schätzer der Menschheit* (Esteemer of Humanity), who recalled "the golden time of classical literature" and "the heroic era of German music," went on for several days in the imperial capital. German liberals throughout Austria celebrated Joseph II together with their political predecessors, the "martyrs of 1848," at both liberal associational meetings and in the municipal governments which they still dominated.[38]

On Thursday, November 25, the Viennese city fathers, along with a deputation of the Viennese *Männergesangverein* (Men's Choral Society) and other organizations, went from the Capuchin Church near the Hofburg, into the Habsburg crypt next door to lay a wreath on the sarcophagus of the emperor. Indeed, the vault was kept open so well wishers could place flowers and wreathes there. So many of them did, according to observers, that it appeared that Joseph II had "only recently been laid to rest." Although the Men's Choral Society sang a Latin dirge in the church, there was no further religious ceremony. Participants then went to the nearby equestrian statue of the Emperor to lay a wreath at its base.[39]

The zenith of the celebrations in Vienna was Sunday, November 28, the eve of the centenary. Tens of thousands of people from throughout the city and its suburbs as well as nearby towns began gathering early that day to pay their respects to the emperor at Josephsplatz, where a banner reading "*Aus Liebe und Dankbarkeit*" (Out of love and gratitude) and "*Dem Schätzer der Menschheit*" (To the esteemer of humanity) hung from two giant obelisks, and the buildings surrounding the square were decorated with the coats of arms and the flags of the crown lands. Crowds also assembled that evening along the route to watch the huge torchlight procession which, upon the sound of a trumpet, wended its way from Stubenplatz along the Ringstrastraße past Schwarzenbergplatz and the Opera House, before turning onto the narrow Operngasse and moving toward the equestrian statue in the center of the city. Onlookers filled the windows and balconies of houses along the Ringstraße and cheering crowds clogged the street. The male participants represented those numerous academic, political, and social groups which laid claim to the liberal, progressive memory of Joseph II.

Liberal student organizations, many dating from 1848, played a large role in the parade and other ceremonies. A civilian band led the way, followed by student groups decked out in full fraternity dress, members of the planning committee, the city council, and district governance, and various academic organizations. Students from the Academy of Art, including three standard bearers in traditional German costume, brought up the rear. Thousands of participants carrying lanterns, laughing, shouting, and singing, indeed, creating a deafening clamor, snarled street traffic, which the police had chosen not to suspend, while making their way to the bronze *Volkskaiser*. Upon their arrival at Josephsplatz, the fraternity students placed their organizational flags upright, then sang their anthem, *Ehre, Freiheit, Vaterland* (Honor, Freedom, Fatherland). The students did not conclude their ceremony with a speech, because imperial officials demanded to see the text in advance. The students rejected this demand, which they considered an attempt to censor homage to the very emperor credited with limiting censorship in 1781. They therefore dropped the planned speech from the program. The result, according to *Neue Freie Presse,* the influential Viennese liberal daily, was the loss of an "appropriate ending" for the festivities.[40]

On the morning of November 29, the day of the centenary of Joseph II's accession to the throne, some three hundred technical university students and professors attended a commemoration of Emperor Joseph II sponsored by members of the *Lese- und Redehalle*. The main speaker addressed Joseph II's church and school reforms, asserting that the emperor really was a good Catholic who merely wanted to lessen the preponderant position of the church in the state, including its dominant position in the schools. He concluded by admonishing his audience to bear in mind not what Joseph II achieved, but rather, what he sought to achieve.[41]

The following day, the *Deutsch-Österreichische Leseverein* held an explicitly secular celebration at the hall of the *Musikverein* (Musical Society) in honor of the emperor's centenary, in which members of the student body of the university in Vienna participated. Among other speakers, the mayor of Vienna, Julius Ritter von Newald, lauded Joseph II's manifold works. First he described the government achievements by which Joseph II provided a "shining example far beyond the borders of Austria." The mayor then moved on to those reforms which helped Vienna to thrive, aiding in its spiritual and material prosperity. Newald concluded by noting that the emperor's ideas on justice and law as well as freedom and equality lived on from generation to generation, that the spirit of his laws had an enlightening effect on the future.[42]

Elsewhere in Vienna, its suburbs, and throughout much of German-speaking Cisleithania, liberal political organizations paid homage to the emperor as embodying the ideas of freedom, Germandom, and imperial unity, in festive ways, with plays, readings, and commemorative meetings of city governments and civic groups. These centenary celebrations were not official imperial undertakings, but rather had been organized at the community level, a reflection of the reserved position the imperial government had taken toward the centenary. Many of the industrializing cities in the hereditary lands and the Bohemian lands credited Joseph II for aiding in the industrial development of the previous century. Columns of light from hilltop fires filled the night sky and candles flickered in the windows of houses in towns and villages which were illuminated in honor of Joseph II. These festivities incorporated traditional and modern elements of celebration: the illumination of towns and villages, the decoration of homes with flags, decorations in imperial black-yellow, and busts of Habsburgs past and present: Joseph II, as well as Emperor Franz Joseph and Empress Elisabeth.[43] Local residents, primarily German speakers representing all social strata, often including school children, organized and attended festivities which included lectures and theatrical performances. In some towns, there were festive religious services—Roman Catholic, Protestant, and Jewish—attended by local imperial officials and employees, as well as the members of numerous associations and other corporate groups.[44]

The Austrian police still sometimes censored individual attempts to honor the *Volkskaiser*. In one case, the owner of Café Niebauer in Leopoldstadt near the Augarten, the park in Vienna's second district dating from 1650 which Joseph II had opened to the public in 1775, placed pictures and banners recalling the emperor in the windows of his establishment.[45] He decorated one window of the café with a portrait of the emperor and his motto. A second window contained a sketch of the entry to the Augarten, above which Joseph II had placed the inscription: "This place of recreation has been dedicated to the People by one who esteems them," accompanied by a poem written by the recently deceased poet-author Anton Langer, author of the *Barrikadenlied* (Song of the Barricades) from 1848. Banners with sayings by and about the emperor inscribed upon them hung in the other windows. The police forced the café owner to remove a banner reading, "'Wird man denn niemals ein Mittel finden, den Feind zu überwinden, ohne dass es so vielen Menschen das Leben kostet?'—Joseph II." (Will a means never be found to overcome the enemy without so many people losing their lives?)[46]

This atmosphere of remembrance, in which well-known Joseph anecdotes were widely repeated, encouraged families to recall their own diverse Joseph legends. One reporter described the home of Viennese friends in which a darkening portrait of Joseph II hung over the portraits of both great-grandparents, because it was the *Volkskaiser* himself who, at the tearful request of the bride-to-be, released the prospective groom from military service so as to make an "honest woman" of her. The release had been accompanied by a cheerful imperial admonishment, "Well! If only the Morals Commission [a reference to Maria Theresia's infamous *Keuschheitskommission,* which he abolished] still existed!" There was also a princely wedding gift, accompanied by a whimsical message, that "The Emperor hoped that the state would soon see its soldier again."[47]

The image of Joseph II putting his hand to the plow during his numerous trips throughout the monarchy, so widespread during the first half of the nineteenth century, retained some resonance during the second half as well. German liberals commemorated the emperor's legendary encounters as "equal among equals" with the peasants of the monarchy in some of the centenary celebrations they held in the Bohemian Lands. In Slawikowitz bei Brünn/Slavíkovice, residents from the Moravian countryside wearing folk dress, were among the participants at a well attended "celebration of peace" at the site where the monumental cast iron statue had been unveiled in 1836. According to German language newspapers, so many residents of the nearby Moravian capital, Brünn/Brno planned to attend that extra trains in addition to the customary mail train were added. Passengers included the city's mayor and city council, members of local organizations, representatives of the German technical university in Brünn/Brno as well as deputations from German-speaking rural communities and Slavic-speaking farmers, who were picked up en route. Before the monument, which incorporated a gilded bas-relief of Joseph II tilling the land, stood the original plow, on loan from the Moravian Provincial Museum.[48] In a formal address from the base of the statue, the regional parliamentary deputy spoke about Joseph II's life, stressing his noble intentions for humanity and his successful efforts to have German made the state language of the monarchy. By contrast, the Czech-language newspaper *Národní listy* downplayed the ceremony. It reported that only Jews from a few villages participated in the celebration at Slawikowitz bei Brünn/Slavíkovice and that due to bad weather, the planned torchlight procession was much smaller than had been anticipated.[49]

The image of Joseph II in the countryside, as a friend to all peasants, who lifted *Leibeigenschaft,* helping free all of them, not only the Germans, remained "safe" and relatively uncontroversial for the duration of the Monarchy, despite the slow nationalization of the countryside. The historic tableau, *Joseph II. Ländliches Fest. Ernte und Weinlese,* which formed part of Emperor Franz Joseph's sixtieth Jubilee Procession in Vienna in June 1908, exemplified the employment of this image. This tableau, emblematic of rural romanticism, presented a rural festival, with harvest and wine production. It symbolized the rural people's feelings about the great emperor and their recognition of what they owed him for freeing the peasants. Neither Emperor Joseph II nor his many reforms found mention outside the title of the tableau, however.[50]

By his centennial, therefore, images of the emperor had begun to occupy a fluid space in the collective memory of Austria. Alongside the popular and liberal interpretations which had formerly predominated, German nationalists began to adopt the figure of Joseph II to symbolize their goals, while German liberals likewise employed the emperor for their newly developing politics of opposition. The former included the liberal-turned-radical-German-nationalist and anti-Semite, Georg Ritter von Schönerer, the *Kornblumenritter*, who used the emperor as an ideological symbol for work in his own parliamentary constituency in Lower Austria. Schönerer stressed the emperor's policy of bringing the fruits of science to the land and building a strong peasantry, and he donated memorial tablets showing Emperor Joseph with his hand on the plow as well as money for statues of "the friend of humanity and the German man, who was also the emperor," to some of the villages in his district.[51] In his congratulatory messages to the Joseph festivities, he encouraged all of the participants to "profess their Germanness." Certainly, some of the more committed German nationalists at Joseph II centenary festivities invoked the *Kornblumenritter* in their speeches. This German liberal-national conjuncture reflects Pieter Judson's assertion that both the liberal and the radical forms of German nationalism derived their organizational style and their ideological content from the traditions of liberalism.[52]

4. Joseph II as a Focus for German Nationalism

In addition to the official and the popular interpretations of the early nineteenth century and the liberal interpretation which became popular at mid-century, another current in the memory of the Emperor Joseph II, one focusing on Joseph II's relationship to the Germans of the monarchy, became increasingly prominent in the last decades of the nineteenth century. Traces of this interpretation were already present in the 1880 celebrations, but it was best embodied in the statues of Joseph II put up primarily in the Bohemian Lands and Lower Austria, and also in Upper Austria and Styria, beginning in November 1881.[53] The German liberal interpretation of the emperor was set in stone—and metal—in the statues of Joseph II which marked the centennial of the lifting of *Leibeigenschaft*. Politically contested from the start, the commemorations incorporated issues of national identity and collective memory, including the meaning the Germans ascribed to their role in "helping" the emperor to lay the foundations for the modern Austrian constitutional state (*Rechtsstaat*). The rhetoric at these unveiling ceremonies was both liberal and national. Both the ceremonial installation of statues of the emperor and the cult that grew up around him in the late nineteenth century mirrored changing political ideologies and commitments. Despite the still predominantly liberal rhetoric about Josephinist reforms, especially the lifting of *Leibeigenschaft* and the issuing of the Edict of Toleration, at the unveiling of the statues, these ceremonies soon came to embody the intensely partisan national politics of the late empire.[54]

The numerous statues unveiled beginning in the early 1880s were not official state projects, rather they represented local responses to the proposal by the editor of the northern Bohemian newspaper, *Leitmeritzer Zeitung*, in May 1879 to commemorate the centenary of the abolition of *Leibeigenschaft*. The suggestion had gained impetus during the recent centenary celebrations of Joseph II's accession to the throne. Many of the German liberals, who organized the centenary festivities that November, were also instrumental in later obtaining statues for their towns. The unveiling ceremonies, with their large scale participation, represented the new German liberal politics of opposition. Although the inscriptions on the statues mainly commemorated Joseph II's abolition of *Leibeigenschaft* or his issuing the Edict of Toleration, they occasionally recalled his enlightened role in promoting knowledge, trade, and industry.

The unveilings celebrated what both liberal and nationalist Germans lauded as Joseph II's centralizing and Germanizing policies as well as the emperor's apparent recognition that the Germans were the most suited among his many peoples to help create "a realm of light, education, toleration, and civilization"—an Austrian nation.[55] They employed the image of one Habsburg ruler—Joseph II—against the rule of another—Emperor Franz Joseph—whom these Germans criticized for his allegedly Slavophile policies. The speeches at the unveilings expanded politics to the crowd, which included women and children. They also reflected the dual creation of Bohemian German identity, in relation to the Habsburgs and Vienna on the one hand, and to the Czechs on the other.

When Ernst von Plener, who in his speeches to the Bohemian Diet regularly invoked Joseph II's progressive achievements, paid homage to the emperor at the unveiling of a statue at Eger/Cheb, in western Bohemia, on 2 October 1887, he stressed the importance of the unitary state. Plener believed this was especially important to the Germans of the Bohemian lands, due to their political losses to the Czechs on the local, provincial, and imperial levels, and because of the other values which the liberals long advocated:

> Joseph II represented for Austria the ideal of the eighteenth century, the founding of the modern state, recognition of human worth and the liberation of the people from chains and maltreatment. He was the first to achieve what we in today's sense call the modern state.[56]

Plener asserted that Joseph II knew a state comprising many nationalities had to have its own language in the interest of unity. Further, he asserted that "governmental and cultural life in Austria were originally German," and thus, the Emperor first created German as the state language of Austria.[57]

During the late nineteenth century and the beginning of the twentieth, many German speakers of the monarchy cited Joseph II himself in the claims they made upon his memory in order to preserve what they considered to be the "Germanness" of Cisleithania. Two of the most popular quotations from Joseph II among the Germans were "I love our entire Fatherland and I am proud to be a German" (*Ich liebe unser gesammtes Vaterland und bin stolz darauf, ein Deutscher zu sein*), sometimes shortened to "I am proud to be a German," and "there is no better sobriquet, than to be called the father of one's people" (*Es gibt keinen schöneren Beinamen, als Vater seines Volkes zu heissen*).⁵⁸

Nationalist Germans increasingly considered Joseph II the representative of their version of Germandom, and in times of political turmoil gathered at the statues, which came to embody the image of him as a Germanizer and centralizer. Thus, in 1897, the image of Joseph II reappeared in multiple ways in conjunction with the months long battle over the Language Ordinances proposed by the Austrian Minister-President, Polish Count Kasimir Badeni. These called for the equality of Czech and German in official usage among imperial-royal civil servants in Bohemia and Moravia, who would be required to demonstrate proficiency in both Czech and German by June 1901. The Language Ordinances did not endear Badeni to German nationalists. After Pan-German Parliamentary deputy Karl Hermann Wolf from Reichenberg/Liberec insulted Badeni on the first day of Parliament in September 1897, Badeni challenged Wolf to a duel. Joseph II's condemnation of duels as barbarism from the age of Tamerlane soon appeared in some German language newspapers, as a calculated insult to the hated Badeni: "I disdain anyone who is ready to sacrifice everything for the sake of vengeance and hatred of an enemy. I consider such a man no better than a Roman gladiator."⁵⁹ Later in the year, Germans throughout the Bohemian lands, and elsewhere, including Graz, the capital of nationally contested Styria, gathered at their statues of Joseph II to first call for Badeni's resignation, and subsequently, to cheer it.⁶⁰

The location of Joseph II in German national ideology in the late nineteenth century is reflected in a picture postcard produced by the Fritz Rasch bookstore in Cilli/Celje, a small, predominantly German town in southern Styria and the site of German-Slovene national tensions. Rasch was one of several firms that produced postcards featuring German national themes, in defense of the Bohemian Germans. One card circulating during the late 1890s explicitly connected Joseph II with Wilhelmine Germany. It featured two stereotypical German men shaking hands against the background of statues of Johannes Schilling's giant Germania (the female allegorical representation of greater Germany), the so-called Niederwald monument, standing guard along the Rhine against the French enemy (part of Wilhelmine Germany's national monument culture), and one of the recently unveiled Emperor Joseph II monuments. The heading read, "Alldeutschland Hurrah!" (Pan-Germany hurrah!), while the bottom portion of the card contained the greeting "Deutscher Heilruf zur Jahreswende!" (A German cheer for the New Year!) together with the first two lines of "Deutschland, Deutschland über alles," which describe the reaches of the German nation.⁶¹

At a gathering of German students from throughout Cisleithania to celebrate the founding of the *Deutschvölkischer Akademikerverband* (German People's Academic Union) in Brünn/Brno's *Deutsches Haus* just before the outbreak of the First World War, a nationalist address discussing the long-time struggle between the two "races" in Moravia harkened back to the golden era of Emperor Joseph II, who had "correctly" appraised and made use of the significance of the German culture and German intellect for the entire Austrian political system. "Everything," lamented the speaker, "that the German people had achieved in Joseph's time had since been lost."[62]

Even when Germans honored Joseph II for reasons other than solely to make declarations of German national pride and to celebrate centralization, national-political elements were sometimes still present in their behavior. For example, when the *Verein der christlichen Deutschen in der Bukowina* (Union of Christian Germans in Bukovina), unveiled a bust of the emperor, whose name was "inscribed in golden letters in the history of Bukovina," at the *Deutsches Haus* in the nationally mixed (German, Jewish, Polish, Romanian, Ruthenian) city of Czernowitz, the provincial capital. Although rhetoric at the unveiling focused mainly on the Edicts of Toleration, it was noted that the first German colonization of Bukovina occurred during Joseph II's reign and that some 125 years later, there were large German communities in the Carpathian area. Thus, Joseph II was lauded for his role in the cultural development of Bukovina, and as an enlightened representative of German centralism and Austrian state thought.[63]

In addition, the consecration of Protestant churches in Cisleithania became increasingly politicized following the foundation of the anti-Roman Catholic *Los von Rom* (Away from Rome) movement, associated with the Pan-German Schönerer in the wake of the Badeni protests. Indeed, a Viennese medical student first employed the term, "*Los von Rom,*" at the German nationalist *Volkstag* in Vienna on 12 December 1897. The movement, with the goal of unifying Austria with Germany and which advocated leaving the Roman Catholic Church and joining the Protestant Church, enjoyed its greatest popularity in northern Bohemia, but also the Alpine provinces Carinthia and Styria at the turn of the century. In rituals connected with the consecration of the Protestant church in the small northern Bohemian town of Warnsdorf/Varnsdorf in 1905, participants in the procession went to the local statue of Joseph II, where they placed a wreath, whose dedication read "To Emperor Joseph II with gratitude for the Edict of Toleration from the Protestant religious community 1781–1905." Their action was more than one of mere religious piety, even if they then went to the city's statue of Franz Joseph I to lay a wreath thanking him for the confessional freedom and equality that dated from 1861.[64]

While the Hungarian and Polish nobility had opposed the limits Joseph II placed on their traditional rights in the late eighteenth century, and some Czech intellectuals, including the founder of modern Slavistics, Josef Dobrovský, as well as the Enlightenment historian František Martin Pelcl, who occupied the first chair of Czech at Charles University in Prague, had early on criticized what they interpreted as Joseph II's state program of centralization and Germanization, there had been little opposition to Joseph's linguistic reforms from the Czech nobility.[65] During the first half of the nineteenth century, there had been little popular Czech opposition to the image of Joseph II, even if there had also been few demonstrations of active support. Despite the lingering positive resonance of the image of Joseph II as the friend of the peasants, by the late nineteenth century Czechs would decry the emperor as a Germanizer and centralizer while Germans praised him for the same reasons. Some Czech political leaders believed that the unveilings of Joseph II statues were above all pretexts for German nationalist demonstrations. They noted that while speakers at the unveilings might employ standard liberal rhetoric about the emperor, the wreaths at the base of the statues bore the *großdeutsch* black-red-gold tricolor, originally a German liberal symbol which enjoyed increased popularity in burgeoning nationalist German circles since Austria and Germany had signed the Dual Alliance in 1879.[66]

Indeed, the entry for Joseph II in the 1898 volume of the Czech-language encyclopedia, *Ottův slovník Naučný,* was not so different from the criticism of the emperor voiced almost two decades earlier in *Národní listy.* It stressed the deleterious effects of centralization (*centralisace*) and Germanization (*germanisace*), which went hand in hand. According to the encyclopedia, both were aimed at "complete eradication" of the Czech element, an interpretation which does not seem to have changed significantly since the Young Czechs condemned the centenary festivities in 1880. On the whole, Czechs appear not to have mounted a fierce challenge to the German appropriation of the memory of Joseph II, but they did sometimes use the example of the emperor to admonish the Germans for what they considered inappropriate behavior. In one case, the local secretary of the Czech National Socialist party, Josef David, during a speech at a memorial service on the first anniversary of the death of carpenter's helper František Pavlík during Czech-German conflict in Brünn/Brno in October 1905, noted, "Today's Germans are unworthy successors to their great master [Joseph II], who respected the freedom of everyone."[67]

6. Joseph II in the Austrian Imagination: Multiple Memories

The memory of Joseph II was not always divisive. He remained a popular figure among the Jews of the Monarchy, who were among the most loyal subjects of the Monarchy. They continued to remember him as the reformer who enacted the Edict of Toleration, thus beginning their road to legal equality, rather than as a Germanizer and a centralizer. It was however, Emperor Franz Joseph, for whom they reserved their real affection. Indeed, the Jews of Cisleithania created a virtual cult of Franz Joseph, revering him for having granted them emancipation and freedom.[68]

Despite the Habsburgs' attempts to control their image and their propagation of cults of memory, ironically, it was the grass roots cult of Joseph II, a challenge to imperial power from the margins, which would be the most popular, longest lasting, and, in the end, the most problematic.[69] Images of the emperor were sites of fluid, contrasting memories which were increasingly democratized, politicized, and nationalized during the late nineteenth and early twentieth centuries. Democratization after the *Ausgleich* in 1867 both complicated and simplified his image, but a hegemonic interpretation of Joseph II as Germanizer and centralizer slowly superseded the others. By the last decade of the monarchy, the most widespread image of the pre-national, absolutist, reformist Catholic emperor, was that of a proto-German, proto-liberal, anti-Clerical ruler.

Although it was not solely the lens of German nationalism through which Joseph II's achievements were perceived after the turn of the century, this interpretation came to dominate the emperor's image among many of the peoples of Cisleithania, especially the Czechs and Germans of the Bohemian lands, but also among anticlerical and nationalist and/or liberal Germans elsewhere in Cisleithania. German rhetoric, both liberal and nationalist, conflated the Josephinist spirit and ideas, "light" and enlightenment, with "German spirit" and (superior) "German culture." Germans accused those who rejected the latter of rejecting the former. By monopolizing the image of Emperor Joseph II in late imperial Cisleithania, by transforming his memory from that of the "esteemer of mankind" to the "esteemer of Germans," nationalist Germans were able to turn an imperial figure against the dynasty. While asserting their loyalty to Vienna and Franz Joseph, nationalist Germans employed Joseph II to attack the politics of the imperial center from the periphery. Especially in the Bohemian lands, they "Germanized" not only Joseph II, but by implication also the entire Habsburg dynasty, making the latter an increasingly less effective centripetal force after the turn of the century.

Notes

* I would like to thank Hugh Agnew for reading various versions of this article and Laurence Cole for providing some of the material used in it.
1. Pieter Judson, *Exclusive Revolutionaries: Liberal Politics, Social Experience, and National Identity in the Austrian Empire, 1848–1918* (Ann Arbor, 1996), 14.
2. Helmut Reinalter, "Die Josephinischen Wurzeln des Österreichischen Katholizismus," *Etudes Danubiennes* 10/1 (1994): 3.
3. Josephinism has been the subject of a large historiography. See Eduard Winter's classic work, *Der Josephinismus und seine Geschichte. Beiträge zur Geistesgeschichte Österreichs 1740–1848* (Brünn, 1943); more recently: Harm Klueting, ed., *Der Josephismus: ausgewählte Quellen zur Geschichte der theresianisch-josephinischen Reformen* (Darmstadt, 1995); and Helmut Reinalter, ed., *Der Josephinismus: Bedeutung, Einflüsse und Wirkungen* (Frankfurt a.M., 1993).
4. On the Josephinist reforms as well as reactions of different Jewish Communities, see for example, Lois C. Dubin, *The Port Jews of Habsburg Trieste: Absolutist Politics and Enlightenment Culture* (Stanford, 1999); Jacob Katz, *Out of the Ghetto: The Social Background of Jewish Emancipation, 1770–1870* (Cambridge, MA, 1973); Joseph Karmiel, *Die Toleranzpolitik Kaiser Josephs II* (Göttingen, 1986); William O. McCagg, *A History of Habsburg Jews, 1670–1918* (Bloomington, 1989); Marsha L. Rozenblit, *Reconstructing a National Identity: The Jews of Habsburg Austria during World War I* (Oxford, 2001); Nancy Sinkoff, *Out of the Shtetl: Making Jews Modern in the Polish Borderlands* (Providence, 2004); also Michael K. Silber, "From Tolerated Aliens to Citizen-Soldiers: Jewish Military Service in the Era of Joseph II," in *Constructing Nationalities in East Central Europe*, ed. Pieter M. Judson and Marsha L. Rozenblit (New York, 2004), 19–39.

5. Steven Beller, *Vienna and the Jews: A Cultural History* (Cambridge, 1989), 128; and Hugo Gold, ed., *Die Juden und Judengemeinden Mährens in Vergangenheit und Gegenwart* (Brünn, 1929), 148. See also the nineteenth-century Jewish historian Heinrich Graetz's description of "Joseph II of glorious memory," who partially removed the "ignominy of a thousand years," in Dubin, *The Port Jews of Habsburg Trieste*, 68; as well as Joseph II in the work of the nineteenth-century Austrian Jewish writer Leopold Kompert in Robertson, "Joseph II in Cultural Memory," 220.

6. See Paul P. Bernard, "Joseph II and the Jews: The Origins of the Toleration Patent of 1782," *Austrian History Yearbook* IV–V (1968–1969): 101–119; and Hugo Gold, *Geschichte der Juden in Wien, Ein Gedenkbuch* (Telaviv, 1966), 25.

7. Cathleen M. Giustino, *Tearing Down Prague's Jewish Town: Ghetto Clearance and the Legacy of Middle-Class Ethnic Politics around 1900* (Boulder, 2003), 167. Also Sigmund Mayer's reference to "Juden(Josefs)stadt" in *Ein jüdischer Kaufman, 1831 bis 1911* (Leipzig, 1911), 151.

8. William M. Johnston, *The Austrian Mind: An Intellectual and Social History, 1848–1938* (Berkeley, 1972), 15–17.

9. Johnston, *The Austrian Mind.*

10. See Wolfgang Häusler, "'Des Kaisers Bildsäule.' Entstehung und politischer Sinngehalt des Wiener Josephsdenkmals," in Niederösterreichische Landesausstellung. *Österreich zur Zeit Kaiser Josephs II. Mitregent Kaiserin Maria Theresias, Kaiser und Landesfürst* Stift Melk, March 29–November 2, 1980 (Vienna, 1980), 288–290; and Eduard Beutner, "Joseph II. Die Geschichte seiner Mythisierung und Entmythisierung in der Literatur (1741–1848). Die Grundlagen und Bausteine der josephinischen Legende" (Habilitationsschrift, Paris-Lodron Universität Salzburg, 1992), 283–301.

11. "Am Denkmahle Kaiser Joseph's II. Bey Errichtung desselben am Joseph's-Platze zu Wien" (Vienna, 1806).

12. See Metodej Zemek, "Joseph II. und Slavikovice," in Niederösterreichische Landesausstellung's *Österreich zur Zeit Kaiser Josephs II*, 291–92; illustrations in the same catalogue; sketches for monuments in Archiv města Brna, XVa č. 28; and the reproductions in Jiří Rak, *Bývali čechové: české historické mýty a stereotypy* (Jinočany, 1994), 142.

13. Apollo-Verein, "Ein Denkmal Kaiser Joseph's II. Eine Anthologie in Poesie und Prosa" (Brünn, 1868), 8; and Carl Richter, *Geschichte der Kaiser Josef-Denkmäler in Böhmen, Mähren, Niederösterreich und Schlesien* (Reichenberg, 1883), 130 and 408.

14. On anonymous anecdotes, see Beutner, "Joseph II. Die Geschichte seiner Mythisierung und Entmythisierung in der Literatur," 280 ff., who notes that anecdotes about Joseph II were published in French (author cited) and Italian (anonymously) in the immediate post-Napoleonic period. See also Ritchie Robertson, "Joseph II in Cultural Memory," in *Cultural Memory and Historical Consciousness in the German-Speaking World since 1500*, ed. Christian Emden and David Midgley (Oxford, 2004), 217, 220–221.

15. Contemporary examples of Joseph II in the Austrian popular imagination are legion. See *Kaiser Josef der Zweite. Gedenkblätter zur hundertjährigen Trauerfeier seines Todes* (Vienna, 1890); Richter, *Geschichte der Kaiser Josef-Denkmäler*, 120; Fest-Ausschuße, "Fest-Schrift zur Enthüllungs-Feier des Denkmals Kaiser Josef II. bei Kletschen am 3. Juli 1881" (Leitmeritz, 1881), 3; and Zemek, "Joseph II. und Slavikovice," 291; and *Reichenberger Zeitung*, 8 November 1880, 1.

16. See *Leitmeritzer Zeitung*, 6 November 1880, 975, on the ruins of a column, with a Latin inscription dedicated to Joseph II, near the Transylvanian border, "where now unfortunately, only opponents of Josephinist ideas govern." Apparently, "hot-blooded" Magyars had destroyed the double eagle atop the column.

17. Herman Hallwich, *Reichenberg und Umgebung. Eine Ortsgeschichte mit specieller Rücksicht auf gewerbliche Entwicklung* (Reichenberg, 1874), 436; *Reichenberger Zeitung*, 3 September 1882, 1.

18. R.J.W. Evans, "Josephinism, 'Austrianness', and the Revolution of 1848," in *The Austrian Enlightenment and its Aftermath*, ed. Ritchie Robertson and Edward Timms (Edinburgh: Edinburgh University Press, 1991), 146–153; and Häusler, "Das Nachleben Josephs II. und des Josephinismus bis zur Revolution von 1848," in Niederösterreichische Landesausstellung, *Österreich zur Zeit Kaiser Josephs II*, 286.
19. Evans, "Josephinism, 'Austrianness', and the Revolution of 1848," 145; and *Neue Freie Presse*, 28 November 1880, 1.
20. University of Colorado Libraries, Special Collections Department, 1848 Collection, J.P. Lyser, "Ein Frühlingstag vor dem Denkmale des Kaisers Joseph des Zweiten. Dem Volke, das Er liebte und schätzte." Robertson discusses other poems dedicated to the Emperor in 1848 in "Joseph II in Cultural Memory," 221.
21. The late Friedrich Prinz wrote widely on Hans Kudlich. Most recently, "Hans Kudlich," in *Nation und Heimat: Beiträge zur böhmischen und sudetendeutschen Geschichte* (Munich, 2003), 217–233, particularly 173.
22. Evans makes this point in "Josephinism, 'Austrianness', and the Revolution of 1848," 155.
23. See for example "Die Religion ist in Gefahr," *2. Gabe des kathol. Volksvereins für Oberösterreich* (Linz, 1873), n.p. [5].
24. Laurence Cole, "The Counter-Reformation's Last Stand: Austria," in *Culture Wars: Secular-Catholic Conflict in Nineteenth-Century Europe*, ed. Christopher Clark and Wolfram Kaiser (Cambridge, 2003), 285–292; and Judson, *Exclusive Revolutionaries*, passim.
25. Judson, *Exclusive Revolutionaries*, 155–159; Richter, *Geschichte der Kaiser Josef-Denkmäler;* and *Stenographischer Bericht XIII Sitzung der dritten Jahres-Session des böhmischen Landtages vom 1878*, 17 October 1881, 278–283, 293, 245–246.
26. *Neue Freie Presse*, 30 November 1880, 2.
27. On the Stremayr language ordinances, see Judson, *Exclusive Revolutionaries*, 196–198; Jeremy King, *Budweisers into Czechs and Germans: A Local History of Bohemian Politics, 1848–1948* (Princeton, 2002), 56; and Otto Urban, *Česká společnost, 1848–1918* (Prague, 1982), 355–358.
28. *Neue Tiroler Stimmen*, 30 November 1880, 1.
29. *Reden von Ernst Freiherrn von Plener, 1873–1911* (Stuttgart, 1911), 202. Plener became known in the 1880s for his national rhetoric and radical party tactics.
30. *Národní listy*, 25 November 1880, 1.
31. On the Bishop of Linz, *Leitmeritzer Zeitung*, 24 November 1880, 1037; *Neue Tiroler Stimmen*, 26 November 1880; and *Reichenberger Zeitung*, 23 November 1880, 1. On his relationship with the Liberals more generally, see Cole, "The Counter-Reformation's Last Stand," in *Culture Wars*, 300–306. On the Cardinal of Vienna, *Das Vaterland*, 29 November 1880, 3; on the Archbishop of Graz, *Das Vaterland*, 26 November 1880, 2.
32. *Reichenberger Zeitung*, 23 November 1880, 1.
33. *Linzer Volksblatt*, 5 December 1880, 1.
34. Daniel Kovář, *Příběhy budějovických pomníků* (České Budějovice, 2000), 69.
35. On the Bishop of Budweis/Budějovice, *Prager Tagblatt*, 29 November 1880, 2. See also *Leitmeritzer Zeitung*, 1 December 1880, 1064; *Mährischer-Schlesischer Grenzbote*, 30 November 1880, 2; 2 December 1880, 3; *Neuigkeits Welt-Blatt*, 27 November 1880, 1; *Neue Freie Presse*, 30 November 1880 (morning edn.), 2; *Prager Tagblatt*, 28 November 1880, 6; and *Wiener Allgemeine Zeitung*, 28 November 1880, 2, and 29 November 1880, 1.
36. *Leitmeritzer Zeitung*, 24 November 1880, 1037.
37. See Daniel Unowsky's essay in this volume; also Unowsky, "'Our gratitude has no limit': Polish Nationalism, Dynastic Patriotism, and the 1880 Imperial Inspection Tour of Galicia," *Austrian History Yearbook* 34 (2003): 166, fn. 73; 169.
38. Judson, *Exclusive Revolutionaries*, 155. Figures from the "classical period of German literature" included Friedrich Schiller, Johann Wolfgang Goethe, and Gotthold Ephraim Lessing.
39. *Wiener Zeitung*, 26 November 1880, 2; on the vault being left open, *Neue Freie Presse*, 28 November 1880, 1.

40. *Neue Freie Presse,* 29 November 1880, 3.
41. *Neue Freie Presse,* 29 November 1880, 3.
42. *Wiener Zeitung,* 26 November 1880, 2; and 1 December 1880, 7–8.
43. *Bohemia,* 16 October 1881, 6; on "the special case of [Protestant] Asch/Aš," see Kristina Kaiserová, *Konfesní myšlení českých němců v 19. a počátkem 20. století* (Úvaly u Prahy, 2003), 85–86.
44. Gustav Frank, *Das Toleranz-Patent Kaiser Joseph II. Urkundliche Geschichte seiner Entstehung und seiner Folgen. Säcular-Festschrift des k.k. evangelischen Oberkirchenrathes A.C. und H.C. in Wien* (Vienna, 1881); *Innsbrucker Nachrichten,* 27 November 1880, 3–4, 1 December 1880, 3; and *Reichenberger Zeitung,* 28 November 1880, 1, 3.
46. On the opening of public parks, see T.C.W. Blanning, *Joseph II* (London, 1994), 64–65.
45. The Augarten itself was the site of numerous stories of Joseph II's encounters with his subjects, as when after meeting the daughter of a poor officer's widow, he helped the widow obtain a pension. For this incident, see *Das Vaterland,* 29 November 1880, 3.
47. *Reichenberger Zeitung,* Feuilleton: "Wiener Kaleidoskopen," 8 November 1880, 1.
48. *Leitmeritzer Zeitung,* 30 November 1880, 966; *Neue Freie Presse,* 29 November 1880, 3; and *Wiener Zeitung,* 1 December 1880, 8.
49. *Národní listy,* 20 November 1905, 1.
50. Elisabeth Grossegger, *Der Kaiser Huldigungs Festzug Wien 1908* (Vienna, 1992), 121, 188–189.
51. In asserting, "For his work in his constituency, he chose the ideological symbol of the *Volkskaiser,* Joseph II, who had made it his policy to build a strong peasantry. Schönerer erected plaques in various villages of his district showing the Emperor Joseph with his hand on the plow. Here the liberal cult of science and public welfare mingled with Habsburg loyalty: Schönerer was clearly still within the framework of the liberal Josephinian tradition," Carl Schorske underestimates the degree to which the image of Joseph II had come to be opposed to the monarchy, "Politics in a New Key," *Fin-de-Siècle Vienna: Politics and Culture* (New York, 1981), 125.
52. For Schönerer, see *Neue Freie Presse,* 16 September 1881, 4; and *Teplitz-Bodenbacher Zeitung,* 15 May 1880, 5; on the national-liberal conjuncture, see Judson, *Exclusive Revolutionaries,* 2–3, 193–223.
53. The statue put up in Wels in 1884 was not part of the jubilee celebration. It was erected by Upper Austrian liberals in connection with the elections held there that year. See Harry Slapnicka, "Das Welser Kaiser-Joseph-Denkmal und die Frühgeschichte des Parteiwesens in Oberösterreich," *Mitteilungen des Oberösterreichischen Landesarchivs* 14 (1984), 449–464.
54. I discuss this topic in greater detail elsewhere, most recently in *Flag Wars and Stone Saints: How the Bohemian Lands Became Czech* (Cambridge, MA, 2007), chapter 1.
55. *Tagesbote aus Mähren und Schlesien,* 17 October 1892 (morning edn.), 1.
56. *Egerer Zeitung,* 5 October 1887, 1.
57. *Egerer Zeitung,* 5 October 1887, 1.
58. *Tagesbote aus Mähren und Schlesien,* 17 October 1892 (morning edn.), 1; in shortened form, see Richter, *Geschichte der Kaiser Josef-Denkmäler,* 248.
59. *Leitmeritzer Zeitung,* 2 October 1897, 1312.
60. *Neue Freie Presse,* 28 November 1897, 7.
61. Although the postcard was sent from Reichenberg/Liberec in August 1898, shortly after the death of former German chancellor Otto von Bismarck on July 30, the legend *Jahreswende,* or new year, indicates that it was published the previous year, possibly as part of the protests against the Badeni language ordinances. The card is reproduced in the color plate section of Kaiserová, *Konfesní myšlení;* for the Niederwald monument, see Sergiusz Michalski, *Public Monuments: Art in Political Bondage 1870–1997* (London, 1998), 58–59.
62. *Tagesbote aus Mähren und Schlesien,* 29 June 1914 (morning edn.), 3.
63. Verein der christlichen Deutschen in der Bukowina, "Festschrift" (Cernowitz, 1903), 1.
64. Kaiserová, *Konfesní myšlení,* 96.

65. On the nobility's opposition to Josephinist reforms, see for example, Ivan T. Berend, *History Derailed: Central and Eastern Europe in the Long Nineteenth Century* (Berkeley, 2003), 34, 52, and 105–107; also Prinz, "František Palacký als Historiograph der böhmischen Stände," *Nation und Heimat*, 122. On the Czech-speaking intelligentsia, see Jiří Štaif, "The Image of the Other in the Nineteenth Century: Historical Scholarship in the Bohemian Lands," *Creating the Other: Ethnic Conflict and Nationalism in Habsburg Central Europe*, ed. Nancy M. Wingfield (New York, 2003), 83–84.
66. *Moravské orlice*, 8 October 1892, 2.
67. Österreichisches Staatsarchiv, Allgemeines Verwaltungsarchiv, Ministerium des Innern, Präsidiale (1900–1918), kar. 2126, 8529/1906, Der k.k. Regierungsrat und Polizei-Direktor to K.k. mähr: Statthalterei-Praesidium!, 30 September 1906.
68. Marsha L. Rozenblit, "Sustaining Austrian 'National' Identity in Crisis: The Dilemma of the Jews in Habsburg Austria, 1914–1919," *Constructing Nationalities in East Central Europe*, 178–79. See also Emperor Franz Joseph's exchange with a Galician Jew in Joseph Roth's *Radetzky March* that Robertson cites as an example of how the memory of Joseph II could live on in disguised form, in "Joseph II in Cultural Memory," 226.
69. On Habsburg attempts to control their image and their propagation of cults of memory, see Andrew Wheatcroft, *The Habsburgs: Embodying Empire* (London, 1995), 251–54, 255. On "image management," Peter Burke, *Eyewitnessing: The Uses of Images as Historical Evidence* (Ithaca, 2001), 72; on "image as argument," Joan B. Landes, *Visualizing the Nation: Gender, Representation, and Revolution in Eighteenth-Century France* (Ithaca, NY, 2001), 24–56.

Chapter 4

THE FLYSPECKS ON PALIVEC'S PORTRAIT
Franz Joseph, the Symbols of Monarchy, and Czech Popular Loyalty

Hugh LeCaine Agnew

The relationship between His Imperial and Apostolic Majesty Franz Joseph I and his "ancient and glorious city of Prague" and "loyal Bohemians"[1] has been the subject of many anecdotes and stories. During his reign, of course, public displays of loyalty and affection from both Czechs and Germans were the norm, although beginning in the 1890s an anti-dynastic tone emerged more insistently in the political protests marking the last decades of the dual monarchy. In independent Czechoslovakia that anti-dynastic element became the norm in its turn, in both popular attitudes and state ideology. The Czechoslovak declaration of independence of 18 October 1918 denounced the Habsburg dynasty as "unworthy of leading our nation" and asserted a Czechoslovak duty "toward humanity and civilization to aid in bringing about its downfall and destruction."[2] The new republic removed all the symbols of the old dynasty, and Masaryk and other Czechoslovak leaders spoke of the need for Czechs to "de-Austrianize" themselves. The terms of their parting thus colored the entire history of the connection between the Habsburg dynasty and the Czechs, reducing it to three centuries of oppression.[3] As the "last" ruler of the dynasty—for in Czech historical consciousness his death in November 1916 truly symbolized the end of the monarchy—Franz Joseph shared this family fate. Like the flyspecked portrait of the emperor that innkeeper Palivec removes from the wall of Josef Švejk's favorite pub, "The Chalice," Franz Joseph vanished from his accustomed location, replaced with a mirror in which the Czechs could see only their own reflection.[4]

With time and the crises of the twentieth century, Czech attitudes to Franz Joseph have mellowed, but however nostalgic Nazi and Soviet domination made them towards the "good old days of Habsburg oppression," they never lost a certain tone of ironic mockery, reflected in Franz Joseph's most common nickname, "starej Procházka" (Old Procházka).[5]

Under that name Franz Joseph figures significantly in one of the plays of the popular Jára Cimrman Theater, *Lijavec* (Deluge, 1982). During the pseudo-academic seminar that typically begins a Cimrman performance, one of the actors describes the historical significance of Franz Joseph by asking the audience to imagine a sixteen-year-old boy on his way to school in Prague in late December 1848. He scrambles over a few barricades, settles onto his bench, and sees on the wall behind the teacher a portrait of the young Franz Joseph. Twenty years pass. It is now 1868: the boy's son goes off to school (the barricades having been cleared away) and behind the teacher is Franz Joseph's portrait. Twenty more years pass. In the year 1888, the grandson goes off to school and behind the teacher there is still a portrait of Franz Joseph. Another twenty years, 1908, and now it is the great-grandson who settles into a school bench and looks at—a portrait of Franz Joseph! "Imagine," concludes the actor, "how tired of each other the Emperor and his peoples were!"[6] In Communist party leader Gustáv Husák's normalized Czechoslovakia, the play's use of the image of Franz Joseph and the deluge clearly had contemporary as well as historical resonance to its listeners. Yet the premise of the joke is still relevant to the historian: the very longevity of the emperor affected how his subjects viewed him during his reign, and how their views changed as the years passed.

Franz Joseph's historians and biographers, however, have typically not devoted much attention to his role as King of Bohemia. The two most recent biographies of Franz Joseph in English essentially ignore this aspect of his position.[7] While the recent study by the Czech historian Otto Urban pays more attention to it, it only does so within a broader framework.[8] Certainly, there is nothing for Bohemia to compare with András Gerő's study of Franz Joseph as King of the Hungarians.[9] To redress this imbalance, the following discussion explores some of the modulations in Czech attitudes to Franz Joseph and the symbols of monarchy during his reign, focusing mainly on the royal visits to the Bohemian capital and the ongoing hopes for a Bohemian coronation. In the process, this essay will trace how traditional forms of dynastic loyalty could be adapted to nationalist politics.

The discussion starts with one of the earliest retrospective analyses of Franz Joseph's reign, the Czech historian Josef Pekař's address at the emperor's memorial service, held at the Czech university in Prague on 4 December 1916. Pekař depicted a much-tried ruler who attempted through gradual adaptation to balance the contesting political forces in his realm, the strongest of which was nationalism. After his reluctant return to constitutionalism in 1861, Franz Joseph spent the remainder of his reign trying to exert the "balancing and facilitating power of the crown," compromising according to the strength of the forces he faced. In the process, he "more than once took leave of ideals dear to him. But ... he continued to labor away at his life's work, a work which we could call seeking equilibrium." Pekař completed this picture of Franz Joseph by citing the monarch's formal farewell to Prague on his final visit to the Bohemian capital in April 1907: "My most longed-for wish would be to see the walls fall that now divide the nations and retard the full development of their rich talents, and thus also of the state's power. I would consider it the greatest happiness if I, who have experienced all the bitterness of the struggle, might one day be able to participate in the joyfulness of national conciliation."[10]

Pekař struck another note that also sounded in later evaluations of the emperor. He emphasized that it was during Franz Joseph's reign that a modern society developed, with new economic, educational, and civic forms. The Czech nation, Pekař asserted, probably benefited from these developments more than any other except the Hungarian. He also referred to the emperor's unrealized desire to carry out a coronation as King of Bohemia, a wish that "remains forever linked in the grateful memory of our nation with the name of Franz Joseph, and the royal rescript of September 12, [1871] will be for us lustrous evidence of princely justice as of our rights, and a pledge of hope that the future will repair what the past let slip away."[11] This is quite an attractive picture, but to what extent was Pekař's account—obviously and of necessity written with an eye to what was possible, decorous, or safe to say on such an occasion and in the middle of an exhausting war—an accurate reflection of his countrymen's attitudes?

Without doubt, the mutual introduction of ruler and subjects could hardly have taken place under less auspicious circumstances. On 2 December 1848, the eighteen-year-old Franz Joseph ascended the throne of an empire still in the throes of revolution. Prague had reposed under martial law since June, Vienna had been tamed in October, but the Constituent Parliament (*Reichsrat*) had reconvened in the Moravian town of Kroměříž/Kremsier to draft a constitution for the empire, while Hungary still resisted the imperial armies. Franz Joseph's accession was a crucial step in the counter-revolution which eventually defeated the Hungarians and aborted the work of the Constituent Parliament. Unfettered by coronation oaths and promises of constitutional rule, his government installed the system of neoabsolutism that forged for the only time in its history a unitary, centralized, bureaucratically administered state out of the Habsburg Monarchy. When he first visited the Bohemian capital as titular King of Bohemia in November 1849, Prague still lay under martial law. All the requisite formal pomp and ceremony accompanied the visit, but any enthusiasm the public displayed was a reflection of the vain hope that the strict regime of military rule would end; otherwise, the Prague public remained indifferent.[12] A return visit in May 1852 was equally disappointing, but in those years Franz Joseph could not count on an enthusiastic reaction to his presence anywhere in his realm, including his residential seat in Vienna.[13]

By the time of Franz Joseph's third visit to Prague during the first half of June 1854, the situation had changed. The new empress and queen Elisabeth accompanied the emperor, on their first official journey as a married couple. A partial political amnesty for sentences arising out of the Revolution of 1848, a relaxation of the administrative regime, and the lifting of martial law had accompanied the wedding. Curiosity to see the beautiful new empress helped bring out more enthusiastic crowds than Franz Joseph had previously experienced. In the words of one later newspaper account, the visit was "like a family celebration," and Prague "pelted the young newlyweds with the most beautiful roses ... and surrounded them with the warmest of best wishes."[14] In spite of the positive impression she made on the Praguers, however, Empress Elisabeth never developed the enthusiasm for Bohemia that she displayed for Hungary and the Hungarians. As her own relationship with her husband cooled, her presence on the Czech scene declined. Although the Czech public in 1854 was willing to let bygones be bygones, complications in foreign affairs quickly undercut any potential new beginning. Before that looming catastrophe had a chance to break, though, Franz Joseph returned in 1858 to unveil a monument on Prague's Malostranské náměstí/Kleinseitner Ring to the victor over revolutionary Italy, Field Marshall Joseph Radetzky.

A monument in Prague to Austria's greatest modern general—and a native Bohemian—was first proposed by the director of the Prague Academy of Fine Arts after the battle of Novara in 1849, and quickly found support in influential circles, especially from Count Franz Thun.[15] He interested the Society of Patriotic Friends of the Arts, which agreed to contribute to the costs. More than one-fourth of the total sum was raised by public donations from around the empire, with the greatest number of contributors among the officers of the northern Italian garrisons. After the court approved the monument, the unveiling was planned for November 1858 to coincide with the venerable hero's ninety-second birthday. Although Radetzky died on 5 January 1858, the presence of the emperor, as well as the fact that the ceremonies were the first major opening of a monument in Prague, still created strong public interest. The square was closed for normal traffic and special tribunes were erected for the paying public (others could purchase tickets to observe the ceremonies from the windows of those fortunate homeowners whose dwellings overlooked the site). The ceremonies proceeded under sunny skies, lighting up the square and the houses decorated with draperies, carpets, and Bohemian red-white or imperial black-yellow banners. Many who were unable to obtain tickets viewed the monument during the days preceding the ceremony. The figure of Radetzky, borne up on a shield by soldiers from every branch of the service (the artilleryman was popularly considered to be from a Bohemian regiment), embodied an Austrianism and *Kaisertreue* shared at that time among many Czechs, especially veterans (see figure 4.1).[16]

Ironically, this flaunting of Austria's military victory over the revolution in Italy in 1848 and 1849 was followed within a year by the disasters at Magenta and Solferino. Those defeats marked the beginning of the end, both of Austria as an Italian power and of neo-absolutism in Austrian internal affairs.[17] When Franz Joseph returned to constitutional rule after this Italian debacle and summoned the Diets of his lands, the question of his coronation as King of Bohemia

Figure 4.1. Photograph of the Radetzky monument in Prague's Malostranské náměstí/Kleinseitner Ring. *Deutsche Arbeit*, 1908

returned to the agenda, as it had not since 1848. On 11 April 1861, Prince Friedrich Schwarzenberg, Cardinal Archbishop of Prague, submitted a motion to the Bohemian Diet to petition the emperor to hold a festive coronation in Prague. Though they recognized him as king according to the Pragmatic Sanction, the archbishop said, Franz Joseph's subjects "longed" for the bond symbolized by the coronation, "the holiest pledge of the sovereign's duty and the subjects' loyalty," which would "bind king and kingdom more closely than cold right, and protect better than the naked sword."[18] The Diet unanimously accepted the archbishop's proposal, and elected a commission to present their request to the emperor and king in person.

Franz Joseph received the Bohemian delegation on April 14, and his response to their request was gratifying. After noting that their shared goal was "to bring the legitimate and established freedom and autonomy of the lands of my crown into harmony with the necessary conditions of the unity of the monarchy," he continued (in Czech): "I will have myself crowned King of Bohemia in Prague, and I am convinced that a new, indissoluble bond of trust and loyalty between my throne and my Bohemian Kingdom will be strengthened by this holy rite."[19] These rhetorical flourishes echoed once more when the diet received the delegation's report on April 15.[20] Soon thereafter, the official *Wiener Zeitung* was printing detailed descriptions of the coronation regalia and accounts of the ceremonies at Ferdinand's coronation in Prague in 1836.[21]

However, the unsettled constitutional situation meant that any Bohemian coronation could not take place immediately. Frustrated by Minister of State Anton von Schmerling's failure to cow the Hungarians, the emperor replaced him in July 1865 with Count Richard Belcredi, who suspended the constitutional provisions of February 1861. The Bohemian Diet welcomed these moves with an address of thanks, expressing the "fervent wish" that they would lead to a Bohemian coronation, "in our kingdom an ancient symbolic manifestation, a mutual guarantee and the highest consecration of an established legal order."[22] Franz Joseph's reply, conveyed to the Diet on 8 January 1866, was again gratifying. He stated that he would "welcome the joyous moment when the success of my great undertaking leads me to my ancient and glorious city of Prague, so that I may carry out according to right and holy custom the act of coronation amidst my loyal Bohemians."[23]

Once more, however, events—this time the Austro-Prussian War of 1866—prevented an early fulfillment of the monarch's promise. Following Austria's defeat near Hradec Králové/Königgrätz on 3 June 1866, and the Prussian withdrawal in September, the emperor visited Prague and toured the battlefields in October and November. His visit was a somber affair, in keeping with the solemnity of the occasion. During the war, the Prussians had published a manifesto "To the Inhabitants of the Glorious Kingdom of Bohemia" promising "full respect for your historical and national rights," and, in the case of a Prussian victory, "the fulfillment of the national longings of the Bohemians and Moravians."[24] Like similar overtures to the Hungarians, this initiative seems to have been much more a diplomatic weapon than a serious attempt to destroy the Austrian empire. In any case, the Czech middle class liberal national leaders remained loyal to the state, in spite of the campaign by the 1848 radical Josef Václav Frič, living in exile in Berlin, to create an independent Czech state within a Central European federation. In return for their loyalty, the Czechs hoped that they and their political demands might be taken more seriously.

Franz Joseph met representatives of the recently created autonomous organs, who petitioned him to take their further development under his protection, but he replied without making any concrete promises. He visited cultural institutions, factories, and other commercial enterprises, and dissolved Prague's status as a fortress city, enabling the dismantling of the city's surviving fortifications and a more rapid urban development. He handed out military decorations and made financial gifts to various institutions significant to the Czech national movement, such as the Bohemian Museum, the Society of Sciences, and the Committee for the National Theater, before leaving to tour the battlefields.[25] The public received Franz Joseph with all due respect and honor, but disappointment with his failure to say anything concrete about the legal position of Bohemia—especially while the settlement with Hungary was gathering speed—helped dampen excessive excitement over the royal presence.[26]

The *Ausgleich* of 1867 left the Czechs and their aristocratic allies without the recognition of Bohemian state rights for which they had hoped. Instead of celebrating a coronation in Prague, they had to watch while the agreement between the crown and the Hungarian political nation was sealed with Franz Joseph's coronation in Budapest on 8 June 1867.[27] Their hopes for a coronation postponed at best, the Czech public could at least look forward to the return of the coronation regalia. The state jewels had been carefully transferred to Vienna for safekeeping as war with Prussia loomed in 1866.[28] The government's decision to return them to Prague by overnight train with few stops turned the state jewels' homecoming into a political issue. In 1791, when Leopold II had returned the regalia to Prague before his own coronation, the Crown of St. Wenceslas met with patriotic manifestations along its route.[29] Although the government reviewed the ceremonies accompanying the crown's earlier return, neither it nor Franz Joseph wanted public demonstrations while the dualistic solution to Austria's constitutional crisis had still to take its final shape.[30] In its first report of the plans, the Young Czech daily *Národní listy* emphasized that the insignia would be sent back "*completely in secret,* so as to avoid any patriotic demonstration," an issue to which the newspaper repeatedly returned.[31]

Národní listy also took issue with voices denying the importance of the occasion. When the German liberal *Tagesbote aus Böhmen* sneered that the crown was nothing more than a piece of Gothic jewelry being misused by Czech nationalist leaders to dupe the people, *Národní listy* indignantly replied that this "golden circlet" had for centuries joined "the three lands of Bohemia, Moravia and Silesia and the fraternal Czech, Moravian and Silesian nation inhabiting them into one whole," and furthermore that "he on whose head the nation places it is bound before God and the world to rule the entire Czech-Moravian-Silesian nation according to the laws it establishes, and thus the crown is a sign to our nation of its independence and sovereignty in union with its crowned King."[32] When the crown jewels finally arrived in Prague, *Národní listy* remarked that the Czechs had hoped to view the crown on their king's head, as promised in 1861. Instead, "for the time being, we bear our crown ourselves ... *This day belongs to us. Today we crown ourselves* with the most noble love, love for our fatherland, love for our language, love for our rights, love for our life!"³³

During the weeks preceding the Hungarian coronation, Czech leaders expressed their rejection of dualism in various ways. František Palacký, a historian and leader of the Old Czech wing of the national liberal movement, led other Czech figures in an ostentatious visit to an ethnographic exhibition in Russia, where they had an audience with Tsar Alexander II. In Bohemia, opposition to dualism took the form of street demonstrations, resolutions from the district representations, and especially the wave of open air mass protest meetings that lasted from 1868 to 1871, known as the "*tábor* movement."³⁴ The Czech national leadership also showed its rejection of the *Ausgleich* by pointedly approaching Franz Joseph directly as King of Bohemia, bypassing the Cisleithanian government whose competence to deal with Bohemia they denied. For its part, the government insisted that Franz Joseph refer all such petitions to its ministers.³⁵

Robbed by the dualist compromise of their hoped for coronation, the Czechs instead turned the laying of the cornerstone of the new National Theater on 16 May 1868 into a patriotic manifestation rivaling previous coronation celebrations (see figure 4.2). The crown was a vibrant symbol during these celebrations, dominating the decorations and featuring prominently in the firework displays accompanying the regatta on the evening of May 15. The festive parade that began the next day was consciously modeled on the coronation processions last seen in Prague in 1836, with participants wearing costumes evoking the age of Bohemia's independence under the estates monarchy in the sixteenth century. At the building site, a replica of the Crown of St. Wenceslas with the coats-of-arms of the three lands of the Bohemian crown surmounted the canopy over the foundation stone (see figure 4.3). František Ladislav Rieger, Palacký's son-in-law and another leader of the Old Czechs, made it the centerpiece of his toast at the concluding banquet on May 17, calling the crown a symbol of the unity of Bohemia and Moravia, their historical rights, and their glory.³⁶ In its editorial on the day of the ceremony itself, *Národní listy* asserted: "We are still here, and as long as we are here, the Czech state is here, the Crown of St. Wenceslas is here … Today we have gathered in Prague for a general diet of the Czech crown. There was no electoral law … each of us brought the diet's program in our hearts, and it has already been voted on among us long ago."³⁷

The celebrations marking the laying of the cornerstone of the National Theater created a mood of national exaltation that cast Franz Joseph's visit to Prague a few weeks later into the shade. The monarch came to Prague to officiate at the opening of the third bridge across the Vltava/Moldau, which was to bear his name for decades. The timing of his visit was ill-conceived: not only had government crackdowns on the ongoing *tábor* movement and the Czech press marked the weeks since the theater celebrations, but the royal presence in Prague from June 21–23 coincided with the anniversary of the execution on Old Town Square in 1621 of the leaders of the Bohemian rebellion against the Habsburgs, which had touched off the Thirty Years' War. *Národní listy* contrasted the current mood

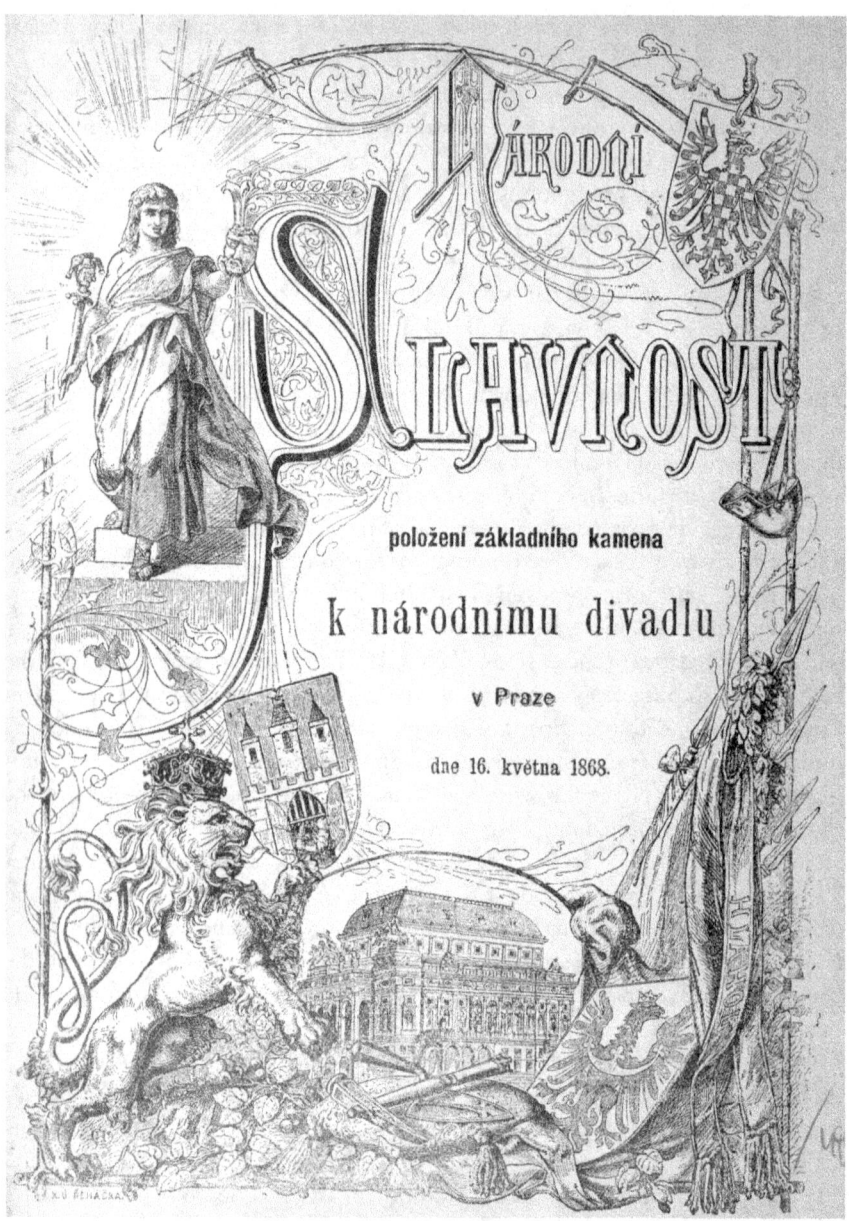

Figure 4.2. Laying of the foundation stones for the Czech National Theater in Prague, May 1868. Servác Heller, *Národní slavnost položení základního kamena k národnímu divadlu v Praze dne 16. května 1868* (Prague, 1868, rpt. 1918).

Klepání na základní kámen'

Figure 4.3. Contemporary illustration of the ceremony at the Czech National Theater construction site, with the canopy decorated with the coats of arms of the Bohemian Crownlands surmounted by the Crown of St. Wenceslas, Prague, 15 May 1868. From Servác Heller, *Národní slavnost položení základního kamena k národnímu divadlu v Praze dne 16. května 1868* (Prague, 1868, rpt. 1918).

with that prevailing in 1866. Then, after the months of war and occupation, the royal visit generated some interest. Now, however, the Czechs had not yet been compensated for their wartime losses and sufferings, and had just seen their historic state rights tossed aside and their land subsumed into the "other" half of the Austro-Hungarian Monarchy, commonly called "Cisleithania."[38]

To reflect that mood, many Czech patriotic organizations arranged to be out of town at the time of the royal visit. The nationalist gymnastic society *Sokol* (Falcon), pleading "previous promises," attended a ceremony dedicating the new banner of the *Sokol* unit in Kolín, while other groups organized trips elsewhere.[39] One favorite destination was the site of the Battle of White Mountain on the outskirts of Prague, where several hundred people gathered to lay laurel wreaths and sing patriotic songs to commemorate the defeat of the Bohemian rebellion in 1620. Prague itself was fittingly decorated with banners, although *Národní listy* noted that the imperial black-yellow predominated and that one house even prominently displayed the German national black-red-gold tricolor. Popular participation was only designated as "appropriate," with the German-speakers most in evidence. When the various singing societies performed, the Czech groups were not present: "in general, the leading Prague Czech societies did not take part in the bridge dedication ceremonies."[40] The Czech university students had planned to hold a meeting of their own on Žofín/Sofien Island in the river, but it was banned. Many of them gathered there anyway, and afterwards a group of them pulled down and tore up the German banner.[41]

In addition to these irritations, Franz Joseph's visit exposed divisions within the government, several of whose ministers had accompanied him. The emperor held preliminary talks with the Bohemian state rights advocates Palacký, Rieger, and their noble ally, Count Heinrich Jaroslav Clam-Martinic. The emperor's foreign minister, Friedrich Beust, joined him in Prague on June 22 to continue the discussions, unbeknownst to the rest of the ministers. Beust's conversations with the state rights leaders got no further than His Majesty's, but they so infuriated the minister-president, Prince Carlos Auersperg, that he left Prague in protest and resigned once he reached Vienna.[42] Although a formal dinner in the Prague castle, to which Palacký and Rieger were invited, was held as planned, the emperor was displeased and made his feelings known.[43] He reportedly urged the Prague police to proceed "firmly and vigorously" against the Czech newspapers, whose articles bordered on treason, and in a conversation with the university rector scolded him for educating "ignoramuses" whose behavior was "a scandal."[44]

Meanwhile, the *tábor* movement continued virtually unabated, as did the authorities' efforts to quash it. Eventually the heavy-handed actions against the organizers, participants, and propagators of these meetings (*Národní listy* was suspended for several months while a state of emergency was proclaimed in Prague and its environs) quelled the demonstrations.[45] In spite of this crackdown, Czech hopes flared briefly again in 1870–71. In an imperial rescript of 26 September 1870, Franz Joseph referred again to the prestige and glory of the Czech crown and to his intention to carry out a coronation. Under Minister-President Count Karl Hohenwart in the summer of 1871, the government negotiated a series of fundamental articles spelling out the relationship of the Bohemian crown to the rest of the Habsburg monarchy, and it appeared as though the state rights program of the Czechs and their aristocratic allies would carry the day. The Bohemian Diet was summoned for mid-September, to hear a rescript from Franz Joseph dated September 12, in which he said: "Having in mind the constitutional position of the Bohemian crown and being conscious of the glory and power which that crown has given us and our predecessors … we gladly recognize the rights of that kingdom and are prepared to renew that recognition through our coronation oath."[46]

International developments after the creation of the German Empire, domestic opposition from German liberals (especially the German-Bohemians), and the warnings of Foreign Minister Friedrich Beust and Hungarian Prime Minister

Count Gyula Andrássy doomed the Fundamental Articles. Hohenwart resigned and the articles were withdrawn. Among some radical nationalists the failure of the 1871 compromise began to change the way they viewed the symbols of monarchy. The rescript of 12 September 1871 was printed with black borders to be hung in windows as a sign of mourning, and even distributed on toilet paper.[47] For most Czechs, however, the failure of their hopes did not entirely spoil Franz Joseph's next visit to Bohemia in September 1874, during which he was greeted with a warmth conspicuously lacking in 1868.

He was greeted, however, as the uncrowned Bohemian king and not as emperor. The Kolín-based newspaper *Koruna česká* remarked that preparations to welcome Franz Joseph in Prague amounted to a demonstration "through which the Czech nation served notice that it was capable of separating the person of the monarch from those of his counselors, in whom it continues to see its political opponents." Adapting the traditional distinction between the good ruler and his evil advisers allowed "His Majesty's most loyal opposition," the Czech nation, to welcome Franz Joseph without compromising its rejection in principle of the dualist constitutional system.[48]

The crown and other symbols of the Bohemian kingdom figured prominently in the decorations that welcomed Franz Joseph in 1874. En route to Prague, the emperor stopped in the western Bohemian town of Plzeň/Pilsen, where he sampled the famous local beer at one of the formal dinners. After his second glass, the emperor reportedly remarked (to the delight of the Czech nationalists), "It's strange that no other brewery has succeeded in brewing such excellent beer, Schwechat and St. Marx's have been sparing no pains!"[49] The locomotive that carried him to Prague bore the Bohemian and Imperial coats of arms, the monogram FJI, and, of course, a representation—this time in flowers—of the Crown of St. Wenceslas. Prague's major squares were hung with banners bearing the crown, lit from behind by gaslights, and on the evening of the emperor's arrival, his monogram was ignited on the balustrade in fireworks, while above it the Crown of St. Wenceslas cast its light, all surrounded by a wreath of gas flames. Thus, in pyrotechnical form at least, the crown symbolically reposed on the head of its rightful bearer.[50]

Franz Joseph's next two journeys to Prague, in August 1879 and June 1880, combined the personal and the political. His son and heir, crown prince Rudolph, served in Bohemia with the 36th Mladá Boleslav/Jungbunzlau regiment during his time in the military. Though primarily undertaken for family reasons, these visits did have a political context, since between 1878 and 1880 the monarchy was undergoing a fundamental reorientation in internal politics.[51] With the fall of the German liberals and the creation of a ministry under the emperor's childhood companion, Count Eduard Taaffe, the Czechs finally abandoned their political abstention and entered the imperial parliament. Taaffe's ministry, supported by the "Iron Ring of the Right," a coalition of Czechs, German clericals, Poles, and some other small parties, remained in office until 1893. The Czechs opened each parliamentary session with a declaration reserving their cherished state rights, but instead of fighting for Bohemian state rights and a possible coronation, they opted for step-by-step bargaining.

Initially this tactic won concessions in language policy, education, and administration. In the long run, however, the decision to enter the *Reichsrat* as part of the Iron Ring accelerated the differentiation between the Old Czechs and the Young Czechs during the later 1880s. The state rights program and coronation became a weapon in their contest, as the Young Czechs turned the apparent decision to shelve it against their opponents. In 1886, the Young Czech journalist Karel Tůma published a pamphlet reviewing the state rights struggle from the 1840s to the rescript of 12 September 1871. In that text, Franz Joseph had recognized "our ancient rights … as valid, and repeated for the fourth time that he was eager to confirm that recognition of our rights through his coronation oath."[52] Fears about this Young Czech approach, in the year of the eight hundredth anniversary of the first Bohemian coronation in 1086 and the fiftieth anniversary of Ferdinand's coronation in 1836, provoked consultation between Bohemian officials and the central government. The Land Marshall, Prince Georg Lobkowitz, sent Taaffe a personal letter asking him to assure Franz Joseph that, if demands for a coronation were raised, "this is only a Young Czech agitation tactic, whose aim is not to expect a coronation, but exclusively and solely to embarrass the Old Czechs and conservative landowners."[53]

Young Czech agitation weakened the pro-government majority in the Bohemian Diet, prompting the Old Czechs to accept Taaffe's invitation late in 1889 to negotiations with the German liberals. Old Czechs and German liberals—each threatened by their own radicals—hoped that a compromise would win them votes, while Taaffe hoped to end the German boycott of the Bohemian diet. The Young Czechs were not invited to the discussions in Vienna in January 1890, where the participants agreed on a series of points (*punktace*) that divided local administrative bodies according to national criteria, in effect splitting Bohemia into German and Czech zones. The German side celebrated the *punktace* as a great victory, but Czech public opinion was overwhelmingly opposed. Rieger insisted that the *punktace* did the Czechs no harm, and in many respects were to their advantage, but to no avail.[54] The turmoil over the *punktace* effectively destroyed the Old Czech party. In the *Reichsrat* elections in 1891, the Young Czechs won a resounding victory and became the dominant force in Czech national politics.[55] During the 1890s, the lawyer Karel Kramář became the Young Czech party's leading exponent of the state rights program, though his use of the state rights did not focus on a coronation as such, but on the legal union and sovereignty of the three lands of the Crown of St. Wenceslas.[56]

Franz Joseph, who had avoided Prague during the relatively "peaceful" decade of the 1880s, faced a tense situation when he next arrived in the autumn of 1891. He came to attend the Provincial Jubilee Exhibition of which he was patron, an undertaking that demonstrated some of the pitfalls that must have kept him away from such events as the opening of the Czech National Theater in 1881 or its reopening in 1883 after the disastrous fire.[57] Originally planned to reflect the achievements of the entire Kingdom of Bohemia in the century since Leopold II's coronation, the exhibition became a political issue when the German Bohemians withdrew following the agitation over the *punktace*. The Czechs then turned what was to have been a Bohemian exhibition into a Czech national manifestation.[58] Thus, when the emperor visited Prague, he also felt impelled to make a state visit to Liberec/Reichenberg, a Bohemian German industrial and cultural center in northern Bohemia.[59] Both Czechs and Germans were disappointed with the outcome, as the emperor—though he clearly found the exhibition's industrial and commercial displays fascinating—said very little at the formal public occasions, and nothing at all about the major political questions of the day.[60]

The Jubilee Exhibition of 1891 did, however, provide an opportunity to make use of the crown and other symbols of the monarchy. The poster design by Vojtěch Hynais prominently featured the Bohemian coat-of-arms surmounted by the Crown of St. Wenceslas, while the commemorative volume published as a memorial to the exhibition used royal emblems repeatedly in its decorations. It also included a standing portrait of Franz Joseph in elaborate robes, resting his hand on a table on which reposed the regalia of the Kingdom of Bohemia: a formal coronation portrait for a coronation that never took place (see figure 4.4).[61] The crown and coat of arms of Bohemia, Moravia, and Silesia had long since become standard graphic elements of any publication that had national aims, to the point where the satirical *Humoristické listy*, in a verse dedicated to the Crown of St. Wenceslas on the eve of Franz Joseph's visit to the exhibition, remarked: "Na průmy slovém paláci/tě postavenou máme,/a v obrázkových novinách/tě často vidíváme;/na uměleckém předmětu/tě také zhusta zříme—/leč tam, kde bysi měla být, tě dosud nevidíme!" (On the industrial palace/We have you displayed,/ And in the illustrated papers/We see you all the time;/On artistic objects, too/We frequently behold you—/But where you really ought to be/Until now we still don't see you!)[62] This rueful doggerel reflects an interesting development: as the longed-for coronation receded endlessly into the future, the Czechs became used to seeing the crown as a national symbol without a concrete connection to Franz Joseph or the dynasty, the coronation portraits notwithstanding. Foreshadowed by *Národní listy* when the crown returned in 1867, by the 1880s this pattern was becoming increasingly common.

Some younger radicals of the fledgling Czech progressive movement used the Jubilee Exhibition to distribute 15,000 copies of a brochure on Czech state rights by Alois Rašín, a law student at the Charles University. Rašín denied that state rights were something "extracted from old parchments," unfitted to life in the modern political age, but he warned against identifying Czech state rights only with the coronation of the king. The coronation promises made by Leopold II, Franz I, or Ferdinand to abide by the law of the land had not been fulfilled, proof that "to demand the renewal of the state rights is by far more consequential than to call *only* for a coronation."[63] In this comment, Rašín echoed a warning already sounded at the time of Franz Joseph's 1874 visit. At that time, *Koruna česká* wrote

Figure 4.4. Idealized coronation portrait of Francis Joseph as King of Bohemia, from the volume commemorating the 1891 Jubilee Exhibition in Prague. *Jubilejní výstava zemská Království českého v Praze 1891* (Prague, 1894).

that, without redress of the injustices it suffered, the "Czech nation could hardly see in [a coronation] much more than a mere ceremony."[64]

In a further action, the radicals distributed a pamphlet called *Císařská slova* [The emperor's words] outside the exhibition grounds. This pamphlet simply reprinted all the statements the emperor had made promising a coronation since 1861.[65] The more the government under Count Franz Thun tried to crack down, the more radical the progressive students' actions became. These actions centered on symbols and sites of myth in the nationalist interpretation of Czech history. The progressive youth gathered on Bethlehem Square in Prague, where the Bohemian reformer Jan Hus once preached, to mark the anniversary of his martyrdom at Constance on 6 July 1415. They marched to White Mountain on the anniversary of that fateful battle, and they staged a mass demonstration on the battlefield at Lipany, where moderate Hussites and Catholics crushed radical Hussites in 1434. By 1893, their agitation was flowing together with demands for universal suffrage by the nascent workers' movement, with which many progressives had close ties. On 15 May 1893, the feast day of St. John of Nepomuk, demonstrators tried to topple a statue of the saint, which they considered an emblem of clericalism and the Counter-Reformation, from the Charles Bridge in Prague into the river below. They also draped a hangman's noose around the neck of an equestrian statue of Emperor Franz I which stood on the embankment, wearing the Bohemian crown and holding the royal scepter.[66] These demonstrations coincided with stormy debates in the Bohemian Diet as the government made a final attempt to salvage at least part of the *punktace*, debates that ended in the tumultuous Young Czech obstruction and the dissolution of the Diet on May 17.

Violent demonstrations assumed more anti-dynastic tones over the summer of 1893. On August 17, crowds of students and workers disrupted a concert on the eve of the emperor's birthday, distributing leaflets promising that what the statue had worn in May, the person would eventually wear.[67] Expecting trouble on September 12, the government broke up a meeting of some 600 people on Žofín/Sophien Island, a meeting which had obtained prior police permission. After the ensuing protest demonstrations, Governor Thun declared a state of emergency in Prague and its surrounding districts. Beginning on 15 January 1894, the Bohemian government staged a trial of seventy-six young defendants who allegedly belonged to a conspiratorial group called "*Omladina*" (Youth). Eventually, sixty-eight defendants were convicted and the sentences handed down totaled ninety-six years in prison. The *Omladina* Trial temporarily damped down radical protests, not least because the state of emergency remained in force for twenty-six months. The Young Czechs' hesitant reaction to the trials probably contributed to the further differentiation of the political scene among the Czechs in Bohemia. The turbulent summer also hastened the eventual fall of Taaffe's government on 11 November 1893.[68]

The fiftieth anniversary in 1898 of Franz Joseph's accession to the throne passed without a royal visit to Prague, but the Bohemian Diet did adopt a special address for the occasion, which repeated the basic state rights principles. Since the German Bohemian delegates walked out, the debate over the text was marked only by a few radical complaints that it was too circumspect. Nevertheless, the Diet was disappointed in Franz Joseph's response, read to them during a brief session at the end of December 1898. Of course, following the assassination of his estranged wife Elisabeth, the emperor had canceled all ostentatious celebration, but in contrast to some of Franz Joseph's earlier formal responses to the Diet, his address restricted itself even more than usual to general platitudes.[69] In any case, so close to the tempestuous fall of Count Kazimir Badeni's government in November 1897 and the acceptance of the language regulations enacted in place of Badeni's by Minister President Baron Paul Gautsch, the leading Czech parties were not yet ready to return to supporting the government. They only reached that stage in 1901, prior to Franz Joseph's penultimate visit to Prague. Under Minister President Ernst Koerber, the central government made some concessions in school and cultural policies in return for a Young Czech agreement to drop obstruction in the imperial parliament. A royal visit to Prague from June 11–18 would seal the deal.[70]

By the time of this, his eleventh formal state visit to Prague, contemporaries were beginning to see Franz Joseph as the balancing, equilibrium-seeking monarch described at his funeral by Joseph Pekař. The Realist journal *Čas* chided *Národní listy* for continuing to distinguish between the government, where the nation "sees and hates failures and flaws," and the person of the monarch.[71] The Viennese social democratic *Arbeiter Zeitung* wrote, "The Emperor's person is the equalizer between Czechs and Germans, the arbiter and link between the tribes ... [The crown] desires to maintain *strict neutrality* in the nationality contest, as it were above the fray."[72] For its own part, *Čas* maintained that the proof would be in what concrete results followed the Young Czech change of policy. In the meantime, there was no doubt the Prague population conducted itself in a completely loyal fashion, at least outwardly. "The question was not whether to decorate or not, but in which colors," as Prague's local patriotism came to the fore. Each of the two nations competed to surpass the other, a spirit which even affected the elementary school children who tried to out-shout the other's "Hoch" or "Sláva."[73] Aiming at a very different audience, *Pražský illustrovaný kurýr* noted the real work towards a compromise would be done in the Diet, where the voters and their mood would decide the issues, not a royal visit.[74]

In Prague, Franz Joseph opened the new bridge over the Vltava/Moldau near the National Theater, replacing the suspension bridge which had been inaugurated sixty years earlier. The city was as carefully and festively decorated as protocol demanded (electric lighting joining gaslights to illuminate the decorations); the emperor visited the usual public institutions and different parts of the city; he spoke both in German and Czech as he always did at his public appearances; and, in a final act of "balance," on June 17 he left Prague for a one day visit to Ústí nad Labem/Aussig, a predominantly German town northwest of Prague. He was accompanied not only by the minister president, but also by the Czech minister without portfolio, Antonín Rezek.[75] As the emperor prepared to leave for Ústí, *Čas* noted that "these festive days have otherwise passed in calm, everything took place precisely according to the established program."⁷⁶ That precise program, the highly ritualized public appearances with their equally ritualized phrases, had now become the main content of a royal visit to the realm. If on earlier occasions a visit by the monarch could play a major role in political affairs, by the beginning of the new century, what was left was on the one hand the "mask of majesty," and on the other an aged, august, but remote symbol whose presence did not dramatically affect the political contests among his subjects.

Little changed between his 1901 visit and Franz Joseph's twelfth and final official visit to Prague in 1907. This time the trip had been preceded in 1906 by a visit to an exhibition in Liberec/Reichenberg "balanced" by a stop in Kutná Hora/Kuttenberg, the hometown of the new Czech minister without portfolio, Bedřich Pacák. On his way back to Vienna, Franz Joseph also stopped in Moravia, where he made some favorable remarks about the recently concluded Moravian Compromise, a political power sharing agreement which some considered a model for a Bohemian settlement.⁷⁷ The compromise in Moravia preserved an unequal and undemocratic franchise in elections to the Moravian Diet, protecting the interests of both Czech and German elites. In contrast, the major political change in Cisleithania between 1901 and Franz Joseph's last visit to Prague in 1907 was the adoption of secret, equal, and direct universal manhood suffrage for elections to the imperial parliament. This electoral reform, sped on its way by mass, often violent demonstrations, suggests that other issues and social interests were pushing the state rights question and the coronation from the center of the political stage.⁷⁸ The 1907 visit to Prague followed hard on the heels of the approval of the new franchise, and speculation again connected this visit to renewed efforts at a Czech-German agreement in Bohemia. *Čas* patted itself on the back for predicting a visit as early as the previous year, but it remained skeptical of the results, considering this sort of symbolic politics ineffectual. *Čas* claimed that, from a more practical point of view, "the Emperor himself ... would perhaps be eager to see his visit memorialized in a series of healthy and attractive workers' or similar social institutions, with which Prague could demonstrate its joy over the democratic consequences of universal manhood suffrage."⁷⁹

The German reaction to the royal visit, at least as reported by *Čas*, was to minimize its significance by making the visit itself the main Czech accomplishment. Young Czech triumphalism over Franz Joseph's presence in Prague fell into this trap, *Čas* argued. It reduced the meaning of the journey to the momentary realization of the dream that a king resided in the Prague castle and sent his decrees throughout the land. In an obvious dig at the Young Czechs, *Čas* concluded: "*political dreams* are not, as far as we know, even one strand of *positive* politics."⁸⁰ Like the Germans, the Realist newspaper appeared to view this royal visit primarily as a Young Czech electoral ploy.⁸¹

As during previous visits, Prague decked itself out to welcome the ruler. Advancing technology allowed the dailies to print photographs of the decorations along the route from the train station to the castle, on Wenceslas Square, and elsewhere in Prague.⁸² And as usual, the "colors war" raged on the streets of Prague, with the Czechs preferring the provincial red-white, and the Germans the black-yellow of the imperial emblem.[83] Though himself succumbing to the fashion of reporting about the decorations, the writer for *Čas* pointed out that the Bohemian lion or the Imperial eagle, used five times per house or fifty times along one street, became boring. "Not even two hundred Bohemian lions ... will make Prague's streets more Czech or more patriotic. Czech manliness, self-consciousness and national strength must be displayed elsewhere and in other ways during the Czech king's visit to Prague!"[84] Even *Čas*, however, described how "the brilliant, merry, vivid colors of white and red simply flooded the streets and squares through which the ruler will ride to the royal Prague castle, the imperial black and yellow displayed by Czechs and Germans penetrating the red-white ocean with their ritual ceremony," and predicted that the emperor would be welcomed warmly.[85]

As the comments in *Čas* suggest, by the time of Franz Joseph's last visit the Czech press reports no longer emphasized merely the loyalty and enthusiasm of the crowds. *Čas* noted that at Franz Joseph's age people should only wish him rest and repose, but that they would welcome him to Prague with gratitude for his support of franchise reform, because he was balancing his visit to the German exhibition the previous year, and because his first visit of state after the passage of the suffrage bill was into the heart of the Czech nation.[86] Yet when the emperor actually arrived, *Čas*'s correspondent almost seemed upset at the welcome he received. Noting that "Praguers are a sincere, excitable, romantic folk," the newspaper claimed that the monarch's welcome proved that the people's "feelings may be easily stirred to the point of intoxication: colors, jubilation, splendor, enthusiasm immediately sweep them away." The cheers from the crowds made the event more festive than the decorations, although *Čas*'s report somehow implied that this mood was transient and superficial. It drove the point home with a vignette comparing the modern Prague of 1907 with the historic "fairy-tale in stone" beneath the Prague castle:

> That stone fairy-tale is our royal Prague, the Prague of the past, of former splendor and glory, which long ago and probably forever drowned in the dim grayness of history. Modern Prague is civic, democratic ... The source of our faith in the future, the expression of our hope of coming expansion, of our national consciousness is civic Prague. We love civic Prague with a passionate love, we believe in it with the devotion of unreserved, democratic conviction. Royal Prague is deserted, but civic Prague is effervescent with creative life; historic Prague shows us what we were, civic Prague is laying the foundations for what we want to become in the future ...[87]

Did monarchs, banners, processions and coronations belong in modern, civic Prague? *Čas* surely leaves the impression that the answer would be in the negative—and yet "the Praguers are a sincere, excitable, romantic folk ..."[88]

Franz Joseph's visit to Prague in 1907 was the monarch's last journey of state to his Bohemian capital. His final jubilee in 1908, the sixtieth anniversary of his accession to the throne in 1848, was celebrated in Vienna and not by royal progresses to his other capitals. The Viennese celebration was to be another great procession, on the model of the parade staged in 1879 to celebrate the emperor's silver wedding anniversary, or the parade planned, but later scaled down, for the fiftieth jubilee of Franz Joseph's reign in 1898. The *"Kaiser-Huldigungs-Festzug"* of 1908 combined tableaux from Habsburg history with a procession of delegations from every land in the empire apart from Hungary, garbed in "traditional" national or peasant costume.[89] The governor of Lower Austria, Count Erich Kielmansegg, claimed, "the festival procession represented the Austrian state idea."[90] Yet political divisions and national quarrels took their toll even here. The Hungarians did not participate on the grounds that Franz Joseph would have to wait for his sixtieth jubilee until 1927, since his coronation had taken place in 1867, not 1848. Czech-German tensions both in Bohemia and Vienna remained high, and the campaign led by Viennese German nationalists against the Czech National Theater's guest performances on the stage of the Theater an der Wien, planned as part of the jubilee celebrations, provoked the Czech nationalists to boycott the procession.[91]

In the Bohemian capital, the jubilee was marked by an exhibition involving both Germans and Czechs, mounted by the Prague Chamber of Commerce and Industry. The atmosphere surrounding it was also soured by the renewed intensity of Czech-German conflicts. Czech nationalists noted that earlier exhibitions had enjoyed widespread Czech enthusiasm, but that the 1908 Jubilee Exhibition, in contrast, "was not like that, for in spite of all the sympathy the exhibition enjoys, the participation of the other nationality … acts like a distinct brake on excitement."[92] Rumors had circulated since the beginning of the year that Franz Joseph would visit the exhibition, but instead its patron, the heir-apparent Archduke Franz Ferdinand, presided at the opening ceremony.[93] In his remarks, delivered partly in Czech and partly in German, Franz Ferdinand reiterated the theme of Franz Joseph's farewell to Prague a year before, calling the exhibition evidence of the loyalty of *"both nations, united here in peaceful competition,"* to the emperor.[94] The Czech interpretation differed, as suggested by a cartoon in *Humoristické listy*. One character informs another that visitors on opening day will pay double, to view Czech-German togetherness (*svornost*): "The Czechs will speak German there, and the Germans will too."[95] Czech attention throughout the fall focused instead on the far from peaceful competition between Czech and German nationalists, in particular the conflicts around the German university students' weekly *Bummel*, or procession through the main commercial center of the city. The running street battles the *Bummel* created, together with Czech-German clashes elsewhere in Bohemia, led to the imposition of martial law in December 1908.[96]

In both Prague and Vienna, then, Franz Joseph's sixtieth year on the throne was marred by discordant overtones. Neither the emperor nor the empire survived until his seventieth jubilee in 1918, and thereafter, like Palivec's flyspecked portrait, Franz Joseph disappeared from Czech public life. Was his disappearance really evidence, though, that a king and a crown were irrelevant anachronisms in a modern society? The foregoing analysis suggests that the answer is more complicated than that. Instead of providing evidence of its irrelevance, the failure of Franz Joseph to carry through a Bohemian coronation underlines the symbolic significance of the crown. Otto Urban notes that Franz Joseph never once during his long reign resigned his royal title. Franz Joseph did not regard it as a mere formality, he would have been glad had he been able to carry out his promises of a coronation, and the defeat of the Fundamental Articles was a political defeat for him, too.[97] Yet Bruce Garver has pointed out that, although Franz Joseph never categorically refused recognition of Bohemian state rights, he always resisted any limits on his prerogatives, no matter how carefully buttressed by the language of tradition and history. As Governor Franz Thun remarked to an Old Czech politician in 1894, "state rights slogans [are] like a red flag to the emperor."[98]

How should one try to square this circle? Perhaps by suggesting that Franz Joseph would have been glad to carry out a Bohemian coronation, provided it delivered in Bohemia the same political outcome which accompanied his coronation in Hungary. In achieving such a resolution, however, Franz Joseph was hampered by the differences between the political situations in Bohemia and Hungary. The ambiguities of a royal coronation in Bohemia could no longer paper over the differences between the ruler, the Czech national leaders, the aristocracy, and the Bohemian Germans.[99] The last named group, divided into centralist German national liberals and more radical German nationalists, found all coquetting with crowns, federalism, and feudal traditions abhorrent. The theater of a coronation would have failed to bridge these cleavages within the Bohemian body politic, cleavages which were only complicated and further deepened by the emergence of socially based political movements including organized working class parties. The Crown of St. Wenceslas was becoming a symbol of division and contestation, no longer one of unity. Instead of fostering "solidarity without consensus," a coronation would have meant, in the "rite makes might" world of symbolic politics, the crown's choosing sides in the nationality strife within Bohemia, while also upsetting the accommodation with the dominant social and national groups (Germans and Hungarians) who underpinned the *Ausgleich* of 1867.[100]

Over time, as hopes faded that a Czech-German compromise in Bohemia would allow a coronation, the symbolic meanings of a royal visit had begun to change. By the time Franz Joseph returned to his Bohemian capital in 1891, he was playing the role of the equilibrium-seeker described by Pekař. Recognizing that the crown was attempting to stay "above the fray," Czech and German nationalists increasingly attacked each other by implying that the other side was at heart disloyal to Franz Joseph and the empire.[101] For their part, Czech nationalists also rejected the role of being one of many Austrian nations over whom the emperor arbitrated.[102] Nonetheless, if Franz Joseph could not carry through a royal coronation without losing his position "above the fray," there was still another role the emperor retained and played to the hilt up to the end of his reign. During his six decades on the throne, Franz Joseph's peoples experienced dramatic economic, social, and cultural developments over which the emperor symbolically presided. The highly ritualized public appearances, openings, dedications, and visits to institutions that were an integral part of a royal visit provided Franz Joseph with a role free of political controversy, but not without social relevance, as *Čas* observed in 1907, and Pekař repeated at Franz Joseph's funeral commemoration.[103] Otto Urban agrees, arguing that while progress under Franz Joseph was hardly a smooth, triumphant procession towards modernization, it was nevertheless progress that the emperor did not hinder. In the end, many of his subjects could paraphrase his own ritual comment at hundreds of official ceremonies: "It was very nice, we were quite pleased."[104]

These changes in the meaning of a royal visit to Bohemia and Franz Joseph's role on such occasions reinforced developments in Czech attitudes to other symbols of monarchy. As we have seen, the crown and other royal emblems retained their power as symbols, almost as nationalist clichés (see figure 4.5). Increasingly, however, the Crown of St. Wenceslas was evoked separately from the concrete person of the monarch or the Habsburg dynasty. By the later nineteenth century, the crown was still venerated, but there was no longer anyone "underneath it."[105] The front page of *Pražský illustrovaný kurýr* on the day of Franz Joseph's arrival in Prague in 1907 illustrates these developments: a picture of the coronation regalia dominates the center, and the silhouette of Hradčany dominates the background of the page, while a reclining two-tailed Bohemian lion fills the entire foreground. Franz Joseph's portrait floats within a wreath of laurels in the upper left of the picture, detached both from the scene of Prague and the coronation regalia.[106] The crown as a symbol was now free to be appropriated, and the Czech nationalist movement did just that, turning it into a Czech *national* symbol which could still be used even after the empire and the dynasty that had borne it had been swept away.[107] Unmarred by the flyspecks that eventually spoiled Franz Joseph's portrait as a *Czech* king, the Crown of St. Wenceslas became a symbol of a specifically *Czech* statehood, just as the Kingdom of Bohemia became identified as a specifically *Czech* state. As a result, the crown has continued to serve the symbolic purposes of the independent Czechoslovak and Czech states down to the present.[108]

Figure 4.5. Detail of graphic decoration featuring the Crown Jewels of the Kingdom of Bohemia, from the volume commemorating the Jubilee Exhibition of 1891 in Prague. *Jubilejní výstava zemská Království českého v Praze 1891* (Prague, 1894).

Notes

1. Otto Urban, *Česká společnost, 1848–1918* (Prague, 1982), 198, quoting the emperor's own words.
2. I am citing the version from the US National Archives posted on the web by Theodore Mills Kelly at <http://www2.tltc.ttu.edu/kelly/Archive/CzSl/10-18-18.html>, accessed 19 October 2004.
3. Jiří Rak, *Bývali Čechové: České historické mýty a stereotypy* (Jinočany, 1994), 137–140.
4. Jaroslav Hašek, *The Good Soldier Švejk and His Fortunes in the World War*, trans. Cecil Parrott (New York, 1974), 7–8. As Palivec explains to the secret police agent Brettschneider, the portrait "did hang there, but the flies used to shit on it, so I put it away in the attic. You know, somebody might be so free as to pass a remark about it and then there could be unpleasantness. I don't want that, do I?"
5. Ivana Čornejová, Jiří Rak, and Vit Vlnas, *Ve stínu tvých křídel: Habsburkové v českých dějinách* (Prague, 1995), 7–26, 232–234. Procházka is a common Czech surname, but it also means a walk or stroll. Supposedly the nickname derives from a photograph of Franz Joseph at the opening of a new bridge in Prague in 1901, with the inscription, "Procházka na mostě" [a stroll on the bridge], but the most recent Czech biographer of Franz Joseph discounts this story as an urban legend. See Otto Urban, *František Josef I.* (Prague, 1999), 170–171.
6. Ladislav Smoljak and Zdeněk Svěrák, "Lijavec," sound recording (Prague, 1994). The text of the play may be found on the internet at <http://www.volny.cz/mmmma/divad-hry/lijavec.html>, accessed 1 November 2004. For a sample of the academic "seminar," see the excerpts—which do not, unfortunately, include the cited passage—on the internet at <http://sobulka.webpark.cz/lijavec.htm>, accessed 1 November 2004.
7. See Steven Beller, *Francis Joseph* (London and New York, 1996); Jean-Paul Bled, *Franz Joseph*, trans. Teresa Bridgeman (New York, 1992).
8. Urban, *František Josef I.* The volume by Čornejová, Rak, and Vlnas, *Ve stínu tvých křídel* (see note 5), should also be mentioned, though it treats Czech attitudes to the dynasty as a whole.
9. András Gerő, *Emperor Francis Joseph, King of the Hungarians*, trans. James Patterson and Enikő Koncz (Boulder, 2001).
10. Josef Pekař, *František Josef I. Přednáška, kterou ve velkém smutečním shromáždění české university Karlovy Ferdinandovy dne 4. prosince 1916 k uctění památky zvěčnělého císaře a krále našeho proslovil Dr. Josef Pekař, řádný profesor rakouských dějin* (Prague, 1916), 5–9. See also *Pražský illustrovaný kurýr*, no. 117, 29 April 1907.
11. Pekař, *František Josef I.*, 10–13. The development of a modern society was also the theme of a volume published during the 1898 Golden Jubilee year by the Czech Academy of Sciences and Art named for Franz Joseph, *Památník na oslavu padesátiletého panovnického jubilea jeho veličenstva císaře a krále Františka Josefa I: Vědecký a umělecký rozvoj v národě českém, 1848–1898*, (Prague: Česká akademie císaře Františka Josefa pro vědy, slovesnost a umění, 1898), and is echoed in Otto Urban, *František Josef I.*, 283.
12. Otto Urban, "Návštěvy Františka Josefa I. v Praze," in *Umění a civilizace jako divadlo světa*, ed. Marta Ottlová and Milan Pospíšil (Prague, 1993), 24–25. See also *Pražský illustrovaný kurýr*, no. 94, 6 April 1907. Franz Joseph had visited Prague once while a mere Archduke, in September 1847.
13. Otto Urban, "Návštěvy Františka Josefa," 25; Peter Urbanitsch, "Pluralist Myth and Nationalist Realities: The Dynastic Myth of the Habsburg Monarchy—a Futile Exercise in the Creation of Identity?" *Austrian History Yearbook* 35 (2004): 112–114.
14. *Pražský illustrovaný kurýr*, no. 94, 6 April 1907.
15. Count Franz Thun-Hohenstein (1809–1870) was a leading conservative Bohemian aristocrat and patron of the arts, who like many of his contemporaries supported to some extent the cultural strivings of Czech nationalism. His nephew, also Count (after 1911 Prince)

Franz Thun-Hohenstein (1847–1916), is mentioned below as governor of Bohemia from 1889–1895.
16. Zdeněk Hojda and Jiří Pokorný, *Pomníky a zapomníky* (Prague and Litomyšl, 1997), 46–50.
17. Otto Urban, "Návštěvy Františka Josefa," 26.
18. Stenographic protocols of the Bohemian Land Diet, session 5, 11 April 1861, from the digital library of the Czech Parliament, < http://www.psp.cz/cgi-bin/lat2/eknih/1861skc/stenprot/005schuz/s005003.htm>, accessed on 27 October 2004. See also Otto Urban, *Česká společnost, 1848–1918*, 166–67.
19. *Wiener Zeitung*, 16 April 1861. See also Jan Muk, *Poslední korunovace českého krále roku 1836*, Bílé knihy, 10 (Prague, 1936), 103.
20. Stenographic protocols of the Bohemian Land Diet, session 7, 15 April 1861, <http://www.psp.cz/eknih/1861skc/stenprot/007schuz/s007002.htm>, accessed on 27 October 2004.
21. *Wiener Zeitung*, 26 April 1861. See also Österreichisches Staatsarchiv (hereafter ÖStA), Vienna, Haus- Hof- und Staatsarchiv, (hereafter HHStA), Neue Zeremoniellakten, 13, R. IV, Böhmische Krönung, 1792, 1835/36, where the presence of these newspaper articles suggests that the Oberhofmeister was at least preparing to plan a coronation ceremony.
22. Otto Urban, *Česká společnost, 1848–1918*, 196.
23. Ibid., 198; Muk, *Poslední korunovace českého krále roku 1836*, 103.
24. Cited in Otto Urban, *Česká společnost, 1848–1918*, 209; see also Otto Urban, "Návštěvy Františka Josefa," 26–27.
25. *Pražský illustrovaný kurýr*, no. 95, 7 April 1907.
26. Otto Urban, "Návštěvy Františka Josefa," 26–27.
27. Alice Freifeld, *Nationalism and the Crowd in Liberal Hungary, 1848–1914* (Washington and Baltimore, 2000), 212–219.
28. ÖStA, Vienna, Allgemeines Verwaltungsarchiv (hereafter AVA), Ministerium des Innern, Präsidiale (hereafter MdI-Präs), 1, carton 2, 2713, 2774/1866.
29. Hugh LeCaine Agnew, "Ambiguities of Ritual: Dynastic Loyalty, Territorial Patriotism and Nationalism in the Last Three Royal Coronations in Bohemia," *Bohemia* 41, no. 1 (2000): 8–9.
30. AVA, MdI-Präs, 1, carton 2, 4010, 4085, 4103, 4182/1867. In the last file, the Viennese police director is explicitly instructed to prevent "any political or national demonstration on this occasion."
31. *Národní listy*, no. 126, 8 August 1867, emphasis in original; ibid., no. 135, 16 August 1867, no. 137, 18 August 1867, no. 140, 21 August 1867 and others.
32. Ibid., no. 144, 25 August 1867.
33. Ibid., no. 148, 29 August 1867. Emphasis in original.
34. Jaroslav Purš, "Tábory v českých zemích v letech 1868–1871 (Příspěvek k problematice národního hnutí)," *Československý časopis historický* 6 (1958): 234–266; 446–470; 661–690. Originally these demonstrations were simply called "meetings" using the English word, but the young historian Jaroslav Goll suggested the term "tábor," because of its historical ties to the Hussite period. See Otto Urban, *Česká společnost, 1848–1918*, 230–233.
35. AVA, MdI-Präs, 1/2, carton 20, 1231/1868, Minister of Interior Giskra to Franz Joseph, 7 January 1868.
36. *Národní listy*, no. 137, 18 May 1868; *Národní pokrok*, no. 150, 19 May 1868.
37. *Národní listy*, no. 135, 16 May 1868. See also Otto Urban, *Česká společnost, 1848–1918*, 230–232.
38. *Národní listy*, no. 167, 19 June 1868. The river Leitha marked the frontier between Lower Austria and the Kingdom of Hungary, so the term Cisleithania was used to describe the non-Hungarian half of the Dual Monarchy. Transleithania was used almost exclusively in a pejorative sense.
39. Ibid., no. 168, 20 June 1868. On the role of the Sokol movement in Czech nationalist politics, see Claire Nolte, *The Sokol in the Czech Lands to 1914: Training for the Nation* (New York, 2002).

40. *Národní listy*, no. 170, 22 June 1868, and no. 171, 23 June 1868.
41. Ibid., no. 170, 22 June 1868; *Národní pokrok*, no. 182, 22 June 1868.
42. Otto Urban, "Návštěvy Františka Josefa," 27; Otto Urban, *Česká společnost, 1848–1918*, 233–234.
43. HHStA, Neue Zeremonial Akten, 334 R. XV, Hofreisen, etc., 1867–1869: 1868/15/266, includes a complete guest list as well as the menu and other details.
44. *Národní listy*, no. 172, 24 June 1868, and no. 174, 28 June 1868.
45. For an exhaustive compilation of all the judicial and administrative actions against the Czech opposition between 1868 and 1873, see Jakub Arbes, *Pláč koruny České, neboli Persekuce lidu českého v letech 1868–1873*, 2d ed. (Prague, 1894).
46. Otto Urban, *Česká společnost, 1848–1918*, 246–52; Muk, *Poslední korunovace českého krále roku 1836*, 103–104.
47. Peter Bugge, "Czech Nation-Building, National Self-Perception and Politics, 1780–1914" (Ph.D. diss., Aarhus: University of Aarhus, 1994), 154.
48. *Koruna česká*, no. 71, 5 September 1874, and no. 72, 9 September 1874. The first article bore the title: "His Majesty the King of Bohemia."
49. *Plzeňské noviny*, no. 73, 10 September 1874. According to the account, the court party thereafter left their wine untouched and drank only Pilsener beer. See also Jaroslav Douša, "Návštěvy Habsburků v Plzni v 19. století," in *Umění a civilizace jako divadlo světa*, ed. Marta Ottlová and Milan Pospíšil (Prague, 1993), 35–36.
50. *Koruna česká*, no. 68, 26 August 1874, and no. 69, 29 August 1874.
51. Otto Urban, *František Josef I.*, 184–185.
52. Karel Tůma, *Královský reskript ze dne 12. září 1871 a jeho význam pro státní naše právo* (Prague, 1886), 64–65.
53. Georg Lobkowitz to Taaffe, 22 October 1886, cited in Hans Peter Hye, "Der Aufstieg der Jungtschechen im böhmischen Landtag im Spiegel der Quellen der Wiener Regierung," in *Bratři Grégrové a česká společnost v druhé polovině 19. století*, ed. Pavla Vošahlíková and Milan Řepa (Prague, 1997), 71–74.
54. Pavel Cibulka, *Politické programy českých národních stran, 1860–1890* (Prague, 2000), 306–315.
55. Bruce Garver, *The Young Czech Party, 1874–1901, and the Emergence of a Multi-Party System* (New Haven, 1978), 146–153; Bugge, "Czech Nation-Building," 188–195.
56. See Stanley B. Winters, "'Tactical Opportunism:' Karel Kramář's Adaptation of Palacký's Concept of the Bohemian 'Staatsrecht,'" *Bohemia* 41 (2000): 26–27. Kramář published his ideas in German and then in a Czech translation: Karel Kramář, *Das böhmische Staatsrecht* (Vienna, 1896); Karel Kramář, *České státní právo* (Prague, 1896).
57. Both openings were accompanied by a performance of Bedřich Smetana's opera in tableaux, "Libuše," which had been consciously conceived as a coronation opera.
58. Catherine Albrecht, "Pride in Production: The Jubilee Exhibition of 1891 and Economic Competition Between Czechs and Germans in Bohemia," *Austrian History Yearbook* 24 (1993): 101–118. See also the commemorative volume of the exhibition, *Jubilejní výstava zemská Království českého v Praze 1891* (Prague, 1894), which has a separate section especially devoted to Franz Joseph's visit.
59. Zdeněk Tobolka, *1891–1914*, vol. III, part 2 of *Politické dějiny československého národa od r. 1848 až do dnešní doby* (Prague, 1936), 43–45.
60. Milan Hlavačka, *Jubilejní výstava 1891* (Prague, 1991), 100–108; Otto Urban, "Návštěvy Františka Josefa," 29.
61. A similar portrait, painted by František Ženíšek in 1894, was displayed as part of an exhibition in Prague during the summer of 2004. See *The Prague Post*, 15 July 2004, online edition, at <http://www.praguepost.com/P03/2004/Art/0715/galler.php>, accessed on 20 August 2004. The article suggests that since the Emperor's hand rests on the rescript of September 1871, the portrait is in its own way a political protest.

62. *Humoristické listy,* no. 38, 18 September 1891.
63. Aloìs Rašín, *české Státní právo,* 4th ed, Epištoly pro lid, 1 (Prague, 1892), 4–5.
64. *Koruna česká,* no. 58, 22 July 1874.
65. *Císařská slova,* 3d ed., Epištoly pro lid, 5 (Prague, 1902).
66. This statue, erected by the Bohemian Estates, was immortalized in Karel Havlíček's epigram in which he called Franz a *trouba* (dunce). In 1919, the statue was removed to the National Museum Lapidarium. See Hojda and Pokorný, *Pomníky a zapomníky,* 42–43. Without fanfare, it was restored to its original place following the disastrous flood in the summer of 2002.
67. Tobolka, *Politické dějiny,* 56–57; Garver, *Young Czech Party,* 182–185.
68. Garver, *Young Czech Party,* 185–187.
69. Otto Urban, *Česká společnost, 1848–1918,* 467, 471.
70. Tobolka, *Politické dějiny,* 308–311.
71. *Čas,* no. 162, 14 June 1901.
72. Ibid. Emphasis in original.
73. Ibid., no. 164, 16 June 1901.
74. *Pražský illustrovaný kurýr,* no. 133, 15 May 1901.
75. Tobolka, *Politické dějiny,* 311–312; Otto Urban, "Návštěvy Františka Josefa," 30; Otto Urban, *Česká společnost, 1848–1918,* 512.
76. *Čas,* no. 164, 16 June 1901.
77. T. Mills Kelly, "Last Best Chance or Last Gasp? The Compromise of 1905 and Czech Politics in Moravia," *Austrian History Yearbook* 34 (2003): 279–301.
78. Bugge, "Czech Nation-Building," 259–266.
79. *Čas,* no. 100, 12 April 1907 and no. 102, 14 April 1907.
80. Ibid., no. 105, 17 April 1907.
81. Ibid., no. 107, 19 April 1907 and no. 108, 20 April 1907.
82. The visit dominates *Pražský illustrovaný kurýr* from number 104, 16 April up to number 117, 29 April 1907. Nearly every issue has several photographs and other illustrations of the decorations or other aspects of the visit.
83. *Čas,* no. 102, 14 April 1907.
84. Ibid.
85. Ibid., no. 103, 15 April 1907.
86. Ibid.
87. Ibid., no. 104, 16 April 1907, final ellipsis in original.
88. Ibid, ellipsis in original. The author of this vignette begins and ends with the same observation about Praguers.
89. For the fullest treatment of this procession, see Elisabeth Grossegger, *Der Kaiser Huldigungs Festzug Wien 1908* (Vienna, 1992).
90. *Národní listy,* afternoon edition, 13 June 1908.
91. *Národní listy* denied Kielmansegg's assertion, pointing out that the Czech nation was represented only by a few "godforsaken Moravian villages," and that as a former minister-president of Cisleithania, Kielmansegg should know that "without the Czech nation there can be no talk of Austria." *Národní listy,* afternoon edition, 13 June 1908. See also ibid., 2 April, 10 April, 11 April, 16 April, 2 June, and 12 June 1908.
92. *Národní listy,* afternoon edition, 14 May 1908.
93. Ibid., 26 February, 21 May, and 13 June 1908.
94. Ibid., 14 May 1908, italics in original.
95. *Humoristické listy,* no. 20, 8 May 1908.
96. See Nancy Wingfield, "Chapter IV, Centers and Peripheries: The Francis Joseph Jubilees," in *Flag Wars and Stone Saints: How the Bohemian Lands Became Czech* (Cambridge, MA, 2007). The pages of the Czech *Národní listy* and the German *Prager Tagblatt* throughout the autumn are full of claims and counter claims regarding the *Bummel* and its effects.

97. Otto Urban, "Návštěvy Františka Josefa," 24–25.
98. Albín Bráf, *Život a dílo: Díl první, Paměti,* ed. Josef Gruber (Prague, 1922), 7; Garver, *Young Czech Party,* 50.
99. For a discussion of the ambiguities of rituals such as coronations, see David I. Kertzer, *Ritual, Politics and Power* (New Haven, 1988), 67–76.
100. Kertzer, *Ritual, Politics and Power,* 102–124.
101. For example, see *Humoristické listy,* no. 38, 18 September 1891; and *Národní listy,* afternoon edition, 17 June 1908.
102. *Národní listy,* 15 April 1908.
103. Pekař, *František Josef I.,* 10.
104. Otto Urban, *František Josef I.,* 283.
105. Bugge, "Czech Nation-Building," 154; Jan Havránek, "Český historismus druhé poloviny 19. století mezi monarchismem a democratismem," in *Historické vědomí v českém umění 19. století,* ed. Tomáš Vlček (Prague, 1981), 32–34.
106. *Pražský illustrovaný kurýr,* no. 104, 17 April 1907.
107. One very quotidian way in which this appropriation may be seen is in the retention of the term *koruna* (crown) for the Czechoslovak, and later Czech, currency.
108. Hugh LeCaine Agnew, "Old States, New Identities? The Czech Republic, Slovakia and Historical Understandings of Statehood," *Nationalities Papers* 28, no. 4 (2000): 619–650.

Chapter 5

CELEBRATING TWO EMPERORS AND A REVOLUTION

The Public Contest to Represent the Polish and Ruthenian Nations in 1880

Daniel L. Unowsky

Scholars who research individual provinces of the Habsburg Monarchy all too often focus solely on the seemingly inevitable march toward increasingly radical and conflicting nationalisms and assume a parallel diminishing of popular imperial loyalties. Studies of particular "nationalities" have tended to focus on the journey of a single designated "ethnie" toward national consciousness to the exclusion of other "national communities" inhabiting the same cities, towns, and rural regions.[1] The role of the imperial center is ignored; nationalists are depicted as free to construct seamless narratives of the national past in a vacuum. Much of the recent work on Galicia, the northeastern border province now divided between Poland and Ukraine, follows the same pattern. This emphasis on the nationalization of one sector of the Galician peasantry—Polish or Ruthenian—obscures the Habsburg context within which Polish and Ukrainian nationalists sought to mobilize their potential national communities.[2]

By concentrating here on three public events that occurred in Galicia in 1880—Franz Joseph's inspection tour of the province in September, the fiftieth anniversary commemorations of the 1830 Polish uprising in the Russian partition in November, and the concurrent Ruthenian marking of the centennial of Joseph II's accession to the throne—I will consider the interaction between the spokespersons of both ethnic groups, the political institutions of the crownland, and the imperial center. As this study demonstrates, in 1880 the imperial center could and did inspire loyalty, self-appointed leaders of national communities could and did incorporate the emperor into their own national stories, and, at least in these examples, those rejecting the imperial center failed to rally their potential national constituency behind an anti-Habsburg version of the national interest.

1. Representing the Nation through the Empire: Franz Joseph in Galicia[3]

Galicia, like many Habsburg provinces, had a diverse population. According to available statistics, in 1880 3,058,400 Polish speakers and 2,549,707 Ukrainian speakers lived in the province, which was among the poorest regions in the Habsburg state.[4] In the western districts of Galicia, well over 80 percent of the inhabitants were Polish speakers. In eastern Galicia, religious, social, and ethnic divisions reinforced each other. Approximately two of every three people living in eastern Galicia were counted as Ruthenians.[5] Here, the vast majority of peasants were Greek Catholic Ukrainian speakers, while nearly all noble landlords and the majority of the urban population were Roman Catholic Polish speakers. Jews, a large and very visible presence in towns and city centers in both halves of Galicia, numbered some 800,000 by 1900.

Emperor Franz Joseph had visited Galicia twice prior to 1880. The emperor's first *Kaiserreise* or inspection tour of Galicia, undertaken in 1851, was one in a series of inspection tours in the years following the revolutions of 1848–49 designed to present the new emperor (and the neoabsolutist order) to provincial populations. The court and central government arranged a spectacular display of imperial power to impress Galicia's population with the vitality of what the official government press referred to as the "monarchical principle."[6] Franz Joseph viewed military parades, visited fortresses, and made triumphant entrances into Galician towns while Habsburg troops and police lined the streets. Polish and Ruthenian peasants cheered the "emperor-liberator" who had confirmed the end of serfdom. Polish nobles could participate in the festivities only as passive courtiers in the emperor's entourage, their appeals for Polish autonomy ignored, their role limited by the revived court apparatus.[7] According to Paweł Popiel, an influential west Galician aristocrat, the 1851 reception for the emperor in Cracow was "loud, because there were many peasants, but cold," because of the hostility of the nobility toward the new regime.[8] Franz Joseph returned to Galicia for military maneuvers in 1855. A more substantial imperial visit planned for 1868 and intended to be the first presentation to Galicia of Franz Joseph as the constitutional monarch of the newly reorganized Austria-Hungary, was cancelled after the Galician Diet issued a provocative resolution calling for the formal institution of provincial autonomy—and thereby challenging the new state structure.[9]

It was not until 1880 that Franz Joseph returned to Galicia. This time, several factors combined to make the 1880 *Kaiserreise* to Galicia a propaganda success for the court, the government, and the dominant Polish conservatives. The wounds of 1846 and 1848 had largely healed; celebrations of the twenty-fifth anniversary of Franz Joseph's accession in 1873 and the twenty-fifth wedding anniversary of the imperial couple in 1879 affirmed the growing personal popularity of the emperor. Due to improvements in the education system, modest increases in literacy rates, and the gradual expansion of the suffrage for the Austrian parliament (*Reichsrat*), Galicia's inhabitants were becoming more aware of events outside of the rural communities that were home to the majority of the population. Newspapers presented this increasingly politically aware public with every detail of the emperor's schedule and published calls from voluntary associations and government institutions urging the population to participate in the reception for the emperor.[10] The political context at the state (Cisleithanian) and provincial levels also proved conducive to a successful *Kaiserreise*. After the fall of the Liberal government in 1879, Austrian Minister-President Eduard Taaffe had to rely on Polish participation in his *Reichsrat* coalition.[11] Cracow conservative nobles (the Stańczyks) and their burgher allies, Polish bureaucrats in the Galician administration, and East Galician magnates comprised the loose coalition of Polish elites who supported Taaffe's Iron Ring and dominated the main political and cultural institutions within the province.[12]

The Stańczyks defined themselves as the moderately reformist element among the traditional Polish aristocracy (*szlachta*). Stańczyk historians of the "Cracow School" decried the recent history of Polish uprisings as detrimental to Polish interests and emphasized instead the principle of "organic work," the cultural and economic strengthening of Polish society within Galicia. Although the dream of an agreement with the dynasty formalizing Polish noble control of the province had been dashed by the Hungarian nobility's achievement of the 1867 Compromise, the Polish conservatives' policy of loyalism had secured the use of the Polish language in schools, courts, and local government in the late 1860s and early 1870s, and seemed poised to gain even greater *de facto* autonomy in Galicia.[13]

The Polish elites now appeared to be ideal partners for Taaffe, who imagined he could forge a stable Cisleithania based on modest suffrage expansion and informal alliances and compromises with provincial elites. In 1880, the Polish conservatives, the court, and the Vienna government used the emperor's presence in the province to present a narrative of the ideal monarchy—one based on the mutual understanding of rights and duties between the emperor, as the symbol of the state, and the Polish conservatives, as the acknowledged legitimate and natural leadership of Galicia.

During the first three weeks of September, enthusiastic crowds greeted the emperor as he knelt before relics of Polish saints held aloft by Roman Catholic priests and signed his name in Polish in school guest books. The imperial visit focused on the two major cities of the province: Cracow and Lemberg/Lwów/L'viv. When Franz Joseph arrived, some 50,000 lined the streets of Cracow, the largest city in western Galicia, the political stronghold of the Stańczyks, and, with its castles, monasteries, and churches, the symbolic capital of the defunct Polish-Lithuanian Commonwealth. At least 100,000 witnessed the emperor's entrance into Lemberg, the provincial capital. Lemberg, an urban island in the rural sea of eastern Galicia, was inhabited by a Polish majority, a significant Jewish population, a long-established Armenian community, a small number of German speakers, and a growing Ruthenian community. Millions throughout the province read panegyric editorials and packed Roman and Greek Catholic churches as well as synagogues to hear sermons equating love for emperor and fatherland with religious duty.

The Galician administration and the Diet (*Sejm*) funded and organized the celebrations, mobilizing the peasantry to cheer for the emperor. The conservatives used the emperor's presence to highlight a series of Polish national institutions—the *Sejm*, the Polish language universities, and the Cracow Academy of Sciences—all of which were gained due to the close relationship between the emperor and the Polish elites. In a central symbolic moment, Franz Joseph designated Cracow's Wawel Castle, the former home of Polish kings and the location of their tombs, an official Habsburg imperial residence.

In sharp contrast to previous imperial tours of the province, citizens' guards rather than army formations and police maintained order, underscoring the loyalty of the citizenry and the popularity of the emperor. The official *Gazeta Lwowska* as well as conservative publications interpreted every remark made by the emperor, no matter how empty of real content or how trivial—"very lovely, I am so pleased to be here"—as support for conservative positions. According to the most important conservative journal, Cracow's *Przegląd Polski,* Galicia, "a crownland, once a partitioned land attached to Austria, today joined to it of its own conviction and action with the noble and wise emperor."[14]

However, not all the 1880 events conformed to the will of the Polish conservatives. In 1851, Franz Joseph laid the foundation stone of Lemberg's Ruthenian National Institute, demonstrating that he was not a Polish king, but rather the Habsburg emperor, father, and protector of all his peoples. In 1880, although most of his movements and speeches were scripted by the Polish conservatives and Polish bureaucrats in the Galician provincial administration, Franz Joseph visited the Ruthenian National Institute and the Greek Catholic Cathedral of St. George. At these events, Ruthenian intellectuals, priests, and politicians proclaimed to the Poles and public opinion in the monarchy as a whole that Galicia was not, and could never be, a purely Polish province. Franz Joseph also insisted on entering Lemberg's two main synagogues, where liberal and orthodox rabbis blessed the emperor, the attending generals, and the accompanying Polish bureaucrats and nobles. At every turn, peasants and widows of soldiers and government workers knelt in the mud before the emperor's carriage to plea for help or threw petitions for financial and legal support into the imperial coach (see figure 5.1). The thousands of petitions for imperial assistance attested to the fact that all was not as harmonious as the ideal Galicia created in media accounts of the inspection tour.

At the same time, Lemberg's Polish democrats rejected the allegedly unquestioning loyalism of the Cracow conservatives, called for a formal reorganization of the monarchy to reflect the strength of the Slavs, and cultivated contacts with

Figure 5.1. Wojciech Kossak, *His Majesty accepts a petition,* 1881. Cracow National Museum.

Poles in the other partitions. However, the Polish democrats were weak and divided in 1880. They lacked a large and vibrant potential constituency. In this largely agricultural province, members of the lower *szlachta,* younger sons of noble families, and Jews constituted the majority of the urban professional classes. Democratic politicians and liberal journalists called on their constituency and readership to participate in the welcome for Franz Joseph. They compared the oppression of Polish culture in neighboring Russian Poland to the relative freedom under the Habsburgs and lauded the emperor for allowing the Poles their own language in schools, churches, and government. Still, although leading Polish democrats actively supported the reception, helping to organize the Lemberg citizens' guard and a special theater performance in honor of the imperial guest, the democratic liberal press insisted that the genuinely enthusiastic crowds cheering for the emperor should not be interpreted as popular support for the conservatives' policies.[15]

On balance, the inspection tour ultimately benefited the Polish ruling elites and provided public support for the conservatives' combination of loyalism and promotion of Polish national interests within the province of Galicia. The conservatives had mobilized the autonomous Galician institutions to control most aspects of the visit. The Viennese liberal press, usually critical of Polish participation in Taaffe's Iron Ring coalition, praised Polish support for a strong imperial state. The Vienna government acknowledged its dependence on the Poles, fortifying the political position of the Polish conservatives in the Vienna parliament and in Galicia. The court and the Cisleithanian government, in league with the

Stańczyks, had successfully produced a public drama displaying the ideal monarchy: one based on the mutual interest of regional elites and the crown, and legitimized by the cheering population.

Nevertheless, two competing public celebrations held just two months after the emperor's departure from Galicia defined the limitations of the unified Stańczyk and Cisleithanian government promotion of the emperor during the *Kaiserreise*. First, the organizers of the Polish nationalist celebration of the 1830–31 uprising rejected the image of conservative unity and progress within Habsburg Galicia on display during the *Kaiserreise*. Second, the Ruthenian commemoration of Joseph II incorporated imperial imagery into a Ruthenian national narrative, which clashed with that projected by the Stańczyks during the imperial inspection tour.

2. "For Your Freedom and Ours!": Commemorating 1830 in 1880

In May 1880, Alfred Młocki, a Galician landowner, democrat, and veteran of the 1863 January Uprising in the Russian partition, formed a committee to organize commemorations of the 1830–31 November Uprising. The committee planned the celebrations to coincide with the anniversary of the storming of the Belvedere Palace in Warsaw on the night of 29–30 November 1830. This event marked the beginning of the Polish-Russian war, which only concluded with the surrender of Warsaw to Tsarist forces in September 1831 and the emigration of thousands of Polish revolutionaries to London, Paris, and elsewhere. According to the Lemberg police, the committee's intermittent meetings in the spring of 1880 at first drew few supporters, mostly townspeople and newspaper editors. Once the committee had developed a firm program of celebrations—encompassing a lecture series, publications, and public celebrations on November 29—democratic representatives to the *Sejm*, including Otto Hausner (one of the most active and vocal anti-*szlachta* voices in the *Sejm*), Piotr Gros, and Tadeusz Romanowicz became involved in its activities.[16]

Although this committee formed in May and planned celebrations for November, it published its program on July 11, just four days after the *Sejm* voted to fund preparations for the September reception of Franz Joseph. The authors of the program thus injected the upcoming celebration of the fiftieth anniversary of the November Uprising into press discussion of the *Kaiserreise* and juxtaposed their Polish patriotism with the "slavish" Habsburg loyalism of the Cracow conservatives. Kazimierz Chlędowski, an official in the Galician administration in 1880 and later Cisleithanian Minister for Galicia, wrote in his memoirs that Polish exiles in Paris and in Switzerland supported the plans to commemorate 1830 and wanted to counter the supposed servility of the Galician Polish conservatives.[17]

Forty-three men signed the program announcing the intention to celebrate the heroes of 1830. In direct opposition to the prevailing Cracow historical school, the authors of the address extolled the fact that "fifty years ago the Polish nation took up arms." The address reclaimed the slogan of the Polish revolutionary heroes:

> 'For Your freedom and ours' ... Although as the end result of this battle [the Polish people] yielded in the face of overwhelming numbers and a mighty foe, it inscribed its deeds in the annals of history, affirming not only its valor, but also its everlasting right to freedom and independence.

The importance of the 1830 uprising did not lie in its defeat, but in its power to inspire Polish identity in present and future generations. "In the post-partition history, the Uprising stands as an epoch. It was not only a magnificent and great battle for eternal national right," but also "reinforced the Polish spirit" and forged Polish national ideals. The Lemberg committee formed to organize commemorations of the November Uprising felt obliged to act, since their brethren in other parts of partitioned Poland could not. In Galicia, Poles had the duty to ensure that "the memory of the celebrations was made to endure into even the most distant years ..."[18]

The Polish conservative elites responded with fury toward what they viewed as a challenge to the upcoming reception of the emperor. The editorials of Cracow's *Czas*, the most important newspaper of western Galicia and the mouthpiece of the Stańczyks, dripped with the acid sarcasm that had marked the *Stańczyk Portfolio* in the late 1860s, the first public statement of the Stańczyks as a coherent group:

> We thought that no one could be found, who could think that such a sad anniversary of a pogrom of the entire nation could be celebrated in any way other than in the solitude of the home, in the solitude of the heart, and in mourning. Meanwhile, the address has convinced us that there are incorrigible and sick people who not only love to celebrate past political mistakes, but desire to embark once again on the path of demonstration.

Czas noted with satisfaction that the only people to sign the address were those who "cultivated the theory of demonstration, or who invariably would rather dedicate themselves to stimulating national sentiment than political understanding." The desire to celebrate "mistakes, defeats, and catastrophes" is nothing more than "a symptom of illness." The editors of *Czas* were firmly committed to a program of "serious work," not one of anachronistic and dangerous dreaming. Above all, the conservatives denounced the timing of the announcement of the commemorations of the November Uprising. The conservatives feared any action that threatened to derail the *Kaiserreise*, as had happened in 1868. The conservatives were also concerned that a celebration of the uprising could turn people away from the growing consensus that violence and revolution had brought nothing to the Polish people but death and failure. The conservatives hoped the politically active public would shun this project and instead, like the majority of the people of Galicia, commemorate the events of 1830–31—as well as the failed efforts to revive Poland in 1846, 1848, and 1863—with prayers that the Polish nation would not again experience "similar suicidal blows, political mistakes, and national disasters."[19]

Dziennik Polski, the progressive Lemberg daily whose editor, Jan Lam, one of Galicia's most popular and acclaimed satirists and, according to historian Maciej Janowski, "the most eminent liberal journalist of Galicia of the 1860s and 1870s," countered the Stańczyks' sarcasm with some of its own.[20] *Dziennik Polski* juxtaposed glorification of the heroes of 1830 with the "black-yellow" servility of the "great Austro-Polish politicians"—meaning the Cracow conservatives, who themselves had once hung the same label on Agenor Gołuchowski, the long-serving governor of Galicia who had sought reconciliation with the dynasty in the 1850s and 1860s. Lam's editorial staff denied that the planned commemorations were a demonstration, and argued that the commemorations themselves and the associated program of publications and lectures would "give to the living generations a picture of sacrifice" seldom seen today, least of all among the current self-designated Polish leadership.[21]

Dziennik Polski deflected the conservative charge that no Polish figure of importance would wish to celebrate the November Uprising by printing a letter originally published in 1876 calling for a celebration in honor of the veterans of 1830. The letter had been signed by leading Cracow conservatives such as Henryk Wodzicki, Paweł Popiel, and the editor of *Czas*, Anton Klobukowski.[22] The paper also published a letter by Ludwik Nabielak, a veteran of the attack on Warsaw on the night of 29–30 November 1830, now living in Paris. Nabielak claimed that a true historical account of the uprising must recognize its popular nature, denied by *Czas*. Further, by subjecting all who disagreed with their version of history to personal attacks, wrote Nabielak, the conservatives only revealed the hollow nature of their current monopoly on power in Galicia.[23]

After Franz Joseph visited Galicia in September, inexpensive publications about the events of 1830 began to raise awareness of the celebrations. By early November, the Lemberg police, who had originally discounted public interest in the commemorations, anticipated a large turnout. Responding to the concerns of the Interior Ministry, the police made great efforts to censor and prevent the distribution of questionable materials relating to the celebrations. Of greatest concern was a series of lectures planned for Lemberg. The police informed Młocki that all lectures had to be approved in advance by the censor or they would be prohibited.[24]

Młocki appealed against the police decision directly to Count Taaffe in the latter's capacity as Interior Minister. Młocki insisted that since the lectures would be presented informally, the lecturers themselves did not have complete manuscripts to submit to the censor. The lecturers were well known honorable people, Młocki continued, who obeyed the law and did not participate in public protests. Since the cancellation of the lectures would result in "general dissatisfaction" among the population, Młocki predicted, the lectures should be allowed to go forward without censorship controls.[25] After his arguments were brushed aside by the Cisleithanian government, Młocki decided to evade the censorship laws by arranging for the lecture series to be given in Lemberg's City Hall on the main Market Square to invited guests only (figure 5.2). The committee quietly spread news about the lectures and sold tickets, with all proceeds going to meet the needs of surviving veterans of Polish uprisings.[26]

Count Alexander Borkowski, a wealthy landowner, member of the *Sejm,* and veteran of the 1830 uprising, gave the first of the five scheduled lectures. Kazmierz Chlędowski termed him the "most extreme orator of the *Sejm*" who always spoke "as though he had a crowd before him." Despite his credentials as an orator, Borkowski did not draw a large crowd.[27] About four hundred people, mostly women, heard Borkowski's half hour speech. The police, clearly dismissive of the influence of women on public opinion, interpreted the predominance of women in the audience as evidence of popular indifference to Polish nationalism and as proof that the evening was a failure.[28] Borkowski began by justifying the revolutionary tradition. He declared the right of national defense to be a natural right of nations. He railed against the policy of "servilism." Borkowski conceded that "organic work," the program of the Polish conservatives, was certainly a means of strengthening "patriotic feelings," but, he continued, a program of organic work alone would only create "slaves" and would work to legitimize the current situation. Were servilism the key to the defense of national rights, he asserted, there would already be a free Poland (at least in Galicia).[29]

Democratic politician and representative to the *Sejm,* Tadeusz Romanowicz, delivered the second lecture on 17 November to a somewhat larger audience. In

Figure 5.2. Market Square in modern Lviv. Photograph by author.

a more historical discussion, Romanowicz described the outbreak of the uprising as a justified reaction to the disregard by the Russian government of the "holiest rights of the Poles." A police observer made note of the weak audience response.[30] Henryk Schmitt, democrat, historian, and member of the Galician School Board, delivered the third and fourth lectures, each lasting over seventy-five minutes. Schmitt blamed the "betrayal" of individuals and the "indecisive" action of the *szlachta* for the ultimate failure of the uprising. In his conclusion, Schmitt directly challenged the Cracow school of historians for labeling the "great struggle" of the entire nation an "unripe and mistaken uprising."[31] The police observer noted that the audience, again composed mostly of women, greeted the lecture with "sparse applause" due to Schmitt's "dry style of presentation."[32]

The most successful of the lectures was the final one in the series. Police reports indicated that the previous four lectures had failed to awaken the interest of the female audiences. Given the efforts by the police, the interior ministry, and the Galician administration to suppress public celebrations of the uprising, one might be tempted to dismiss these descriptions as wishful thinking were it not for the altogether different assessment of the fifth and last of the lectures. Democratic activist, writer, and feminist leader, Felicie Bobeerska-Wasilewska attracted a very large crowd, estimated at nearly seven hundred, and received an enthusiastic reception. Bobeerska-Wasilewska lionized the role of Polish women in cultivating national identity and Polish values. She spoke of the actions of individual women in the defense of the "Fatherland" during the uprising. To cries of "Poland lives," Bobeerska-Wasilewska called on Polish women to raise their children in the spirit of those who died in defense of the nation, thus challenging the conservatives whose program did not reserve to women such a heroic role in the narrative of the Polish nation.[33]

Although major figures in the Polish democratic movement presented these lectures, they did not resonate beyond the City Hall itself. The censors prevented newspaper reporting on the content of the speeches, limiting the public impact to the few who actually attended. The democrats did, however, have some limited success in mobilizing the urban populations in Lemberg and Cracow to participate in public commemorations. The most extensive celebrations took place in Lemberg, the political base of the Polish democrats. On 28 November 1880, the Jewish academic youth sponsored a service in honor of the fallen in the liberal Temple on the Old Market Square (one of two synagogues Franz Joseph had visited in September).[34] Some veterans of the 1830 uprising as well as members of the city council and many other non-Jews came to the Temple and joined in singing a psalm of David in Polish translation.[35]

On 29 November, students, pupils, veterans, and large crowds gathered in Lemberg's Dominican church for mass in honor of the fallen at 9 am. At 11 am, the veterans walked to the city Casino. There, five hundred invited guests honored close to two hundred veterans of the November Uprising. Democratic politician Otto Hausner delivered the first of several speeches, whose nationalistic content prompted the censor to prevent their publication in the press. In a cutting reference to conservative claims of achievement, Hausner admitted that in Galicia Poles were free to be Poles, but that this meant only that they were free to mourn their dead, prevented by the conservative Catholic clergy from planning church celebrations. Hausner recalled the heroic deeds of 1830, and compared the leaders of the present generation unfavorably to the heroes of the past, voicing the hope that the children of today would rise to follow in the footsteps of the generation of 1830. Each of the surviving revolutionaries received a medal of honor—on one side a symbolic figure of Poland held a banner bearing the revolutionary Polish motto, "For Your Freedom and Ours," while the other side read "Poland to the heroes of the November Uprising on the fiftieth anniversary."[36] In the evening, in the City Hall, Romanowicz, Młocki, and Hausner again toasted the veterans and Poland.[37]

Even in Cracow, their political base, the conservatives could not suppress public celebrations of 1830, defined by the conservatives as a misguided waste of Polish lives. In the Dominican church below Wawel Castle—the Catholic hierarchy forbade any commemorations in Wawel Cathedral, the burial site of Polish kings—several dozen veterans sat in places of honor, hundreds of students and others filled the church, and amateur choirs sang under the direction of Wawel's cathedral organist. At 6 pm. in the hall of Hotel Saski, over two hundred people gathered to listen to music and speeches in honor of the veterans. Lemberg's democratic *Dziennik Polski* interpreted the Cracow festivities as a popular protest against *Czas* and the conservatives. Despite the gloating of the Lemberg democratic press, however, the Cracow conservatives did succeed in preventing the Cracow celebrations from becoming as nationalistic as those in the provincial capital. Polish patriots and Stańczyk allies, like Cracow's mayor Mikołaj Zyblikiewicz and historian Józef Majer, the president of the Cracow Academy of Sciences, played prominent—and moderating—roles in these celebrations.[38]

Ultimately, however, the liberal democratic challenge to conservative hegemony had been a limited one. Censorship prevented news of the lecture series from disseminating outside the urban centers. Aside from events in Cracow and Lemberg, the festivities differed little from the modest commemorations organized on the local level in years past, certainly nothing like the extraordinary outpouring of popular participation which had characterized Franz Joseph's recent visit to the province. The urban democrats had no contacts with the rural population, which remained suspicious of activity meant to reconstitute or memorialize a Polish state which, for many, still evoked serfdom and oppression rather than national pride. One of the most widely circulated newspapers directed at the Polish peasantry, *Wieniec,* agreed with *Czas,* and called on peasants to limit their participation to quiet tributes to the fallen.[39] The Catholic hierarchy forbade church celebrations beyond mourning, and the Galician administration and the police attempted to minimize public discussions about the celebrations.[40]

3. Joseph II: Emperor-Liberator of the Ruthenians

In contrast to the Polish democratic commemorations of 1830, the Ruthenian celebrations on 29 November 1880, marking the centennial anniversary of Joseph II's accession to sole rulership of the Habsburg lands and the associated All-Party Ruthenian Meeting in Lemberg held the following day, posed a serious challenge to the narrative of provincial unity presented by Polish conservatives during Franz Joseph's September inspection tour of the province. The Ruthenian November events had their origin in the efforts by the major Ruthenian political and cultural institutions to organize a united Ruthenian reception for Franz Joseph. Ruthenians were all but shut out of the Polish conservative dominated official reception committee for the emperor. Greek Catholic Metropolitan Sembratovych and Greek Catholic Bishop Stupnicki of Przemyśl sat on the committee, but there were no delegates from major Ruthenian cultural or political organizations. In mid August, Russophiles (Ruthenians who advocated cultural and/or political solidarity with the Russian people) grouped around the newspaper *Slovo* (The Word) called for an all-Ruthenian political meeting to take place in Lemberg in early September. Participants at this meeting were to formulate a list of grievances to hand to the emperor when he arrived in the provincial capital.[41] However, the national populists or Ukrainophiles (Ruthenians who promoted the idea of a separate Ukrainian language and nation) close to the rival newspaper *Dilo* (The Deed) hoped to "welcome the emperor as the protector of freedom and equality ..."[42] The national populists wanted to demonstrate to the imperial visitor and to the wider population of the state that Ruthenians were Austrian patriots rather than supporters of the Russian Tsar, as the Polish language press claimed.[43]

In the end, Ruthenian intellectuals, the Greek Catholic hierarchy, and the major Ruthenian associations and institutions represented on a committee set up to organize a Ruthenian welcome for Franz Joseph decided not to confront the emperor with lists of complaints. Instead, the various Ruthenian factions set aside disagreements over their national orientation in order to present a unified front of imperial loyalty and Ruthenian self-assertion in the presence of the emperor. However, at the insistence of Russophile delegates, the reception committee agreed to support the convening of a Ruthenian political meeting at a later date. Indeed, as soon as Franz Joseph left the province, the movement began to organize a Ruthenian meeting in conjunction with the celebration of Joseph II, which was to be a "national celebration of freedom and equality"[44] and an opportunity to protest against Polish oppression of Ruthenian rights and dignity.

Throughout German-speaking Austria, German liberals, whose governing coalition Ruthenian deputies to the Cisleithanian *Reichsrat* had supported in the 1870s, were preparing to celebrate Joseph II, the emperor they deemed the father of the ideals of centralism and liberal reform. This was planned as a monarchy-wide assertion of the continued vitality of the German liberals who fell from power in 1879 and opposed Taaffe's coalition of conservatives and federalists.[45]

Ruthenians in Lemberg also intended to celebrate Joseph II, but infused the memory of this emperor with very different content. They would not celebrate Joseph II as a "reformer of empty liberal phrases and centralism," but would rather commemorate him for his promotion of the material and spiritual advance of the Ruthenian people.[46] The Ruthenians viewed Joseph II as the champion of the Ruthenian peasantry, evidenced by his efforts to moderate the burdens of serfdom and his support for raising the educational level of the Greek Catholic clergy.[47]

In the first half of October, 1880, the executive committee of *Prosvita* (Enlightenment), an association founded in 1868 to spread Ukrainian language and consciousness among the peasantry, held a meeting at which national populists determined to promote Joseph II celebrations all over Galicia and to work with other Ruthenian associations based in the Ruthenian National Institute in Lemberg.[48] For its part, the Ruthenian Council (*Rada Ruska*) sent out invitations to all the major Ruthenian associations to join them in preparing celebrations. The initiatives merged, and delegations from the Ruthenian organizations, the same ones which had sent representatives to the Ruthenian committee to welcome the emperor, gathered on 24 October in the Stauropegion Institute, one of the oldest Ruthenian cultural organizations, under the chairmanship of Teofil Pavlykiv, one of the leaders of the Ruthenian Council.

The "Committee to Celebrate Joseph II" began preparing to make the Joseph II commemorations and the upcoming Ruthenian Meeting "a new sign of the existence and unity of all Ruthenians."[49] As *Dilo* wrote, "Now, as Halicka Rus' prepares for the celebration of the one-hundredth anniversary of the accession of Joseph II and of his reforms," Ruthenians faced a new opportunity for enhancing the "solidarity of all Ruthenians," not only those in Lemberg, but of all Ruthenians in Galicia.[50] A subcommittee then began to prepare a political resolution to be passed at the all-party Ruthenian Meeting. Pavlykiv was the official chair of this subcommittee, but *Dilo* editor Volodymyr Barvins'kyi authored the final resolution.[51]

In several open addresses to the Ruthenian People, the committee published information about the planned church services and other celebrations in honor of Joseph II scheduled for 29 November, and about the Meeting planned for the following day.[52] The committee also voted to send a delegation led by Vasyl' Kovals'kyi to place flowers on the coffin of Joseph II in Vienna.[53] In his capacity as president of the National Institute, Kovals'kyi had served as host to Franz Joseph during the emperor's visit to this central Ruthenian institution. Kovals'kyi was a member of the *Sejm*, the *Reichsrat*, and, in later decades, the Supreme Court in Vienna.

On the morning of 29 November, the same day Polish democrats marked the failed November Uprising of 1830, commemorative services were held in honor of Joseph II in the Greek Catholic Cathedral of St. George (figure 5.3). Hundreds of Ruthenians, many of whom were in Lemberg for the Ruthenian Meeting, crowded into the church and stood outside on the street.[54] That evening, in the great hall of the National Institute, which was decorated with flowers and

Figure 5.3. St. George Cathedral in modern Lviv. Photograph by author.

portraits of Joseph II (as it had been with flowers and portraits of Franz Joseph just two months before), the Ruthenian intelligentsia, school children, and peasants, packed the room for an evening of speeches and music. To the cheers of the audience, Barvins'kyi denounced the Poles and their Jewish allies for oppressing the Ruthenian people and praised the Habsburg acquisition of Galicia as the beginning of the emancipation of the Ruthenians from spiritual and physical slavery. Choirs sang the *Kantata in honor of the visit of His Majesty Emperor Franz Joseph I to Galicia,* just as they had when Franz Joseph visited Ruthenian institutions in September.[55] At least two hundred peasants from small towns joined a crowd estimated at six hundred.[56] Outside of Lemberg, Galicia's Greek Catholic churches held special services to honor the memory of the "Emperor-Liberator."[57]

The church services at St. George opened the festivities for the Joseph II celebrations and were followed by a much more nationalistic event at the National Institute the next day (figure 5.4). According to the national populist newspaper *Dilo,* "Never before had any Ruthenian national manifestation or public gathering been so imposing" as the November 30 Ruthenian Meeting.[58] Prominent Russophiles and national populists spoke to the audience, declaring Ruthenian loyalty to Franz Joseph, the heir to Joseph II, and decrying the nefarious policies of the oppressive Poles. Ivan Naumovych, a Greek Catholic Priest, received the most positive audience response.[59] Naumovych edited the popular peasant oriented publication *Nauka,* and had been one of the founders of the Russophile Kachkovs'kyi Society in 1874, which—with its network of rural reading rooms and publications—was the largest Ruthenian voluntary association in 1880.[60] In his speech to the Ruthenian Meeting, Naumovych used folk references and called for the Ruthenians to organize in order to break through the "intellectual domination" of the Jews in the countryside, prompting the representative of the police to warn him against inciting the crowd.[61]

Figure 5.4. Ruthenian National Institute in modern Lviv. Photograph by author.

The participants accepted the resolution authored by Volodymyr Barvins'kyi and approved by the committee overseeing the celebrations. This Ruthenian Resolution reiterated demands made by Ruthenian deputies to the *Sejm* and the *Reichsrat* since 1848. The resolution insisted that the Ruthenians' national rights under the 1867 constitution regarding language use in schools, the bureaucracy, the courts, and public life be enforced, and that election manipulation by the Polish dominated Galician Election Committee cease. Though the resolution declared the Ruthenians loyal to the dynasty and the state, it also made clear that this loyalty was conditional. The Ruthenians would not back a government that failed to support them in their quest for the fulfillment of their constitutional rights. The resolution demanded economic assistance to enable the peasant population to overcome the "harmful influence" of the Jews, and it also dealt specifically with issues surrounding the provincial school system. Despite the guarantees in article 19 of the Austrian constitution, the Poles had not conceded equality to Ukrainian in the schools, often offering Ukrainian only as an optional choice even in regions almost wholly populated by Ukrainian speakers. Finally, in words echoing sentiments found often in the pages of *Dilo,* the resolution called on all Ruthenians to work with their united strength for the achievement of their rights.[62]

The same day the national meeting passed the political resolution in Lemberg, Kovals'kyi laid a wreath on the simple coffin of Joseph II in the imperial crypt in Vienna's Capuchin Church with the words: "Galician Ruthenians—To Emperor Joseph II—1880." The Ruthenian delegation was the only non-German delegation to participate in the Austro-German liberal-dominated celebrations of Joseph II in Vienna. The previous evening, a massive crowd, including representatives from German communities from Bukovina and other Habsburg provinces, followed a torchlight procession and converged on Josephsplatz, where an equestrian statue of Joseph II guards one of the entrances to the imperial palace.[63] The *Wiener Allgemeine Zeitung* described the Joseph II celebrations held all over German-speaking Austria as "an imposing celebration of the liberal population of Austria, a demonstration for the unity of the empire, and a protest of the entire Austrian people against the presently dominant clerical-federal tendencies favored by the government."[64]

The Polish democrats attempted to undermine the Ruthenian celebration of Joseph II. *Dziennik Polski* printed a pamphlet written in Ukrainian, which was distributed everywhere Joseph II celebrations took place. This pamphlet, "Address to the Ruthenian People," allegedly written by a "Friend of the Gathering," reminded the Ruthenian peasantry that while Joseph II had freed them from personal servitude almost one hundred years before, the Greek Catholic clergy continued to charge them inflated fees for ecclesiastical duties well beyond what Joseph II had decreed.[65] Police confiscated copies of this pamphlet all over eastern Galicia, and the Lemberg police expended some energy—in vain—in an attempt to discover its author.[66]

Cracow's conservative organ *Czas* and Lemberg's liberal democratic *Dziennik Polski* highlighted this supposed irony and ridiculed both the Joseph II celebrations and the Ruthenian Meeting. Polish democrats and conservatives claimed that the great hall of the National Institute, which they alleged could only seat 300, was far from full for the great national meeting. The Polish papers feigned sympathy for the poor Ruthenian peasants who had to "sit for several hours like mannequins with printed resolutions in hand." The Polish press also claimed that the ignorant peasants did not know for whom they should cheer. The confused peasants present at the Meeting supposedly cheered at the mention of a member of the aristocratic Czartoryski family before the speaker had a chance to denounce this Polish magnate for oppressing Ruthenian national rights.[67]

The Polish press also challenged the central assertions of the Joseph II celebrations and the Meeting. The democratic newspapers argued that serfdom had never existed in Galicia, and that the peasantry had been better off within Poland-Lithuania than under Russia and Prussia. They noted that the abuse of peasants by the landlords described in national terms at the Meeting was experienced by Polish as well as Ukrainian-speaking peasants, and therefore should not be understood as a Ruthenian national issue.

The Joseph II celebrations and the Ruthenian Meeting were, however, by no means the fiascos depicted in the Polish language press. Peasants, intellectuals, and priests did pack the main hall of the National Institute. The correspondent of Vienna's *Neue Freie Presse* claimed that 2,534 attended this event, and the Russophile *Slovo* estimated the crowd at 2,500.[68] Even the 1,400 cited in police reports suggests that the Polish press accounts were less than accurate.[69] The celebrations also succeeded in disseminating a specific interpretation of Galician politics. The Resolution was printed and distributed through newspapers and pamphlets to reading rooms all over Galicia, thus successfully bridging the gap between the small Ruthenian urban intelligentsia and the rural masses. As never before, the monarchy-wide press, especially German liberal journalists who enthusiastically commemorated Joseph II as a liberal centralist, also took notice of the grievances of the Ruthenians and wove these grievances into their own critique of the Slavic supporters of Taaffe's federalist-leaning Iron Ring.

The Austro-German Liberal press claimed that this Meeting was called and dominated by the populists.[70] Contemporary reports in the democratic Polish press, however, credited the "Moscophiles" with control over the Joseph II celebrations and the Meeting, and sarcastically wondered how the populists could have allowed themselves to be duped into promoting the Moscophile agenda.[71] Nevertheless, the 1880 Meeting was not an exclusively national populist congress or a Russophile event. *Slovo*, the Ruthenian Council, and other Russophile associations joined *Dilo* and the national populists in organizing the 29–30 November events. All the major Ruthenian associations supported the Joseph II celebrations, most of all the grass roots Russophile Kachkovs'kyi society and the national populist Prosvita.[72] At the Meeting itself, Russophiles such as the president of the Ruthenian Council and Naumovych, held leadership positions and delivered well-received speeches as did Ukrainophiles like Volodymyr Barvins'kyi.[73]

In late October, a month before the commemorations of the 1830 uprising and the Joseph II celebrations, Cracow conservatives, not surprisingly, had criticized both of the planned events. For them, Polish democrats and Ruthenian agitators jointly threatened to undermine the harmony and unity of the society that had been evident during the emperor's visit. *Czas* claimed at once to champion legitimate Ruthenian interests and to work for Polish national goals. They invoked the recent reception of the emperor to justify these seemingly mutually exclusive contentions:

> The Poles do not need any demonstration of patriotism or of loyalty. Our province at every step gives proof with facts, not historical anniversaries or historical memories, that its Polishness is the very foundation of its loyalty to the monarchy and the state. The reception of the emperor in Galicia was more than a demonstration, it was a sign and historical fact, directed toward the future, supported by the existing relations in the present moment. It was, it can be said, a great plebiscite ... the voices of masses of people affirmed better than any uprising or Josephinist celebration that the people of both tribes are one nationality, in agreement in their national feelings, and want to stand with Austria.
>
> No demonstration will weaken this great plebiscite ...
>
> ... When our province came forward for the reception of the Monarch in the full brilliance of tradition and Polish insignia, behind the *szlachta* in [traditional dress] came the people, and in both capitals of the province every strata presented a magnificent picture of national unity ...[74]

Czas insisted that the reception of Franz Joseph had proven once again that only the conservative nobles could unite all Polish factions and the Ruthenian masses into one harmonious Galician society. The commemoration of the uprising and the Joseph II celebrations, designed to shatter this vision of unity, could not, according to *Czas,* alter reality. The reception of the emperor had verified that the Polish population backed the conservative definition of Polish national interests, and that Ruthenians approved of the Polish nobility's patriarchal concern for Ruthenian welfare:

> Who among us does not preserve in grateful memory the numerous multitudes of kind-hearted Ruthenians, who along with citizens from the eastern part of our province arrived in Cracow for the reception of His Majesty? We saw in these deputations representatives of Ruthenian towns and villages and Uniate Priests, and at the head [of these delegations were] *szlachta* in robes.

Czas blamed the agitation on "Moscophiles," and vowed that this agitation would not weaken the great expression of solidarity manifested during Franz Joseph's visit.[75]

In the end, however, the Cracow conservatives appeared satisfied with the limited success of both celebrations. The celebration of the 1830 uprising had not led to massive demonstrations opposed to the conservatives' continued leadership. After the Joseph II celebrations and the Ruthenian Meeting, *Czas* was less concerned about the Ruthenian demonstration. "The Ruthenian Meeting took place, but despite that, and for this we thank God, it did not break up … any of the institutions, which according to the decisions and resolutions of the Meeting so cruelly oppress three million Ruthenians." The resolutions were, *Czas* gloated, only repetitions of what the Ruthenians had repeated year after year in the Vienna parliament and the *Sejm*.[76]

Conclusions

In 1880, the popularity of Franz Joseph proved useful to both Polish conservatives and Ruthenian intellectuals. Revered by the peasantry, his presence and association with Polish and Ruthenian leaders legitimized their status before their respective constituencies. During Franz Joseph's visit, Polish magnates joined Polish bureaucrats and Ruthenian priests and professors—as well as rabbis—at the imperial table, acknowledged by Habsburg court etiquette as worthy of imperial recognition. Unlike earlier visits, however, in the context of a vibrant independent press and an expanding reading public, imperial ceremonial could not define the hierarchy of society. Ruthenian intellectuals and the Polish conservatives incorporated heroic Habsburgs into their competing national narratives, creating very different histories of the province, contrasting interpretations of the present, and incompatible visions of the future.

For the Polish conservatives, Franz Joseph was a symbol of the transfer of control from the imperial center to the provincial elites. The Polish conservatives used Franz Joseph's visit to Galicia to prove to the emperor, their Polish constituency, their new political partners in the Iron Ring, as well as to the German liberals, the efficacy of their strategy of loyalism and Polish cultural progress under conservative political hegemony. Aside from a few oblique references to Poles in the other partitions, they focused on achieving Polish national and cultural goals within a Habsburg-loyal Galicia. The Polish elites in turn basked in the sacred aura of the political authority wielded by the emperor. The conservatives succeeded in mobilizing the population to participate in the celebrations within a framework that presented a unified province populated by quaint and colorful Ukrainian and Polish-speaking peasants and Jews marching loyally forward under the leadership of the *szlachta*.

For Ruthenian intellectuals, Franz Joseph was a symbol of rights denied to Ruthenians by the Polish elites. They endeavored to use the presence of the emperor to legitimize their struggle for equality in Galicia. When Franz Joseph arrived at St. George Cathedral and the National Institute in September, he recognized the cultural progress of the Ruthenian people, presented to him by the Ruthenian committee. The Ruthenian network of voluntary societies and cultural organizations received signs of imperial favor. Ruthenian notables—priests, professors, lawyers, members of the *Sejm* and the *Reichsrat*—presented themselves to the emperor, receiving acknowledgment of their leadership position, and implicitly countering the claims of the Polish conservatives to speak in the name of all inhabitants of the province.

Polish democrats had joined with the conservatives to present a united Polish reception for Franz Joseph. However, in the commemorations of the November Uprising, the democrats revealed a wholly different set of national symbols, challenging the program of conservative loyalism that had determined Galician politics for two decades. While the conservatives praised Franz Joseph as the symbol of the success of their policy of organic work and political realism and of the union of Polish and Austrian interests, Polish democrats looked to the revolutionary tradition for the alter egos of the conservatives. They lionized a list of uncompromised Polish heroes—veterans of the 1830–31 and 1863 uprisings—and related a version of Polish history that redefined the Galician present and, through their emphasis on the other partitions, implied the need for political action directed toward a Polish future outside of the Habsburg Monarchy. Though their program challenged conservative hegemony within the Polish national community, it failed to provoke an enthusiastic response among the masses of Galician Poles. In 1880, at least, such an appeal to an anti-Habsburg Polish nationalism proved less attractive than the Polish conservatives' or the Ruthenian intellectuals' incorporation of Habsburg dynastic symbols into their respective national narratives.

With the Joseph II celebrations and the Ruthenian Meeting in late November, Ruthenians again merged dynastic and ethnic history, as the Polish conservatives had done repeatedly during Franz Joseph's visit. For the Ruthenians, Franz Joseph embodied the ideal of national equality and Ruthenian economic and educational progress, which, like the many reforms of Joseph II, had been opposed by the Polish nobility and perverted into Polish domination over the Ruthenian people. The Ruthenian organizations used the popularity of the dynasty to disseminate this specifically Ruthenian conception of history and politics. The Ruthenian associations succeeded in publicizing their alternative view of Galician history to their constituents. Throughout the province, Ruthenian peasants attended religious celebrations in which the still very influential clergy described the relationship between the population and the state and dynasty in very different terms to the hegemonic Polish conservatives. *Prosvita* and the Kachkovs'kyi Society distributed pamphlets and other information, including copies of *Nauka*, to the peasantry. They learned of the unified Ruthenian reception of the emperor, the Ruthenian national celebration of Joseph II, and the Ruthenian resolution defining a common list of grievances against Polish domination.

These three public events could not have provided much solace to the imperial center. The stable monarchy imagined by Franz Joseph and Taaffe, one anchored by agreements between the center and entrenched regional elites, never came into existence. In Galicia, as elsewhere in the monarchy outside of Hungary, moderate and conservative politicians, nobles, and economic leaders were facing the pressures unleashed by the expansion of suffrage and the realization of the civil freedoms inherent in the constitutional system adopted in 1867. In Galicia, at the moment of conservative consolidation of provincial power, the Stańczyk coalition was already under siege by Polish nationalists unsatisfied with Polish cultural achievements within Habsburg Galicia, and by Ruthenians politically organizing to assert their rights under the Austrian constitution—rights denied them by the ruling Polish elites. Ruthenians and Polish democrats interpreted the importance of Franz Joseph's presence in September in very different ways from the Polish conservatives: for the Polish democrats, Habsburg Galicia was a beacon of hope in the dark era of the partitions, an era they hoped would come to an end in the not too distant future; for the Ruthenians, Franz Joseph and his predecessor Joseph II became rallying cries for their agenda of national assertion. The imperial inspection tour could draw the attention of the population and inspire gratifying scenes of public acclamation, but, as the Polish and Ruthenian events of November confirmed, it was not sufficient to channel public discourse about the state, province, and nationalities into a single narrative of unity and unconditional loyalty.

Notes

1. On "ethnie" and nationalism, see the work of Anthony Smith, especially *The Ethnic Origins of Nations* (London, 1987).
2. For important recent work on Galicia, see, among others, Alison Fleig Frank, *Oil Empire. Visions of Prosperity in Austrian Galicia* (Cambridge, MA, 2005); Christopher Hann and Paul Magosci, eds., *Galicia: A Multicultured Land* (Toronto, 2005); Kai Struve, *Bauern und Nation in Galicia. Über Zugehörigkeit und soziale Emanzipation im 19. Jahrhundert* (Göttingen, 2005); Harald Binder, "Making and Defending a Polish Town: 'Lwów' (Lemberg), 1848–1914," *Austrian History Yearbook* 34 (2003): 211–240; Keely Stauter-Halsted, *The Nation in the Village: The Genesis of Peasant National Identity in Austrian Poland*, 1848–1914 (Ithaca, 2001).
3. For a much more extensive discussion of the 1880 *Kaiserreise*, see Daniel Unowsky, "'Our Gratitude Has No Limit': Polish Nationalism, Dynastic Patriotism, and the 1880 Imperial Inspection Tour of Galicia," *Austrian History Yearbook* 34 (2003): 145–171.
4. These statistics are drawn from John-Paul Himka, "Dimensions of a Triangle: Polish-Ukrainian-Jewish Relations in Austrian Galicia," in *Polin: Studies in Polish Jewry. Volume 12. Focusing on Galicia: Jews, Poles, and Ukrainians 1772–1918*, ed. Israel Bartal and Antony Polonsky (London and Portland, OR, 1999), 26. Determining ethnicity/national identity from the Habsburg censuses is a problematic endeavor. There were Greek Catholics who viewed themselves as Polish patriots (Cracow's mayor in 1880, Mikołaj Zyblikiewicz, for example) as well as Polish speaking peasants who identified themselves as Ruthenians. Leila P. Everett, "The Rise of Jewish National Politics in Galicia, 1905–1907," in *Nationbuilding and the Politics of Nationalism. Essays on Austrian Galicia*, ed. Andrei S. Markovits and Frank E. Sysyn (Cambridge, MA, 1982), 149–150, footnote 2. The Habsburg censuses did not offer the possibility of choosing Yiddish. Before 1867, the majority of Jews were counted as German speakers; the majority of Galicia's Jews were numbered among the Polish speakers in 1880.
5. "Ruthenian" (*rusyny* in Ukrainian; *Ruthenen* in German) is used here to distinguish between an ethnic designation (Ruthenian) and the national orientations of Ruthenian leaders and factions. I employ "Ukrainian" when referring to the language spoken by Ruthenians, although this too is a very complicated question. In this I follow John-Paul Himka, *Religion*

and Nationality in Western Ukraine: The Greek Catholic Church and the Ruthenian National Movement in Galicia, 1867–1900 (Montreal & Kingston, 1999) and Alison Fleig Frank, Oil Empire.

6. *Gazeta Lwowska,* 2 October 1851.
7. On the revival of the Habsburg court after the 1848 revolutions and the 1851 inspection tour of Galicia, see Daniel Unowsky, "Reasserting Empire: Habsburg Imperial Celebrations after the Revolutions of 1848–1849, " in *Staging the Past: The Politics of Commemoration in Habsburg Central Europe, 1848 to the Present,* ed. Maria Bucur and Nancy Wingfield (West Lafayette, 2001), 13–45.
8. Paweł Popiel, *Pamiętniki Pawła Popiela, 1807–1892* (Kraków, 1927), 124.
9. For a more extensive treatment of the 1868 events, see Daniel Unowsky, *The Pomp and Politics of Patriotism: Imperial Celebrations in Habsburg Austria, 1848–1916* (Lafayette, 2005), 46–50.
10. On literacy, see Adalbert Rom, "Der Bildungsgrad der Bevölkerung Österreichs und seine Entwicklung seit 1880 mit besonderer Berücksichtigung der Sudeten- und Karpatenländer," *Statist. Monatsschrift* 40 (NF 19) 1914. Harald Binder documents the growth of newspaper circulation in Galicia in "Die polnische Presse in der Habsburgermonarchie" and "Die ukrainische Presse in der Habsburgermonarchie," in *Die Habsburgermonarchie 1848–1918, Bd. 8: Politische Öffentlichkeit und Zivilgesellschaf: Die Presse als Faktor der politischen Mobilisierung,* ed. Helmut Rumpler and Peter Urbanitsch (Wien, 2006), 2037–2090 and 2091–2116.
11. William Jenks, *Austria under the Iron Ring, 1879–1893* (Charlottesville, 1965).
12. On politics in Galicia, see Harald Binder, *Galizien in Wien. Parteien. Wahlen, Fraktionen und Abgeordnete im Übergang zur Massenpolitik* (Wien, 2004).
13. On the Polish conservatives, see Michal Jaskólski, *Kaduceus Polski. Mysl polityczna konserwatystów krakowskich, 1866–1934* (Warszawa, 1990); Lawrence Orton, "The Stańczyk Portfolio and the Politics of Galician Loyalism" in *The Polish Review,* XXVII 1982; Jakub Forst-Battaglia, *Die polnischen Konservativen Galiziens und die Slawen (1866–1879),* (Diss., University of Vienna, 1975); Kazimierz Wyka, *Teka Stańczyka na tle historii Galicji w latach 1849–1869* (Wrocław, 1951); Wilhelm Feldman, *Stronnicwa i programy polityczne w Galicyi, 1846–1906* (Cracow, 1907).
14. *Przegląd Polski,* year XV, second issue, 1880, 6–38.
15. *Gazeta Narodowa,* 31 August 1880, 1; *Gazeta Narodowa,* 1 September 1880, 1. Conservative journalists made similar comparisons with the plight of those living in the Russian partition. *Czas,* 21 September 1880, 1; *Czas,* 22 September 1880, 1. HHStA, NZA, r. XV, Hofreisen 1880, ct. 367 [Loebenstein to the Office of the Grand Court Master, 17 September 1880].
16. L'viv Oblast State Archive (DALO), 350/1/ 2378/21 [Z. 825, pr. 20 July 1880. Police Direction to Interior Ministry]. The Lemberg police kept the Interior Ministry and Taaffe apprised of the state of preparations for the November celebrations. On the Polish democrats, see Maciej Janowski, *Inteligencja wobec wyzwań nowoczesności. Dylematy ideowe polskiej demokracji liberalnej w Galicji w latach 1889–1914* (Warsaw, 1996); Zbigniew Fras, *Democraci w życiu politycznym Galicji w latach 1848–1873* (Wroclaw, 1997).
17. Chlędowski, *Pamiętniki,* 398–399.
18. *Dziennik Polski,* 11 July 1880, 1.
19. *Czas,* 13 July 1880, 1.
20. Maciej Janowski, *Polish Liberal Thought before 1918* (Budapest and New York, 2004), 163. The semi-official organ of the foreign ministry in Vienna, *Fremden-Blatt,* termed *Dziennik Polski* the "main organ of the Lemberg liberals." *Fremden-Blatt* (evening edition), 7 September 1880, 1. For detailed discussion of the Galician press, see Binder, "Die polnische Presse" and "Die ukrainische Presse"; Józef Myśliński, "Prasa Polska w Galicji w dobie autonomicznej (1867–1918)" in *Prasa Polska w Latach 1864–1918,* ed. Jerzy Lojka (Warsaw, 1976), 114–176.

21. *Dziennik Polski*, 15 July 1880, 1.
22. *Dziennik Polski*, 20 July 1880, 1.
23. *Dziennik Polski*, 4 August 1880, 1.
24. DALO, 350/1/2378/33–38.
25. DALO, 350/1/ 2378/125–129.
26. DALO, 350/1/ 2378/39. *Neue Freie Presse* reported on the police and Galician administration injunctions against such speeches without prior approval. *Neue Freie Presse* (morning edition), 7 November 1880, 7; *Neue Freie Presse* (morning edition), 9 November 1880, 3; *Neue Freie Presse* (morning edition), 16 November 1880, 9. The Polish press printed little about the lecture series. *Gazeta Narodowa*, a Lemberg newspaper controlled by Polish nationalists and progressives, did describe Romanowicz's speech and advertised for the next three lectures: *Gazeta Narodowa*, 20 November 1880, 3.
27. Chlędowski, *Pamiątka*, vol. 1, 273.
28. Clearly, as recent research has shown, the police observer misinterpreted the central role women have played in national movements. For women and Polish nationalism, see, among others, Rudolf Jaworski and Bianka Pietrow-Ennker, eds., *Women in Polish Society* (Boulder, 1992); Anna Żarnowska and Andrzej Szwarc, eds., *Kobieta i społeczęnstwo na ziemiach Polskich w XIX* (Warsaw, 1990); Bogna Lorence-Kot, "Klementyna Tanska Hoffmanowa: Cultural Nationalism and a New Formula for Polish Womanhood," in *Women in European Culture and Society*, ed. Karen Offen. A special issue of History of European Ideas, vol. 8, nr. 4/5, 1987; Sławomira Walczewska, *Damy, rycerze i feministki* (Cracow, 1999).
29. DALO, 350/1/ 2378/111 [Pr. 1268, 15 November 1880. Betreffend die am 14 dm von Alexander Gf Borkowski gehaltenen Vorlesung].
30. DALO, 350/1/ 2378/116 [Bericht 18 November 1880. Betreffend die von Tadeus Romanovicz am 17 dm. abgehaltenen Vorlesung über den pol. November Aufstand].
31. DALO, 350/1/2378/130 [Pr. 1311, 25 November 1880. Bericht betreffend die vierte Vorlesung über den November Aufstand].
32. DALO 350/1/ 2378/119–122 [Pr. 1302. Betreffend die dritte am 21. dm. von Heinrich Schmitt gehalten Vorlesung über den November Aufstand].
33. DALO, 350/1/2378/134 [Pr. 1328, 29 November 1880. Betreffend die funften und letzte Vorlesung über den November Aufstand].
34. *Dziennik Polski*, 18 November 1880, 1.
35. DALO, 350/1/2378/47.
36. DALO, 350/1/2378/26–27, 45–51.
37. *Gazeta Narodowa*, 30 November 1880 and 1–2 December 1880; *Dziennik Polski*, 1 December 1880, 1.
38. *Dziennik Polski*, 5 December 1880, 1. The participation of prominent conservatives in the celebrations after the failure of the conservatives to prevent the festivities is a tactic Cracow conservatives would employ in later years during national festivals such as the 1894 celebrations in honor of Kościuszko and the 1898 festivities for Adam Mickiewicz.
39. *Wieniec*, 7 October 1880, 167. Rural activist and anti-Semitic priest Father Stanisław Stojałowski published *Wieniec* and *Pszczółka*, among other popular publications aimed at the peasant audience.
40. *Neue Freie Presse* reported on the cancellation of a planned public distribution of medals to the living veterans of the November Uprising, and on the orders of the episcopate that only mourning services would be tolerated in churches. *Neue Freie Presse* (morning edition), 20 November 1880, 3.
41. *Slovo*, 12 August 1880, 1.
42. On Ruthenian associations, political organizations, and national orientation, see Anna Veronika Wendland, *Die Russophilen in Galizien. Ukrainische Konservative zwischen Österreich und Russland, 1848–1915* (Wien, 2001); Wendland, "Die Rückkehr der Russophilen in die ukrainische Geschichte: Neue Aspekte der ukrainischen Nationsbildung in Galizien,

1848–1914," *Jahrbücher für Geschichte Osteuropas* 49 (2001): 178–199; John Paul Himka, "The Greek Catholic Church and the Ukrainian Nation in Galicia," in *Religious Compromise, Political Salvation. The Greek Catholic Church and Nation-Building in Eastern Europe*, ed. James Niessen (Pittsburgh, 1993). Paul Magosci defines Russophiles and Old Ruthenians (*starorusyny*) as separate groupings. Magocsi, "Old Ruthenianism and Russophilism: A New Conceptual Framework for Analyzing National Ideologies in Late 19th Century Eastern Galicia," in *American Contributions to the Ninth International Congress of Slavists, Vol. II: Literature, Poetics, History*, ed. Paul Debreczeny (Columbus, 1983), 310.

43. *Dilo*, 21 August 1880, 1–2.
44. *Dilo*, 25 September 1880, 1–2.
45. See Nancy Wingfield, "Emperor Joseph II in the Austrian Imagination up to 1914" in this volume.
46. *Dilo*, 30 October 1880, 1.
47. On the reforms of Maria Theresia and Joseph II see, among others, P.G.M. Dickson, *Finance and Government under Maria Theresia, 1740–1780* (Oxford, 1987); T.C.W. Blanning, *Joseph II;* Derek Beales, *Joseph II* (Cambridge, 1987); Roman Rosdolsky, *Untertan und Staat in Galizien: Die Reformen von Maria Theresia und Joseph II* (Mainz am Rhein, 1992); Kieniewicz, *The Emancipation of the Polish Peasantry* (Chicago and London, 1969).
48. *Dilo*, 19 October 1880, 4.
49. *Dilo*, 23 October 1880, 4; *Slovo*, not surprisingly, credits the Ruthenian Council for initiating a joint Ruthenian Josephine celebration, *Slovo*, 9 October 1880, 1; *Slovo*, 28 October 1880, 1. The Lemberg police reported, erroneously, that the entire preparations were taking place under the auspices of the Ruthenian Council. In a later report to the Interior Ministry, the Lemberg police corrected this mistake, and described the celebrations as the product of all the major Ruthenian factions; DALO, 350/1/2378/58–66 [Pr. 1190, 29 October 1880. Über von den Ruthenen in November beabsichtigte Veranstaltung einer Gedenkfeier der Thronbesteigung weiland Sr. Majestät des Kaisers Joseph II; Pr. 1269].
50. *Dilo*, 23 October 1880, 1.
51. *Dilo, Slovo*, and the Lemberg Police Direction confirm the central role played by Barvins'kyi; *Dilo*, 27 October 1880, 3; *Slovo*, 28 October 1880, 2.
52. *Dilo*, 13 November 1880, 1.
53. *Dilo*, 3 November 1880, 1.
54. DALO, 350/1/2378/84 [Pr. 1331, 30 November 1880. Bericht vom 30/11 über die von den Ruthenen am 29 November 1880 veranstalteten Kaiser Josephsfeier].
55. *Dilo*, 1 December 1880, 3.
56. DALO, 350/1/2378/84.
57. Central State Historical Archives, L'viv (TsDIA-L), 146/7/4215/5. In Tłumacz, for example, an estimated 2,000 people came to services in honor of Joseph II, and seventeen priests joined to perform the mass.
58. *Dilo*, 1 December 1880, 1–3.
59. This charismatic leader was convicted in the 1882 Russophile treason trial and sentenced to eight months in prison. Excommunicated by the Vatican, Naumovych converted to Russian Orthodoxy in 1885 and went into exile in Russian Ukraine in 1886. Wendland, *Die Russophilen in Galizien*, 201–236. See also Himka, *Religion and Nationality in Western Ukraine*, 73–97.
60. The Kachkovs'kyi Society founded by Russophiles "facilitated communication between the Ruthenian elite and the rural population," thereby functioning as "an important basis for national mobilization." Wendland, "Die Rückkehr der Russophilen," 185. In 1880, The Kachkovs'kyi Society had approximately 6,000 members. Magocsi views this association as "an ideological child of the so-called Old Ruthenian (*starorusyny*) movement." Magocsi, "The Kachkovs'kyi Society and the National Revival in Nineteenth-Century East Galicia," *Harvard Ukrainian Studies* XV (1991): 49–87.

61. DALO, 350/1/2378/83–91 [Pr. 1347, 1 December 1880, über den am 30 November dj abgehaltenen Ruthenischen Partheitag].
62. All of the major Ruthenian newspapers reported on the Joseph II celebrations, the Meeting, and the "Resolution presented by the committee for the josephinian celebrations for the approval of the National Ruthenian Meeting": *Nauka,* November/December, 1880; *Dilo,* 1 December 1880, 1–3; 4 December 1880, 1, 4; *Slovo,* 30 November 1880, 1–4; 1 December 1880, 1; 7 December 1880, 1–3.
63. *Dilo,* 17 November 1880, 3, describes the wreathe. For a description of the events in Vienna, see *Wiener Allgemeine Zeitung* (afternoon edition), 30 November 1880, 2.
64. *Wiener Allgemeine Zeitung* (morning edition), 30 November 1880, 1.
65. A copy of this pamphlet can be found in TsDIA-L, 146/7/4215/17.
66. TsDIA-L, 146/7/4215/19.
67. *Gazeta Narodowa,* 2 December 1880, 1–2; *Czas,* 2 December 1880, 1–2. The Czartoryski family was one of the leading Polish noble families supporting the reform movement of the 1780s. Prince Adam J. Czartoryski led the Polish exile organization set up after the failure of the 1830 uprising, which was based in the Hotel Lambert in Paris.
68. *Neue Freie Presse* (evening edition), 30 November 1880. *Slovo,* 30 November 1880, 3; 2 December 1880, 1.
69. DALO, 350/1/2378/91–100.
70. The *Neue Freie Presse* correspondent clearly did not understand the differences between the various Ruthenian factions. The paper reported that these 2,534 participants were all "Young Ruthenians," another designation for the Ukrainophiles. In reality, the audience, like the speakers, were drawn from all of the major Ruthenian factions and organizations. In an earlier report, the *Neue Freie Presse* had reported that the Ruthenian Council and the Old Ruthenians were sponsoring the Joseph II festivities. *Neue Freie Presse* (morning edition), 31 October 1880, 3. Scholars have also tended to interpret the 1880 political meeting as a specifically national populist undertaking. See the entry on national populism in the *Encyclopedia of Ukraine,* vol. IV (Toronto and Buffalo, 1993), 154–155.
71. *Gazeta Narodowa,* 3 December 1880, 1.
72. For examples of Russophile participation in these events, see *Slovo,* 14 December 1880, 1.
73. The Lemberg police initially reported that the Meeting and Joseph II celebrations were the production of the Ruthenian Council, but later informed the *Statthalterei* and interior ministry that in fact all the Ruthenian factions had joined together for both the celebrations and the Meeting. See DALO, 350/1/2378/56–58.
74. *Czas,* 27 October 1880, 1.
75. *Czas,* 26 October 1880, 1.
76. *Czas,* 2 December 1880, 1.

Chapter 6

EMPRESS ELISABETH AS HUNGARIAN QUEEN
The Uses of Celebrity Monarchism*

Alice Freifeld

Over four million people have seen the musical *Elisabeth* since its premier in 1992, making it the most successful German language musical to date. In this melodrama, the once most beautiful sovereign in Europe descends to her doom, with her assassin, Luigi Luccheni, insisting he is merely the agent of her death wish. The musical gained its poignancy from the real life ending which befell the Empress, her son, the monarchy itself, and their public, for whom all ended tragically in assassination, suicide, war, and political abyss. A *Variety* reviewer likened the musical to a sort of *Cliffs Notes* of the Habsburg dynasty and suggested the American audience "think of Scarlett O'Hara, Evita, and Jackie Kennedy meeting on the Danube."[1] The centenary of Elisabeth's assassination in 1998 followed in the wake of the death of Princess Diana and the parallels became popular fare.[2] While intellectuals may have wished to scoff at the public outpouring for Diana and the rebounding spotlight on Elisabeth (nicknamed Sisi/Sissi),[3] both have reminded us of the touchstone played by the personal in politics, by family tragedy amongst the great, and the cultural significance of celebrity monarchism since the onset of the mass press.

Elisabeth, as the wife of the Emperor Franz Joseph, appeared on no bureaucratic organizational flow chart, but she had direct access to the Emperor for her causes. Like other royal consorts, she did not herself possess the power to impose policy or govern, but she could serve as a conduit. Her comfort and intimacy with Hungarian culture and its political elite gave added substance to her ceremonial and public role as advocate. Lithography spread word of her beauty across the land. As a sovereign in the newspaper age, her celebrity was reinforced around a set of motifs: while the Emperor had in 1849 defeated the revolutionary war for independence, she learned Magyar, brought Magyar back into the Buda social circles and her court in Vienna, and raised her children to be fluent in the language. She was an accomplished equestrian who parleyed well with the Magyar magnate class, seeking solace in their company at her hunting lodge in Gödöllő. With her son Rudolf's sensational suicide, and then her own assassination, the melodrama of Elisabeth's family life gained real cult status.

In any age Elisabeth's beauty would have been legendary, but in the new age of photography and the lithograph it seemed palpable. We now know how much daily energy, exercise, and misery went into keeping Elisabeth one of the wonders of the age. But we sometimes forget how she helped define something new in the 1860s—a celebrity monarchism which fed a love-hate relationship with the crowd.[4] Wounded soldiers would hang her picture above their beds; inexpensive reproductions allowed the portrait of the beautiful young queen to adorn peasant homes as an icon. Elisabeth filled the public sphere with the glamour of a new monarchism and gave royalty a human face.[5]

Elisabeth's image was not only captured in paint and lithographs and then in photographs, but it was touched up and altered. Photomontages were built of the idyllic family, when in fact Elisabeth was photographed with her dogs but never with her children. In one such picture, her breasts and shoulders were enhanced; in another, sideburns were added to make the coiffure more stylish. As Elisabeth grew older and shied away from cameras, previous images were "aged" and reissued. This emphasis on image may seem unsurprising today in the age of film celebrity, anorexia, and plastic surgery. But we need only compare the paintings of Elisabeth and her family with Francisco Goya's portrait of the Spanish Queen Maria Louisa in *The Family of Charles IV* (1800), in which she stood for the family portrait, unselfconsciously, blemishes and all.

Hungarian scholars and museum curators concede *Erzsébet Királyné* (Queen Elisabeth) has been the most popular figure in modern Hungarian history.[6] "Elisabeth" or "Queen Elisabeth" boulevards, plazas, and districts are found not only in Budapest but throughout Hungary, including village roads, small town thoroughfares, and country markets. Ordinary people lived and worked on Elisabeth streets or partied in Queen Elisabeth grand hotels, restaurants, and spas. Modern bridges, docks, and other symbols of progress were given her name, as well as a college for women, daycare centers, sanatoriums, and hospitals. Even prosaic grain mills and military barracks were named after her. The image of Elisabeth and Franz Joseph, husband and wife, were available to average people through memorabilia and inexpensive items for use or display in their homes (figure 6.1).

Her popularity began and developed in her lifetime, but given the ubiquity and exaggerations of the image, it is no wonder that historians eschew the hyperbole and romance that surrounds her. András Gerő scoffs at the kitsch and historically naive narrative encasing Elisabeth, although he concedes that Queen

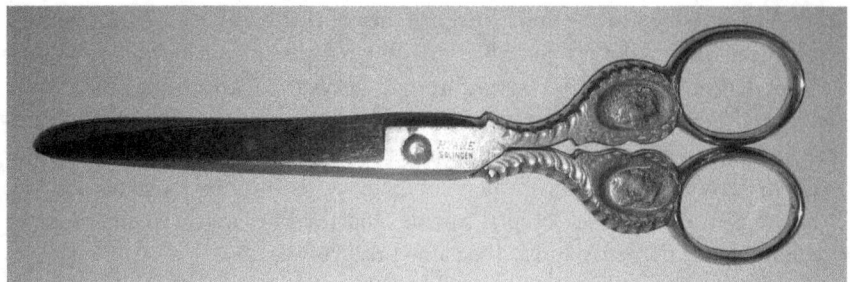

Figure 6.1. Jugendstil scissors decorated with portraits of Franz Joseph (bottom) and Elisabeth (top). Royal Palace of Gödöllő Museum.

Elisabeth "became the object of a national cult, which cherishes her memory and the faith it has invested in her to the present day."[7] Gerő emphasizes the limitations of Elisabeth's influence, which were simply advisory, and in any case only a form of stopgap in the void left by her unsympathetic and utterly uncharismatic husband, the occupier of Hungary.[8] In Gerő's biography of Franz Joseph, he takes a more Kossuthite position which downplays the benefits of Dualism to Hungary.

Elisabeth's couture itself connotes the age, both its romance and tight lacing.[9] Her beauty was memorialized in Franz Winterhalter's portraits, particularly a set of three in 1864, which were then reproduced across the monarchy in busts and statues. The image of Elisabeth dressed in a white gown with bare shoulders and stars studded in her long braided hair reappeared recently, worn by Emmy Rossum, in the movie "Phantom of the Opera." After the Monarchy fell, Elisabeth became a film icon. Carla Nelsen played her in a silent film of 1920. Charles Boyer played her doomed son with Wagnerian excess in the French hit *Mayerling* in 1936. The German exile Max Ophuls completed *De Mayerling á Sarajevo* just before the Wehrmacht arrived in 1940. He placed Elisabeth's fate in a chain of Habsburg melodramas resulting in World War I and spawning Nazism. Ava Gardner depicted Elisabeth as aloof and detached in Hollywood's remake of *Mayerling* in 1968, with Omar Sharif as Rudolf and James Mason as Franz Joseph.

Within Austria, Elisabeth seems to have become more comprehensible to the Viennese only in the 1920s. She seemed prophetic in her "forebodings" and solitude. In the disjointed First Republic, Elisabeth enjoyed a "posthumous homage."[10] For the shell-shocked and guilt-ridden Austrians of the early Second Republic, thoughts of Elisabeth were a soothing dalliance in that void between doom and the better world of yesteryear. In *Sissi*, a film trilogy produced in the mid 1950s, she was a talisman of a wholesome normality. During the Christmas season, the soap opera continues to be replayed endlessly on Central European television, now in a restored and colorized version. The series begins as an almost perfect love story, and with its perky young emperor's bride, remains happy romantic fare. It was love at first sight that moved Emperor Franz Joseph to marry Sissi, a free-spirited fifteen-year-old. Catapulted into the role of empress at sixteen, she handled herself with intelligence and uncommon maturity. Stunning in her crinolines, born the year Queen Victoria ascended to the throne in Britain, Elisabeth found herself emotionally trapped by the staid court and political intrigue in Vienna. The death of her first child to measles in Hungary and the defeat of the monarchy to Prussia brought anguish and crisis. The trilogy ended with Elisabeth at the top of her game, as the star—Queen of Hungary, reconciling her country and her marriage, and bearing her Hungarian child, her favorite, Marie Valerie, in 1868. Elisabeth was played by Romy Schneider, who would complain later that the Sissi image stuck to her like porridge.[11] The filmmaker Ruth Beckermann gives a good sense of the family oriented Sissi trilogy's impact when she recalls watching it with her mother. Both mother and daughter were transfixed by the poignant melodrama, cozy in their home, while Elisabeth was tightly laced into her crinolines and surrounded by old furniture, none of which had been inherited.[12]

Sissi and the Austrian past have continued to appeal to PG audiences excluded from the more explicit adult fare of German language film. The Sissi industry has spanned the generations. *Sissi* morphed into a PG Disney-like princess in a Hungarian full length cartoon, a children's video game, as well as Sissi Barbie dolls available in both run-of-the-mill blonde and collector brunette models. Elisabeth made a cult of her hair, which was dark blond but dyed chestnut and reached to her toes. Many at the time tried to copy her, but few could grow their hair that long, and lacked the leisure and skilled hairdressers to do so successfully. Stories occasionally appeared in the serious press about ladies whose dye jobs went badly wrong.[13] Today, cafés, apricot liqueurs, hotels, and travel agencies sport Elisabeth's name.

Of her three major public roles—Bavarian Duchess, Austrian Empress, Hungarian Queen—the Bavarian was the least political. The Bavarian Sissi Museum is housed in the Center for Unusual Museums, alongside museums for chamber pots, scents, and Easter bunnies. The image of a flighty woman, lonely, and tangential to politics has meshed well in the tourist trade with the flamboyant and isolated castle of her Wittelsbach cousin, Ludwig II. A Sissi museum opened in the imperial palace (Hofburg) in Vienna in 2004, gathering the famous paintings of the empress and the objects of her official station, such as the imperial china, silver, and glassware. The museum underscores her personal beauty, the opulence of court life, and her celebrity role, granting audiences to her people.

The Gödöllő hunting lodge and palace, thirty miles east of Budapest, where Elisabeth spent much of her time, fell into terrible disrepair under Communism when it served as a nursing home for the elderly. Now restored, it is a museum and showcase for a summer concert series, and there are ambitious plans to rebuild the stable areas as well. In Hungary, Sissi kitsch is consumed less widely, reserved more exclusively for tourist spots and souvenirs. Yet, on a different level, appreciation of Elisabeth remains high, higher than in the German-speaking world.[14] Hungary has been remembered as the site of her most decisive political act and genuine personal comfort. Elisabeth visited Hungary at least once a year between

1868 and 1897, usually staying at her hunting lodge in Gödöllő in the fall and traveling to Budapest when duty called.[15] The Gödöllő estate provided Sissi with grounds of her own, to paraphrase Virginia Woolf. She longed for a getaway, a place to ride her horses in peace, and to socialize on her own terms. Hungary afforded Elisabeth that retreat. Her youngest daughter Maria Valerie was primarily raised in Gödöllő; the family sometimes celebrated Elisabeth's birthday on December 24 and the Christmas and New Year holidays there. As aches and pains began to plague Elisabeth, the avid horseback rider turned to fencing. Instead of lengthy walks in the forest, she sought warmer, new exotic climates, and built a palace on Corfu.

Elisabeth's appeal in her lifetime was never that of a vacuous Barbie doll. She identified with Heinrich Heine, emulated his style and sentiments in her own poetry, read Hungarian literature widely and sought out the literary intelligentsia of Hungary. She seldom smiled for the camera lens or the painter's brush. She was a profoundly melancholy person, and it was empathy for her sadness that in large part drew Hungarians toward her. The reexamination of gender roles has stimulated new images of the unhappy Elisabeth. In Ruth Beckermann's 1999 film, *A fleeting Passage to the Orient,* Beckermann took advantage of the familiarity of Elisabeth's image, and used it as a vehicle for examining the angst of the modern woman. By following the incognito travels of the cosmopolitan Empress of Austria to Egypt, Beckerman explored her own complicated identity as a postwar Austrian Jewess. Her Elisabeth transcended the usual caricature of Elisabeth as marginalized, neurotic, willful, self-absorbed, and much too anxious about weight and looks, or bedeviled by her sharp intellect. Beckermann tapped into the role of the empress "as central to an affirmative postwar Austrian identity" in order to escape the one-dimensional notions of Austrian national identity.[16]

As a day-to-day political actor, Elisabeth was only an erratic and occasional player; yet, she did at least once a decade become a lightening rod, magnetizing attention and effecting historic events. In the Hungarian arena, Elisabeth had a four-fold political role: first, in helping to defuse the Hungarian martyrology of revolutionary defeat in the 1850s; second, in fashioning Dualism between 1863 and 1867; third, as a justifying icon of the Compromise in representing liberal values, espousing greater rights for women, sympathy for Jews, and skepticism about the monarchy's future. Finally, she has come to symbolize a martyrdom that is personal, familial, but also one identified with the fall of the Kingdom of St. Stephen and Hungary's sense of having lost its way in the twentieth century.

1. The Imperial Tour of Hungary in 1857

While in Germany the defeated revolution of 1848 would be remembered as "the crazy year"—the year the people went mad—in Hungary it would remain the touchstone of radical and national politics. Hungary experienced a form of "total revolution" in 1848, e.g., the creation of a constitutional and parliamentary system, and the abolition of serfdom. In the War of Independence, Habsburg armies were expelled for almost a year before Russian intervention in the east and a resurgent Austrian counter-revolution in the west extinguished the revolution and scattered the revolutionaries. Under the state of siege, Hungarian men were under suspicion. While it was politic for revolutionaries to lay low and to "manly" bear wounds, women could still publicly exhibit the nation's suffering, albeit in a restrained or indirect fashion. The brief imprisonment of revolutionary leader Lajos Kossuth's mother and sister, and the arrest, mistreatment, and flogging of activist women in the immediate aftermath of the defeat incurred notoriety and indignation throughout Europe and America. In the 1850s, the crinoline clothed matron in the countryside came into her own with her quasi-secret cult of the disappointed revolution, or the lost cause. Hungarian women became the key purveyors of a new martyrology of revolutionary defeat. They were freer to do so than their male counterparts and were effective in projecting a new politics of pain. In one district, peasant women stitched the border pattern of the illegal Kossuth bank notes into their traditional costumes.[17] Legal reprisals followed with the enforcing of an ever-stricter dress code.

In this restricted atmosphere, the imperial romance and marriage of 1854 received due attention in the Hungarian press. The arrival in Austria of the "German woman" and mother-to-be of the Monarchy was noted.[18] Blue-and-white Bavarian flags fluttered alongside the imperial double eagle on the ship and dock. The emperor did announce, as was customary, a package of political amnesties in honor of his marriage, and rumors credited pressure from Elisabeth. Word spread that in Bavaria she had had a Hungarian teacher, János Majláth, who introduced her to the storybook world of Hungarian fiction and acquainted her with Hungary's unhappy past.

However, it was not until the imperial couple's tour three years later that Elisabeth made her public mark in Hungary. On 4 May 1857, the imperial couple sailed down the Danube to the twin cities of Pest and Buda. Amidst a sea of red and white flags, Franz Joseph alighted once again as "Lieutenant Red Legs," wearing military whites with a red stripe down the leg rather than a Hungarian uniform. However, the sight of Elisabeth with a brilliant diadem and dress adorned in Hungarian red, white, and green colors generated wild enthusiasm.[19] "I am pleased that once again I could come here and show the empress the nice fatherland," Franz Joseph replied to the mayor's official welcome. The emperor sought to deflect the continuing resentment toward him onto the hopeful signs of an improving standard of living and his new consort, Elisabeth. After guilds and officials greeted the sovereign, a 150 man banderium of the medieval tribes of Jasygen and Cuman in fur robes paraded on horses fitted with white-and-blue cockades.[20] On this tour, several hundred thousand Hungarians came out to see the sovereigns, and Elisabeth was the central attraction.[21]

When the imperial couple visited the Óbuda ship works, the sight of Elisabeth adorned in red, white, and green colors generated genuine enthusiasm as they walked through a cordon of 2,600 workers.[22] In their honor, Ferenc Erkel produced an opera called "St. Elisabeth." The magnates appeared *en masse* in the full brilliance of their national costumes, and Elisabeth and Franz Joseph were greeted with an extended ovation. The theater was "national ground" where Hungarian, not German, was the language of the hour. Franz Joseph also appeared for a public occasion in a Hussar uniform next to Elisabeth in attire befitting a Hungarian lady (see figure 6.2).[23] The sovereign couple also visited a ball in the German theater attended by the bureaucracy and the German and Jewish middle class.[24]

Figure 6.2. Elisabeth in Hungarian folk dress. Royal Palace of Gödöllő Museum.

The imperial couple's appearance at such events could legitimize a variety of social shifts already underway. In particular, by wearing western fashion that was designed with a Hungarian flare, Elisabeth reflected and anticipated the politicization of fashion in Hungary. She was one of the beauties of her age, with luscious long hair and an extraordinary figure—a sixteen-inch waist, thin but relatively tall, and full figured. She was corseted and poured into her dresses, which were made of mounds of fabric, but were sewn with no folds in order to accentuate her waistline. After almost a decade of enforced isolation, Hungarian fashion was poised to take notice. That year, the first women's fashion store opened on Pest's Váci Street. No longer was the promenade just for the regime's supporters (those who were "*gutgesinnt*"), who spoke German and dressed in "German attire." Contemporaries described Váci Street as "an open salon where everyone can step in without an entry card or differences in rank."[25] Elisabeth's influence was felt most directly on the magnates, bureaucrats, and merchants, for whom it would become fashionable, even pragmatic, to incorporate a Hungarian idiom into their dress and speech. During the carnival season of 1857, Pest law students made their toilet an overt nationalist statement. Fashion statements became a substitute form of politics.

Hungarian fashion was an artful construction rather far from the "true genre figures" it imitated.[26] Commerce from and to the capital led to a modified and homogenized folk style, which could be embraced by the urban classes and Hungarian elites as symbols of national identity. By wearing nationally inspired gowns, the empress gave an added elegance and legitimacy to this fashion trend. With the abolishment of serfdom and increasing prosperity, Hungarian peasants were in the mood to experiment. Costumes became more colorful and they began integrating new materials and products brought in by cheaper transportation and railroad lines. Ideas and designs were borrowed from other villages, and village products were marketed almost as trademark goods to urban dwellers. Through this flow from one village to another and from urban to rural areas a new national folk culture would be constructed.[27] Between 1859 and 1861, almost the whole country would dress in Hungarian national costumes for Carnival, and then also for daily wear. Women wore red, white, and green, donned Hungarian hats and promenaded with partners who wore traditional embroidered cloaks and pants, with feathers in their hats.[28]

Tragedy struck on the last leg of the 1857 tour when Elisabeth and Franz Joseph's two-year-old daughter, Princess Sophie, came down with the measles and died. The image of the empress distraught and in tears, rushing with her husband back from Debrecen to her daughter in Buda touched a population in which resentment at defeat and occupation in 1849 remained keen.[29] On this issue the official press was informative, and Hungarians were swept up in the Habsburg family tragedy. The public did not know the full despair of the mother who had brought her sickly child to Buda despite her doctor's warning and her mother-in-law's pleas. However, in this second personal drama in Franz Joseph's tenure (the 1853 assassination attempt by an Hungarian tailor being the first), the Hungarian public could identify with the couple's grief and felt part of the genuine family drama.[30]

Elisabeth was disconsolate and melancholy. Mourning became public when the imperial couple went on a pilgrimage to the Mariazell shrine in Styria, near the Hungarian border. By appending a pilgrimage to the funeral rite, the sovereigns dramatized the tragedy and accentuated the pious nature of the dynasty. A pilgrimage of thirty thousand Hungarians to Mariazell followed. To a degree that most Hungarians, certainly Hungarian nationalists, were unwilling to admit, the tour of 1857 built some new connections with the public. This had not been like the colorless tour undertaken by Franz Joseph in 1852, with its Potemkin village crowds. The conscripted nature of Franz Joseph's reception five years before had underscored his unpopularity with the magnates and the indifference of the public. Although real concessions were still not forthcoming in 1857, Elisabeth's presence had inserted something more genuine into the interaction between the sovereign and his subjects. In the midst of neoabsolutism, a new celebrity monarchism was being born. This was also part of a European trend, for which the glamorous Bonapartist Empress Eugénie had set the tone in the 1850s. The British Queen Victoria's melodramatic, unrelenting public mourning for Prince Albert diverted public interest further onto both Elisabeth and Eugénie. The mixture of allure and a problematic persona drew public attention toward Elisabeth, who eventually upstaged Eugénie.[31]

The tour of 1857 had a beautiful, bereaved heroine. Thoughts of a reconciled future began to attach itself to Elisabeth. The lore around Elisabeth credits her with more power than she really held as Queen, but it is accurate in emphasizing Elisabeth's mediating role between Hungarian political culture and the court. The tour hinted at a public dynamic which was bringing the ruling house and the public closer together. In Hungary, the stiff and wary greetings were receding, unlike in Italy where the reception in 1856/57 remained cold and testy. The Habsburg's Italian domains would soon secede and become absorbed into an Italian nation-state. Hungary was physically fully within the boundaries of the monarchy, and although the people were disgruntled, they had nowhere else to go.

2. Elisabeth's Appeal

Shattered by guilt about the death of her child, the rupture in Elisabeth's marriage came out into the open when she fled to Madeira after Austria's defeat in Italy in 1859. Elisabeth seemed to have withdrawn completely, virtually abandoning the role of empress. But when Hungarian national politics revived and produced a deadlock between the court and the Hungarian moderates, she returned, and became active, focused, and single-minded. She surprised the court in 1863 by taking up the study of Hungarian, and amazed those at court even more by actually learning it. She helped stampede Hungarian Habsburg bureaucrats and society into learning the language and engaging its culture, reversing a decade of

Germanization.³² Furthermore, she made known her regret at past repression, apologized for the execution of the Arad martyrs (thirteen Hungarian revolutionaries shot in 1849), and departed on a much publicized pilgrimage to pray for reconciliation with Hungary. Between 1863 and 1868, Elisabeth allowed her own opinions to be projected onto the political world. Archduchess Sophia, the mother-in-law she despised, had championed the Czechs and distrusted the Hungarians; Elisabeth reversed the equation.

In the summer of 1865, Elisabeth presented Franz Joseph with a "your-mother-or-me" ultimatum. She resented that her mother-in-law, who was also her aunt, had assumed control of raising Elisabeth's children. Elisabeth mobilized herself around the issue of Rudolf's "future," insisting that his tutor be dismissed and that the emperor sign a statement giving her "complete autonomy in everything which concerns my children," and demanding that "all matters which affect me personally will be determined solely by me."³³ At the same time, Elisabeth became allowed herself to be seen as a linchpin of Hungarian strategy behind the scenes. Elisabeth's study of Hungarian intensified when Ida Ferenczy entered her entourage in the fall of 1864; she served as a conduit between Elisabeth and Hungarian politicians and literati.³⁴ Ferenczy remained Elisabeth's loyal assistant throughout her life and cemented Elisabeth's connection to Hungarian culture. Her Magyarophilia turned into a Magyaromania.³⁵ By the following year, she purged her retinue of all those who could not speak Hungarian. At a formal dinner, she attracted attention with the statement that, "if the emperor's cause goes badly in Italy it pains me, but if it goes badly in Hungary, it is death to me."³⁶

On 8 January 1866, accompanied by her eight Hungarian ladies-in-waiting, Elisabeth formally received a large Hungarian deputation in Vienna. The Prince Primate Scitovszky, as leader of the national delegation, praised Elisabeth for "learning our language and the hours of work and attention involved. It ties the nation to the throne with a tighter cord."³⁷ He invited her to visit Buda-Pest, to which Elisabeth replied in Magyar that she had no "dearer wish than to return to that beautiful city."³⁸ She lingered with her guests and had her first meeting with Count Gyula Andrássy. Elisabeth cultivated the interest shown toward her by the dashing, dark Andrássy, who would for his part call Elisabeth "our lovely Providence." Something clicked between them, making it easier for Andrássy to serve as Elisabeth's advisor and confidant in this critical year, but also well beyond, as friend and political ally. Andrássy moved from tainted supporter of the defeated revolution to first prime minister of Hungary under Dualism and then imperial foreign minister.³⁹

With war approaching, Franz Joseph needed to bolster support and therefore made a trip to Hungary with Elisabeth. The "hereditary royal couple"—to use the Hungarian phrase of the moment—arrived in Buda-Pest on 29 January 1866. During this visit, she confirmed Hungarian impressions of her partisanship and of her public role as Hungary's advocate. On February 1, Elisabeth addressed the parliament in flawless, and seemingly spontaneous, Magyar, thanking the Hungarians for their enthusiastic reception.⁴⁰ At the court ball that evening, Elisabeth demurred that she did not understand politics, to which the novelist Mór Jókai responded, "The highest politics is to win a country's heart, and you certainly understand that."[41] The city was still abuzz three days later in praise of her pronunciation and artful use of the language.[42] "Not in three hundred years" had a Hungarian queen spoken the language, the press proclaimed.[43] Elisabeth was alternately identified with earlier Queen Elisabeths of Hungary or St. Elisabeth of the thirteenth century. She promoted the latter, and Franz Liszt composed a "St. Elisabeth Oratorio," which he conducted for the Pest Summer Music Festival of 1865. This embellished the allusion with musical genius, added an air of serendipity, and brought further attention to the queen in popular culture. The composer, hitherto only nominally Hungarian—practically German—was discovering his Magyar roots.[44]

Elisabeth, as a heroine, induced a cultural change only possible "by the intervention of someone of such a high position, where power, fame, and good nature intersected."[45] Women in Buda's inner circle were suddenly expected "to speak in their mother tongue," the press reported.[46] Elisabeth could be ruthless in her insistence that Hungarian be spoken within Hungary. During a visit to a convent school, Elisabeth spoke in Hungarian to the Mother Superior, who was Italian and did not understand her. The empress retorted in her coldest and haughtiest manner that next time she expected to be answered in Magyar. True to her word Elisabeth returned, only to find that the Mother Superior had taken to her bed with a sudden illness. Undaunted, the empress went to the Mother Superior's room, said something in Hungarian, which the woman did not understand, and left abruptly. Shortly afterward, the unfortunate woman resigned her post.[47]

"The ice is breaking. We are full of hope," wrote Nándor Zichy in February 1866.[48] A month later, he jotted down in his diary that "time is flying, and we're just bustling, preparing, listening to everything."[49] "Ferenc Deák and the emperor are now like two men standing at a door, each wanting to thrust the other through, so as not to be the first to step into unfamiliar territory."[50] Elisabeth's last words on the train platform after her six week Pest visit were, "I hope soon to return to my dear, dear Hungary."[51]

During the 1866 Austro-Prussian War, Franz Joseph turned to Elisabeth for help. It would be the one and only time in Franz Joseph's long reign when he permitted his wife so much political sway. Elisabeth's great achievement in these critical months was to upstage Lajos Kossuth, who was in exile in Italy.[52] Kossuth's wartime proclamation of 23 June 1866 calling for the overthrow of the monarchy concluded with the words, "I embody a principle called 1849." Hungary had been isolated then, he said, but now, as an ally of Prussia, "we are neither alone nor abandoned," and will reap the fruits of Hungarian efforts in 1849.[53] However, Elisabeth countered Kossuth's invocation of 1849 by in effect reenacting the year 1740, when Maria Theresia called upon the Hungarians to save the monarchy in its struggle against Prussia.

"The burning desire for revenge against Prussia, the uncertainty of the international situation, the untenableness of the Hungarian conditions, and the effective intervention of Empress Elizabeth (called the 'beautiful Providence' by the Magyars), in favor of the Magyar standpoint were victorious over the resistance of the Emperor," even Oscar Jászi later wrote, and caused Franz Joseph to accept "that whole program against which he carried on a bloody war and pressed during two decades ..."[54] It was a curious circumstance: the anti-liberal Prussian Minister President, Otto von Bismarck, was the ally of the liberal revolutionary Kossuth, while the compromisers of the Deák camp opposed Bismarck and Kossuth in the name of liberal constitutionalism. The speed of Prussian victory brought the undoing of Kossuth's insurrection fantasy. The Hungarian Legion of 1,500 men recruited from captured Hungarian soldiers was never employed in the war. The 1849 option ended in a fiasco.

Franz Joseph dispatched Elisabeth to Buda after the defeat at Sadowa (Königgrätz) on 3 July 1866 concluded the Austro-Prussian War: "Take the children to Buda and be my advocate there. Hold the people in check as best as you can, and we shall find a way."[55] Only Ida Ferenczy accompanied her and the children. The principal architects of Dualism, Deák and Andrássy, were there to greet her, and the six kilometer drive from the station to the castle of Buda was triumphal.[56] Elisabeth was received in Pest on July 10 by tens of thousands of cheering people.

One of Elisabeth's duties was to visit hospitals. Franz Joseph wrote: "The poor soldiers are certainly very consoled that you come to the hospital," and he inquired whether there were enough nurses for the wounded. On September 5, while Elisabeth visited the military hospital in the converted stables of the Gödöllő estate, she was charmed by the castle, its vast forest, and its equestrian potential. She toured the town of about "fifty-two houses," by her estimate. Franz Joseph warned her, "Don't look at the palace as if you want to buy it, at the moment we don't have the money ..."[57]

Elisabeth played a critical role in bringing about the reconciliation between Hungary and the Monarchy. She was in constant communication with Andrássy, in meetings, correspondence, and through intermediaries.[58] He would come to understand her inferences in poetry, responding in verse himself.[59] Ensconced in Buda, she bombarded Vienna with her solution: appoint Andrássy Minister of Foreign Affairs and thereby keep Hungary attached to the Monarchy. Archduchess Sophia was horrified, viewing Dualism as rewarding the disloyal, sacrificing the interests of the loyal, and violating tradition, especially since no Habsburg had ever been crowned in Hungary without also being crowned in Bohemia. Elisabeth remained deaf to the pleas from Prague, and the Czechs were placed in the former role of the Hungarians as the slighted and embittered opponents of the status quo. Franz Joseph chided Elisabeth for her "exclusively Hungarian point of view," which he felt "slight[ed] those lands which have endured unspeakable sufferings with steadfast fidelity." She responded by begging him "in Rudolf's name not to lose this one chance at the last moment." She insisted that he see Andrássy,[60] informing him that "Andrássy is inclined at this moment, when shipwreck threatens the state, to do anything in his power to save it. Whatever he has, his intellect, national influence he places at your feet."[61]

Implicit here is that Andrássy was to fight the internal struggle to disarm the Kossuthite position within Hungary. Hungary would be required to display more than simple fealty; the compromise was to forge a dual loyalty to the emperor-king and nation. Hungarians were never all united in one opinion, but this compromise did lead to a national consensus in favor of Hungarian identity and Habsburg loyalty, both of which would develop popular forms and coexist simultaneously in official and popular culture, as well as on the personal level. The Hungarian public would credit every concession wrested from Franz Joseph to Elisabeth's influence, just as every setback was blamed on her mother-in-law.

Once Franz Joseph made the decision for an agreement, he called Ferenc Deák to Vienna for secret negotiations and telegrammed Elisabeth to suspend further negotiations with Andrássy.[62] When Elisabeth returned to Vienna in the fall, she responded to the court's hostility to her Hungarian partisanship by adding five more Magyar ladies-in-waiting to her retinue and defiantly engaging in her service the liberal Hungarian Jewish journalist Max Falk,[63] who had been arrested in Vienna for a censorship violation.[64] In Hungary, each political party developed its own press organ, and through Falk, Elisabeth was championed by the *Pester Lloyd*, the preeminent mainstream Hungarian daily. It was published in German and would for decades reflect Falk's assimilationist stance. Elisabeth's celebrity was thus tied to the possibilities of the newspaper age.

During the year and a half between her visit to Pest in early 1866 and coronation day, 8 June 1867, Elisabeth was central to the pageantry of Compromise. Through her shone the new, human face of Habsburg royalty. Citizens clamored for a glimpse of her. For military parades, Elisabeth shed the lace frills and rode alongside her spouse. Her "Amazon attire" (riding garb) was "simple and tasteful," the *Pester Lloyd* reported. An avid equestrian, Elisabeth was pleased at the opportunity to ride, since in Vienna she was expected to attend such events in a carriage. When rumors spread in Buda-Pest that she could be seen riding her horse in the City Park, the carriage traffic became snarled.[65] The image of the empress as equestrian, skilled and spirited, met with rapturous public approval. (A later tale of 1876 has a stag wandering out of the City Park onto an elegant thoroughfare and running amok in the commercial stalls in front of the Opera House. The animal was pursued and killed by a hunting group led by Queen Elisabeth).[66]

No day seemed to pass without some new article on Elisabeth. "In the pleasing figure, royal dignity and feminine appeal are in exceptionally dignified harmony."[67] Dubbed Hungary's "guardian angel," she was even credited by much of the populace as the guardian of feminine virtues.[68] Preparations for the coronation were presented to the public in the language of a drawn out courtship, a pseudo-romance highlighting Elisabeth and Count Andrássy. In so far as dualism was acted out as a marriage, the Hungarians played the role of the wife, and Elisabeth represented Hungary's role in the unique personal union which was established. Family tragedy did hang over the event when Franz Joseph's brother, Emperor Maximilian of Mexico, was executed only five days before the coronation, but the ceremonies went ahead as planned.

Eighteen days before the coronation, Kossuth published his "Cassandra Letter," condemning the Compromise as a surrender of national independence. "Tomorrow we have the coronation," the liberal József Eötvös wrote in his diary. "The people will try out whether they can like the sovereign. That they learn this is much more important than any ceremony."[69] Three aspects of this ceremony were unique. It was the first of its kind to be held in Buda-Pest, and the first to acquire a true crowd dimension; it was also the one and only time the queen was crowned in the same ceremony as the king. So while the coronation might have appeared to be an archaic rite and great effort was made to conform meticulously to tradition, the event's novel features were carefully designed to appeal to its various publics. The crowning of the queen without a separate ceremony more closely mimicked a wedding ritual. Queens had customarily been crowned apart from the central ceremony, often the following day, but Franz Joseph made the ceremonial request that his queen be crowned before the assembled officials. Count Andrássy was named acting palatine and crowned the king. The three principals were all on the coronation dais at the same time. Elisabeth was anointed by the Primate of Hungary, handed the staff and orb, and then her shoulder was grazed by the crown (figure 6.2).

Elisabeth wrote Rudolph that she had received "a really big cheer," which was so deafening that the sound almost blew the roofs off the houses, and that she was buried under flowers.[70] The literature on Elisabeth describes this as her crowning moment; she is radiant in her success.[71] A "coronation child" was subsequently borne by the thirty-one-year-old queen on 22 April 1868 in Buda. The popular press followed the pregnancy closely, speculating about the future dynastic heir. Would it be a boy, named István, after the first king of Hungary?[72] Speculation as to a possible cadet line of Hungarian kings being established through this child ended when she was born a healthy girl, Marie Valerie. In honor of the coronation, the Hungarian parliament purchased the estate at Gödöllő for 1,840,000 forints and presented it to the royal couple. Here, in Hungary, Elisabeth could play her role as a free spirit: riding her horses, thrilling in the peasant bareback races at the lodge in Gödöllő, and socializing there with gallant magnates on the hunt, or imbibing literature with a sharp political bite. Elisabeth liked being in Gödöllő, and she arranged a nursemaid for her baby and tutors for the two older children there. From her home base at Gödöllő, she traveled up to Buda about every other day to take care of business. In 1869, for example, Elisabeth spent more than 130 days in Buda and Gödöllő. Gödöllő was Marie Valerie's primary home; she played with the local children and spoke Hungarian as her first language.[73]

Among historians, dismissing Elisabeth as simply a neurotic recluse has run hand in hand with missing the significance of the Coronation of 1867 and the Compromise and Dualist system it sanctioned. The Compromise and Coronation of 1867 completed a shift in Hungarian loyalty, after which Franz Joseph and Elisabeth were commonly referred to in Hungary as "King" and "Queen." It is simply incorrect to assume that Franz Joseph expected to be referred to as emperor everywhere in the Monarchy. The phrase "Emperor and King" could be used in Hungary for formal occasions, but by speaking of the sovereign as "our king," Hungarian patriotism was at one with imperial loyalty. Kossuth and some of his supporters remained dogged in their opposition, but the alliance between the Hungarian political elite and the dynasty had been reinvigorated.

The construction of a new state in 1867, indeed a new concept of a state, gained public manifestation in festivity. The dualist state drew upon the arcane rituals of Habsburg tradition and nineteenth-century crowd politics. The subsuming of multiple loyalties into the definition of identity as a Magyar and a Habsburg subject was novel. Out of defeat—first Hungarian in 1849, then dynastic and Kossuthite in 1866—a chastened compromise was forged, in which multiple loyalties coexisted, including that of Magyar; Habsburg subject; local identification to place; profession; and religion. Elisabeth and her son Rudolph aligned with the liberal forces in Hungary, which were open to Jewish emancipation and assimilation; to economic free trade and urban growth. Elisabeth's poetic sensibility relished the potentials of the intelligentsia and education. Hungarian liberals would dominate Hungarian parliamentary politics throughout her lifetime, though with lessening vitality.

Nevertheless, this dynastic-national-liberal alliance shortchanged other nationalities within the monarchy. What was seen as compensatory from the Hungarian perspective, was understood as exclusionary by Czechs, Croats, Romanians, Serbs, and Slovaks, all of whom protested at the outcome. Hungarian liberalism, with its literacy campaign in Magyar and its promise of widening suffrage rights only to the educated, blindsided the system to the disenfranchisement of the kingdom's minorities—Slovaks, Romanians, Croats, etc.—who remained dissatisfied. The disaffection the Compromise caused amongst the other nationalities would eventually come to haunt the system.

3. The Veiled Icon

After two decades of demystifying monarchy, Hungarian nationalists found themselves ready to venerate it. An appearance by the sovereign couple, however brief and rare, would inevitably produce tremendous excitement. The legitimating crowd had become a participant, separating itself from the principles of its erstwhile leader, Kossuth, although without abandoning the myth of 1848. Ferenc Deák, the architect of the legal arrangements of the Compromise, moved awkwardly into the role of parliamentary leader. He was a private, unostentatious man who had shunned the excesses of revolution and nationalist crowd politics. Incorruptible himself, he was unable to corral the greed of his followers once in power. Queen Elisabeth mourned Deák's death in 1876. Kossuth, the committed antidynast and Deák's political opponent, sent an open letter praising what "Queen Elisabeth accomplished. I respect her for her gentle, noble spirit."[74] The lithograph by Mihály Zichy of Elisabeth kneeling before Deák's casket in homage to the architect of Dualism would become a central image in the iconography of the monarchy, familiar to virtually every Hungarian. Despite the dark, somber colors, a hopefulness seemed to generate out of the lofty, albeit funereal theme.[75] In paying her respects to Deák, Elisabeth elevated the national grief into a legitimation of Dualism. Yet, for all practical purposes, it was also her last political act.

During the 1880s, Elisabeth added a new identity to her existing Bavarian, Austrian, and Hungarian one, that of the royal Philhellene. She assumed the antipolitical stance of the aristocratic radical, anticipating the extinction of monarchism, and affecting an aestheticism which reflected her sympathy both toward Heine and her unbalanced cousin King Ludwig II of Bavaria.[76] When Elisabeth's son, the liberal Crown Prince Rudolf, committed suicide on 30 January 1889, a requiem was held in Buda. The public lined the streets and squares from the railroad station to the Buda fortress to watch the king ride by in an open wagon. The queen, darkly veiled, followed in a closed carriage.[77] The following year Gyula Andrássy, her confidant of many years, died as well. She had become the *mater dolorosa* of liberal monarchism, convinced that the monarchy would not outlive her husband. She decided it was an "expensive ornament," which would soon enough bore the crowd and be discarded.[78] In her poetry, she was Titania, the fairy queen, with the admiring crowds as the jackasses of a midsummer night's dream. In truth, Elisabeth had long tired of public adulation. It was as a disappointed, withdrawn wife that she would live out the rest of her life. In 1892, the twenty-fifth anniversary of the Compromise, she did not come to Budapest for the festivities, such as they were. Hungarians were also not in the mood to celebrate, preoccupied by a government crisis over church/state relations.

As a recluse, Elisabeth generally faded from public view. She did appear, however, at the 1896 Millennium celebration. She previewed the exhibits in a hour-and-a-half tour, spending twenty minutes with Mihály Munkácsy's painting, *Ecce homo*. At Queen Elisabeth's death Kálmán Mikszáth, novelist and parliamentarian, recalled her appearance at the opening ceremony in the throne room in "When We Saw Her Last," which is worth quoting here at length:

> Sitting beside her husband, "everything she wore was black, everything, everything. Her hair was tied in Hungarian style with a black veil; the hairpins and jewels were all black. Just her face was white and immeasurably sad ... A Mater Dolorosa. Ah, it was still the old face, the one we remember from pleasant pictures: thin, regal lines, her bangs ... like silk drawn across her forehead," her hair "more beautiful than any crown ... The picture was the same, only it was as if it was in a fog ... There she sat quietly, almost emotionless, ... not a single movement or glance indicated her interest. She was like a white statue with her sad white face."
>
> The King focused on the speaker, "a word, a thought seems to capture his attention, but there is nothing written on the Queen's face. ... When her name is mentioned in the speech not even her eyebrows raise. They can speak of the statue to the statue.
>
> But at the sound of the Queen's name the cheering erupts. And what a cheer it is! as if an emotional torrent broke forth from their hearts. The yellow marble walls of the throne room shake. It was such an amazing sound, impossible to write down or explain. In this cheer there was a chant, the ringing of bells, the roar of the sea, ...

prompting the impassive sovereign's head to move. Slightly, almost imperceptibly she nodded thank you ... The burst of cheering got louder, and it did not want to stop for minutes. It raised upward and upward to the rafters and shook the rafters. The nation's great men and government leaders were not satisfied with the intoxicating screaming, they waved their hats and caps, and a thick forest appeared above the people's heads out of eagle and heron feathers; a cool breeze blew in the warm air. Few queens have ever had such a fan ...

"The white face suddenly started to blush ... more and more. At first it just wasn't so white anymore, then it was like fresh milk, as if it was tinged with pink, then it was red as life, completely red ... Next to King Franz Joseph sat a completely bright red Queen. It only lasted a minute. Her eyes opened wide, and the old brightness twinkled out of them. And out of the eyes, which once could laugh so that they were able to cheer up a sad country, a teardrop appeared. Hundreds and hundreds saw that dear little drop. This was the reciprocity. A happy country could cheer up the Queen. But it only lasted for a second. The regal woman lifted a lace handkerchief to her eye and wiped away the tear." The cheering stopped, the speaker resumed ... "In a moment a Queen in mourning once again was sitting next to the king, a Mater Dolorosa, pale, quiet, without feeling, like a white rigid statue, which reminded one of a sweet face."[79]

After the ceremony, the Queen left immediately and the king dutifully proceeded through the crowded park of pavilions. Franz Joseph's final persona as "Jóska" (Joey), the kindly, sorely tested grandfather had become iconic enough to fill the space, and he was always dutiful and predictable. This was to be the last major public festival in which the Compromise between the king and the Hungarian elite was publicly acclaimed, although Elisabeth actually did visit Hungary again the next year. She stopped in at Gerbaud's confectioners in Budapest with her older daughter Gizella, where they were serenaded by the Munczi Gypsy band.

The storm of affection for Elisabeth at the Millennium came from the national leaders—an age group which had grown up with the Elisabeth cult. Amongst them were magnates and bourgeoisie, politicians, and publicists, those who not only negotiated with the monarchy but also with the Hungarian public. The privileged and powerful grew as Budapest mushroomed; new nobles were inducted during rites that accompanied the Millennium celebrations and all such royal/imperial visits.

4. Martyrdom

On 10 September 1898, Elisabeth was fatally stabbed by an Italian anarchist on a public quay in the little resort of Territet on the shores of Lake Geneva. She did not realize the seriousness of her wound, because she was so tightly packed into her Victorian-style stays. Luigi Luccheni had planned to assassinate Henri, Duke of Orleans, but the French Pretender had already left Geneva. He then considered traveling to Rome to kill King Humbert, but he lacked the funds. The assassin finally chose an ineffectual imperial target, an estranged matron, because it was easy. Elisabeth's political star had passed with the death of her son, of

Andrássy before him, and with the general passing of a chastened liberal national Hungarian vision. Real grief was felt at the murder of the frail, unhappy recluse, but it was not a concern about the loss of her political leverage.[80]

Elisabeth's public sadness, dressed in mourning for her daughter, then her son, had given soul to her image. Now she herself became an object of the rituals of mourning. The empire grieved not only in the expected ways, with theaters and public places being closed, but also by declaring an official day of mourning on which all work was halted.[81] When the Hungarian delegation arrived in Vienna on the eve of the funeral, they discovered that on the wall of the Capuchin church it read, "*Elisabetha Imperatrix Austria.*" The banner "*Regina Hungariae*" was quickly added.[82] The conservative Prime Minister Dezső Bánffy declared, "never has a Queen been mourned more authentically and with greater grief than our admired Queen Elisabeth, who was not just our Queen, but our nation's sincerely beloved mother."[83]

Indeed, the Hungarians were widely acknowledged as the primary mourners for the queen, and their grief even spanned the Atlantic. The *New York Times* devoted a paragraph of her obituary to her "Happy Life in Hungary."[84] Two thousand mourners at the Hungarian Literary Society in New York City listened to Gypsy music and speeches recalling Elisabeth's good works and her image kneeling before Ferenc Deák's coffin. A Democratic Party politician, W. Bourke Cockran, impressed to orate on a woman he did not know, gave a speech which reflected the sentiments of the time. Elisabeth was linked to the martyrdom of Lincoln. Cockran conjectured that "the Empress died as she had lived, a useful death." Her death served as an awakening of the public to the dangers of a rising tide of terrorism.[85] Her death seemed to put governments and political leaders on notice and widened the fear of vulnerability. Anarchists had killed the Spanish prime minister a year before; the French president four years earlier. Within weeks of Elisabeth's death, a plot was uncovered to kill the German emperor; two years later the king of Italy would be murdered, and a year thereafter, President McKinley. Within six weeks of Elisabeth's murder, the International Anti-Anarchist Conference convened, which was attended by twenty-one nations and established the first mechanisms for formal coordination of international policing, out of which came Interpol.[86]

Within five days of Elisabeth's death, 100,000 forints had been collected in Hungary for a statue of the queen. "If her grave is in Vienna, she should have a statue in Budapest, the city which she so loved," a leading journal announced.[87] The fundraising campaign for her statue was the most successful in Hungarian history. By 1900, the collection totaled 1.5 million crowns and continued to grow.[88] At the time, the only other statue to a Habsburg in the Kingdom of St. Stephen was an equestrian statue of Maria Theresia, recently unveiled in Bratislava. Another was planned for the Palatine Joseph and erected in Pest in 1907.

Busts of Elisabeth proliferated within a year of her murder, but the competition for her statue in the capital moved along laboriously. While sculptors and architects were able to produce a coherent vision for a Kossuth Mausoleum, the same

Figure 6.3. In loving remembrance of our Queen, 1837–1896. Royal Palace of Gödöllő Museum.

architects produced conflicting and convoluted designs for the Elisabeth statue. For Kossuth, the cemetery park framed his mausoleum. The site chosen for Elisabeth, in contrast, was almost too spectacular. The monument was to fill a whole swathe of the Buda hillside, so as to be seen from across the Danube in Pest too. However, the difficulty of extolling a queen and empress on a grand scale while still capturing the young beauty and a sensitive, withdrawn woman seems to underscore the nuanced roles she had played. By 1913, designs were scaling down the edifice and incorporating landscaped park space on the Palace Hill site. World War I then intervened and the project ran aground.

Franz Joseph had begun as a villain, and Elisabeth may have been an expensive ornament; however, she added charm, softening the image of the monarchy. Her intellect and connection to Hungary's great men cemented a bond with Hungarians. By the outbreak of World War I, Hungarian patriotism could coalesce around the old king and country. Hungarians would, indeed, remain nostalgic adherents to the monarchy, retaining the illusion of a regency during the interwar period. After the fall of the Habsburg Monarchy in 1918, plans for the Elisabeth statue proceeded. An earlier, more restrained design was agreed upon. The statue was encased in a cupola, and Elisabeth was seated in mounds of crinoline. The sculptor, György Zala, was a safe choice. Placed on Oath Square on the Pest bridgehead of the Elisabeth bridge, it was dedicated with full pomp and ceremony by the regency of Miklós Horthy in 1932.

Elisabeth's statue was removed in 1953 and placed in storage. In 1986, as part of the revival of interest in the Dualist period during the final decade of "Goulash Communism," it was restored. Currently, the statue is located on the Buda side of the bridge in a square caught between a busy overpass and a highway. About ten feet away lies a desecrated Communist plaque, which commemorates an anti-fascist demonstration held in that square in 1944. Elisabeth's statue has shed its cupola, making it possible to see the Buda cliffs behind her, with St. Gellért anointing the city and, at the mountain top, the mammoth, yet soaring Statue of Liberation (one of the few Communist monuments that has withstood the hostile postmortem to a failed regime). While the Communist figure seems to hurl victory out across the Danube, Elisabeth stands stiff, erect, and unobtrusive in the park-like space where twenty-first century students may lounge on their way to and from the nearby University of Technology.

Figure 6.4, Embroidered wall hanging, artist unknown (approx. 3′ × 2′), expressing Hungarian war enthusiasm at the outbreak of World War I. From the top clockwise: "Long live the King! Long Live the Homeland!" "That's How They Should Return" "Our beloved King Franz Joseph I" "Magyars win!" (Wall hangings were a form of handiwork that commonly decorated kitchens in rural homes. They generally included well-known aphorisms extolling a clean house and light family scenes, although women sometimes stitched playful messages and more serious ones.)

In one of the more famous postmortems of the Monarchy, Oscar Jászi assessed the role of celebrity monarchism. In *The Dissolution of the Habsburg Monarchy* (1929), Jászi included both dynasticism and socialism among the centripetal forces which could pull the monarchy together. Jászi regrets the fall of the monarchy, but judged its artificiality as an impediment toward both the creation of an authentically democratic society and the heeding of socialist and ethnic voices. Jászi's assessment of the urgency of suffrage reform and the recognition of national minority rights was prophetic, but his own liberal party was ineffectual in its attempts to steer the mass demonstrations taking place between 1907 and 1912. Unlike the socialists, the Liberals lacked the party discipline to keep demonstrations from unraveling into crowd violence, and they lacked a charismatic or cult figure like Elisabeth to draw public attention. "The prestige of the imperial family was until the end more than a purely military or power position," Jászi conceded, and "it was based on very widely spread mass feelings in many more traditional parts of the monarchy under the influence of school and church." Jászi was impatient with the mystical, pre-modern nature of dynasty and took a critical view of Franz Joseph, who was so "rigidly isolated" that "the very idea of the people was for him ... devoid of life and blood." Yet, on balance, Jászi perhaps did not appreciate the link between the demonstrators' demands for political reform and their identification with "Uncle Jóska" or his martyred wife.[89]

Even at their most passive, a frozen Elisabeth or a stiff Franz Joseph without the leavening presence of his spouse, were at significant times able to elicit genuine emotion. One of the most curious of these moments was the unwelcome fortieth anniversary of the Compromise in 1907. With the reigning nationalist coalition adamantly blocking any suffrage reform, Franz Joseph expressed his reluctance to attend the jubilee. But when he arrived in Budapest on June 6, he experienced one of his most unusual receptions. Social democrats staged a monarchist demonstration, lining the streets awaiting their king, who was dangling the threat of expanded suffrage before the Hungarian government. Forty thousand workers formed a cordon along the route. There was no subject-like waving of hats; rather the public raised their hats politely and cried out "Long live universal secret suffrage!" They also cheered, "Long live our King!" and even "Long live our people's King!" The unperturbed Monarch saluted gratefully, but stiffly, over and over again as his carriage sped to the Buda Castle.[90] Later that year, the first Elisabeth Museum opened in the Buda Castle. It placed on display the famous Hungarian dress, as well as some of her favorite things, including her portraits and busts of Heine, thereby laying the foundations for the veneration that was to come.

Notes

* I wish to thank Ildikó Faludi and Margit Szabó of the Royal Palace of Gödöllő Museum for their generous assistance and for opening the storehouse of their collection for use in this article. The scissors and the cup shown in figures 6.1 and 6.3 were provided courtesy of the

Education and Cultural Ministry and are found in the collection of the Royal Palace of Gödöllő Museum.
1. Larry Lash, http://www.variety.com, Nov. 3, 2003.
2. Renate Daimler, *Diana & Sisi* (Vienna, 1998); Margit Szabó, *Sisi and Diana* (Budapest 2005). For a sociological study on Elisabeth in relation to the other female consorts of her time, see Lisa Fischer, *Schattenwürfe in die Zukunft. Kaiserin Elisabeth und die Frauen ihrer Zeit* (Vienna, 1998). See also Andrew Sinclair, *Death by Fame; A Life of Elisabeth, Empress of Austria* (NY, 1999), 194–207.
3. Elisabeth was nicknamed Sisi, but some of the popular films and dolls have used Sissi with a double 's'.
4. See Brigitte Hamann, *Elisabeth: Kaiserin wider Willen* (Vienna and Munich, 1982); Gyöngyvér Czére, *A koronás szépaszzony (Erzsébet magyar királyné)* (Budapest, 1989); Emil Niederhauser, *Merénylet Erzsébet királyné* (Budapest, 1985). See, for example, the last chapter of Captain Walter Wyatt, *Hungarian Celebrities* (London, 1871).
5. On celebrity monarchism and some of the other themes in this essay, see Alice Freifeld, *Nationalism and the Crowd in Liberal Hungary, 1848–1914* (Washington, D.C. and Baltimore, 2000), 153.
6. Antal Tóth, "Erzsébet királyné kultuszáról," in *Városi Helytörténeti Gyűjtemény Kiállítása Erzsébet Királyné Születésének 150. Évfordulójára* (Gödöllő, 1987), 3; Péter Polónyi, "Erzsébet királyné és Gödöllő," in *Kiállítása Erzsébet Királyné Születésének*, 11.
7. András Gerő, "A Hungarian Cult: Queen Elisabeth of Bavaria," in *Modern Hungarian Society in the Making, The Unfinished Experience* (Budapest, London, New York, 1995 (orig., *Magyar Polgárosodás*, [Budapest, 1993]), 236.
8. András Gerő, *Ferenc József, a magyarok királya* (Budapest, 1988), 109; English translation: *Emperor Francis Joseph, King of the Hungarians* (Boulder, CO and NY, 2001), 207.
9. Even Elisabeth's eating disorder is revisited and turned to an *absurdum*. Rossum apparently discovered that the tight lacing of the dress made it difficult to eat, so she ate only soft ice cream during the filming. Accessed at <http://www.uno.hu/news/story/154358>
10. Karl Tschuppik, *The Empress Elizabeth of Austria*, trans. Eric Sutton (New York, 1930), 263.
11. Schneider's short, tragic life only seemed to confirm the connection. From her beginnings as a Shirley Temple-like adolescent, proper and demure, Romy Schneider became a beauty, the German Marilyn Monroe, only to die from a heart attack and a broken heart after her son's premature death.
12. www.ruthbeckerman.com
13. Hamann, *Elisabeth*, 204; László Tarr, *A Délibábok Országa* (Budapest, 1976), 242.
14. Daniel Szabó shared with me a collection of contemporary commentary in newspapers and popular culture on Queen Elisabeth in Hungary, gathered for the preparation of the guidebook to the Gödöllő exhibition commemorating Queen Elisabeth's 150th birthday anniversary.
15. Ildikó Faludi, *A Gödöllő Kastély* (Gödöllő, 1998); Gerő, "A Hungarian Cult," 233.
16. See Christina Guenther, (unpublished paper) "Ruth Beckermann's *Ein flüchtiger Zug nach dem Orient,"* Panel: Travel, Exile, Immigration: Coordinates of Modern Homelessness. Visualizing Invisibility, German Studies Association annual meeting (Washington, D.C., 2003).
17. György Szabad, *Hungarian Political Trends Between the Revolution and the Compromise (1849–1867)* (Budapest, 1977), 63.
18. *Budapesti Hirlap,* 25 April 1854.
19. *Pester Lloyd,* 8 May 1857.
20. *Pester Lloyd,* 5 May 1857.
21. *Pester Lloyd,* 8 May 1857.
22. *Pester Lloyd,* 8 May 1857.
23. Walter Rogge, *Österreich von Világos bis zur Gegenwart* (Leipzig, 1872), vol. 1, 482.
24. Rogge, *Österreich*, vol. 1, 482–483. On the German theater, see Wolfgang Binal, *Deutschsprachiges Theater in Budapest* (Vienna, 1972).

25. Károly Vadnai cited in Láslzo Tarr, *A régi Váci Utca regényes krónikája* (Budapest, 1984), 13.
26. Ibid.
27. See Tamás Hofer, "Peasant Culture and Urban Culture in the Period of Modernization. Delineation of a Problem Area Based on Data from Hungary," in *The Peasant and the City in Eastern Europe. Interpenetrating Structures,* ed. Irene Portis Winner and Thomas G. Winner (Cambridge, MA, 1984), 117.
28. Gellért Váry, 1843–1926, diary excerpt, "A Bach-korszak csongrádon," in *A föld megőszült, emlékiratok, naplók az abszolutizmus (Bach) korából,* Gyula Tóth, ed. (Budapest, 1985), 28.
29. *Pester Lloyd,* 3 June 1857.
30. *Pester Lloyd,* 31 May 1857.
31. Fischer, *Schattenwürfe in die Zukunft.*
32. *Pesti Napló,* 4 February 1866; Imre Visi, *Tisza Kálmán politikai jellemrajz a tizéves jubilaeum alkalmából* (Bratislava-Budapest, 1885), 7.
33. Joan Haslip, *The Lonely Empress: A Biography of Elizabeth of Austria* (Cleveland, 1965), 178–179.
34. See Mária Kiss Tolnay, *Kedves Idám! Erzsébet Királyné, Ferenc József, Andrássy Gyula és Schratt Katalin Levelei Ferenczy Idához* (Budapest, 1992).
35. Serious study of Hungarian began in February 1863; see Hans Rödhammer, ed., *Elisabeth. Kaiserin von Österreich und Königin von Ungarn, 1837–1898* (Linz, 1983), 322.
36. Hamann, *Elisabeth,* 227.
37. *A Hon,* 2 January 1866.
38. Tolnay, *Kedves Idám!,* 31; Haslip, *The Lonely Empress,* 186.
39. Tarr, *A délibábok országa,* 12.
40. Rödhammer, *Elisabeth,* 131.
41. Margit Szabó, ... *gödöllői lakos vagyok ...; Erzsébet királyné a kastélyban* (Gödöllő, 2002), 28.
42. *Pesti Napló,* 4 February 1866; *Vasárnapi Ujság,* 11 February 1866.
43. Ibid.
44. *Pester Lloyd,* 2 August 1865.
45. *Pesti Napló,* 4 February 1866.
46. Ibid.
47. Haslip, *The Lonely Empress,* 188–189.
48. Sándor Pethő, ed., *Emlékkönyv Zichy Nándor Gróf születésének századik évfordulójára, 1829–1929* (Budapest, 1929), diary entry of 26 February 1866, 49; Ferenc Bonitz, *Gróf Zichy Nándor, élet- és jellemrajz* (Budapest, 1912), 96–109.
49. Pethő, *Emlékkönyv Zichy Nándor Gróf,* 2 March 1866, 49.
50. Pethő, *Emlékkönyv Zichy Nándor Gróf,* 4 March 1866, 5.
51. Haslip, *The Lonely Empress,* 189.
52. Their rivalry persisted into the 1890s when ostentatious mourning for both again became an affirmation or rejection of the *Ausgleich.* See Anonymous, *The Marytrdom of an Empress* (New York, 1900).
53. A. Kienast, *Die Legion Klapka* (Vienna, 1900), 100.
54. Oscar Jászi, *The Dissolution of the Habsburg Monarchy* (Chicago, 1929), 107.
55. Haslip, *The Lonely Empress,* 195.
56. Ibid., 194.
57. Cited in Szabó, *gödöllői lakos vagyok,* 13.
58. For the correspondence through Ida Ferenczy, see Tolnay, *Kedves Idám!*
59. Tolnay, *Kedves Idám!,* 61–62.
60. Haslip, *The Lonely Empress,* 196.
61. Szabó, *gödöllői lakos vagyok,* 11.
62. Ibid.
63. Mrs. Bánffy, born Ágnes Esterházy, Duchess Stefónia Almásy-Wenckheim, Duchess Katalin Andrássy-Kendeffy, Duchess Gabriella Andrássy-Pálffy, Duchess Franciska Bombelles-Hunyady. Országos Levéltár, (Miniszterelnökség), 1867 K26 ME Segédkönyv.

64. Brigitte Hamann, *The Reluctant Empress. A Biography of Empress Elisabeth of Austria* (New York, 1986), 165.
65. *Pester Lloyd,* 7 May 1867.
66. Tarr, *Délibábok Országa,* 229.
67. *Vasárnapi Ujság,* 11 February 1866.
68. Lajos Bátorfi, *Tiz év emléke Zalában, 1867–1876* (Nagy-Kanizsa, 1878), 141.
69. Imre Lukinich, ed., *B. Eötvös József naplójegyzetek; Gondolatok, 1864–1868* (Budapest, 1941), 7 June 1867, 233.
70. Péter Búsbach, *Egy viharos emberöltő, korrajz* (Budapest, 1899), 209–210. The eight-year-old Rudolf would describe the coronation in his German essay book, "Die ungarische Königskrönung," which captured both the excitement and the tedium of the event ("much Latin was read") in Hamann, *Elisabeth,* 387–388.
71. Szabó, *gödöllői lakos vagyok,* 19.
72. *Vasárnapi Ujság,* 1868, cited in Szabó, *gödöllői lakos vagyok,* 23.
73. Later, however, Marie Valerie married a Habsburg cousin for love, Franz-Salvatore of Habsburg-Tuscany, dropped the Hungarian, and became the mother of ten children.
74. *Pesti Hirlap,* 24 April 1879.
75. Kornél Ábrányi, Jr., "A kiegyezés," in *Nemzeti dicsőségünk: fényes korszakok a magyar nemzet történelméből,* ed. János Hock (Budapest, 1906), 281. For a description of the funeral, see Judit Lakner, *Halál a századfordulón* (Budapest, 1993), 27.
76. For other examples of anti-political or aristocratic radicalism in the 1880s, see Peter Bergmann, *Nietzsche, "the last Antipolitical German"* (Bloomington, 1987), 182.
77. *Neues Politisches Volksblatt,* 12 February 1889.
78. Empress Elisabeth, *Das poetische Tagebuch,* ed. Brigitte Hamann (Vienna, 1984), 341.
79. *Vasarnapi Ujság,* 18 September 1898, 645.
80. OL, K26 ME, packet 446. See Emil Niederhauser, *Merénylet Erzsébet királyné ellen* (Budapest, 1985), 25. On the "chastened crowd," see Freifeld, *Nationalism and the Crowd,* chapter 1.
81. Tóth, "Erzsébet királyné kultuszáról," 6.
82. Hamann, *Reluctant Empress,* 371.
83. Gyula Gábel, *Erzsébet, Királyasszony Emlékének. Hódolt Magyarország Nagy Királynéjának* (Budapest, 1905), 41.
84. *New York Times,* 11 September 1898.
85. "The Empress Laid at Rest," *New York Times,* 17 September 1898.
86. The Empress's assassination resonated abroad. The anarchist Emma Goldman was touring the United States at the time of the assassination delivering a series of lectures, among them one on "The New Woman." Although Goldman considered Luccheni's act a "folly" with "no propagandistic value," she refused to condemn the murder itself. "He was a victim no less than the Empress; I refused to join in the savage condemnation of the one or in the sickening sentimentality expressed for the other." Goldman's public stance on the assassination brought her a storm of opprobrium and police surveillance. Emma Goldman, *Living My Life* (New York, 1931), vol. 1, chapter 18.
87. *Vasárnapi Újság,* 25 September 1898.
88. O. Farkas Zsuzsa, "Az Erzsébet királné emlékmü pályázat," in *Kiállítása Erzsébet Királyné Születésének,* 18.
89. Jászi, *The Dissolution of the Habsburg Monarchy,* 140, 154.
90. T.M. Islamow, "Die ungarländische Arbeiterbewegung zur Zeit der Koalitionsregierung (1907–1909)," *Acta Historica,* vol. 16 (1970), 109.

Chapter 7

STATE RITUAL AND RITUAL PARODY

Croatian Student Protest and the Limits of Loyalty
at the End of the Nineteenth Century*

Sarah A. Kent

Having come to the Habsburg throne at a time of revolution, Emperor Franz Joseph (1848–1916) confronted the difficulty of reconciling the competing interests of a multitude of peoples to life in a multinational state. One of the central mechanisms that he and his advisers employed was the revitalization of court ritual and Catholic tradition, which bound the aristocracy and the church hierarchy to the monarch. The incorporation of local elites and the wider populace into this process was achieved not only through official holidays celebrating the royal family and Catholic feast-days but also through the renovation of the imperial inspection tour (*Kaiserreise*), which would be undertaken by Franz Joseph and members of his family in order to promote the dynasty as the personification of empire.[1] Such celebrations aimed to garner support for the empire, in part on the basis of the concrete benefits the populace received as imperial citizens, and to gloss over any local tensions that threatened the tranquility of the empire.

Masquerading as part of a long historic tradition, these state rituals in the nineteenth century were in many ways as modern as the nationalism they sought to tame.[2] Especially problematical, however, was the fact that expressions of loyalty to the dynasty were not necessarily coterminous with the acceptance of imperial policy, and the meaning of state ritual could become hotly contested political territory at the local level. Such was the case on the occasion of Franz Joseph's trip to Zagreb in 1895, when the most famous incident in late nineteenth-century Croatian history—the burning of a facsimile of a Hungarian flag by law students from the University of Zagreb—took place. On the one side stood Franz Joseph, King of Croatia, and the astute, if much hated, viceroy, Count Karl Khuen-Hédervárý, who viewed the monarch and Hungarian rule as inseparably bound; on the other stood nationalist Croatian students, who were willing to pledge allegiance to the monarch, but not to Magyar domination.[3]

The aim of this article is to examine how, in the Kingdom of Croatia-Slavonia, this tense dynamic called into question the effectiveness of "celebrity monarchy," which is understood here as the attempt to shore up monarchy in the modern period through the innovation and renovation of imperial traditions which placed the monarch at the center of political and media attention.[4] Beginning with a description of the political background to the monarch's trip, the analysis concentrates on the student response to the king's visit. This took the form of street demonstrations which protested against political arrangements in the Hungarian half of the monarchy by assaulting the most basic of state symbols, the Hungarian flag. Finally, the discussion turns to the trial of the 54 students who were charged with disturbing the peace during the king's visit.

1. Croatian Politics and the Royal Visit

Franz Joseph came to Zagreb in October 1895 to celebrate the progress that the Kingdom of Croatia-Slavonia had made since his last visit in 1869 and to demonstrate the concrete benefits which the inhabitants of the kingdom had enjoyed under the dualistic system introduced in 1867. The centerpiece of Franz Joseph's visit to Zagreb in 1895 was the opening of the newly constructed Croatian Theater, a symbol of the vitality of Croatian national life; in addition, the mustard-colored theater, which was designed by the Viennese architects Helmer and Fellner, was a visible link to a shared Habsburg heritage. As with all such state visits, imperial protocol strictly regulated the event, which only began to be finalized late in the summer of 1895. Viceroy Khuen-Hédervárý had himself composed the first draft of the program, which was then turned over to provincial and city government officials. They worked hard to achieve a celebration which would portray Franz Joseph as the object of adoration, the embodiment of empire, and the fulfillment of local aspirations.

From the moment of his arrival at the Zagreb train station, Franz Joseph was embedded in a ritual which was a symbolic representation of empire. His train pulled into the new station of the Hungarian State Railway, a mark of progress, but the crowd outside the train station stood in prearranged social corporations, such as those of "university citizens" (*sveučilišni građani*) and volunteer firemen, distinguished by dress. On his way to the viceroy's palace in the upper city, which was the traditional seat of power, the king passed under a victory arch festooned with Hungarian and Croatian flags. A peasant guard of honor in national costume accompanied the king on the parade through the city, and presentations of delegations to the king once he had arrived at the viceroy's palace followed a rigid, predetermined hierarchical order. During his stay, the king laid the keystone of the new Croatian Theater and attended the opening performance; he inspected schools, the military base in Zagreb, orphanages, and churches. Everywhere he was greeted with short patriotic speeches paying homage to the dynasty and to the empire.

Although the emerging middle class in Zagreb was generally supportive of the monarchy, many of its members were specifically critical of local political conditions, and the complex past of the various Croatian kingdoms provided the basis for numerous contradictory interpretations of their status within the empire.[5] The Croato-Hungarian Agreement (*Nagodba*) of 1868, which supplemented the Austro-Hungarian Compromise (*Ausgleich*) of 1867, was supposed to resolve these disputes by guaranteeing Croatian autonomy in internal affairs, and the *Nagodba* declared the political result to be "one and the same state union [*državna zajednica*]"[6] with a single crown and a single coronation,[7] but this apparent simplicity was belied by the actual complexity of the situation.[8] The *Nagodba*, for example, refers to the "Dalmatian, Croatian, and Slavonian kingdoms" as if they were a compact unit, and the Magyars pledged themselves to work for their integration; in reality, Dalmatia continued to be in the Austrian half of the monarchy until 1918.[9] Even the agreement's subsequent revisions did not resolve these disputes, which meant that the Croatian nationalist defense was highly legalistic.[10]

The attitude towards the *Nagodba* became a critical factor in political party formation after 1868. The three major political parties in Croatia-Slavonia in the 1880s were the National Party (*Narodna Stranka*), the Independent National Party (*Nezavisna Narodna Stranka*), and the Party of Rights (*Stranka Prava*).[11] The governmental National Party, which was composed primarily of nobles, Serbs, and Jews, supported close cooperation with Hungary.[12] Given the small franchise and the widespread electoral corruption during the last two decades of the nineteenth century, the National Party invariably won the majority of seats in the Croatian *Sabor*, or Diet. The Independent National Party, whose members came largely from the middle-aged urban intelligentsia and the hierarchy of the Roman Catholic Church, believed that the Magyars should be forced to live up to the spirit and the letter of the *Nagodba*. The radical nationalist Party of Rights, whose support came primarily from non-voters and the younger urban intelligentsia, rejected the *Nagodba* as inimical to Croatian state rights.[13]

Locally, therefore, Franz Joseph's visit occurred within the context of the political achievements of Count Karl Khuen-Héderváry, a Hungarian magnate who had been appointed *ban* (viceroy) of the kingdom in the aftermath of the peasant rebellions in the fall of 1883.[14] In twelve years, the viceroy had succeeded in creating a ruling coalition based on unionist Croats, Serbs, and Jews, mostly members of the National Party, and had eliminated effective political opposition. The revision of the parliamentary rules of procedure in 1885 made possible the exclusion of members of the opposition from entire sessions of the *Sabor*. Subsequently, the radical nationalist Party of Rights was removed from parliamentary life with the persecution and prosecution of its party leader, David Starčević, and the Independent National Party lost its last political stronghold when the National Party seized control of the Zagreb city government in the early 1890s. Attempts to create a united opposition were stymied, which ensured that, by 1895, the viceroy had completed the so-called pacification of the Croatia.[15]

Behind Khuen-Héderváry's apparent political success, however, lurked the regime's on-going difficulties in keeping political protest at bay. Electoral politics in the kingdom were relatively easy to manipulate because just under two percent of the population were allowed the vote in the 1890s and the regime had gerrymandered electoral districts to secure a majority in the *Sabor*. Furthermore, the state was the largest employer for the educated, and in the mid-1880s, Khuen-Héderváry's administration had introduced harsher disciplinary measures for government employees who did not vote for the government party. Despite an active oppositional press and sometimes inflammatory speeches in the *Sabor*, the nationalist critiques remained somewhat muted, since appointments in the civil service required the invocation of "political correctness"[16] in the 1880s–90s, and those who translated nationalist words into deeds faced disciplinary action and dismissal.[17] Although a university education was the main channel for the creation of a local elite dependent on the state for employment, students were to some degree protected during their academic program by the autonomy of the university and by a traditional tolerance towards some measure of youthful hotheadedness. By the 1890s, Croatian university students were inclined to radical nationalist politics, and no students at the university were more infected with these ideas than those studying at the Law Faculty.[18]

2. Zagreb University and Student Radicalism

The participation of university students distinguished the celebrations in 1895 from the king's earlier visit in 1869, because the University of Zagreb had only been founded in 1874. A university education conferred special privileges and responsibilities on its beneficiaries: the growing bureaucracy was an increasingly important instrument in the management of empire, and higher education shortened military service and ensured voting rights. As Table 7.1 shows, overall enrollments at the University of Zagreb increased by 25 percent (from 308 to

Table 7.1. Enrollment at the University of Zagreb by Faculty[19]

	1875/76		1885/86		1895/96	
	No.	Percent	No.	Percent	No.	Percent
Faculty of Theology	73	2	92	29	66	17
Faculty of Law	189	61	184	58	203	53
Faculty of Philosophy	46	15	43	13	113	30
Total	308	100	319	100	382	100

382 students) over the first twenty years of the institution's existence. The number of law students, however, increased only 10 percent by the 1895/96 academic year, whereas two times as many students were enrolling in the disciplines in the Faculty of Philosophy. Nevertheless, law continued to be the most popular subject of study because a law degree opened a variety of careers in the civil service and the judiciary, as well as the possibility of practicing law.

Although the published and unpublished statistics on the background of students at the University of Zagreb are flawed,[20] students from peasant backgrounds appear to compose a stable percentage of the enrolled students—between 19 to 21 percent of the students enrolled for the 1875/76, 1885/86, and 1895/96 school years. What peasants were studying, however, appears to have shifted over time, for the number studying law increased from 15 to 22 percent; their absolute numbers increased from 28 in 1875/76 to 44 in 1895/95 (see Table 7.2). More important, however, is the fact that almost twice as many law students from all social backgrounds received some sort of financial aid in 1895/96 than did law students in 1875/76 (119 as opposed to 64), and the number receiving full fee remission jumped from 17 to 64.[21] These figures are not surprising given the long-term depression that resulted from the crash of the Viennese stock market in 1873, which reflected the lack of native capital in the Kingdom of Croatia-Slavonia, and the consequences of the twenty-year agricultural depression that was just ending in the mid-1890s. In short, the student body at the law faculty in 1895 was more diverse than twenty years before, but also more impoverished, which played a major role in determining their perception of the benefits of dualism, and thus also in shaping their attitudes towards Franz Joseph's visit.

Since the provincial government and the bureaucracy envisioned popular participation during the king's visits on the basis of social corporations, "university citizens" were assigned roles in a predetermined hierarchy, which involved them wearing identifiable markers of their social position. On 4 October 1895, Rector Franjo Spevec submitted a rush order for fifty-one ceremonial outfits from the Company of Moritz Tiller in Budapest. This ceremonial attire consisted of a silk-lined black shirt with a Persian collar, a black military-style coat with braid and with a cape on the left shoulder, stockings, a fur hat with a feather, a cere-

Table 7.2. Enrollments at the Faculty of Law by Social Background[22]

Faculty of Law	1875/76		1885/86		1895/96	
	No.	Percent	No.	Percent	No.	Percent
Professions	48	25	76	41	74	36
Peasantry	28	15	24	13	44	22
Crafts	20	11	14	7	21	10
Commerce/Transport	10	5	20	11	34	17
Other Backgrounds	31	16	22	12	30	15
Unknown	52	28	28	15	0	0
Total	189	100	184	99	203	100

monial sword with black velvet and gold fittings, a black sword belt, a black necktie, a pair of golden rosettas for shoes, and three pairs of gloves.[23] The cost was 175 forints, which few students could afford, so Rector Spevec first approached Minister Iso Kršnjavi and then the viceroy himself in order to work out a deal whereby the government paid for the outfits and students were to repay the government in installments.[24] Students who could not afford the gala uniform at all were to wear black suits to all festivities.

In the presence of the king, university students performed their ritual role admirably. On October 8, the mayor of Zagreb informed the rector that appropriately attired university students were to participate in five activities: the reception at the train station, the laying of the foundation stone at the theater, the evening serenade of the king, Franz Joseph's visit to the university, and his departure.[25] In addition, the rector selected a limited number of students to receive invitations to the royal ball and the opening of the new theater.[26] In these venues, the students joined in the celebration of the monarch, who passed like an icon through the events. This patriotic expression was quite in keeping with the views of such opposition leaders as attorney Josip Frank, who believed that a pro-dynastic position was critical for promoting Croatian national interests.[27]

Unexpectedly, however, on three separate occasions when the king was not present, students from the University of Zagreb were involved in street disturbances and political protests. The first disturbance occurred on the first day of the king's visit, immediately after the initial parade in which Franz Joseph and his retinue went in carriages from the Zagreb train station to the upper city via Zrinjevac, Jelačić Square, Ilica, and Mesnička Street. Just off Ilica stands a small Serbian Orthodox Church, and there the crowd, which had just greeted the monarch, began to pelt the church with stones and inkpots. The reason later cited for the disturbance was that the church was hung with a Serbian, not a Croatian, flag in celebration of the monarch's visit. Ivan Frank, one of Josip Frank's sons, was in the crowd with several of his friends, and in depositions before the trial several policemen claimed that he yelled, "Tear it down!" and threw a stone at the church.

The second disturbance emerged out of the assault on the Serbian Orthodox church. Ivan Frank's brother Vladimir heard the crowd decide to go to the victory arch north of the train station in order to take down the Hungarian flag that hung there. After surging through the streets, the crowd arrived at the arch and someone broke open the door at the base with a shovel.[28] Vladimir Frank went up the stairs and untied the flag, which fell onto one of the supporting allegorical figures; in their effort to get the flag down, members of the crowd damaged the figure. A policeman showed up and drew his sword, whereupon the students present ceremoniously drew their swords but then withdrew, and officials hoisted the Hungarian flag back up.[29] Later that night, some Magyars who worked for the Hungarian State Railway attacked the Frank brothers and beat them up in revenge for their assault on the Hungarian flag.

The most serious of the student protests occurred on October 16, on the last day of the king's visit. After the king had visited Zagreb city hall, the law students returned to the faculty, where registration for fall semester was taking place. Students—among them the future leader of the peasant party, Stjepan Radić[30]—began debating the actions of the two Frank brothers in the assault on the Orthodox church and in removing the Hungarian flag. Some students argued that the rabble rousing actions were inappropriate because they were members of the educated intelligentsia. In this vein, after a somewhat formless meeting in groups huddled in the corridors of the law faculty, the students came to an agreement that they should protest against the use of the Hungarian flag as a symbol of Magyar supremacy in a way that was peaceful, "spontaneous," and "corporative." An unidentified student brought a facsimile of the Hungarian tricolor, which had been commissioned the day before from seamstress Margarita Wastler; another student went to collect the official university banner, which constituted another symbol designating the students' corporative status.[31]

At 11 am, the students set off on their demonstration. Although they could have taken a shorter and more direct route, they chose to march eight abreast down Frankopan Street and then to turn right onto Ilica. Not only were these two of the main streets in Zagreb, but the route was actually a mirror image of the king's path from the new train station to the upper city. Vladimir Vidrić carried the university banner at the head of the procession and was flanked by two students in ceremonial dress with swords drawn. Students in ceremonial dress walked at the front, along the sides, and at the rear, while those in ordinary suits formed the inside of the procession. As the students proceeded, they encountered colleagues on the streets who joined the group, but they rebuffed non-students who wanted to join because the demonstration was to be a corporative statement of "university citizens." By the time the group had reached Jelačić Square it numbered between 70 and 80 students.[32]

Although by the 1890s the centrality of Jelačić Square in the urban design of Zagreb had been superseded by the city's growth, the square remained a gathering point where Kaptol (the medieval ecclesiastical city) and Gradec (the medieval civil city) met the nineteenth-century lower city (*doljnji grad*) which stretched southward towards the Sava River.[33] The peasant market place was located on Jelačić Square and at its western end, where Ilica debouched, stood a bronze statue of Ban Jelačić, erected in 1866. The Zagreb city government had initially proposed in 1854 to honor Jelačić's contribution to Croatia, where the memory of the heady days of 1848 was still alive. The general, who had led Croatian military forces into Hungary to help quell the revolution there, thus represented the loyalty of the Croatian nation to the House of Habsburg. In addition, although Bishop Josip Juraj Strossmayer promoted the Croatian sculptor Vatroslav Donegani from Rijeka in the competition, the Zagreb city government gave the commission to Viennese sculptor Anton Dominik Fernkorn, who was already well known for his equine statues of Prince Eugene of Savoy and Archduke Karl in Vienna.[34] The statue was thus a twofold symbol of Croatia's Habsburg legacy.

While the placement and orientation of the statue derived from Fernkorn's assessment of the square's spatial framework,[35] the political symbolism of the 1848 hero on horseback with his sword drawn and pointed north towards Hungary was not lost on contemporaries, and public celebration of Jelačić's achievements had ceased after the implementation of the dualistic system in 1867.[36] Now, in 1895, the university students stopped their procession at the foot of the statue and arranged themselves in a square. Those in ceremonial dress drew their swords, and the facsimile of the Hungarian flag (which had been hidden during the procession)[37] was stretched over four swords. The students shouted: "Long live the Croatian king! Praise Jelačić! Down with the Magyars [*Abzug mađari*]!" They then poured spirits on the flag, raised it into the air, and set it on fire. After repeating the same three slogans, the students sheathed their swords, marched back to the university in orderly fashion, and returned the university banner to storage. They then decided to send a laurel wreath to Franz Joseph with the inscription, "[From] Croatian university citizens to their Croatian king after the protest against the tyranny of the Magyars." The entire event had taken place in about half an hour.

3. Student Identity and the Performance of Honor

How do these 1895 demonstrations fit in with general student conduct in Zagreb at the end of the nineteenth century? Government regulation enjoined municipal police and local courts to report student arrests, fines, and punishments to the university rectorate, which opened up the possibility of further punishment if the behavior was out of keeping with the prestige of the institution and the standards of expected behavior. The vast majority of disciplinary cases in the year 1895—as in the preceding twenty years—received little disciplinary response from the university because most incidents concerned offensive behavior in public places—that is to say, drunkenness, urination, impolite behavior towards public officials (usually policemen), fighting (often in connection with gambling), and behaving impolitely towards women on the street. The most serious case in 1895 involved an impecunious student who offered his student identification card in return for a prostitute's favors; he then beat her up to get his ID card back. The severe reprimand which he received from the university resulted not because he had frequented a brothel, nor because he had assaulted a prostitute, but because he had misused an official document, which violated an executive order issued by the Provincial Government in 1887.[38]

The fact that the local authorities reported few political cases to the university does not mean that students were politically quiescent: students sometimes engaged in organized political activity such as collecting money for political parties; they commonly attended sessions of the *Sabor* and the courts, and, as the published transcripts of those institutions testify, disrupted the proceedings with wolf whistles and the thumping of feet so that the gallery frequently had to be cleared. As a result, attendance at important political trials required admission tickets. Conservatives tolerated some degree of public display of opposition, in large part because many of the well known government supporters in the 1890s had themselves been members of the political opposition as young men during the heady days of the 1840s or 1860s. The conservatives did, however, demand that student protest remain within the bounds of social hierarchy and civility. The rowdier students therefore aimed to ensure that they would not be caught for the expression of their political opinions. Under cover of night, for example, they pelted the houses of many an unpopular politician with eggs while chanting political slogans and insults or singing nationalistic songs.

An exception to clandestine activity was Stjepan Radić (1871–1929), the intellectual progenitor of the flag burning incident. Unlike most of the students at the University of Zagreb, Radić came from a peasant family near Sisak and had experienced first hand the economic difficulties resulting from the European-wide agricultural depression. Radić early expressed a pan-Slav orientation and had even traveled to Russia. Like many peasants, Radić viewed the representatives of the state with some hostility, which as a *Gymnasium* student in Zagreb, he directed against the government of Khuen-Hédervary. In 1889, for example, he had been arrested for shouting "Glory to Zrinski, down with the tyrant Hédervary!" at a performance of the Croatian national opera *Nikola Subić Zrinski*. Later that year, he ran into problems with the grammar school for political agitation and was put under psychiatric observation at the Zagreb hospital. He was expelled from the University of Zagreb in 1893 for participation in a patriotic demonstration in Sisak and from Prague University in 1894 for involvement in student demonstrations. He won some renown for being ejected from the Hungarian State Railways for refusing to understand a ticket collector who spoke only Hungarian in a train traveling on Croatian soil.[39]

As Radić makes clear in his autobiographical writings, his acts were firmly based in the concept of honor which regulated the actions of the educated male, and this belief was widely shared by university students.[40] As the students who participated in the flag burning began to be arrested, a number of students reported to the police station and presented themselves for arrest—whether they had participated in the event or not—in an act of solidarity with their fellow students. Furthermore, during the five-day trial, which opened on 11 November 1895, the students collectively refused responsibility for breaking the law. Rather, they tried to turn the tables on the prosecution. All of the students insisted that the procession was a "spontaneous" decision. Since the majority of the students involved in the demonstration studied law, they were well aware of the legal context of intent, and they sought to escape culpability by characterizing their act as impromptu. The weak link in their argument was of course the existence of the facsimile of the Hungarian flag.

The students collectively characterized their protest as one committed by citizens faithful to the dynasty. Radić stated, as did others, that they would not have participated in a protest which took place in the presence of the king because that would have denoted disrespect for his person and the institution of the monarchy. Furthermore, Radić maintained that the order of the three slogans demonstrated dynastic fidelity. The students first shouted, "Long live the Croatian king!" to represent the organic connection between the monarch and his loyal Croatian subjects. The second slogan—"Praise Jelačić!"—invoked the historic loyalty which Jelačić and the Croats demonstrated to the Habsburgs during the revolutions of 1848. The third slogan—"Down with the Magyars"—was thus contextualized by implicit reference to Magyar disloyalty to the monarch during the revolutions of 1848. Nonetheless, through direct contrast of Croats and Magyars, the students were also explicitly challenging dualism.

With varying success, the students attempted to introduce the idea that the source of their outrage was the use of Hungarian flags during the 1895 celebrations, which they claimed was a violation of the Croato-Hungarian Agreement of 1868.[41] In different ways, they therefore justified their actions as a protest against what they saw as the illegal use of Hungarian flags on Croatian soil.[42] Radić added that the students were politically aware and were upset that Croatia's parity with Hungary was being ignored during the visit, for the use of Hungarian flags was just a symbol of the actual precedence that Minister-President Dezső Bánffy and his retinue enjoyed during the public ceremonies. Radić also emphasized the care with which students determined their action: "We did not want to demonstrate like the rabble with its muscles, but as human beings (*ljudi*) with our convictions."[43] Other students mentioned that the decision to stage a corporative parade to Jelačić Square was based on a desire to avoid a confrontation with the police and to prevent the possibility of a riot.[44] The students thus argued that they wanted to protest against the illegal violation of the *Nagodba* in a way befitting their status in Croatian society. Such a protest, they believed, was not only a suitable action but a patriotic duty for the educated; hence too, their acting as a corporation.[45]

This concept of appropriate behavior was stated in another way by Heneberg, who claimed that "had we wanted to incite the people, we would have processed through the entire city and collected workers and craftsmen and convinced them to revolt and incited the people against the Magyars. We didn't do that because we didn't want to do that."[46] In addition, several of the students mentioned that many of the people who happened to be on Jelačić Square during the demonstration approved of their action. Dabčević claimed that individuals shouted "*Živjeli!* [Long may they live!]" and women waved their umbrellas and blew kisses.[47] Milan Krištof claimed that not only children but "excellent people [*odlični ljudi*] collected the ashes [from the incinerated flag], and I saw one priest who put the ash in his pocket. When a gentleman asked why he was doing that, he said, to put away for remembrance."[48] Significantly, those who approved of the corporative statement, according to the students, were clearly members of the urban, educated middle class—women with umbrellas, a priest, and a gentleman.

The students thus maintained that they were performing a set of rights and responsibilities which pertained to the kingdom's educated elite. They also believed they were adhering to a strict code of honor: each was willing to admit what he himself had done personally, but none saw anyone else speak or act. Radić articulated the position most clearly: the students practiced collegiality and did not want to denounce anyone.[49] The prosecution also harped on honor—that is, on the breach of honor—for Rector Spevec had called the students together to extract a promise that they would behave themselves during the celebration. Several of the students mentioned they had only promised to behave themselves at the university and that Spevec had commented that whatever happened outside of the university was not his concern.[50] Perhaps most telling was the fact that the students disputed the prosecution's interpretation of their oath to the rector: several argued that they had done nothing embarrassing when in the king's physical presence.

The results of the trial were a foregone conclusion, for the presiding judge truncated the students' testimony and silenced their attorneys when they tried to engage in a political justification for the flag burning; the judge even ignored the oral testimony of witnesses for the prosecution when it contradicted their signed, sworn depositions taken before the trial.[51] The trial itself became the subject of daily editorials in the press, both in Croatia and in the rest of the Monarchy, and donations poured in from all over Croatia-Slavonia to help the students financially.[52] Despite this popular support, sentences from two- to six-months' imprisonment were handed out to the defendants, and at the end of November they were sent to Bjelovar to serve their time. There, the local judge, Šišman Herrnheiser, met them with the words, "Gentlemen! I greet you because every true and honorable Croat approves of what you have done! You will be well received in my jail, but please have some consideration for me and my position!"[53]

Conclusions

Franz Joseph left Zagreb on October 16 believing that his visit had been an unqualified success as an exercise in monarchical display. As he wrote to Katarina Schratt from Gödöllő on October 18, "My stay in Zagreb pleased me greatly and was disturbed only at the end by an outrage by some student loafers which was very disagreeable but very much exaggerated by the newspapers. My reception was a very cordial, patriotic one, with great order and correct behavior by the public."[54] Khuen-Héderváry, a more astute observer of Croatian politics, was less sanguine about the meaning of the protest. The day after Franz Joseph left Zagreb, Minister Kršnjavi recorded in his diary that he was summoned to appear before the viceroy, who angrily informed him that "because you obtained national costumes for the students, they therefore became unruly and created a scandal. I foresaw that. As a result, I no longer had the situation under control. You have spoiled the directions of my policies."[55]

For the young men who so adeptly manipulated the symbolic universe of late Habsburg Croatia, the demonstration formed part of their initiation into nationalist politics.[56] Acting as a cohesive social corporation was effective precisely because these "loafers" were the future political and social elite of the kingdom. The widespread support for their action through public donations showed they were not alone in rejecting the viceroy's coercive "pacification" of the kingdom. The nature of the street violence in 1895 was anti-Serbian and, more profoundly, anti-Magyar, but the students took great pains to promote their actions as pro-dynastic, both through the wreath sent to the king and through their statements in court. By attempting to uncouple the monarch from the solution he had found in 1867, they were also implicitly stating how and where their loyalty had its limits.

Viceroy Khuen-Hédervary well understood the political importance of the protest, but he realized too that the students' demonstration on Jelačić Square was a parody of the reception for the king, one which mocked the effectiveness of imperial ritual itself. That parody was not just satirical in nature, but a deadly serious, corporative demonstration against dualism and the Hungarian state idea. Furthermore, the viceroy knew that, if the physical presence of the king was necessary for the maintenance of political order among the educated urban intelligentsia, his policies were potentially endangered over the long term, for Franz Joseph had not been in Zagreb since 1869 and he was never to visit the Croatian capital again.

Notes

* I would like to thank Daniel Unowsky and Laurence Cole for their helpful editorial work, as well as James P. Krokar and Howard Eissenstat for their comments on the final draft of this article. The research was supported by the University of Wisconsin University Personnel Development Committee, IREX, the Institut za međunarodnu suradnju, and the Institut za suvremenu povijest. I would especially like to thank the Rectorate of the University of Zagreb for the use of its archives.

1. On the Habsburg court, see Brigitte Hamann, "Der Wiener Hof und die Hofgesellschaft in der zweiten Hälfte des 19. Jahrhunderts," in *Hof und Hofgesellschaft in den deutschen Staaten im 19. und beginnenden 20. Jahrhundert*, ed. Karl Möckl (Boppard am Rhein, 1990), 61–78; Jean-Paul Bled describes Franz Joseph's centrality to court life in "La Cour de François-Joseph," in *Hof, Kultur und Politik im 19. Jahrhundert: Akten des 18. Deutsch-französischen Historikerkolloquiums Darmstadt vom 27.–30. September 1982*, ed. Karl Ferdinand Werner (Bonn, 1982), 169–182. Marie Tanner discusses the creation of the Habsburg family myth that reached its height under the Spanish Habsburgs in *The Last Descendant of Aeneas: The Habsburgs and the Mythic Image of the Emperor* (New Haven, 1993). Anna Coreth examines the use of Catholic piety in *Pietas Austriaca: Österreichische Frömmigkeit im Barock* (Vienna, 1982). See, as well Daniel L. Unowsky, *The Pomp and Politics of Patriotism: Imperial Celebrations in Habsburg Austria, 1848–1916* (West Lafayette, 2005); Andrea Blöchl, "Die Kaisergedenktage," in *Der Kampf um das Gedächtnis. Öffentliche Gedenktage in Mitteleuropa*, ed. Emil Brix and Hannes Stekl (Vienna 1997), 117–144.

2. Eric J. Hobsbawm and Terence Ranger, eds., *The Invention of Tradition* (Cambridge, 1983). On the reframing of state ritual to address national identity, see the essays by Laurence Cole, Jeremy King, Keely Stauter-Halsted, and Nancy Wingfield in *Staging the Past: The Politics of Commemoration in Habsburg Central Europe, 1848 to the Present,* ed. Maria Bucur and Nancy Wingfield (West Lafayette, 2001).

3. For a brief summary of the crisis in the Hungarian Liberal Party at the turn of the century, see Arthur J. May, *The Habsburg Monarchy, 1867–1914* (New York, 1951), 346–358. For

an analysis of the crisis that centers on the politicians Dezső Bánffy and István Tisza, see Gabor Vermes, *István Tisza* (Boulder, 1985), 76–85. On the appeal of the Hungarian opposition, see Alice Freifeld, *Nationalism and the Crowd in Liberal Hungary, 1848–1914* (Washington, D.C. and Baltimore, 2000), 282–289.

4. This has become a subject of considerable interest in the last two decades. The approach owes much to Clifford Geertz's work in anthropology and "thick description" applied to state ritual; to Eric Hobsbawm's historical work on "invented" traditions; and to Benedict Anderson's study of "imagined communities." Political scientist Daniel I. Kerzer discusses ritual in the context of democracies as well, in *Ritual, Politics, and Power* (New Haven, 1988). For stimulating essays on state ritual in Europe, see Sean Wilentz, ed., *Rites of Power: Symbolism, Ritual, and Politics since the Middle Ages* (Philadelphia, 1985), and Bucur and Wingfield, *Staging the Past*. For an application to the Russian autocracy, see Richard Wortman's two-volume *Scenarios of Power: Myth and Ceremony* (Princeton, 1995 and 2000).

5. These historical disputes include the relationship of the kingdoms of Croatia, Slavonia, and Dalmatia with Hungary as a result of the Pacta Conventa of 1102, when the Árpád dynasty was elected to the Croatian and Dalmatian kingship; the election of Ferdinand of Habsburg in 1526–1527; the Pragmatic Sanction, which the Croats ratified in 1712 and the Hungarians in 1723; the Croatian participation in the revolt against Joseph II's legislation in 1790–1791; and the Magyar deposition of the Habsburgs during the revolutions of 1848.

6. This is opposed to *državno jedinstvo*, which carries the connotation of a unitary state. Article 48 of the Nagodba, in *Hrvatske pravice*, ed. Petar Požar (Ljubljana, 1990), 149–150, 164. For a discussion of the debate over this terminology in 1867, see Mirjana Gross and Agneza Szabo, *Prema hrvatskome građanskom društvu: Društveni razvoj u civilnoj Hrvatskoj i Slavoniji šezdesetih i sedamdesetih godina 19. stoljeća* (Zagreb, 1992), 224–225.

7. A separate coronation ceremony in Croatia fell into disuse in the medieval period. After the Pacta Conventa in 1102, Koloman had himself crowned in Biograd na moru; Lovre Katić claims that the Árpád kings ceased to crown themselves as Croatian and Dalmatian king after Bela III because the Croats wanted to save themselves the costs of a separate coronation, Lovre Katić, *Pregled povijesti Hrvata* (Zagreb, 1938), 114. Ferdo Šišić mentions that some doubt exists whether Koloman's son, Stjepan II, and his great-grandnephew, Stjepan III (who both ruled before Bela III) were crowned; Šišić, *Pregled povijesti hrvatskoga naroda* (Zagreb, 1975), 179–182. Stephen Gazi maintains that Bela IV eliminated the separate coronation in *A History of Croatia* (reprint, New York, 1993), 47. Tomislav Rauchar agrees that no separate coronations in Croatia were held after Bela IV and gives the fullest discussion of the central issues behind coronation—the geographical definition of the Croatian state and its continued existence as an independent entity after 1102; see Rauchar, *Hrvatsko srednjovjekovlje* (Zagreb, 1997), 44–46, 61–65, and especially 74–76. Ivan Beuc discusses the issue of coronation, especially in connection with the Pragmatic Sanction and the 1723 law which affirmed the indissoluble union of Hungary and Croatia in Beuc, *Povijest institutucija državne vlasti u Hrvatskoj (1527–1945)* (Zagreb, 1969), 11–14, 171. The *Nagodba* reaffirmed that a single coronation was valid for the crownlands in the Hungarian half of the monarchy; see Article 2 in *Požar,* 150. Since Franz Joseph was crowned in Budapest in 1867, before the *Nagodba* was negotiated, the Croatian *Sabor* declined to send representatives on the basis that the relations between Hungary and Croatia were not legally defined.

8. The complexity extends to the political situation in Croatia, where the *Nagodba* was opposed by both unionists and the opposition; the meeting of the *Sabor* that passed the *Nagodba*, to quote Mirjana Gross "would have been illegal even if the electoral results were not achieved by violence because the electoral law was not passed in the *Sabor* but was imposed, and the preceding *Sabor* had twice asserted that it would not recognize the legality of deputies elected on the basis of an imposed law." See Gross and Szabo, *Prema hrvatskome građanskom društvu,* 223.

9. Under the provisions of the *Nagodba*, Budapest was supposed to work towards the territorial unification of the Triune Kingdom—that is, the unification of Dalmatia, Croatia, and Slavonia. Article 65, ibid., 167. The *Nagodba* was, however, bedeviled by the so-called rag (*krpica*), which contained the draft on the status of Rijeka passed by the Hungarian parliament (but not the Croatian *Sabor*) and was pasted over article 66 of the Croatian version, which the king signed. See ibid., 227–232.
10. Such provisions as those on the financial arrangements, on the number of deputies to the Budapest parliament, and on the viceroy's title were superseded by other legislation in 1873, 1881, 1889, 1891, and 1906.
11. For a general survey of the history of these political parties, see Jaroslav Šidak, et al., *Povijest hrvatskog naroda 1860–1914* (Zagreb, 1968). For a useful summary in English, see Ivo Banac, *The National Question in Yugoslavia: Origins, History, Politics* (Ithaca, 1984), 85–96.
12. As Nick Miller points out, aside from the Serbian Club within the National Party, the Serbian opposition had difficulty achieving representation in the *Sabor* because of the high tax qualification for voting. See his *Between Nation and State: Serbian Politics in Croatia before the First World War* (Pittsburgh, 1997), 38. For a more extended treatment of Serbs in Croatia during the Khuen-Hédervary period, see Mato Artuković, *Ideologija srpsko-hrvatskih sporova (Srbobran 1884–1902)* (Zagreb, 1991).
13. The theoretician of the party was Ante Starčević; his nephew David Starčević was the political leader of the party in the *Sabor* until his arrest and conviction for professional misconduct in 1888. Josip Frank became the political leader of the party, which he took on a new trajectory towards accommodation with Vienna. As a consequence, on the eve of Franz Joseph's visit to Zagreb, the Party of Rights was splitting into two factions—the Domovinaši (after the party's newspaper) and the Frankovci, or members of the Party of Pure Rights (*Čista stranka prava*). For the seminal work on the history of the Party of Rights [hereafter, *Pravaštvo*], see Mirjana Gross, *Izvorno pravaštvo: Ideologija, agitacije, pokret* (Zagreb, 2000).
14. On the peasant rebellion in Croatia and its aftermath, see Manuela Dobos, *The Croatian Peasant Uprising of 1883* (PhD Diss., Columbia University, 1974) and Dragutin Pavličević, *Narodni pokret 1883. u Hrvatskoj* (Zagreb, 1980).
15. Milan Marjanović described the viceroy succinctly: "Energetically, coldly, with cunning, seeing through people and using their weaknesses, [Khuen-Hédervary] began to put into effect dualism and to consolidate the supremacy of the 'Hungarian state idea' during his twenty year rule in Croatia." See Milan Marjanović, *Savremena Hrvatska* (Belgrade, 1913), 146. Croatian histories almost universally condemn *Khuenovština* for corruption, political coercion, and the politics of divide and conquer. The most notable exception is Martin Polić's *Ban Dragutin Grof Khuen-Hédervary i njegovo doba,* which was published in Zagreb in 1901, before the end of Khuen-Hédervary's tenure in office. Polić was a member of the governmental National Party. Popular misconceptions of Khuen-Hédervary's removal derive in part from the contemporary attitude in Croatia and in part from the stress that more popular accounts (often written by journalists) give to Croatian, rather than to Habsburg and Hungarian, politics. For examples see Lovre Katić, *Pregled povijesti Hrvata,* and Josip Horvat, *Politička povijest Hrvatske* (reprint, Zagreb, 1989).
16. Khuen-Hédervary's administration actually used the term "politically correct" (*političko korektno*), along with the term "politically suitable" (*političko podobno*), in appointments of civil servants and in granting attorneys and public notaries the right to practice.
17. In 1900, 20 percent of the population of Zagreb consisted of civil servants and the professions, as opposed to under two percent for Croatia-Slavonia as a whole. See Božena Vranješ-Šoljan, *Stanovništvo gradova Banske Hrvatske na prijelazu stoljeća* (Zagreb, 1991), 99–102, 147–148. On the dependence of the professional middle classes during the 1880s and 1890s, see Šidak, et al., *Povijest hrvatskog naroda 1860–1914,* 139–143; Rene Lovrenčić, *Geneza politike "Novog kursa"* (Zagreb, 1972), 27–33. On the profession of attorneys, a traditional free profession, but one that required state appointment in Croatia-Slavonia, see

Sarah A. Kent, *Attorneys in Zagreb, Croatia, 1884–1894* (PhD Diss., Indiana University, 1988), 110–16, 122–126.

18. On the periodisation of student political opinions and on the difficulty of tracking precise groups, see Mirjana Gross, "Studentski pokret 1875–1914," in *Spomenica u povodu 300-godišnjice Sveučilište u Zagrebu*, ed. Jaroslav Šidak (Zagreb, 1969), 451, 455–461.
19. Calculated from Table 5 in "Statistički podaci," in *Spomenica o 25-godišnjem postojanju Sveučilišta Franje Josipa I. u Zagrebu* (Zagreb, 1900), 154–155.
20. See Table 7.2 for information about the total number of students whose social background was unknown.
21. Kent, *Attorneys in Zagreb*, 33.
22. Calculated from Table 5 in "Statistički podaci."
23. Rektorat, Sveučilište u Zagrebu, 1895/380. This gala uniform was derived from the traditional dress for Croatian nobles, which was also customary for the Hungarian nobility and for the members of the Hungarian home guard.
24. Iso Kršnjavi, *Zapisci: Iza kulisa hrvatske politike* (Zagreb, 1986), vol. 1, 90.
25. Rektorat, Sveučilište u Zagrebu, 1895/388.
26. Rektorat, Sveučilište u Zagrebu, 1895/377 and 1895/392.
27. On Josip Frank's involvement in exciting the 1895 demonstration, see Gross, *Pravaštvo*, 816–818, and Lovrenčić, *Geneza politike "Novog kursa,"* 41.
28. Frank maintained that this person was "a simple man" (*priprosti čovjek*); a witness for the prosecution claimed that it was a law student. Testimony of Vladimir Frank in *Hrvatski đaci pred sudom: Stenogram suđenje hrvatskim sveučilištarcima u Zagrebu* (Zagreb, 1995), 140–143.
29. Testimony of Atila pl. Botke, a Magyar employed by the Hungarian state railways. His testimony was given in German. Ibid. 146.
30. Radić had already been expelled from both the University of Zagreb and Prague University for his political activities, but was considering enrolling at the University of Budapest. See Mark Biondich, *Stjepan Radić, the Croat Peasant Party, and the Politics of Mass Mobilization, 1904–1928* (Toronto, 2000), 35–37.
31. Wastler, who was called as a witness, could not identify the student. The prosecution claimed that Milan Dörwald and Gjuro Balaško were probably the ones who purchased the flag. Testimony of Milan Dörwald, *Hrvatski đaci*, 121–122.
32. The two policemen maintained that there were a total of forty or fifty students (ibid., 14). Stjepan Radić claimed in his cross-examination that the group had 200 people (ibid., 34), a claim that he repeats in *Uzničke uspomene* (Zagreb, 1929), vol. 1, 56.
33. Originally, the square was called Harmica, but the Zagreb city government changed the name to Jelačić Square after the revolution of 1848. For a discussion of the nineteenth-century plans for the urban development of Zagreb, see Snježana Knežević, *Zagrebačka zelena potkova* (Zagreb, 1996), 28–34.
34. On the history of the Fernkorn statue, see Božena Kličinović, "Anton Dominik Fernkorn: Spomenik Banu Josipu Jelačiću," in *Anton Dominik Fernkorn*, ed. Vladimir Maleković (Zagreb, 1990), 5–15. The initial sketch of the statue had Jelačić on a galloping horse, but Fernkorn revised the proposal after seeing the square so that only one foot of the horse is lifted. See Kličinović, "Anton Dominik Fernkorn," 8, 47, and 60. Olga Maruševski quotes Adolfo d'Avrilo who perceived the statue as pointing towards Vienna, in *Od Manduševca do Trga Republike* (Zagreb, 1987), 40. For a popular version that emphasizes the restoration of the statue in 1990, see Zvonimir Milčec, *Povratak bana (Spomenik hrvatskog ponosa i hrvatskog srama)* (Zagreb, 1990).
35. See Kličinović, "Anton Dominik Fernkorn," 8. For a detailed description of the buildings on Jelačić Square, see Gjuro Szabo, *Stari Zagreb* (reprint, Zagreb, 1990), 116–118.
36. See Pavo Barišič, "Gedenktage in Kroatien als Medium der Geschichtserzählung," in Brix and Stekl, *Der Kampf um das Gedächtnis*, 340. As Gj. Szabo comments, "It would perhaps have been hard to have erected the statue by the following year," 116.

37. Dr. Aleksander pl. Rakodczay, president of the court, to Vladimir Vidrić, *Hrvatski đaci*, 27.
38. Rektorat, Sveučilište u Zagrebu, 1895/208.
39. The most recent treatment of Radić in English is Biondich, *Stjepan Radić*, which covers Radic's early life on 28–39. Radić's own autobiographical writings, such as *Praški zapisi*, trans. Dušan Karpatský (Zagreb, 1985), and *Uzničke uspomene* (Zagreb, 1929), give a fuller picture of his youthful protests.
40. No work has been done specifically on Croatian concepts of honor, but see Ute Frevert, *Men of Honour: Social History of the Duel* (London, 1995); Kevin McAleer, *Dueling: The Cult of Honor in Fin-de-Siècle Germany* (Princeton, 1994), especially his discussion about dueling and the *Bildungsbürgertum*, 203–208. István Deák discusses dueling and honor in the Habsburg officer corps in *Beyond Nationalism: A Social and Political History of the Habsburg Officer Corps, 1848–1918* (New York, 1992), especially 130–136.
41. See, for example, Testimony of Vladimir Vidrić, *Hrvatski đaci*, 31.
42. Ibid.
43. Testimony of Radić, ibid., 33–34.
44. Ibid., 38.
45. Testimony of Ante Fabrio, ibid., 47.
46. Testimony of Josip Heneberg, ibid., 50.
47. Testimony of Ante Dabčević, ibid., 42.
48. Testimony of Milan Krištof, ibid., 55.
49. Testimony of Radić, ibid., 36. He was quite right that under Austrian law private citizens were not required to denounce others. See Elgin Drda, *Die Entwicklung der Majestätsbeleidigung in der Österreichischen Rechtsgeschichte unter besonderer Berücksichtigung der Ära Kaiser Franz Josephs* (Vienna, 1992), 161–162.
50. See, for example, the testimony of Vladimir Vidrić and of Ante Dabčević, *Hrvatski đaci*, 29, 42.
51. In Ivan Frank's trial, for example, the policemen who had stated in a written deposition that they heard him shout and saw him throw a stone would not testify to that in court. Ibid., 130–137.
52. On the fund created for students, see Gross, *Pravaštvo*, 818–819, and Lovrenčić, *Geneza politike "Novog kursa,"* 41.
53. Cited in Horvat, *Politička povijest Hrvatske*, vol. 1, 235.
54. Brigitte Hamann, ed., *Meine liebe, gute Freundin! Die Briefe Kaiser Franz Josephs an Katharine Schratt* (Vienna, 1992), 329.
55. Several days later, Kršnjavi recorded that "[the idea] that my permission to the boys to obtain national costumes for the celebration caused a demonstration is foolishness. The principle loudmouth and instigator [Stjepan Radić] was not wearing national costume." As a face-saving measure, the viceroy did not dismiss Kršnjavi from office until the following year. Kršnjavi, *Zapisci*, vol. 1, 91–92.
56. Barred from the University of Zagreb, most of the students continued their studies in Prague and profited from study under Professor T.G. Masaryk. One group became involved in the politics of the New Course, which sought Serb-Croat cooperation; see Lovrenčić, *Geneza politike "Novog kursa."* With his brother Ante, Stjepan Radić founded the Croatian Peasant Party in 1904, which went on to become the most popular party in the interwar period after the introduction of the democratic vote. See Biondich, *Stjepan Radić*. For the further development of the Party of Rights after the turn of the century, see the final chapters of Mirjana Gross, *Povijest pravaške ideologije* (Zagreb, 1973).

Chapter 8

COLLECTIVE IDENTIFICATIONS AND AUSTRO-HUNGARIAN JEWS (1914–1918)
The Contradictions and Travails of Avigdor Hameiri*

Alon Rachamimov

Avigdor Hameiri (born Feuerstein, 1890–1970) was one of the most significant literary masons in modern Hebrew literature. Besides being the most prolific World War I memoirist in the Hebrew language, the Austro-Hungarian born writer pioneered the expressionist style in Hebrew poetry, edited his own literary journal, authored children's literature, composed travel journals, and translated into Hebrew numerous works from Hungarian, German, and Yiddish. Despite his manifold contributions, Hameiri is primarily remembered today as the lyricist of two songs: the sentimental poem *Me'al pisgat har ha-tsofim* (On Top of Mt. Scopus) and the children's favorite *Ten katef* (Give a Shoulder).[1] Although he received the highest literary awards of the state of Israel, Hameiri felt unappreciated and rejected throughout his life by the literary establishment, believing that his Hungarian, Austro-Hungarian, and Central European background made him a pariah among the Eastern European born *literati*.[2] Thus, in 1955 when he decided to write his autobiography, Hameiri preferred the language of his youth, Hungarian, to the language which had made his literary reputation for five decades. Accordingly, forty-eight years after publishing his first poem in Hebrew, Hameiri returned to his Hungarian roots, declaring that only the readers of the Hungarian-language daily *Új kelet* (New East) may find some interest in his life.[3]

This adamant return to the language of his youth may appear to be the offended reaction of an aging man. However, as this chapter will show, Hameiri's oscillation between various cultural, political, and national force fields did not begin in his sunset years. From his early years among the Hassidim of the Carpatho-Rus' region of upper Hungary, through his youth in Pozsony (Pressburg/Bratislava) and Budapest, during his years on the Galician front and in Russian war captivity, and indeed throughout his life, Hameiri identified with a complex, constantly shifting, and seemingly contradictory mix of cultural and political constructs: be it various shades of Zionism, Hungarian national myths, the image of the decadent "damned poet," Habsburg loyalism, and central European cosmopolitan pacifism. Sensitive, temperamental, and prone to pathos, Hameiri left in the many genres he employed numerous indications of his dilemmas and conflicting emotions. Although often contradictory and inconsistent, Hameiri's life story nonetheless exemplifies a crucial point about Austro-Hungarian Jewry in general, namely that identification processes had as much to do with the ever changing social, cultural, and political context as with individual temperament and personal ambitions. Thus, as the context shifted dramatically, especially during the turbulent years of 1914–1921, individual Jews such as Hameiri continuously shuffled and re-shuffled various identification combinations, experiencing a tortuous process whose outcome was, for many, unclear.

By following very closely the personal history of one individual, this chapter aims to highlight the various forces, fears, and considerations that went into Jewish collective identifications in the last years of Austria-Hungary's existence.[4] Although it is obvious that arguments based on one case study should proceed carefully with general assertions, I would like nonetheless to suggest that Avigdor Hameiri's prolific and self-conscious writings about his war experiences clearly reveal the degree to which Jewish identification processes could be contextual, angst-ridden, and laden with contradictory tendencies. The extent to which Hameiri was aware of his inner struggles regarding the notions of "loyalty," "fatherland," and "patriotism," coupled with his cognizance of the gap between feelings and actions, make him a wonderful case study to illuminate the complexities of collective identification among Habsburg Jews. Thus, although it is absolutely clear that Hameiri was a Magyar patriot and Habsburg loyalist in terms of his actions, his feelings and reasoning were much more turbulent and multifaceted.

By focusing on Hameiri, this study aims to examine closely the extent to which one can assert that Habsburg Jews were indeed, in Steven Beller's words, "enthusiastic about the dynastic supra-national state."[5] Through the analysis of Avigdor Hameiri's autobiographical and literary writings, I seek to illuminate the degree to which collective identifications and loyalties among Habsburg Jews could be part of an intricate web of issues. Gender, occupation, life-style, and class could at times be just as crucial as the more commonly examined issues of language, religion, ethnicity, and politics. In short, my concern here is to assess how and where Habsburg loyalties fitted into the wider matrix of markers that combine together in the process of self-identification.

To undertake the investigation in a systematic manner, this chapter will first look at the theoretical issues arising from the scholarly discussion about the attachments and loyalties of Austro-Hungarian Jews in the period between the

Ausgleich of 1867 and the dissolution of the monarchy in 1918. I will argue in this respect that one needs to distinguish between "loyalty to the state," which required adherence to a set of known rules of conduct and to which the Jewish population in both halves of the monarchy adhered, and "identification with the state," which involved a complex set of issues and was consequently contextual and limited. The second and the third sections of this essay will return to Avigdor Hameiri, following his life before the war, during his odyssey at the front, and in Russian captivity.

In structuring the essay in this particular manner, two unorthodox theoretical choices are made. First, the term "identification" is preferred to the more commonly used term "identity." This conceptual modification is designed to shift the emphasis toward the identifying individual, and away from culturally and politically constructed categories. Such an approach highlights Hameiri's shifting, manifold, and contextual attachments, without precluding the possibility that many people could have shared his dilemmas and choices. In other words, the emphasis here is on the process ("identification") rather than the product ("identity"). This choice follows Rogers Brubaker's recent line of argument that "identity" has become an overused and unproductive analytical tool in the social sciences.[6] The second unorthodox choice proceeds from the first and involves the protagonist's first and last name. Avigdor Hameiri did not use the name "Hameiri" before migrating to Mandatory Palestine in 1921. Prior to that time, he intermittently used his birth name "Feuerstein;" a Yiddish-spelled version of his name, "Fayersteyn" (פאירשטין); a Hungarian-sounding name, "Albert Kova"; and, for a very brief time in Russia, also the name, "Anton Germanovich Slezak."[7] This contextual usage of names is extremely significant, and scholars of East-Central European history have long been very sensitive to it when dealing with place names. Using a certain place name in anachronistic fashion automatically privileges a later stage in the historical development, while diminishing the significance of prior stages. To avoid similar teleological pitfalls, the practice applied to place names could and should also be extended to individuals. Hence, I refer in the following pages to the same person by the name most befitting a particular context: "Feuerstein," "Fayersteyn," "Kova," "Hameiri," and sometimes even a mixed form, such as "Feuerstein/Kova".

1. Jewish identification processes and Habsburg loyalty in Austria-Hungary

The Jews of Austria-Hungary are usually depicted in historical narratives as among the most loyal of all "imperial and royal" (*k.u.k.*) subjects.[8] Despite great diversity in terms of religiosity, place of residence, income, and language of daily use, the estimated two million plus Jews of the dual state appear—as Marsha Rozenblit recently phrased it—as "intensely loyal" both to the dynasty and to the existence of the Habsburg Monarchy.[9] Whether perceived primarily as a modern capitalist group, wishing to take advantage of large scale market conditions in Central and Eastern Europe (as Oskar Jászi had argued); as an ethnic group wishing to preserve its sense of unity in an increasingly nationalist and contentious environment; or as a religious minority, praying to the health of the *"KIRAH"*[10] as the guarantor of its religious freedoms—from all these points of view, the Jews of Austria-Hungary appear deeply committed to the existence of the monarchy and quintessentially "loyal to the emperor" (*kaisertreu*).

Furthermore, according to Rozenblit, "Jewish loyalty to Austria-Hungary grew during World War I. Jews shared the patriotism and sense of common purpose that galvanized most Habsburg subjects in 1914, and sustained them through four endless years of bloody slaughter."[11] Despite relentless sniping from anti-Semitic circles, who emphasized "Jewish under-representation" among those killed in action, an estimated 275,000–400,000 Jews served in the Habsburg armed forces during the First World War, with the figure of 300,000 as the one usually cited.[12] Jews were highly represented among Habsburg reserve officers: prior to World War I, they constituted some eighteen percent of all reserve officers and as much as one third in the Hungarian National Guard, the *Honvéd*.[13] According to Erwin A. Schmidl, the significant expansion of the Austro-Hungarian officer corps during the war brought in officers from other backgrounds and lowered the ratio of Jews among reserve officers to about ten percent (although this was still two and a half times their proportion in the overall population).[14] These figures stand in stark contrast to Austria-Hungary's chief ally, Imperial Germany, where thirty thousand Jewish cadets sought a commission as reserve officers in the Prussian army between 1885 and 1914, yet not one of them was admitted.[15]

In explaining this staunch imperial loyalty, scholars of *fin-de-siècle* Austria-Hungary usually rely on two interconnected arguments: one pertaining primarily to the Austrian half of the monarchy and a second to the Hungarian half. Regarding the Austrian half (Cisleithania), historians employ what I would call a "pre-modern" argument. In other words, Jewish pre-modern distinctness (understood in ethnic or religious terms, or conversely as the identification of "Jews" as such by non-Jews) was best accommodated by a benign pre-modern state (dynastically constructed, tradition-bound with an a-national ruling elite).[16] The very fact that the Austrian half of the Habsburg monarchy was not a nation-state gave Jews relatively more "inner-space" than was available in most other countries, making them in Hannah Arendt's words "the 'state people' par excellence."[17] Furthermore, the intensification of anti-Semitism in the *fin-de-siècle*, the growing difficulties in shedding much or all of this pre-modern distinctness, and the vociferous demands of national movements to restructure "backward" Austria along "modern" national lines, cemented this "pre-modern pact" between Jews and the Habsburg dynastic state. Thus, approached from this perspective, it is not surprising that, after the dissolution of the monarchy in 1918, the greatest Habsburg "nostalgists"—such as Josef Roth or Stefan Zweig—were Jewish.[18]

In the Hungarian half of the monarchy (Transleithania), Jewish state loyalty is usually understood to have been mediated through the language of Magyar patriotism.[19] The rapid linguistic Magyarization of Jews in the middle decades of the nineteenth century, and the concurrent rise of many of them to economic and cultural prominence, made Hungarian Jews partners in the cause of Magyar nationalism. According to Michael Silber, after the Compromise of 1867 the Hungarian half of the dual monarchy adopted the model of French "civic nationalism," which allowed for religious pluralism and even some measure of ethnic distinctness as long as the supremacy of Magyar nationalism was not challenged.[20] In other words, as long as Hungarian Jews publicly accepted Magyar patriotism, they could articulate as much of their pre-modern uniqueness as they wished: from a vague sense of ethnic distinctness, through Reform (*Neolog*) Judaism to Orthodoxy and ultra-Orthodoxy.[21]

Notwithstanding this undisputed allegiance to the Austro-Hungarian state, one cannot, however, assume automatically that Jews had been really enthusiastic about the dynastic, supra-national state. After all, there is a difference between loyalty to the state, which requires adherence to a set of known rules of conduct, and collective identification, which rests on the assumption that the self and the collective are in some way inextricably intertwined. Jewish loyalty to the dual monarchy could indeed have emanated from powerful emotional attachments to Austria-Hungary, but could also just have reflected the behavior of dutiful citizens, whose dilemmas of collective identification remained a separate issue.

A substantial portion of the work done on Habsburg Jewry in the past three decades has been devoted exactly to illuminating the dilemmas of Jewish collective identification in the context of *fin-de-siècle* national conflict. George Barany, Gary Cohen, Hillel Kieval, Marsha Rozenblit, Dimitry Shumsky, Michael Silber, Robert Wistrich, and many others, have approached this complicated issue and attempted to make sense of it through the application of different historical methodologies.[22] Despite the obvious differences between these individual studies, it is possible to identify two broad interpretative approaches that have emerged in recent decades in relation to this issue.

The first approach highlights the development during the nineteenth century of new, "hybrid" or "hyphenated identities." According to this view, the legal emancipation of Jews in central Europe led to increased integration of Jews into non-Jewish society. This integration, which most often occurred through embourgeoisement, included also the acquisition of surrounding cultures ("acculturation") and some of their objects of collective identification. Now living in closer daily contact with German, Magyar, Polish, and in some cases Czech speakers, Jews began to graft their pre-modern sense of distinctness onto that of the neighboring populations. The Habsburg state for its part helped to sustain this hyphenated identity by forcing Jews to declare one of the "recognized" languages as their "language of daily use" (while not recognizing Yiddish as an option), or to declare affiliation to a "recognized nationality" in places where national cadastres were in use (without recognizing "Jewish" as a recognized national affiliation). From the perspective of the state, Judaism constituted solely a religious category which could and should have been combined with other categories of self-identification. According to the "hyphenated" approach, *fin-de-siècle* anti-Semitism, when coupled with increased national tensions, led either to new and ever-more-complex hyphenated solutions, such as "Czecho-German-Jewry," as recently suggested by Dimitry Shumsky, or conversely, to the nationalization of pre-modern distinctness through the development of a separate Jewish national identity (either in the autonomist or Zionist variant).[23]

The second approach argues for a fragmentation of Jewish pre-modern distinctness during the nineteenth century. It takes a cue—albeit immensely amplifying it—from the works of Salo Baron, Jacob Katz, and Yosef Haim Yerushalmi, who have pointed to the destructiveness of emancipation on the social structures and cultural practices supporting the Jewish sense of collectivity.[24] In the works of Scott Spector or Jacques le Rider, the Jewish pre-modern sense of distinctness is presented as unable to find legitimate public expression, outside perhaps religious or Zionist circles.[25] "Hyphenated" constructs were eventually challenged either from within Jewish communities or from non-Jewish circles, preventing stable and long-term identifications with these paradigms of co-existence. The inability of these "hybrid" constructs to provide a basis for imagining a secure future found expression among sensitive Jewish contemporaries in "identity crises" or in escape to an aesthetic "in-between" existence.[26] Thus, in Scott Spector's view, the "Prague circle" of writers—placed "in a historical moment between an irrecoverable past and an as yet unimaginable future"—could function as a kind of seismograph exposing "conflicts beneath the surface of European modernity."[27] The "fragmentation approach" has been most convincing when focusing on small groups and individuals, and in incorporating theoretical, mainly postmodern, insights. Still, apart from studies focusing on small groups in the Austrian half of the monarchy, there is not yet a large enough body of work supporting the claim that large sections of the Jewish population had only fragmented cultural constructs with which to identify.

Although both these interpretative approaches have been productive in exposing Jewish subjectivities at the close of the nineteenth century, it is the latter of these two approaches which offers more potential as a starting point for reconstructing an individual sense of self and the ways in which it may have impacted on loyalty to the state. Significantly, proceeding in this way also allows for many objects of identification to be equal partners in the formation of a person's mental makeup. Gender identifications, occupational identifications, local attachments, and other *foci* of identification can all be examined in discerning collective attachments, but without privileging national identification as the cornerstone of one's sense of individuality. Unlike the "hyphenated approach," it takes account of the fact that a myriad of collective identifications might be simultaneously attractive to an individual, while not presupposing that these were fundamentally different from—or conflictual with—one another. Thus, collective identifications need not have automatically belonged to different categories (e.g., religious Jewish vs. Magyar national), or have had different strengths (e.g., strong German cultural identification vs. a weak Czech one). In short, it was possible for individual Jews to have been simultaneously moved by Magyar and by Jewish notions of collectivity, without necessarily being worried that one impinged on the other. The fact that the state defined them as qualitatively different, and privileged one attachment over the other, does not necessarily mean that individuals also saw it this way.

2. "Avigdor Feuerstein": a Jewish life in late Habsburg Hungary

Avigdor Hameiri was born in 1890 as Avigdor Feuerstein in the tiny village of Odavidhaza located in the Carpatho-Rus' area of the Hungarian part of the Habsburg Monarchy.[28] The region, which consisted at the time of four counties (*Comitat*)—Ungh, Ugocsa, Bereg, and Marmaros—was one of the most poverty-stricken regions in the whole of Austria-Hungary. The majority of Carpatho-Rus' Jews resided in small villages in the countryside and were as destitute as their Rusyn, Romanian, Slovak, Roma, and Hungarian speaking neighbors: they "walked barefoot. ... dressed in worn-out rags that clung to their bodies due to lack of underwear," observed a representative of the American Jewish Joint Distribution Committee after World War I.[29]

Estimated at approximately 90,000 people in 1890, Carpatho-Rus' Jews made up about one-sixth of the total population of the region, and unlike in any other place in contemporary Europe, they were predominantly employed in agriculture and forestry. Whether earning their livelihood as peasants, owning or leasing small plots of land, being employed as loggers, porters, and coachmen in the wood industry, or working as peddlers and wandering artisans, the majority of Jews barely made a living much above subsistence level. Many were recorded in official reports as beggars who roamed the surrounding regions looking for handouts.[30] As descendents of Galician Jews who crossed the Carpathians in the latter part of the eighteenth century and the first half of the nineteenth century, the Jewish population of the region also tended to be deeply devout. They were inclined to follow Hassidic devotional customs whether or not they formally associated themselves with one of the ultra-Orthodox Hassidic courts of the regions. The influence of ultra-Orthodoxy was especially strong in the home region of the young Avigdor Feuerstein along the Latorica river, where the *Munkaczer Rebbes* from the Shapira rabbinic family pressed for what one modern commentator described as "the most extreme version of Hungarian ultra-Orthodoxy."[31]

Orphaned at a very young age, Feuerstein grew up in his maternal grandfather's house in what he would later call "the poorest and darkest place of human settlement on earth."[32] His beloved grandfather, a devout Orthodox Jew with mystical inclinations, showed a profound love for the Hebrew language, possessing a collection of religious and secular Hebrew books. The fact that his grandfather "made his love for the Hebrew language into a rite [*pulkhan*]," led the young Feuerstein—according to his recollections—to base his Jewish national identification predominantly on the Hebrew language.[33] As a young pupil in the *cheder* (Jewish Orthodox religious school), Avigdor Feuerstein bestowed Hebrew and biblical names on the local topography: "the Latorica river was the Jordan, Munkács was Jerusalem, its clock tower was the Tower of David ... and the ruins of the old religious seminary [in Munkács] were the Western Wall."[34]

However, Feuerstein's early experiences were conflictual and emotionally charged, due to the intense resistance of the local Hassidim to any secular use of Hebrew, coupled with the brutality of his uncle, who as the local *melamed* (teacher) beat him because of his non-approved forays into Hebrew. Munkács in particular figured menacingly as "the fiercest and most sinister hornet's nest at war with any form of light, especially Hebrew culture."[35] The literary scholar, Hana Yaoz, described two symbolic groupings pertaining to Judaism which would later figure prominently in Hameiri's work: representations of a pure and loving mother (the Hebrew language and the Jewish people) contrasted with images depicting a stern and vengeful father (religion and God).[36] Hameiri, who identified throughout his life with the figure of an orphaned child, bounced around in his writings between these two Freudian poles, unable to extricate himself from their grip. Thus, in his 1955 recollections, Hameiri described his youthful years in terms of a double existence. On the one hand, he received a Jewish Orthodox upbringing in a prestigious Hungarian *yeshivot*, while on the other hand, he belonged to "a small and secret group of Zionists, meeting 'clandestinely'" and "conversing amongst themselves solely in Hebrew."[37] This dual experience of Judaism, as an object of both longing and agony, would come to make his Jewish identification ridden with conflict and guilt.

Expelled from the famous Pressburg (Pozsony/Bratislava) Orthodox Yeshiva at the age of fifteen, "in part because of Zionist activities," the young Feuerstein moved to Budapest to continue his studies at the *gymnázium* of the Budapest Rabbinical Seminary. Although the seminary was a state-sponsored institute aimed at disseminating Hungarian culture and patriotism among rabbinical students (and through it among Hungarian Jewry), it was at the same time also a center for the study of medieval and modern Hebrew literature. The seminary's journal, *Magyar Zsidó Szemle* (Hungarian Jewish Review), regularly published reviews in Hungarian of modern Hebrew works, while simultaneously translating Hungarian poetry into Hebrew. Although as an institution it eschewed the fledgling Zionist movement ("with all its force" according to Hameiri), the seminary did allow faculty members to lend a helping hand to various cultural projects associated with the revival of Hebrew, most notably Eliezer Ben Yehuda's great dictionary. According to Moshe Carmilly-Weinberger, the purpose of all this was "to build a cultural bridge between Jerusalem and Budapest." In this context, there emerged the formulation—printed in every textbook of Jewish studies in Hungarian schools—"we are Hungarians of the Israelite faith; our forefathers were Abraham, Isaac and Jacob." Thus, Feuerstein's early poetic activity within the seminary's literary circle could be best understood as part of a larger attempt to weave together two equally bright strands: Hungarian and Hebrew cultures.[38]

Following his matriculation from the *gymnázium*, Avigdor Feuerstein embarked on a career as journalist and night editor in the Hungarian language press, publishing in the Zionist weekly *Mult és Jövő* (Past and Future) as well as in a host of other Hungarian language newspapers. It was in the context of his budding journalistic career that he began using the Hungarian name, Albert Kova.[39] At the same time, he plunged head on into the bohemian lifestyle of what he called "the night-owl":

> Getting-up at five o'clock in the afternoon. Sitting at a café for two hours or more. Poems, short stories, essays. Then: first a visit to the newspaper. Then: the obligatory concert or theater show till ten or later. After all this: the hard labor of creating the newspaper till three o'clock ... and after work who goes to sleep? In convivial company until the morning light. Socializing: music, art, philosophy, woman, dance, and science.[40]

The poet Itamar Yaoz-Kest, who edited one of Hameiri's anthologies, argued that Feuerstein/Kova closely identified at that period (and to a certain degree afterwards, too) with the romantic figure of the "poet ablaze." This image of the poet's vocation had been developed during the *fin-de-siècle* by French "damned poets" such as Verlaine, Rimbaud, and Baudelaire, and filtered into turn-of-the century Hungary through the radical "New Poems" (*Új versek*) of Endre Ady.[41] The calling which Feuerstein/Kova seems to have envisioned himself as following at the time, was that of a poet who wrote fervently and truthfully, drank hard (including absinth, a staple drink of the "damned"), and lived mostly at night. He saw himself as a cosmopolitan lover, believing in "the international language of wine and love," and stressing—in the manner of contemporary pacifist writers such as Ivan Bloch and Norman Angel—the futility of armed conflict. Yet, Feuerstein/Kova was also firmly committed to specifically Hebrew and Hungarian national literary agendas and their political, patently non-cosmopolitan implications.

In this context, the young Avigdor Feuerstein managed to catch the attention of the greatest Hebrew and Hungarian poets of the time, respectively Haim Nahman Bialik and Endre Ady. With Bialik, it was Hameiri's "powerful Hungarian tone" and his "willingness to stray from well-trodden roads" which recommended the young writer to the "Hebrew National Bard."[42] Although his first book of Hebrew verse, published in 1912 as *Meshirei Avigdor Fayersteyn* (the Poems of Avigdor Feuerstein), received mixed reviews in the Hebrew language press of the time, Bialik was impressed. In 1913, when they met for the first time during the eleventh Zionist congress in Vienna, Bialik was kind enough to quote a line from Fayersteyn's poems, and say "it is very beautiful, really beautiful."[43] Bialik would become a much more immediate influence in 1917, when Fayersteyn would join his literary entourage in Odessa. However, the main artistic and personal inspiration in 1913 was Endre Ady and his powerful poetry.

In Endre Ady, Feuerstein found a close mentor and a role model for combining "East" and "West," cosmopolitanism and national identification. He regarded Ady as one of the most important innovators of literary decadence:

> [He created] a new meaning for nationalism: an individualistic meaning, freeing the nationally-inclined writer from the rough chains of politics and putting him in touch

with his instinctive racial qualities. And that in an archaic-biblical style. In his love poems you remember the Song of Songs, in his overall lyricism Isaiah, in his anger Hosea, in his grief Jeremiah ...[44]

Ady in his eyes possessed the "soul of a Magyar seer" in the same mold of a biblical prophet and Feuerstein/Kova became part of his following. Not unreasonably, Itamar Yaoz-Kest concluded that Hameiri saw himself as a Hebrew version of Endre Ady.[45]

Thus, the outbreak of the First World War found the twenty-four-year-old Avigdor/Albert Feuerstein/Fayersteyn/Kova as a relatively accomplished poet with good contacts and influential patrons. At his newspaper, the telephone operator and telegraph ticker constantly fed him information about far away places and the hustle and the bustle of big city life in Budapest. In less than two and a half decades before World War I, he went through a variety of Jewish experiences: Hassidism, ultra-Orthodoxy, positive-historical Judaism (at the Theological Seminary), and Budapest bohemian decadence. Like many of his contemporaries, he was completely astounded by the outbreak of war in the summer of 1914 and by the intrusion of the state into his daily routines. The war would prompt him into a different course and to unexpected choices, while unleashing in him a creative energy which would fuel him for the next two decades.

3. The experience of war 1914–18

Avigdor Hameiri's war writings are vast. The literary scholar, Avner Holtzman, has pointed out that Hameiri is the only Hebrew writer whose experiences at the front and in war captivity assumed a central place in his artistic output.[46] Although over a hundred Hebrew writers served in the various armies fighting in the First World War, and although thirty of them wrote about their war experiences, no one published as much and with such intensity: two autobiographical "non-fiction novels," *Ha-Shigaon ha-gadol* (The Great Madness, 1929) and *Be-Gehenom shel mata* (Hell on Earth, 1932), twenty-seven short stories, fifty poems, and one play.[47]

Like other important war writers Hameiri approached the subject with a pacifist sensibility, attempting to probe the meanings and implications of the words "loyalty," "*moledet*" (fatherland or *Heimat*), "us," and "them." Perhaps more than others, he was continuing his own private search, which had begun years earlier in Odavidhaza, but was now being reworked against a backdrop of cataclysmic world events. Thus, the structure of his two autobiographical novels is that of a *Bildungsroman*, where the hero—amidst great misery, pain, and destruction—attempts to sort out his various identifications, conflicts, and desires, before deciding eventually to forsake his birthplace for the "real" *moledet* in mandatory Palestine.

During the six years covered by *Ha-Shigaon ha-gadol* and *Begehenom shel mata*, the hero gradually loses trust in the Habsburg monarchy, its institutions, and its emperor, while loosening the emotional bonds which tied him to Hungary and Hungarian patriotism. The symbolic climax comes in the administration of a *Get* (traditional Jewish writ of divorce) "to Madame Hungaria" by a fellow Jewish officer who takes the hand of Avigdor Feuerstein and encourages him to part with Hungary in this mock ceremony. It is interesting to note that, in this scene, it is not Feuerstein himself who initiates this emotional parting. However, once divorced from Hungary, he declares his thrill to be married solely to his Jewish wife.

The fact that during these six years Feuerstein/Hameiri was forcibly cut off from what he called his "civilian essence," gave him a new vantage point from which to examine his life. It had also opened the gates for new sensations which either had not existed before the war, or could not have been acknowledged: the exhilaration of close masculine bonding with a group of beloved friends; the agony of constant degradation; the illicit pleasures of exercising authority and humiliating others who "deserve it"; and in one shocking case, a sense of contentment derived from murdering a fellow ensign (*Fähnrich*), who had slept with the wife of another officer while on leave. What makes Feuerstein/Hameiri's writing so exceptional is his constant awareness of the contradictory nature of some of his feelings, choices, and actions. He is relentless in his self-criticism and self-loathing: spitting at his reflection in the mirror after behaving cowardly towards a disgraced friend, or calling himself, in one of his poems from 1917, "The King of Filth" (*Melekh ha-Skhi*).[48] This complexity, and the ways in which it translated into questions of identification and loyalty, can be illustrated by way of three examples: his enlistment to the Habsburg army in the summer of 1914, his portrayal of Jewish soldiers at the front, and his perception of the emperor-king.

The last days of peace in the summer of 1914 find Feuerstein/Kova drinking and hanging out with his reporter buddies and a group of five foreign women in the Royal Orpheum nightclub in Budapest. One of his companions, Dr. Garrey, gives a speech in a drunken stupor, claiming that a great war would constitute an immense catharsis, "after which we will emerge as a patient who had had all the puss drained out from his wound."[49] Feuerstein dismisses this as the alcohol talking, and is sure that Garrey will return to their previous stance of condemning war as futile. Yet, the outbreak of war leads Garrey to be deeply affected by the patriotic crowd, announcing to Feuerstein his intention of volunteering. Feuerstein in turn bursts out laughing, saying to him jocularly: "You are quite a guy! Go, go my war hero, the fatherland is in danger!" This draws an angry reaction from Garrey who looks at Feuerstein with disgust and cries: "Jew! ... how could you even know the meaning of the word fatherland?"[50]

Hana Yaoz has argued that this anti-Semitic utterance from one of his closest drinking companions unleashed a kind of "Dreyfus crisis" in Hameiri, similar to the one experienced two decades earlier by the founder of political Zionism, Theodore Herzl.[51] However, the comparison is not totally apt because Feuerstein, in contrast to Herzl, did not give up on the state. Rather, he attempted to prove his loyalty and patriotism. This questioning of his identification with the Hungarian fatherland led him to seek immediate enlistment, although he was not yet obliged to do so. He was especially moved by the military clerk's reference to his birthplace in the Carpathian mountains and to the fact that this was the *moledet* which "the savage Cossacks are threatening to overrun."[52] When he was rudely yelled at by the recruiting officer, Feuerstein was aware that he was having his first pangs of regret, and admits feeling like an idiot for rushing to volunteer. He quickly changes his mind again after some encouraging words in coarse language from the *Feldwebel* (Sergeant), who assures him: "With us you will finally become a human being. Your hands will not be covered anymore in ink and the rest of all of your nonsense!" Although feeling like a fool, especially when he learns that Dr. Garrey with all of his patriotic bravura sought deferral rather than immediate enlistment, Feuerstein reports feeling "pride and happiness." "Why deny it," he acknowledged, "I was happy."

However, this fleeting sense of pride and happiness cannot be disentangled from its immediate cause, namely anti-Semitic prejudice. Throughout *Ha-Shigaon ha-gadol,* this dynamic recurs in one form or another: Feuerstein is pressed to prove his patriotism and his manliness in the face of anti-Semitic hostility, prevalent predominantly among Habsburg reserve officers. Yet, once Feuerstein proves his courage, thereby experiencing a moment of self-satisfaction, he is faced with the resentment of those who interpret his endeavors as an attempt to make them look bad. Consequently, in Hameiri's war literature, Austro-Hungarian Jewish soldiers are forever caught between a rock and a hard place, without a truly "honorable" course of action. Either they were unjustly perceived as not patriotic enough, or were seen as individualistic show-offs who lacked *esprit-de-corps:*

> After ten days of horrendous fighting near Częstochowa with heavy casualties [it became known] that all the Jewish officers in our Regiment, almost without exception, have proved themselves as heroic without peer ... and that most of the [heroic deeds] in this battle were done by Jews, the rest by Hungarian officers, but none by the Austrian officers. Although it was a coincidence, it was still a fact.[53]

This last incident led, according to Hameiri, to an outbreak of animosity toward Jewish officers, and to the court martial of a Jewish platoon commander on trumped up charges.

In Hameiri's writing, the only course open to Jewish soldiers was to hide their "Jewishness" as much as they could. This was indeed the message conveyed to him on numerous occasions by his superior officers. "You don't have to be always a Jew!", one of his commanders advised him during his officer training course, while his battalion commander—who later turns out to be himself of Jewish origin—inquires, "Why are you so proud of being a Jew?"[54] When Feuerstein answers, "that there is nothing really to be proud of, but when expected to be ashamed of it, I become proud," he gets into a heated exchange with his commander, who tells him: "This entire stinking Jewish package should go to hell!"[55] As a result of this dispute, *Unteroffizier* Feuerstein is sent prematurely to the front— instead of receiving a cushy assignment in the rear—and is denied officer's rank.

In Hameiri's narrative, there is no doubt that not hiding his proud Jewish identification led to discrimination and dangerous assignments.

Yet, a frontline assignment is not necessarily a punishment in Hameiri's world. Like other Great War writers, he is scathing in his portrayal of civilian life during the war, and is especially nasty in his descriptions of women. After being injured at the front for the second time, Feuerstein is sent to recuperate at a Budapest hospital, where he sees nothing but whoring "and the abyss of mankind in all its filth and cowardice."[56] The same Budapest nightlife which Feuerstein/Kova enjoyed so much, "which was known to me so intimately, is occupied now by completely different beings: worm-people who despise everyone who comes from the front."[57] Thus, the only option available to a decent citizen, a proud Jew, and a manly soldier is the front.

Indeed, one of the main rewards of Jewish soldierly pride is a heightened sense of manliness. Immediately upon his enlistment, Fayersteyn pens a poem entitled *Ketem Adom* [a Red Stain], in which he anticipates his "withering muscles becoming meshed steel."[58] As the war progresses, Feuerstein feels intense bonding with the mostly common peasant soldiers assigned to his command. He shares his parcels with them, and expresses his love and responsibility in knightly gestures. In *Ha-Shigaon ha-gadol,* for example, Hameiri lengthily quotes his Calvinist *Oberleutnant*—one of the few non-odious officers in the book—who maintains that, because Jews were allowed for the first time in two thousand years to display their prowess, the "result was a gush of natural heroism."[59] Hameiri's ecstatic representation of Jewish warriors was one of the earliest expositions of Jewish martial ideals in Hebrew literature, and, according to Avner Holtzman, "the most comprehensive portrayal of Jewish Great War soldiers."[60] The fact that it was written by a self-proclaimed pacifist is in itself a striking indication of the inherent tensions embedded in early Jewish nationalism.

The reverse side of Jewish heroism is the unmanly conduct of converts to Christianity or of Jews who are ashamed of their Jewish origin. Some of the most despicable characters presented in Hameiri's writing are discovered later on to be ex-Jews. They are petty, ugly, and prone to anti-Semitic vitriol, in order to curry favor with their superiors. Although Hameiri assures the readers in the introduction to *Ha-Shigaon Ha-gadol* that his narrative is accurately based on his wartime diaries, it is clear that he arranged the material so converts would always be exposed as dishonorable characters. The most despicable of all Jew-baiters in the regiment, the provincial actor Andras Madi, confesses his Jewish origin only before his execution for attempting to flee the front. Thus, in Hameiri's narrative, there is a strong link between Jewish pride, manliness, heroism, and patriotism, while Jewish shame, effete behavior, cowardice, and fake patriotism are also intimately linked.

Thus, the fact that the Habsburg army did not appreciate the fighting spirit of its Jewish soldiers is presented in the narrative as cruel ingratitude. Proud Jewish soldiers were not only courageous and manly, but also Habsburg loyalists and, in the case of Hungarian Jews, also supporters of the Magyar nation. In a moving scene, Feuerstein meets the elderly major-general (*Feldmarschalleutnant*), Eduard von Schweitzer, a veteran of the 1866 war and one of five Jewish officers to reach the rank of general in the Habsburg armed forces.[61] Coughing and full of tears, Schweitzer tells Feuerstein that "it is a cruel *moledet*, my dear boy, cruel, cruel, because she knows we love her so."[62]

The image of the Emperor-King, Franz Joseph, evolves in *Ha-Shigaon ha-gadol* and *Be-gehenom shel mata*, becoming complex and ambivalent. Thus, in the beginning of his narrative, Hameiri depicts Franz Joseph as a beloved figure of his childhood "a tender, aged man, whose life was filled with sorrow … this old king I envisioned as a friend of my old grandfather … coming to celebrate an opening of a synagogue, listening to the prayers and answering Amen." Even when drawn to radical socialism, "hating all kings with all of my heart. I could not bring myself to hate the old king. The most I could do was view him as a nice operetta king with a paper crown and a wooden sword." However, the carnage of war, coupled with the inability of commanding officers to explain the purpose of all this devastation, darkens the image of Franz Joseph among his troops. In one hilarious scene, Feuerstein is ordered to prepare a list of the "ten virtues of war." Being a man of letters, Feuerstein comes up with a list that begins with "strengthens the muscles," and ends with "grants our deaths a heroic quality." His commander looks at his list for a split second and calls it "filth." He then recites the ten official virtues: "it destroys, kills, murders, flattens, annihilates, uproots, obliterates, demolishes, wipes out and buries." Later on, when his own troops inquire who willed this war, he tells them "His Royal Highness, Our Commander, Emperor Franz Joseph." As a result, the men in the company begin spitting and cursing their sovereign profusely. "I wanted to tell them," writes Hameiri, "that he didn't want the war either, but I thought it over and kept quiet … poor Franz Joseph! His good soldiers direct at him the nastiest and most obscene curses with all of their hearts."[63]

Even after he falls captive in June 1916, Feuerstein still cannot deny his emotional attachment to the dying emperor-king, despite his conviction that the old man is responsible for the war. Like a sizeable section of Austro-Hungarian POWs in Russia, Feuerstein is delighted by the arrival of new clothes from the Dual Monarchy, and reports that many prisoners credited—incorrectly—Franz Joseph as buying the garments from his own funds.[64] When many of these clothes are stolen, his Jewish comrade, Margulies, the *yeshiva* student, feels sorry for Franz Joseph: "Poor old man! He spends and here it is stolen."[65] Despite a pool of warm feelings to Franz Joseph, the person of the emperor-king disappears completely from the narrative once the old sovereign dies in November 1916. Feuerstein knows little about the new Emperor-King Karl and does not seem to care much either. The state becomes either an uncaring entity ("not worth the life of a flea"), or is reduced to his remote Magyar fatherland.

Ultimately, even the memory of Hungary fades in the period covered by *Be-Gehenom shel mata* and the various writings produced during Hameiri's stay in Odessa from 1919–1921. Whereas he could still be amazed in 1915 by "the miraculous assimilatory powers of the Magyar nation which cannot be rivaled anywhere in the world,"[66] he is quite despondent about Hungary's future in the fall of 1916:

> I will not be deceitful: I have that [dreaded] feeling that they will defeat us, poor Hungary. We, who unwillingly follow Germany and Austria singing sad parting songs, have the role of a light-headed apache who follows his Viennese mistress … and dies for her while this whore is searching for another lover.[67]

A year later, after a serious bout of typhus which almost killed him, Feuerstein finds little energy to care about Hungary and its fate in the war. Using the name Anton Germanovich Slezak, he managed to be sent to Kiev. From there, through his various contacts among Hebrew *literati,* he found his way to Odessa, one of the most important centers of Hebrew culture. Thus, between the fall of 1917 until he left Odessa in 1921, Hungary recurs in his writings only once, when all Hungarian citizens are ordered to return to Hungary to join Béla Kun's revolutionary forces in the summer of 1919. In this context, Avigdor Fayersteyn writes in his diary: "I will not go because I have a choice: if they force a weapon into my hands, I will use the first bullet to free myself from this hell."[68]

Sailing from Odessa in the summer of 1921, Fayersteyn set out for Mandatory Palestine with a large group of Hebrew writers and intellectuals. Soon after his arrival, he would begin publishing in Hebrew under the name "Hameiri," which he would keep until his death in 1970. He would visit Hungary again only in 1930. Upon visiting his hometown of Odavidhaza, now part of Czechoslovakia, Hameiri finds that all its magical powers of biblical allusion are gone: "the land of Israel in the Carpathian valley … is just like the Land of Israel on the Dead Sea" and that turned out to be not very much. His *Heimat* region has become hollow, its Hassidic crowd remained loathsome, but the new *moledet* had lost its magical appeal as well. During the remaining years of his life, he would make choices and take actions, but eventually concede that none of them truly reflected the manner in which he felt. "I have two souls," he wrote in one of his poems, "one residing on the banks of eastern rivers/with reflections of peace in her eyes/ the second lies on western rivers/dreaming a scarlet dream." In another poem, he said with resignation: "my soul is the daughter of Shem, Ham and Japheth."

Conclusion: the contradictions of identification processes

Habsburg Jews have been presented in the historiography as intensely loyal, and it is obviously true that most of them dutifully did what the state required them to do during the First World War. Hameiri's own wartime record would suggest that perhaps he was also one of those intensely loyal citizens: volunteering to fight at the beginning of the war, injured twice in battle, and earning a medal for bravery. However, Hameiri's personal story and his portrayal of the behavior of other Jewish soldiers leads one to question whether this behavior was truly the outcome of intense attachment. During the war, Hameiri's emotional attachments slowly drifted away from the Habsburg monarchy and from the Magyar fatherland.

In his journey, Hameiri was probably not alone. After the war, when his home region of Carpatho-Rus' was incorporated into the newly established state of Czechoslovakia, under the new designation of Subcarpathian Rus' (*Podkarpatská Rus*), ninety-five percent of "Jews by religion" declared themselves to be also "Jews by nationality."[69] In comparison, in Bohemia the westernmost province of the new state, only twenty percent of Jews by religion declared themselves to be Jews by nationality. This trend continued also in the 1930 Czechoslovak census, when out of 102,542 Jews living in Subcarpathian Rus', 95,002 declared themselves to be "Jewish by Nationality," 3,870 professed to being "Magyar by nationality," 708 declared themselves as "Rusyns," 130 declared themselves as "German by nationality," and a paltry 80 declared themselves to be "Czechoslovak."[70] When most of the region was annexed to Hungary in the years 1938-39, following the First Vienna Award, 104,642 Jews declared Yiddish to be their mother tongue, rather than declaring Hungarian. Based on these figures, Yeshayahu Jelinek concluded that the Jews of Carpatho-Rus', in contrast to their coreligionists from other parts of pre-World War I Hungary, "relinquished without difficulty their Hungarian identity, adopted during the final decades of Hungarian rule."[71]

In the final analysis, subjective feelings of attachment were just one factor in a complex matrix of rejections and attractions which changed and shifted in the latter part of the nineteenth century and first half of the twentieth century. Context was often more important than conviction and ideology, and instinctive, murky thought could be at times more typical than clarity of vision. The Great War was an important juncture in this respect, because it uprooted people from established routines, suggested new possibilities for envisioning the future, and encouraged a reassessment of old traditions and attachments. However, in saying this, it must be emphasized that these considerations were not unique to Jews. Recent studies clearly demonstrate that soldiers fighting in all armies during World War I experienced conflicting feelings, dissonance, and periods of despair.[72] It cannot be otherwise when a person is exposed to so many new and demanding experiences. Great War writers represented such perplexity very well, and in this sense too, the figure of Avigdor/Albert Feuerstein/Fayersteyn/Kova/Hameiri was very much part of that more universal trend.

Notes

* An earlier version of this essay appeared in Hungary in *Múlt és jövő* [Past and Future] (2006/1): 45–61, and in Germany in the *Simon Dubnow Jahrbuch,* 5 (2006): 135–157.
1. For assessments of Hameiri's unfulfilled potential, see most recently Pinhas Genosar, "Baderekh le-shira be-mivta sephardi: Avigdor Hameiri ve-hapolmus al ha-mishkal ha-syllabo-

toni," [On the way to Sephardic accentuated poetry: Avigdor Hameiri and the Controversy over the Syllabo-Tonic Meter], *Iyunim be-Tkumat Israel,* 11 (2001), 447–464; see also Hameiri's most systematic literary scholar, Avner Holtzman, *Avigdor Hameiri ve-sifrut ha-milkhama* [Avigdor Hameiri and War Literature] (Tel Aviv, 1986); Ehud Ben Ezer, "Ha-Shigaon ha-gadol le-Avigdor Hameiri," [The Great Madness by Avigdor Hameiri], in *Ahavat sofrim* [The Love of Authors], ed. Israel Eliraz (Tel Aviv, 1984), 114–115. For the few literary scholars who still examine his work, Hameiri's output as a memoirist is seen primarily as a distinctive "Jewish voice" among the war generation writers. Thus, like another former Austro-Hungarian Jewish writer, Max Brod, Hameiri is perceived today first and foremost as a facilitator, who helped usher in modernism, but contributed little of intrinsic and lasting value. On Brod, see Scott Spector, *Prague Territories: National Conflict and Cultural Innovation in Franz Kafka's Fin-de Siècle* (Berkeley, Los Angeles and London, 2000), 60-67, 210–217; Hillel Kieval, *Languages of Community: The Jewish Experience in the Czech Lands* (Berkeley, Los Angeles and London, 2000), 216–220; id., *The Making of Czech Jewry: National Conflict and Jewish Society in Bohemia 1870–1918* (Oxford and New York, 1988), 139–140; Max Brod, *Streitbares Leben 1884–1968* (Munich, 1969).
2. No less a figure than the "Hebrew National Poet," Haim Nahman Bialik, emphasized Hameiri's "Hungarianess" and contrasted it with the Russian flavor of most other Hebrew writers. On Hameiri's uneasy relationship with Bialik, see Avigdor Hameiri, *Bialik al atar* [Bialik ex tempore] (Tel Aviv, 1962); Itamar Yaoz-Kest, "Avigdor Hameiri ve-shirato," [Avigdor Hameiri and his Poetry], *Avigdor Hameiri: yalkut shirim* [Avigdor Hameiri: Poetic Anthology] (Jerusalem, 1976), 7–25; Pinhas Genosar, "Ba-derekh le-shira be-mivta sephardi," 452–458; Holtzman, *Avigdor Hameiri,* 37–39.
3. Avigdor Hameiri to David Zakai, *Gnazim Archive,* Avigdor Hameiri Collection.
4. Jacques Le Rider, *Modernity and the Crises of Identity: Culture and Society in Fin-de-Siècle Vienna,* translated from the French by Rosemary Morris (New York, 1993).
5. Steven Beller, "Patriotism and National Identity of Habsburg Jewry, 1860–1914," *Leo Baeck Institute Yearbook* XLI (1996): 215–238.
6. It has become, writes Brubaker, "a deeply ambiguous term," harboring simultaneously two conflicting tendencies. On the one hand, it assumes some kind of "hard" foundation—be it gender, racial, ethnic, religious, class—otherwise the group of people under discussion would have no common denominator, yet, on the other hand, there is an insistence that all identities are "soft," i.e. fluid, negotiated, constructed, and ever changing. Rogers Brubaker, *Ethnicity without Groups* (Cambridge, MA, 2004), 4, 28–31, 33–41. See also, Peter Wagner, "Identity as Selfhood and *Problématique,*" in *Identities: Time, Difference and Boundaries,* ed. Heidrun Friese (New York and Oxford, 2002), 32–55.
7. Even after settling on the Hebrew "Hameiri," he transliterated it at various moments as "Hammeiri," "Hammeïri," "Hamme'iry," and "Hammèiri." See *Agudat Hasofrim* [The Writers Association]: *Gnazim Archive,* Avigdor Hameiri Collection.
8. On this, see Marsha Rozenblit, *Reconstructing a National Identity: The Jews of Habsburg Austria during World War I* (New York and Oxford, 2001); David Rechter, *The Jews of Vienna and the First World War* (London and Portland Oregon, 2001); William O. McCagg, Jr., *A History of Habsburg Jews 1670–1918* (Bloomington and Indianapolis, 1992); István Deák, *Beyond Nationalism: A Social and Political History of the Habsburg Officer Corps 1848–1918* (New York and Oxford, 1990); Erwin A. Schmidl, *Juden in der k.(u.)k. Armee 1788–1918/Jews in the Habsburg Armed Forces* (Eisenstadt, 1989); Oscar Jászi, *The Dissolution of the Habsburg Monarchy* (Chicago, 1961; orig. 1929).
9. Rozenblit, *Reconstructing a National Identity,* 4. According to the last official census in 1910, there were 1,325,856 Jews in the Austrian half of the monarchy and 932,416 Jews in the Hungarian half.
10. The acronym "KIRAH" stands for the Hebrew *Keisar yarum hodo* (His Majesty the Emperor).
11. Rozenblit, *Reconstructing a National Identity,* 4.

12. See Schmidl, *Juden in der k.(u).k. Armee*, 142–144; Deák, *Beyond Nationalism*, 195–197.
13. Schmidl, *Juden in der k.(u).k. Armee*, 135–136.
14. Schmidl, *Juden in der k.(u).k. Armee*, 144; Robert Kann, *A History of the Habsburg Empire 1526–1918* (Berkeley, Los Angeles, and London, 1974), 606.
15. Schmidl, *Juden in der k.(u).k. Armee*, 142–145; Werner Angress, "Prussia's Army and the Jewish Reserve Officer Controversy Before World War I," *Leo Baeck Institute Yearbook* XVII (1972): 19–42.
16. See Rozenblit, *Reconstructing a National Identity*, 3–38.
17. Quoted from Carl Schorske, *Fin-de-Siècle Vienna: Politics and Culture* (New York, 1981), 125.
18. See Stefan Zweig, *The World of Yesterday*, (New York, 1943); Joseph Roth, *Radetzky March*, (New York, 1933); Joseph Roth, *Die Kapuzinergruft*, (Cologne, 1950); See also Michael Stanislawski, *Autobiographical Jews: Essays in Jewish Self-Fashioning* (Seattle, 2004), ch. 4.
19. Michael Silber, "Pa'amei lev ha-ivri be-eretz hagar," [A Hebrew Heart Beats in Hungary], *Kathedra* 73/3 (Sept 1994): 84–105. id., "The Entrance of Jews into Hungarian Society in the Vormärz: The Case of the 'Casinos'," in *Assimilation and Community: The Jews in Nineteenth-Century Europe*, ed. Jonathan Frankel and Steven J. Zipperstein (Cambridge, 1992), 284–323; id., "The Historical Experience of German Jewry and its Impact on Haskalah and Reform in Hungary," in *Toward Modernity: The European Jewish Model*, ed. Jacob Katz (New Brunswick, NJ, 1986); McCagg, *A History of Habsburg Jews*, ch. 8; Péter Hanak, "Problems of Jewish Assimilation in Austria-Hungary in the Nineteenth Century," in *The Power of the Past: Essays for Eric Hobsbawm*, ed. Pat Thane, Geoffrey Crossick, and Roderick Floud (Cambridge, 1984), 235–250; George Barany, "Magyar Jew or Jewish Magyar: Reflections on the Question of Assimilation," in *Jews and Non-Jews in Eastern Europe*, ed. Bela Vago and George Mosse (New York, Toronto, and Jerusalem, 1974), 51–98.
20. Michael K. Silber, "The Rise of Ethnicism and the Emergence of Jewish Nationalism: The Paradoxical Dialectic of Jewish Collective Identities in the Mid-Nineteenth Century" (paper presented at the conference *Jews in a Multi-Ethnic Network*), University of Haifa, 20 December, 2004.
21. Silber, "Pa'amei lev ha-ivri be-eretz hagar."
22. Barany, "Magyar Jew or Jewish Magyar"; Gary Cohen, "Jews in German Society: Prague 1860–1914," *Central European History*, 10 (1977), 28–54; id., "Education, Social Mobility and the Austrian Jews," in *Bildungswesen und Sozialstruktur in Mitteleuropa im 19. und 20. Jahrhundert*, ed. Victor Karady and Wolfgang Mitter (Cologne and Vienna, 1990), 141–161; Kieval, *Languages of Community*; id., *The Making of Czech Jewry*; Marsha Rozenblit, *The Jews of Vienna 1867–1914: Assimilation and Identity* (Albany, 1983); id., *Reconstructing a National Identity*; id., "The Assertion of Identity: Jewish Student Nationalism at the University of Vienna before the First World War," *Leo Baeck Institute Yearbook* 27 (1982): 171–186; Dimitry Shumsky, "Historiografia, leumiut ve-du-leumiut: yahadut checho-germanit, zionei prag u-mekorot ha-gisha ha-du-leumit shel Hugo Bergmann," [Historiography, Nationalism and Bi-Nationalism: Czech-German Jewry, the Prague Zionists, and the Origins of the Bi-National Approach of Hugo Bergmann], *Zion* LXIX n. 1 (2004): 45–80; Silber, "The Rise of Ethnicism and the Emergence of Jewish Nationalism"; id., "A Hebrew Heart Beats in Hungary"; Michael Silber, "The Entrance of Jews into Hungarian Society in the Vormärz"; Robert Wistrich, *The Jews of Vienna in the Age of Franz Joseph* (Oxford, 1989).
23. Shumsky, "Historiografia, leumiut ve-du-leumiut," and compare the critique of the Shumsky thesis by Martin Wein, "Yehudim czecho-germanim ve-tu lo? T'guva le-ma'amaro shel dimitry shumsky," [Only Czecho-German Jews? A Response to Dimitry Shumsky], *Zion*, LXX n. 3 (2005): 383–392. Shumsky emphasizes that his construct of "Czecho-German Jews" applies to "the socio-cultural position" of some Jews, not to the totality of Jews in Bohemia and Moravia. He further stresses that what is being described is an "experience" and not an "identity." Yet, the notion of a "Czecho-German Jewry" might easily be misinter-

preted as referring to the majority of Bohemian Jews and as describing a constructed "identity." Shumsky clarifies this issue nicely in his reply to Wein; see Dimitry Shumsky "Yehudim czecho-germanim" [Czecho-German Jews], *Zion,* LXX n. 3 (2005): 393–399.
24. Salo Baron, "The Modern Age," in *Great Ages and Ideas of the Jewish People,* ed. Leo Schwartz (New York: The Modern Library, 1957), 315–484; Jacob Katz, *Tradition and Crisis: Jewish Society at the End of the Middle Ages* (Syracuse, 2000) [originally published in Hebrew as Masoret u-Mashber, 1958]; Yosef Haim Yerushalmi, *Zakhor: Jewish History and Jewish Memory,* forward by Harold Bloom (Seattle and London, 1982), second printing 1996, ch. 4.
25. Spector, *Prague Territories,* preface, ix–xi; Le Rider, *Modernity and the Crises of Identity,* introduction, 1–7. This line of argumentation is also present in Jeremy King's comments regarding Jewish collective identification in the nineteenth century, see his "The Nationalization of East Central Europe: Ethnicism, Ethnicity, and Beyond," in *Staging the Past: The Politics of Commemoration in Habsburg Central Europe, 1848 to the Present,* ed. Maria Bucur and Nancy M. Wingfield (West Lafayette, 2001), 127.
26. The idea of "identity crisis" is derived from Erik Erikson's work in the 1950s, especially his *Childhood and Society* (New York, 1950), part 3. Erikson's concept of identity rested on the idea of integrating various givens, needs, capacities, identifications, defenses, and roles into a sense of continuity, unity, and wholeness. On the rough road to "identity integration," a person may experience unresolved conflicts which result in "identity crises." Although contemporary psychoanalytic literature rejects much of Erik Erikson's work, his notions of "identity" and "identity crisis" gained a broad appeal in cultural studies. See Stephen Seligman and Rebecca Shahmoon Shanok, "Subjectivity, Complexity and the Social World: Erikson's Identity Concept and Contemporary Relational Theories," *Psychoanalytic Dialogues,* 5 (4) 1995, 537–565.
27. Spector, *Prague Territories,* x.
28. Odavidhaza is today Stare Davydkovo in Ukraine. As explained above, the rule I follow regarding place names is the same used for personal names, i.e., the name used at the time, as it applies to the specific context. In this article, the name most often given is the Hungarian official place name. Thus, the largest town in the region (population 17,200 in 1910) was officially known as Munkács in Hungarian, but was rendered also as Munkacz or Minkacz in Yiddish, Mukacheve in Ukrainian, Mukachiv in Rusyn, Mukačevo in Slovak, and Munkatsch in German.
29. Yeshayahu Jelinek, *Ha-golah le-raglei ha-karpatim: yehudei Carpatho-Rus' ve-Mukachevo 1848–1948* [Exile in the Foothills of the Carpathians: The Jews of Carpatho-Rus' and Mukachevo 1848–1948] (Tel Aviv, 2003), 36, 46–60.
30. Ibid., 35–37.
31. Allan Nadler, "The War on Modernity of R. Hayyim Elazar Shapira of Munkacz," *Modern Judaism,* 14:3 (October 1994): 233.
32. Hameiri, *Masa be-europa ha-prait* [A Trip in Ferocious Europe] (Jerusalem, 1938), 143.
33. Hameiri, Brief Autobiographical Essay.
34. Avigdor Hameiri, *Masa be-europa ha-prait,* 140.
35. Avigdor Hameiri, Brief Autobiographical Essay, in *Gnazim* Archive (Tel Aviv), Avigdor Hameiri Collection: Microfilm Section. On Munkács, see Aviezer Ravitzky, "Munkács and Jerusalem: Ultra-Orthodox Opposition to Zionism and Agudaism," *Zionism and Religion,* eds. Shmuel Almog, Jehuda Reinharz, and Anita Shapira (Hanover and London, 1998), 67–89; Allan Nadler, "The War on Modernity of R. Hayyim Elazar Shapira of Munkacz," *Modern Judaism,* 14:3 (October 1994): 233–264.
36. Hana Yaoz, "Livtei zehut ve-livtei kiyumiut yehudit be-yetsirat Hameiri" [Identity Dilemmas and Jewish Existential Dilemmas in Hameiri's Work], *Zehut* 3 (1983): 217–224.
37. Hameiri, Brief Autobiographical Essay.

38. Moshe Carmilly-Weinberger, "The Similarities and Relationship between the Jüdisch-Theologisches Seminar (Breslau) and the Rabbinical Seminary (Budapest)," *Leo Baeck Institute Yearbook*, XLIV (1999): 3–22; id., "Hebrew Language and Literature," in *The Rabbinical Seminary in Budapest 1877–1977*, ed. Moshe Carmilly-Weinberger (New York, 1986), 205–214.
39. Itamar Yaoz-Kest, "Avigdor Hameiri ve-shirato," 7.
40. Avigdor Hameiri, *Ha-shigaon ha-gadol: reshimot katsin ivri ba-milkhama ha-gdola* [The Great Madness: The Notes of a Hebrew Officer in the Great War], Dvir Edition edited by Avner Holtzman and Dan Meron (Tel Aviv, 1989), 15.
41. Yaoz-Kest, "Avigdor Hameiri ve-shirato," 11–13. In Hungary, Endre Ady was the quintessential "poet ablaze," working feverishly as a poet and a journalist, drinking hard, challenging bourgeois conventions, and perceiving his home country through an intense love-hate prism. See Péter Hanák, "The Start of Endre Ady's Literary Career (1903–1905)," in id., *The Garden and the Workshop: Essays on the Cultural History of Vienna and Budapest* (Princeton, 1998), 110–134.
42. Less generous souls among the Hebrew *literati* suggested that Fayersteyn's "uniqueness" consisted not in the quality of his poetry, but in the fact that he was a Hebrew voice writing in assimilationist Budapest rather than the Hebrew culture centers of Odessa and Warsaw. See Yaoz-Kest, "Avigdor Hameiri ve-shirato."
43. However, Bialik was mainly interested to know whether the young "scoundrel" [*Kundas*] had studied Talmud during his childhood. When Fayersteyn answered in the affirmative, stating that he went both to a *cheder* and a *yeshiva*, Bialik became distraught and lamented that he had not met yet "a Hebrew poet" without intensive religious education and that he was not sure whether it was possible to become one outside the confines of a *yeshiva*. Hameiri, *Bialik al atar*, 10–11.
44. Quoted after Yaoz-Kest, "Avigdor Hameiri ve-shirato," 12.
45. Ibid., 11–12. Hameiri was undoubtedly also attracted to Ady's usage of biblical allusion and metaphor. See Hanák, The Start of Endre Ady's Literary Career, 110–111.
46. Holtzman, *Avigdor Hameiri ve-sifrut ha-milkhama*, 31–39.
47. A "non-fiction novel," according to Holtzman, claims the "authority of reality" by referring to the outside experiential world while leaving the author enough room to exercise "aesthetic control." Thus, although Hameiri argued in the preface to *Ha-Shigaon ha-gadol* that he "did not embellish the facts, nor made them uglier; did not add nor subtract anything," it is clear that certain facts could not have occurred in the way Hameiri described them. The chronology at certain times is patently flawed, dialogue is arranged to increase dramatic effect, etc. Still, as Michael Stanislawski has recently argued, all autobiographical writing is essentially of "constructivist nature" and cannot be approached as "unmediated factual account." Michael Stanislawski, *Autobiographical Jews*, 3–7. On the classification of Hameiri's war literature according to genres, see Holtzman, *Avigdor Hameiri*, 31–42, 54–57.
48. Self-loathing was also a recurrent theme in the work of Hameiri's mentor, Endre Ady.
49. Hameiri, *Ha-shigaon ha-gadol*, 13.
50. Ibid., 19–20.
51. Yaoz, "Identity Dilemmas and Jewish Existential Dilemmas in Hameiri's Work," 218. According to legend, Herzl conceived the idea for a Jewish state as a response to the accusations against Alfred Dreyfus, and the latter's formal degradation in Paris on 5 January, 1895. As a correspondent for the *Neue Freie* Presse, Herzl was present at the degradation ceremony at the École Militaire, and was shocked by the widespread anti-Semitism which he encountered on the streets of Paris. It should be noted, however, that Herzl conceived the idea of a mass exodus of Jews from Europe over a period of a few months spanning the autumn of 1894 and the winter of 1895. Although deeply shocked by the Dreyfus affair, it was most probably "the last straw," which convinced him "of the necessity of Jewish exodus

from Europe." Amos Elon, *Herzl,* (New York, 1975), 126–127. See also Steven Beller, *Herzl* (London, 1991), ch. 2; Alex Bein, *Theodore Herzl: A Biography* (Philadelphia, 1941), 108–120.
52. Here, and for what follows Hameiri, *Ha-shigaon ha-gadol,* 24–25.
53. Ibid., 122–123.
54. Ibid., 81–84.
55. Ibid., 83.
56. Ibid., 200.
57. Ibid., 200.
58. Avigdor Hameiri, *Sefer ha-shirim* (Tel Aviv, 1932), 186. See also Hameiri, *Ha-shigaon ha-gadol,* 30.
59. Hameiri, *Ha-shigaon ha-gadol,* 213.
60. Holtzman, *Avigdor Hameiri,* 36.
61. The question of who should be counted as a "Jewish general" is a delicate and very problematic one. Schmidl lists five, while Deák—who counts also converted Jews—lists twenty-five. It is clear that an officer who converted to Christianity had far greater chances of promotion. Schmidl, *Juden in der k.(u.)k. Armee,* 124–9; Deák, *Beyond Nationalism,* 196.
62. Hameiri, *Ha-shigaon ha-gadol,* 28.
63. Ibid., 165.
64. Avigdor Hameiri, *Be-gehenom shel mata: reshimot katsin ivri be-shevi Russia* [Hell on Earth: The Notes of a Hebrew Officer in Russian Captivity], Dvir Edition edited by Avner Holtzman and Dan Meron (Tel Aviv, 1989), 150–153. On the Austro-Hungarian POW relief effort and its perception by the prisoners, see Alon Rachamimov, *POWs and the Great War: Captivity on the Eastern Front* (Oxford and New York, 2002), chs. 5–6.
65. Hameiri, *Be-gehenom shel mata,* 152.
66. Hameiri, *Ha-shigaon ha-gadol,* 112.
67. Hameiri, *Be-gehenom shel mata,* 111–112.
68. Ibid., 438.
69. Jelinek, *Ha-golah le-raglei ha-karpatim,* 25–26. Jelinek bases his figures on Hungarian and Czech sources. Ezra Mendelsohn, who uses different sources, comes up with slightly different figures for 1921 in Subcarpathian Rus': Jewish 86.81 percent, Hungarian 7.49 percent, Rusyn 3.85 percent, Czechoslovak 0.78 percent. Ezra Mendelsohn, *The Jews of East Central Europe between the World Wars* (Bloomington, 1983), 146–152. Interwar Czechoslovakia registered the "nationality" of its citizens, based usually on the self-declaration of the "mother tongue." It thus created a category of "Hebrew and Yiddish" declarations which did not exist in either the Austrian or the Hungarian part of the Habsburg Monarchy. However, as Joseph Rothschild pointed out, "Hebrew and Yiddish" declarations could be just as tactical as pre-war declarations and should not be necessarily understood as indicative of deeply ingrained ethnic identification. By trying to stay out of the Czech-German or Slovak-Magyar conflicts, Jews in interwar Czechoslovakia could have resorted to non-alignment as the best option. Joseph Rothschild, *East Central Europe between the Two World Wars* (Seattle, 1974), 86–90.
70. Jelinek, *Ha-golah le-raglei ha-karpatim,* 25–26.
71. Ibid., 26.
72. On this, see Leonard Smith, *Between Mutiny and Obedience: The case of the French Fifth Infantry Division during World War* I (Princeton, 1994); Wilhelm Deist, "Verdeckter Militärstreik im Kriegsjahr 1918" in *Der Krieg des kleinen Mannes,* ed. Wolfram Wette (Munich 1992), 146–147; Richard Holmes, *Acts of War: The Behavior of Men in Battle* (New York, 1986); Allan Wildeman, *The End of the Russian Imperial Army: The Old Army and the Soldiers' Revolt (March–April 1917)* (Princeton, 1980); Tony Ashworth, *Trench Warfare: the Live and Let Live System* (New York, 1980).

Chapter 9

REPRESENTING CONSTITUTIONAL MONARCHY IN LATE NINETEENTH AND EARLY TWENTIETH-CENTURY BRITAIN, GERMANY, AND AUSTRIA*

Christiane Wolf

Until 1914, Europe was a continent dominated by monarchies. Even the new "nation-states" which emerged during the nineteenth century were founded as monarchies. Despite the obvious persistence of dynastic states, however, there have been relatively few sustained efforts at examining how monarchies met the challenges of modern society, chief among them being the idea of "the nation" and the force of nationalism. In short, the "nationalization" of society became an existential question for numerous states including the British Empire, the new German Empire, and the multinational Habsburg Monarchy.

Over the last decade and more, a growing body of work has begun to explore the issue of how effectively dynasties could act as sources of integration in a changing social and political environment by looking at such phenomena as royal ceremonies and public rituals, the changing image of individual rulers, and the constitutional and political role played by the monarch.[1] Yet, if this work generally points to a remarkable popularity of European monarchs around the end of the nineteenth century, it must be noted that very little of it is explicitly comparative in nature.[2] As a result, long standing assumptions regarding the differences between "Western" constitutional monarchies and "Eastern" autocracies have not been subjected to close analysis and overlap in many respects with the traditional distinctions made between Western European "civic nationalism" and Eastern European "ethnic nationalism."

Such observations are especially pertinent to the history of the Habsburg Monarchy, given that both contemporaries and later generations have viewed the nationalities question as the fundamental problem for the multinational state. Whereas nationalism framed in the context of an imperial mission might increase the popularity of the German and British monarchs, nationalism posed a direct threat to the very existence of Austria-Hungary. According to an article on the Habsburg Monarchy published in the left-liberal *Berliner Tagblatt* in 1913, Austria-Hungary was the only great power of Europe that was not a nation-state. Instead of national homogeneity bolstering state unity, Austria-Hungary's fifty-two million inhabitants were riven by national divisions: some twelve million Germans, ten million Hungarians, three million Romanians, and twenty-six million Slavs, divided into many different national groups, lived in the chaotic Habsburg polity. For this Berlin-based newspaper, the "Panslavism" of the Bohemians, the rise of "south Slavic nationalism," and the establishment of the Magyars as the "ruling nation" in Hungary constituted serious threats to the survival of the state.[3] Just as Joseph Roth illustrated in his 1932 novel, *The Radetzky March*, standard works on the Habsburg Monarchy underscore the "unstoppable and undeniable" yearning of the nationalities for independence, a wish that could not in the end be fulfilled within the structure of the monarchy.[4]

From this perspective, the labeling of the Danubian monarchy as a creation doomed to destruction may seem understandable. However, by focusing on the nationalities problems and assuming that the demise of the monarchy was inevitable, scholars have neglected the centripetal forces which also shaped the monarchy. At the end of the 1980s, Alan Sked pointed to those developments that supported the maintenance of the Habsburg state.[5] More recent work has sought to show how identification with the state and the emperor did not just exist in the traditional supranational institutions of the army, church, and bureaucracy, but received popular support as well.[6]

While scholars are starting to address the previously neglected question of the effectiveness of Emperor Franz Joseph as a symbol of the unified state, the historiography on the Habsburg Monarchy has devoted little attention to the wider implications of the central constitutional role of the dynasty, despite the fact that demands for democratization and the strengthening of parliamentary power were—along with the rise of nationalism—among the most significant trends in nineteenth century European history. Indeed, popular pressure in favor of constitutional forms of government challenged all European dynasties—the Habsburg, Hohenzollern, and Saxe-Coburg included—as the most visible symbols of actual or potential arbitrary rule.[7] As David Cannadine has argued in an influential article on the British monarchy, the interplay between the "political power of the monarch," the latter's "personal character and standing," and the "attitude of the media" is a crucial element in understanding the meanings of royal ritual and ceremonial in the modern era.[8]

By examining the public debates in Great Britain, Germany, and the Habsburg Monarchy on the position of the ruler in the constitution, this article considers from a comparative perspective the degree to which Emperor Franz Joseph could act as a meaningful figure of integration in the Habsburg Monarchy. In particular, the public discourse on the popular perception of the monarchs will be explored through a close reading of the contemporary press.[9] In all three countries, the expansion of the mass press enabled journalism to achieve greater influence than had been the case in the past (and arguably, than is the case today). As Edith Walther has concisely put it, "when the young democracies were learning to walk, when pictures could not yet move, when the newspaper was the only source of information, interest in the printed word was probably never greater."[10]

Whereas scholarship since the 1980s has come to revise substantially previous views regarding the modernization of political culture in the Austro-Hungarian and German Empires,[11] the powerful position of both emperors within their respective constitutional frameworks is nevertheless still emphasized—in contrast to the British Queen Victoria's retreat from politics.[12] Certainly, the real power wielded by the rulers differed greatly in the three states under consideration, as did the willingness of the dynasties to adapt to demands for change.[13] Great Britain had long since embarked on its transformation into a constitutional monarchy, and by the 1850s, the British monarch's role had become largely ceremonial.[14] In contrast, the Habsburg Monarchy only began flirting with constitutional experiments after the losses in the war against France and Piedmont in 1859 (aside from the brief interlude of 1848–49).[15] The German Empire was, of course, founded as a constitutional monarchy in 1871, but the precise role of the emperor in the constitutional structure was never clearly delineated.[16]

An examination of their actual constitutional powers does not, however, clarify the question of the popular image of the monarchs regarding their position as head of state. Generally speaking, the scope of monarchical action has not been re-evaluated by historians and only the recent study by Johannes Paulmann properly differentiates between the real political authority held by the monarch and the public perception of the monarch's power.[17] In contrast to Franz Joseph's role, for example, the constitutional position of the German Emperor Wilhelm II was critically debated by his contemporaries and remains controversial. More particularly, David Cannadine has argued that the stability of the late Victorian British monarchy can be attributed to its renunciation of direct political power.[18] Does it follow, then, that the wide-ranging powers of the German and Austrian emperors were responsible for the downfall of the German and Austrian monarchies? John Cannon seems to support this contention when he writes that "had the British monarchy retained its powers, it would almost certainly have perished in the cataclysm that swept away the continental monarchies during the Great War."[19] Considering the evident popularity of the German and Austrian emperors around 1900, it is necessary to examine the validity of this thesis in a European context.

Great Britain

Whatever others might have thought, Queen Victoria (1837–1901) clearly believed that her role as British sovereign included active interventions in political events, and she did so via numerous orders and commentaries to her Prime Ministers. In the often quoted words of MP Charles Dilke, "the Queen does interfere. Constantly."[20] Even after the death of her husband, Prince Albert, and Victoria's retreat from public life, she maintained her interest and continued her interventions in political events in her empire. She corresponded tirelessly with her ministers, read cabinet memoranda daily, and expected detailed reports from her prime ministers. She was hardly non-partisan. Indeed, her strong preference or distaste for the prime minister of the day determined her views of the party to which he belonged.

In her study of Victoria's role as mediator between Liberals and Conservatives in the government crisis of 1884, Corinne Comstock-Weston documented the great influence Victoria was able to wield.[21] Victoria did not consider the function of the monarch to be limited to representative functions, and she reserved for herself an active role in political events, even if executive power was essentially exercised by her ministers. She complained about her loss of power and the corresponding rise of parliamentary power as an affront, which had to be strictly opposed. She did not want to be the queen of a democracy, and for her the tasks of a monarch included political activity. However, the public image of Victoria as a model constitutional monarch was never seriously undermined by her political actions. Her interventions rarely had serious ramifications, and she avoided public confrontations with parliament.[22]

On balance, therefore, Victoria's popularity and her actual political activity had little relation with one another. This is demonstrated by the fact that although her partisan political behavior was increasingly well known—her antipathy towards Gladstone and her positive stance toward the Conservatives, for example, were widely reported—she was never more popular than in the last decades of her long reign. Indeed, as Geoffrey Searle has noted, "the 'rehabilitation of monarchy' was one of the most startling developments of the late Victorian period."[23]

The fact that Victoria's partisanship did not provoke any larger public debate can be attributed above all to the successful cultivation of the image of Victoria as empress, a mother figure for the entire British Empire who seemingly stood above politics. As late as the middle of the nineteenth century, the empire had been the subject of vigorous public criticism, mostly on the part of liberals and radicals who argued that the costs of colonies outweighed their benefits. However, the expansion of the empire and the appointment of Disraeli as prime minister in 1874 fundamentally transformed views of empire and ushered in a new era of popular interest in all imperial matters. In speeches before his election, the Prime Minister blamed the Liberals for indifference toward the colonies and called for a new mission for Great Britain, emphasizing the consolidation and expansion of the empire. Queen Victoria shared Disraeli's enthusiasm for colonial questions and warmly embraced his 1876 proposal to award her the title of Empress of India. Not only the Queen, but also the population, displayed increasing interest in the growing empire. For example, a trip by the Prince of Wales to India in 1875 and the regular exhibitions in London on people and art from throughout the empire met with great public acclaim.[24]

The successful nationalization of the empress as a universally recognized living symbol of the British Empire ensured that Victoria's public preference for certain politicians did not have any broader impact on her own popularity in the last decades of her reign . In fact, newspaper reports explicitly played on the contribution of the dynasty to the existence of the empire. Thus, the conservative *Morning Post* commented on Victoria's Diamond Jubilee in 1897 that, "as a Republic, the nation might have been rich and prosperous ... , but without a Monarch at its heart it could never have held the Imperial position it now holds in the world."[25] Certainly, some newspapers like *The Times* attempted to depict Victoria as a convinced constitutional monarch who never displayed partisanship.[26] Other newspapers, however, made no attempt to hide Victoria's preferences for one or another minister, although they did not question or criticize the queen for taking sides in political disputes. Such was the case with the *Illustrated London Press* and *Daily Mail,* which were examples of the "new journalism," characterized by "shorter paragraphs, larger and more informative headlines, and the increasing use of illustrations."[27] In terms of their political direction, these newspapers by the 1880s turned ever more toward an all-encompassing imperialism. According to the *Illustrated London Press* special edition celebrating Victoria's Diamond Jubilee, Victoria's partisan tendencies never shattered the constitutional framework within which the queen acted. After all, it inferred, such preferences were only human—and even more so for a female: "she would be more than mortal and less than a woman if she had not" played political favorites.[28]

At the same time, the popular perception of Victoria as the ideal constitutional monarch also limited the room for maneuver for republicans, who had enjoyed widespread appeal in the 1870s. The protests of those who argued for scrapping the monarchy were reduced to a simple cost-benefit analysis, which was doomed to failure once the queen returned to public life after the end of her private mourning for her husband and became increasingly associated with the popular imperialist program of her governments. Even such a dyed-in-the-wool republican as the socialist politician Keir Hardie acknowledged that there were more important problems than the monarchical form of government: "we might get rid of the royal family without getting rid of a single one of our burdens." After all, socialists in republican systems had to fight against capitalist structures just as much as the British socialists had to struggle against rapacious capitalists in monarchist Great Britain:

> In this country loyalty to the Queen is used by the profit-mongers to blind the eyes of the people, in America loyalty to the flag serves the same purpose. Law and order

... must have a symbol, and anything will serve. Therefore, until the system of wealth production be changed it is not worth while exchanging a queen for a president.[29]

The renewed emphasis of the British socialist movement on social problems and everyday concerns and its turn away from confrontation with the monarchical system contrasted sharply with the direction taken by social democrats in the German Empire. The limited sphere of action left to the Labor Party thus illustrates the broad acceptance that the monarchy had come to enjoy among the British population. Even in Ireland, a radical nationalist paper like *The Nation* was willing to attribute to Queen Victoria a popularity that was in sharp contrast to the political relationship which the Irish national movement had with London.[30]

Overall, however, it is clear that the acceptance of Victoria had not been automatic, for it had emerged mainly from the 1880s onward. Just as significantly, this popularity was achieved irrespective of Victoria's inclination to political interference, for it was only with the accession of George V in 1910 that Britain acquired a "politically neutral monarchy."[31]

The German Empire

If, despite not being "apolitical," Queen Victoria came to occupy a position beyond criticism by the end of her reign, the person of German Emperor Wilhelm II (1888–1918) contrasted noticeably, for he was contested throughout his reign. The vaguely defined legal position of the emperor within the new constitution of 1871 created the impression that he had considerable powers, which was greatly enhanced by Wilhelm's personal style of rule.[32] His conception of the office of emperor was very difficult to limit constitutionally, and this situation created both demands and uncertainties, which opened the monarch up to criticism.[33]

The public behavior of the emperor—his speeches and other official appearances, as well as the publication of private conversations—led many contemporaries to term his reign a "personal regime."[34] Among historians, it is above all the work of John Röhl which has moved the emperor to the center of scholarly debates concerning the later German Empire. Influenced by the work of Norbert Elias, Röhl has described Wilhelm's rule as a form of "kingship mechanism," emphasizing the powerful position occupied by the emperor.[35] While there is still no consensus as to the real extent of Wilhelm's authority, a focal point in the debate over Wilhelm's "personal regime" continues to be the *Daily Telegraph* Affair, which highlighted for contemporaries the problematic position of the emperor in the constitution and led to one of the worst crises of the monarchy before World War I. Here, however, my focus is less on the actual power structures, and much more on the question of how public discussion evaluated Wilhelm in his constitutional role at the time of this scandal. For contemporaries, the affair combined the question of imperial authority with popular expectations of the monarch.

The *Daily Telegraph* Affair was instigated by the publication of a conversation which the emperor had in November 1907 as a private citizen with his English host, Colonel Stuart-Wortley, at Highcliff Castle.[36] Shortly after the publication of the article in November 1908 in the *Daily Telegraph,* the interview became publicly known in Germany as well. The storm that broke out focused initially on the content, because the emperor stated that he himself had developed a plan of defense against the Boers during Britain's recent war in South Africa and had sent it to his grandmother, Queen Victoria, as proof of his friendship with Great Britain. Unfortunately for the emperor, that was not a sentiment shared by most of his fellow Germans. Almost the entire German press corps criticized the emperor's behavior and called for his "personal regime" to be reined in. This, it was assumed, would result in more circumspect public behavior on the part of the emperor.

While Emperor Wilhelm's open contempt for the German Social Democratic Party (SPD) set the tone for his relationship with social democracy even before the *Daily Telegraph* interview, the affair led to an intensification of SPD attacks on the personal regime.[37] Revisionists within the SPD were prepared to work in a parliament under Wilhelm, but the latter's persistent demonization of the party alienated even the revisionists. Nevertheless, Social Democrats accepted the existence of the monarchy as long as they did not consider a republic to be a better alternative, and they did not focus their critique of the political system on the dismantling of the monarchy. Instead, they aimed much more at the enhancement of parliamentary power.[38] Such a constitutional change was not, however, central to the middle class parties. In concordance with the Catholic press, liberal newspapers desired the reinstatement of the constitution, rather than a substantial transformation of the governing system.[39] The political actions taken by the emperor independently of parliament and the chancellor were, according to the south German Catholic *Augsburger Postzeitung,* "against the spirit and letter of the constitution."[40]

From Catholic to social democratic newspapers, therefore, the German press unanimously condemned the emperor's conception of politics. Even the conservative media criticized the emperor's conduct and published a statement from the Conservative Party which called on the emperor to conduct himself with greater discretion in foreign policy.[41] Nevertheless, the Conservatives did not link this criticism of the emperor's behavior to a general wish for a stronger parliamentary role in the governing of the state. As an institution, the *Reichstag* itself issued only general criticism of the emperor after the *Daily Telegraph* Affair and it accepted Wilhelm's declaration that he would restrict himself to his constitutionally defined role. Fear of social democratic electoral victories united the parties from the Conservatives to the National Liberals in their rejection of an increase in the power of the *Reichstag.*[42] Even most of the left liberal representatives shied away from a strengthening of parliament. They believed that Germany lacked the necessary preconditions for an English-style constitutional monarchy. The left liberal Friedrich von Payer, for example, argued that Germany did not have a stable consensus like that found in the British Parliament.[43]

Clear criticism of the emperor also had its limits, as politicians and journalists were cautious about humiliating the emperor by demanding public guarantees of more constitutional behavior. According to the Catholic Center newspaper *Germania,* "one cannot demand a public humiliation of the emperor. Such an act would impact not only the person of the ruler, but also the office of emperor and the nation."[44] Indeed, the very reason *Germania* moderated its criticisms of the emperor went to the heart of what lay behind the original outrage: the *Daily Telegraph* Affair had called into question the meaning of the emperor as the embodiment of the nation.

Despite the crisis-ridden nature of his ruling style, it is important to realize that Wilhelm II had in fact become a powerful integrative symbol of the new nation-state.[45] This success derived from Wilhelm's strong desire to be the emperor of all Germans—rather than, like his grandfather Wilhelm I, to be Prussian King—and from the fact that Wilhelm II became the strongest advocate for a vigorous German imperialism. Certainly this consensus was potentially fragile, but imperialism had such strong mass resonance that even reluctant groups could not completely and permanently escape its attraction. Thus, for example, emperor and empire were included in Sunday prayer services in Catholic churches along with those for the Bavarian king.[46]

Seen from this perspective, the *Daily Telegraph* Affair was so severe because the monarch's political gaffes undermined his claim to interpret foreign policy in accordance with the will of the people and to represent Germany in the diplomatic arena. The emperor's ability to embody the nation was further damaged by the general consensus across the political spectrum from the right to the left-liberals that German prestige depended directly on the emperor.[47] In other words, it was not just Conservatives who demanded a strong monarch, almost the entire spectrum of public opinion agreed that "a great people" had to have a strong ruler.[48] All parties—with the partial exception of the Social Democratic Party—were unified in viewing the emperor as the leader of the nation, even if this was embedded in very different political programs.[49] Because the significance of the emperor as the leader of the nation was perceived as fundamental to domestic and international perceptions of the German Empire, opposition to Wilhelm II's style of rule arose when the illusion of the great leader threatened to dissolve, namely when his foreign policy misadventures revealed "the inadequate political skills of the emperor."[50]

Above all, the emperor's desire for an expansive *Weltpolitik* had raised public expectations that he would promote German national interests on the world stage. The "imperial idea" thus became the "most widely effective integrating symbol of the German Empire."[51] This strong personalization of German politics, which stands out in comparison with the British case, was demonstrated especially in Wilhelm's role as patron of the German fleet, which was portrayed as the guarantee for a strong German position in international power politics.[52] These expectations for success derived in part from Wilhelm's own ambition to project himself to the German public as the personification of the imperial idea, and in part from the popular image of Bismarck, as Christopher Clark has suggested.[53] Very swiftly after Bismarck's resignation, a Bismarck myth had emerged which transformed the former Chancellor into a charismatic figure, divorced from historical context.[54] Through the figure of Bismarck, a conception of the ruler developed which was indebted to the leadership principle and not solely bound by traditional conceptions of the monarchy.

By personally pushing the position of emperor beyond its constitutionally defined powers, Wilhelm subjected the office to the same kind of expectations of success that were inspired by the Bismarck myth. Yet, the expectations bound up with the emperor's leadership qualities proved impossible—for Wilhelm, at least—to fulfill, notwithstanding the apparently greater legal powers he possessed when compared to the British monarch.[55]

The Habsburg Monarchy

Often dubbed "the last monarch of the old school," Emperor Franz Joseph (1848–1916) enjoyed an important position in the political structure of the Habsburg Monarchy, one that showed more similarities to the German than the British case. Raised in accordance with the ideal of an absolute monarch, he believed throughout his life that the existence of the Habsburg Monarchy depended on protecting his prerogatives.[56] Franz Joseph therefore frustrated the hopes placed in him for a constitutional transformation of the state when he acceded to the Habsburg throne at the age of eighteen. It soon became clear that the young emperor was not yet prepared to rule as a constitutional monarch, and many of his subjects blamed him for the decision to jettison the constitutional reforms of 1848–49, even if it was believed that he may have been manipulated by his powerful advisor, Prince Felix von Schwarzenberg, and his mother, the Archduchess Sophie.[57]

While the focus of this analysis is on imperial Austria, it should be noted that the revocation of constitutional reforms was particularly unpopular in Hungary, where the rebellion against Habsburg rule had been finally quelled with the assistance of Russian troops.[58] After the victory of 1849, the new regime attempted to stifle all movements for national emancipation, and the relationship between the Hungarian population and the dynasty was strained for the best part of two decades. In this respect, it is not surprising that the first and only attempt to assassinate Franz Joseph was undertaken by a Hungarian apprentice tailor, János Libényi.[59] The assassination attempt made public the bitterness of many Hungarians toward Franz Joseph, even if it led to a wave of sympathy for the lightly wounded ruler in other provinces. Nevertheless, even in other regions of the monarchy, there were clearly some who would not have been saddened had the attempt on Franz Joseph's life succeeded, as one mocking poem sung on the streets of Vienna shortly after Libényi's execution suggested:

On the Semmering Heath,
A tailor was executed,
But he deserved his fate,
For how could a tailor have cut so poorly?[60]

The massive foreign policy failure, military disaster, and near bankruptcy of state finances that comprised the 1859 war against Piedmont and France put an end to the neo-absolutist system of the 1850s. The fact that Franz Joseph had personally tried to lead the campaign in Northern Italy ensured that his popularity suffered greatly during this crisis. Although the constitutional reforms of the early 1860s were positively received in many parts of the western Habsburg Monarchy, the humiliating loss against the Prussians at Königgrätz in 1866 was to have far-reaching implications. Soon after the war began, the initial euphoria that had greeted the outbreak of the conflict turned to dismay over the imminent catastrophe. The mood among the German-Austrian population was so negative that Franz Joseph wrote a bewildered note to his wife asking her to show herself in public more often, in order to strengthen the morale of the Viennese. As the emperor traveled from Schönbrunn Palace to the center of Vienna, the crowds lining the streets greeted him with catcalls and demands for his abdication.[61]

The seething domestic unrest was only becalmed by the sealing of the Compromise or *Ausgleich* with Hungary in 1867. The decision for Dualism and against federalism at least pacified the restive crowds in Hungary, but in return led to a noticeable cooling in the relationship between Franz Joseph and his Slavic subjects.[62] As is well known, the Compromise transformed the unitary state into the Dual Monarchy, now officially named Austria-Hungary, its two halves joined together in personal union by the Habsburg monarch, Emperor of Austria and King of Hungary. Austria (officially referred to as "the Lands and Kingdoms represented in the *Reichsrat*," but colloquially known as Cisleithania, or simply, Austria) and Hungary, had separate representative institutions, administrations, and legal systems, but a joint foreign policy and a central military organization. For Austria, undoubtedly one of the most important results of the Compromise was the December constitution of 1867 (also known as the Fundamental Laws).[63] Franz Joseph had to overcome his most deeply held convictions before he approved the Compromise and the constitution, but he recognized their necessity if the state was to be saved from crisis.[64]

Certainly, the Austrian constitution trimmed the monarch's prerogatives, but it did not seriously call his authority into question. The emperor named and had the power to dismiss all ministers, who were responsible to him alone. The Austrian ministerial cabinet was an imperial rather than a parliamentary government.[65] Furthermore, Franz Joseph officially called into session the *Reichsrat*, as well as the provincial Diets, and could dissolve them too. Through his extensive emergency powers, Franz Joseph could rule by decree without deferring to the parliament in times of crisis.[66] Foreign policy and the military remained under the direct authority of the emperor. Franz Joseph enjoyed and protected these powers as long as he lived, countering sharply any challenges to his preeminence in military and foreign policy.⁶⁷ Despite the extensive authority wielded by the emperor, however, the parliament was not powerless. It played a crucial role in shaping legislation and, through its budgetary powers had some means of control over policy; also, the government always sought to find a majority in the *Reichsrat*, even if this was not always easy to achieve.⁶⁸

Not unlike the situation in Great Britain, however, neither Franz Joseph's actual constitutional position nor his self-conception as monarch ultimately proved decisive in the formation of his public image. For example, the articles published in the German language press in Cisleithania on the occasion of Franz Joseph's fiftieth and sixtieth jubilees as emperor emphasized the non-partisan nature of the emperor, a non-partisanship which the liberal *Neue Freie Presse* and other major newspapers claimed Franz Joseph had publicly expressed at the beginning of his reign and to which he, supposedly, remained committed.⁶⁹ The jubilee publications made no effort to engage critically with Franz Joseph's early unpopularity in the face of the brutal actions he authorized to suppress the revolution of 1848 or his long and bitter refusal to grant a constitution. Instead, the era of neo-absolutist rule was depicted as a phase of unfortunate errors ultimately brought to a close with the constitution of 1867. Thus, the new constitution enabled Franz Joseph finally to succeed in countering the negative influences that had informed his policies in the early years of his reign: "so he has become again and remains a constitutional emperor and king, is praised as a model constitutional monarch throughout the world, and is honored in Hungary as in Austria."⁷⁰ Franz Joseph was lauded by almost all papers as "a shining model" of a monarch who thinks and acts only within the framework of the constitution.⁷¹ This was, quite definitely, a reflection of Austria's more stringent laws on *lèse-majesté*, which meant criticism like that voiced towards Wilhelm II in Germany could never have happened in Austria.⁷² Still, critics of the regime always had the option of expressing their disapproval by ignoring official events, whereas the commentary in Austria's German language press was striking for its warmness of tone.

After 1867, Franz Joseph certainly endeavored to rule in accordance with the constitution and he carefully respected the letter of the law, even if he never became a true believer in the merits of constitutional governance.⁷³ Despite this reality, the image of Franz Joseph as a convinced representative of monarchical constitutionalism completely overshadowed his personal views on the subject. This view of Franz Joseph was shared even by foreign observers. According to the *Berliner Tagblatt*, for example, Franz Joseph was a "deeply devoted constitutional ruler like the Empress of England or the King of Italy."⁷⁴ In view of the actual powers available to Franz Joseph, the comparison to the heads of state in Italy and Great Britain might seem strained; nonetheless, even the Austrian press distinguished between the actions of the ministers and those of Franz Joseph.⁷⁵ For example, the Christian Social *Reichspost* justified its critique of Franz Joseph's speeches to open the *Reichsrat* on the grounds that his words were "the work of the responsible ministries." According to this paper, the emperor determined the correct "fundamentals of foreign policy," although the "execution of his policies"—for which the ministers were responsible—gave rise to a great deal of concern.[76] Since Franz Joseph allegedly had no responsibility for day-to-day political matters, he could not be blamed for political failures.

In some respects, this "apolitical" image can be seen as making a virtue out of necessity, because, in view of the problems faced by the government, a partisan intervention by the emperor would have been extremely damaging to his popularity as an integrating figure for the monarchy as a whole. Above all else, the nationalities conflicts made constructive policies difficult to formulate and carry through. The various nationalities strove for some kind of realization of their national interests: Hungarian politicians demanded greater autonomy (and some called for independence); Germans liberals demanded a centralized unified state; Czech parties based their programs on "Bohemian State Right."[77] At the same time, the endeavors of the various nationalities to lay claims on the emperor for their own nation constituted an ever greater challenge for the maintenance of state unity.[78] The case of the Czechs clearly illustrates this dilemma, as the efforts to have Franz Joseph crowned King of Bohemia suggest.[79]

In practice, therefore, the complexity of the Habsburg Monarchy's many national conflicts limited the possibility of "nationalizing" the person of the emperor in the same way that could occur in Britain and Germany. Yet, the conflictual situation still left other ways of constructing an imperial image; indeed, it perhaps made the idea of an integrative emperor more credible. Particularly around the turn of the century, the imperial parliament became the site of wild scenes, with screaming accusations and violent confrontations. At times, obstruction and near riots became daily occurrences.[80] This parliamentary paralysis led to a decline in the public standing of the *Reichsrat*. Many Viennese expressed their outrage at the delay of important social legislation by demonstrating in front of the parliamentary building.[81] Nevertheless, minority groups of radical nationalists in the *Reichsrat* obstructed the moderate majority and, through disruptive tactics, contributed to the gradual radicalization of moderate representatives.[82] Cooperation between the various parties represented in the *Reichsrat* was already difficult, irrespective of the actions of the radical nationalists, because there was no fundamental consensus about the state.[83] The legitimacy of the state was not in and of itself questioned, but there was disagreement as to what the basic structure of the Habsburg Monarchy should be. The result was an escalating brutalization of parliamentary interaction, legislative paralysis, and resort to rule by emergency decree under the provisions of article 14 of the constitution.

In this context of perceived political crisis, the constitutional role of Franz Joseph had to be distanced as far as possible from practical politics if his image was to have a positive integrating effect. The cult of personality, which developed around Franz Joseph and intensified in the last decades of his life, had its genesis in the depoliticization of the emperor. In this context, it was not important that Franz Joseph did not actually give up the reins of power. Of greater significance was the potential for creating a fiction of non-partisanship around his person in a way that elevated him above the political fray. In the end, this trend did not contribute to a resolution of the nationalities conflicts, but it did establish the emperor as a focal point for an emotional connection to the state. In this sense, it did have a stabilizing effect on the Habsburg Monarchy.

Franz Joseph's reticent demeanor, his absolute devotion to duty, his life story, which was seen as being touched by personal tragedies not of his own making, as well as his advancing age, elevated him in the popular imagination. Golo Mann offers this trenchant characterization of the image of the "old Emperor":

> The emperor was enthroned above his peoples, a man from a mythical world, who as a youth was the head of the counter-revolution of 1848, and as an old man had become experienced and pessimistic. The people loved or admired him, his austere lifestyle, his worthy dedication to duty. No boasting speeches here, no dubious indiscretions, just rising in summer and winter at 5 a.m. and working into the night for the good of his peoples, as the old man understood it. [84]

On the rare occasions when Franz Joseph was seen to express a clear political preference, this was interpreted as being non-partisan and for the benefit of all his peoples. For example, his public support for universal manhood suffrage in 1907 resulted in a sharp rise in his personal popularity. Needless to say, the emperor's engagement on behalf of electoral reform did not stem from an inner commitment to democracy, but rather reflected political calculations. He hoped that electoral expansion would drive out the "devil" of national hatred.[85] Even his harsher critics, the social democrats, struck a conciliatory tone, and not only because of Franz Joseph's sixtieth jubilee.

> However, in contemplation of the reality, that the most recent act of this monarch was the promotion of electoral reform, that the emperor, whose reign began with the reversal of the gains of the revolution, became in the twilight of his life a trustworthy and fervent promoter of the rights of the people, the past dims and sinks with all of its failures into the sea of forgetting. That his jubilee day made possible the remembrance of this deed is to Franz Joseph's glory and fortune.[86]

Franz Joseph's advocacy of electoral reform was the basis of the very different stance taken toward monarchy by the Austrian social democrats in comparison to the position of their socialist comrades in the German Empire. In a letter written to Karl Kautsky marking the opening of the new *Reichsrat* term, Victor Adler expressed the positive view held by the Austrian social democrats:

> More important, however, the emperor, with whose help we in Austria defeated the Junkers, stands in Hungary in a battle for life and death with the [Hungarian] Junkers … we would clumsily spit in the soup of our Hungarian comrades, were we purposefully to weaken the position of the emperor and the cause of electoral reform by loud demonstrations. In Germany, the situation is entirely different, and what would be in my opinion a necessity of simplest good sense would be perhaps utter folly outside [of Austria]. It would actually be rather odd if I had to explain to you … why social democrats cannot breathe in the same room with Wilhelm, while that is quite possible

with Franz Joseph without giving away any of their dignity and without the slightest alteration of any of their principle positions.[87]

The stabilizing effect of the integration of social democracy into the state through the institution of universal manhood suffrage should not be underestimated, even if the real aim of this measure, namely the amelioration of the nationalities conflicts, was not achieved.[88] What did remain was the belief held by broad strata of the population that the emperor intervened on behalf of the needs and wishes of his peoples.[89]

Franz Joseph's support for universal manhood suffrage was depicted in many newspapers as an expression of the love and concern of the emperor for his subjects. The apolitical *Illustrierte Wiener Extrablatt* praised the emperor as "the People's Monarch" who "gives and receives love."[90] According to this popular illustrated paper, Franz Joseph had demonstrated impressively that a great ruler was greatest when he yields rather than rejects.[91] The *Reichspost* also saw in the electoral reform proof of the successful cooperation between ruler and people.[92] The image of the emperor as the protector of the rights of his peoples can also be seen in how public opinion in Austria viewed the interpellation of the non-Hungarian minorities in the Hungarian parliament during the debates on electoral reform in Hungary. The authors of the interpellation cited the words of their king who, according to the Romanian representative Blad, had promised to grant his peoples universal suffrage.[93] Even the ruling party in Hungary, according to the social democratic *Arbeiter-Zeitung*, could not simply ignore this "pact with the people in Hungary."[94]

Fundamental for the representation of the unity of Emperor and People was the image of Franz Joseph as the loving father of his subjects, for which he was repeatedly praised by much of the middle-class press during the jubilee and beyond. In a typical 1908 jubilee commentary, the *Deutsche Volksblatt* claimed that over the course of his sixty-year reign, Franz Joseph had always desired to be the father, not the ruler of his people.[95] And just as a father loves his children, so noted most newspapers, children also love their father. While commenting on the 1908 jubilee, the *Reichspost* noted that "certainly we peoples of Austria are untamed children and are always beating each other bloody, often about some trivial matter ... however, we do not tolerate any attacks on our emperor, our father."[96]

According to the *Illustrierte Wiener Extrablatt*, love of Franz Joseph had become a matter of the heart for every individual in Austria-Hungary. "There are countries with *königstreuen* parties. The term itself does not exist here. We have replaced it with imperial and royal loyal nations, with millions of subjects who are divided by language but joined in sentiment."[97] In its coverage of the 1908 historical procession around the Viennese Ringstrasse, the centerpiece of Franz Joseph's sixtieth jubilee, the *Neue Freie Presse* evaluated the love of Franz Joseph as fundamental for the existence of Austria-Hungary:

> How these peoples love their emperor, who has brought to fruition the greatest of all miracles: so many nations, each of which has its own special interests, have been welded

together into to a strong, great, indivisible whole ... Austria is stronger than ever, nourished with an inexhaustible living force that derives from love of monarch.[98]

An important aspect of this paternalistic image was the markedly religious element in the last years of reign.[99] The Homage of the Children on his sixtieth jubilee in 1908 was especially rich in religious imagery. In an analogy to Christ, the event, according to the *Illustrierte Wiener Extrablatt*, was devised entirely with the intention of preparing a joyful event to honor the much tried emperor. The event evoked the suffering path of Christ and his moving words: "let the children come to me." And so, the newspaper reported, the people sent their children in their thousands to the lonely monarch.[100] Finally, the *Neue Freie Presse* utilized the savior myth to characterize the relationship between the emperor and his subjects: "there once was an emperor in Austria, he was the heart of our people ... This life overwhelmed him with travails; it has taken from him what could be taken ... and in return it has given him nothing, nothing but love. However, that love will save Austria."[101]

Here, in the hopes for salvation, there emerges a true sense of the role of Franz Joseph as a palliative for the difficulties of the Habsburg state. The merging of the principle of divine right with a sentimental and religious elevation of the peoples' bond with the emperor illustrates a great desire for an integrating symbol which could provide stability and continuity within the Habsburg Monarchy. Franz Joseph was ascribed an almost mythic role beyond the formal political authority ceded to the monarch by the constitution, and it is no coincidence that the German language press expressed this most strongly of all. The desperate sense of urgency implicit in the plea by the *Neue Freie Presse* reveals some of the fault lines in the jubilee celebrations. This was true in different ways of 1898, when the Hungarians did not get involved (arguing that 1867, not 1848, was the relevant date),[102] and 1908, when the Czechs famously boycotted the historical celebration in Vienna.[103] It is also the case that the paternalist image of Franz Joseph could be contested by liberals and socialists among national minorities such as the Italians, who felt excluded from the political system because of the lack of local autonomy.[104]

From this point of view, disputes arising over imperial celebrations imitated conflicts over the nature of the Habsburg state. Yet, as Daniel Unowsky suggests, such "difficulties did not, for the most part, reflect antagonism toward the emperor or the state itself."[105] The image of Franz Joseph at the head of the empire did, on balance, have an integrative effect, even while different interpretations of that image abounded. Arguably, what was much more problematic was the fact that this symbolic position seemingly placed the burden of the future of the monarchy on the shoulders of an aging emperor, and, in the end, did not prove transferable to Franz Joseph's successor.[106] Hence, the depoliticization and sentimentalization of the image of Franz Joseph was also an expression of resignation from the possibility of formulating an active and effective role for the emperor in the nationalities conflicts.

Conclusion

In an era when monarchy constituted only one among many possible governmental forms, the ability of dynasties to survive depended in part at least on their attractiveness as potential symbols of identification. As this analysis suggests, this proved to be far more important than the actual powers exercised within the framework of their respective state constitutions. In both Great Britain and the German Empire, the nationalization of monarchy had an integrative impact, albeit for different reasons. Where the retreat of Queen Victoria from active politics corresponded with the image of a "loving mother of the empire," the active role that Wilhelm II sought to play in domestic and foreign policy was expected of the "Leader of the Nation." In contrast to Wilhelm II, but showing similarities to Victoria, the image of Franz Joseph as "the Father of His Peoples" was designed to transcend the nationalities conflicts in imperial Austria. The cult of personality around Franz Joseph became increasingly depoliticized, sentimentalized, and religiously inflected, and enhanced the popularity of the monarch.

One corollary of these developments was that the reputation of the German and the Austrian parliaments suffered due to the fact that the popularity of both Franz Joseph and Wilhelm was anchored outside of their constitutional roles.[107] In the British case, a little bit of monarchical magic, according to Prochaska, could be transferred by association onto the parliament itself. The fact that the British Queen refused for years to open parliament was interpreted as a loss of legitimacy for this representative body: "her refusal to open Parliament damaged the symbolic link between the cabinet and the nation and reflected badly on Parliament."[108] In the case of Franz Joseph, closer ties between parliament and the monarchy would have implied the formulation of an active political role, but this was almost impossible if the non-partisan image was to be preserved.

The personification of the state in the figure of Franz Joseph constructed a symbolic role which the emperor had in common with the monarchs of European nation-states. The role of Franz Joseph, Wilhelm II, and Victoria as the symbolic embodiments of their respective states, whether defined as national or multinational, made them, according to Johannes Paulmann, "personified representations of the national prestige" and disagreement between monarch and people endangered this unity.[109] The position of monarchs as the "first diplomat" of the country was also of great significance, because the monarch's reputation abroad was assumed to be transferable, according to *Die Neue Freie Presse*, to the nation itself.[110] Sympathy for the emperor was, therefore, "precious political capital for the empire."[111] This personalization of foreign policy was a European-wide phenomenon, and awarded the monarch a great deal of influence beyond that defined by constitutional statute. Edward VII, for example, was portrayed in the German and Austrian press as an extremely gifted diplomat, as "ruler of the English world empire," although in consideration of the constitutional limitations on the English monarch, such a designation hardly corresponded with the king's real scope of action.[112]

The new symbolic link between monarch and state signified an immense increase in popularity for all three monarchs. For Emperor Wilhelm II and Queen Victoria, this status had its origin in the successful transformation of these rulers into recognized symbols of their respective countries, even though they differed substantially in terms of the actual powers they exercised. However, through his supranational and non-partisan public stance, Franz Joseph did become a recognized and widely revered symbol of the Habsburg Monarchy. It was clear, however, that in the era of nationalism and nation-states, Franz Joseph's efforts to counter nationalism were subject to the same conditions which governed the success of the monarchs of the nation-states. "The political survival of dynasties and their form of rule" remained dependent on the success or failure of the state.[113] None of the European monarchs could elude this pressure to succeed—not even the legendary old emperor.

Notes

* This article was translated from the German by Daniel L. Unowsky.
1. For an overview, see Wolfgang Weber, "Einleitung," in *Der Fürst. Ideen und Wirklichkeit in der europäischen Geschichte*, ed. Wolfgang Weber (Cologne and Vienna, 1998), 1–26.
2. See, however: Johannes Paulmann, *Pomp und Politik. Monarchenbegegnungen in Europa zwischen Ancien Regime und Erstem Weltkrieg* (Munich, 2000).
3. *Berliner Tagblatt*, 21 January 1913. The analysis of nationalism offered by the *Berliner Tagblatt* reflected the Austro-Germans' fear of losing their leading role in the Habsburg state to the non-German speaking majority.
4. Among others, see Robert Kann, "Zur Problematik der Nationalitätenfrage in der Habsburgermonarchie 1848–1918," in *Die Habsburgermonarchie 1848–1918. Bd.III Die Völker des Reiches Teilbd. 2*, ed. Adam Wandruszka, (Vienna, 1980), 1304–1338, here 1337; William Johnston, *The Austrian Mind. An Intellectual and Social History, 1848–1938* (Los Angeles, 1972); Carl Schorske, *Fin-de-Siecle Vienna. Politics and Culture* (New York, 1980); A.J.P. Taylor, *The Habsburg Monarchy, 1809–1918* (Chicago, 1976). Recent surveys of Habsburg history that deal with this topic include Jean Bérenger, *Histoire de l'Empire des Habsbourg, 1273–1918* (Paris, 1990); Charles Ingrao, *The Habsburg Monarchy: 1618–1815* (Cambridge, 1994); Robin Okey, *The Habsburg Monarchy c.1765–1918* (Basingstoke, 2001).
5. Alan Sked, *The Decline and Fall of the Habsburg Empire, 1815–1918* (London, 1989).
6. See, among others: Daniel Unowsky, *The Pomp and Politics of Patriotism: Imperial Celebrations in Habsburg Austria, 1848–1916* (Purdue University Press, 2005); Unowsky, "Reasserting Empire: Habsburg Imperial Celebrations after the Revolutions of 1848–1849," in *Staging the Past: The Politics of Commemoration in Habsburg Central Europe, 1848 to the Present*, ed. Maria Bucur and Nancy Wingfield (West Lafayette, 2001), 13–45; Laurence Cole, *Für Gott, Kaiser und Vaterland. Nationale Identität der deutschsprachigen Bevölkerung Tirols, 1860–1914* (Frankfurt, 2000); id., "Vom Glanz der Montur. Zum dynastischen Kult der Habsburger und seiner Vermittlung durch militärische Vorbilder im 19. Jahrhundert. Ein Bericht über 'work in progress,'" *Österreichische Zeitschrift für Geschichtswissenschaften* 7 (1996): 577–591; Peter Urbanitsch, "Pluralist Myth and Nationalist Realities: The Dynastic Myth of the Habsburg Monarchy—a Futile Exercise in the Creation of Identity?" *Austrian History Yearbook* 35 (2004): 101–141; Ernst Bruckmüller, "Die österreichische Revolution und der Habsburgmythos des 19. Jahrhunderts," in *Bewegung im Reich der Immobilität. Rev-*

olutionen in der Habsburgermonarchie 1848–1849, ed. Hubert Lengauer and Primus Heinz Kucher (Vienna, 2000), 1–33; Emil Brix and Hannes Stekl, eds., *Der Kampf um das Gedächtnis. Öffentliche Gedenktage in Mitteleuropa* (Vienna, 1997).

7. Arno J. Mayer, *Adelsmacht und Bürgertum. Die Krise der europäischen Gesellschaft 1848–1914* (Munich, 1984).

8. David Cannadine, "The Context, Performance and Meaning of Ritual. The British Monarchy and the 'Invention of Tradition', c.1820–1977," in *The Invention of Tradition*, ed. Eric J. Hobsbawm and Terence Ranger (Cambridge, 1983), 101–164.

9. A total of sixty-four newspapers and journals published in the German Empire, Great Britain, and Cisleithania serve here as source material. I use only German language publications from the Habsburg Monarchy and, therefore, my comments in relation to the Habsburg Monarchy are informed by this German language perspective. A study focused on these same questions using publications in the other major languages of Cisleithania would certainly add greatly to the conclusions drawn from the German language source material.

10. Edith Walther, *Österreichische Tageszeitungen der Jahrhundertwende* (Vienna, 1994), 42. The interaction between editorial strategy and public opinion formation is very difficult to quantify objectively. One can assume that a relationship between the reader and editor or publisher existed, wherein the latter wanted to increase circulation, and therefore could not ignore the spirit of the times or the wishes of the reader, while, at the same time, and more or less depending on the orientation of the newspaper, the editorial staff wanted to convey its own political and cultural viewpoint to the reader. For the relationship between monarchy and mass press in the German Empire, see Martin Kohlrausch, *Der Monarch im Skandal. Die Logik der Massenmedien und die Transformation der wilhelminischen Monarchie* (Berlin, 2005).

11. John Boyer, *Culture and Political Crisis in Vienna. Christian Socialism in Power, 1897–1918* (Chicago, 1995); Pieter Judson, *Exclusive Revolutionaries: Liberal Politics, Social Experience, and National Identity in the Austrian Empire, 1848–1914* (Ann Arbor, 1996); Gary Cohen, "Neither absolutism nor anarchy: new narratives on society and government in late imperial Austria," *Austrian History Yearbook* 29 Pt.1 (1998): 37–61; James Shedel, "Fin de Siecle or Jahrhundertwende. The Question of an Austrian Sonderweg," in *Rethinking Vienna 1900*, ed. Steven Beller, (New York, 2001), 80–105. On the German *Sonderweg*, see David Blackbourn, *Class, Religion and Local Politics in Wilhelmine Germany. The Centre Party in Württemberg before 1914* (New Haven, 1990); Geoff Eley and David Blackbourn, *The Peculiarities of German History. Bourgeois Sciety and Politics in Nineteenth-Century Germany* (Oxford, 1984); Geoff Eley, *Wilhelminismus, Nationalismus, Faschismus. Zur historischen Kontinuität in Deutschland* (Münster, 1991); Margaret Anderson, *Practicing Democracy: Elections and Political Culture in Imperial Germany* (Princeton, 2000); Martin Kirsch, *Monarch und Parlament im 19. Jahrhundert* (Göttingen, 1999).

12. John Cannon, *The Modern British Monarchy;* Cannadine, "The Context, Performance and Meaning of Ritual"; Jean Paul Bled, *Franz Joseph. 'Der letzte Monarch der alten Schule.'* (Vienna, 1988); Alexander Novotny, "Der Monarch und seine Ratgeber" in, *Die Habsburgermonarchie 1848–1981. Bd.II Verwaltung und Rechtswesen*, ed. Adam Wandruszka (Vienna, 1975), 57–95.

13. On the constitutional position of the monarchs in these three states, see Berthold Sutter and Ernst Bruckmüller, "Der Reichsrat, das Parlament in der westlichen Reichshälfte Österreich-Ungarns (1861–1918)," in *Parlamentarismus in Österreich*, ed. Ernst Bruckmüller (Vienna, 2001), 60–109; Helmut Rumpler and Peter Urbanitsch, eds., *Die Habsburgermonarchie 1848–1918. Bd.VII Verfassung und Parlamentarismus* (Vienna, 2000); Frank Hardie, *The Political Influence of Queen Victoria 1861–1901* (London, 1963); Dorothy Thompson, *Queen Victoria. Gender and Power* (London, 1990); Richard Williams, *The Contentious Crown. Public Discussion of the British Monarchy in the Reign of Queen Victoria* (Aldershot, 1997); William Kuhn, *Democratic Royalism. The Transformation of the British Monarchy, 1861–*

1914 (London, 1996); John C.G. Röhl, *Kaiser, Hof und Staat, Wilhelm II. und die deutsche Politik* (Munich, 1995); John C.G. Röhl and Nicolaus Sombart, eds., *Kaiser Wilhelm II. New Interpretations* (Cambridge, 1982); John C.G. Röhl, *Der Ort Kaiser Wilhelms in der deutschen Geschichte* (Munich, 1991); Isabel Hull, *The Entourage of Kaiser Wilhelm II* (Cambridge, 1982); Thomas Nipperdey, *Deutsche Geschichte, 1866–1918. Bd.2 Machtstaat vor der Demokratie* (Munich, 1998).

14. For a general overview of this constitutional change, see Eric Hobsbawm, *Age of Empire 1875–1914* (London, 1989).
15. F. Glatz and R. Melville, eds., *Gesellschaft, Politik und Verfassung in der Habsburgermonarchie 1830–1918* (Stuttgart, 1987).
16. On this topic, see Nipperdey, *Deutsche Geschichte*.
17. Paulmann, *Pomp und Politik*.
18. David Cannadine, "The Context, Performance and Meaning of Ritual," 118.
19. Cannon, *The Modern British Monarchy*, 4; William Kuhn, *Democratic Royalism*, 8.
20. Williams, *The Contentious Crown*. Charles Dilke was a member of parliament for the Liberals, but was also well known for his republican views. Stanley Weintraub, *Victoria. Biography of a Queen* (London, 1987), 445.
21. Corinne Comstock-Weston, "The Royal Mediation in 1884," *The English Historical Review* 82 (1967): 296–322.
22. Williams, *Contentious Crown*, 134.
23. Geoffrey Searle, *A New England? Peace and War 1886–1918* (Oxford, 2004), 121.
24. On these points, see: David Cannadine, *Ornamentalism. How the British saw their Empire* (London, 2001), 101; John Mackenzie, *Propaganda and Empire. The Manipulation of British Public Opinion, 1880–1960* (Manchester, 1984), 2; Mackenzie, *The Victorian Vision. Inventing New Britain* (London, 2001), 22; Jan Morris, *Pax Britannica. The Climax of an Empire* (London, 1968), 26.
25. *Morning Post*, 1 July 1897.
26. *The Times*, 22 June 1897. *The Times*, independent in its political orientation, or, less flatteringly, "modifying its political opinions when it found that its circulation was being adversely affected"—was despite—or perhaps in fact because of this flexibility, the newspaper with the largest circulation and most influence in all of Great Britain. "It was recognised by friend and foe alike that *The Times* could make and unmake governments." Geoffrey A. Cranfield, *The Press and Society—From Craxton to Northcliffe* (London, 1978), 154ff.
27. Alan J. Lee, *The Origins of the Popular Press in England 1855–1914* (London, 1976), 120.
28. *Illustrated London Press, Jubilee edition*, 22 June 1897. See also the liberal *Daily News*, 21 June 1897; the politically independent Scottish *Aberdeen Evening Gazette*, 23 July 1897; and the workers' paper *The Star*, 30 June 1897. Scholars have evaluated the importance of Victoria's gender for the contemporary perception of the constitutional stance of the monarch in very different ways. Margaret Homans argues that the association of Victoria with the women of the middle classes of England facilitated England's path to constitutional democracy and symbolic monarchy. This was because the qualities that were expected of a monarch in a constitutional democracy in the nineteenth century were very similar to those expected of women from the middle strata of society in this period. Just like the women of her era, the Queen was duty-bound not to actively interfere in politics. Victoria served as the public, visual symbol of national identity, just as a housewife was expected to represent the status of her spouse. See: Margaret Homans, "'To the Queen's Private Apartments'. Royal Family Portraiture and the Construction of Victoria's Sovereign Obedience," *Victorian Studies* 37 (1993/94): 1–41. In contrast, Richard Williams asserts that many women believed their struggle for emancipation and the vote was reflected in the queen's political position. Even the weekly *Reynold's Newspaper*, popular among the lower middle classes, pointed out Victoria's central role in the women's question: "Her life had one great use. It has taught us the power we are willfully allowing to got to waste in the womanhood of the

nation. ... No longer can be argued ... that women are unfitted for public duties." Quoted in Williams, *Contentious Crown*, 145. See also Thompson, *Queen Victoria*, 145.
29. *Labour Leader,* 19 June 1897.
30. *The Nation,* 10 July 1897. The relationship between the Irish and Queen Victoria was of course ambivalent, and was affected by the identification of Irish nationalism with Roman Catholicism in the course of the nineteenth century. See: R.F.G. Holmes, "Ulster Presbyterians and Irish Nationalism," in *Religion and National Identity,* ed. Stuart Mews (Oxford, 1982), 535–549. The complex relationship between Ireland and the British monarchy cannot be dealt with here, but compare for an overview: Morris, *Pax Britannica;* W.E. Vaughan, *A New History of Ireland: Ireland under the Union.* Volume 6 (Oxford, 1996); Charles Townshend, *Ireland: the 20th Century* (Oxford, 1999).
31. Searle, *A New England?,* 121.
32. The powers of the monarch were defined in the constitution of the German Empire under the section "Presidium," which declared the Prussian King to be German Emperor. The *Berliner Tagblatt* summarized the powers of the emperor as follows: "He opens and closes the *Reichstag,* he summons the *Bundesrat,* he names the German Chancellor, he is responsible for the completion and declaration of the laws of the empire and for carrying them out." *Berliner Tagblatt,* 1.10.1908. In addition to these powers, the German Emperor also had command over the armed forces. Nipperdey, *Deutsche Geschichte,* 99.
33. *Berliner Tagblatt,* 1 October 1909, *Die Jugendzeitschrift. Der gute Kamerad,* Band 25, 1911. Nipperdey, *Deutsche Geschichte,* 85.
34. See among others, Elisabeth Fehrenbach, *Wandlungen des deutschen Kaisergedankens 1871–1918* (Munich, 1969).
35. John C.G. Röhl, *Wilhelm II. The Kaiser's Personal Monarchy, 1888–1900* (Cambridge, 2004); Röhl, *Kaiser, Hof und Staat;* Röhl and Sombart, *Kaiser Wilhelm II;* Röhl, *Der Ort Kaiser Wilhelms;* Hull, *The Entourage of Kaiser Wilhelm II.*
36. Terence Cole, "The Daily Telegraph affair and its aftermath: the Kaiser, Bülow and the Reichstag, 1908–1909," in *New Interpretations,* ed. Röhl and Sombart, 249–268, 253. Also, Peter Winzen, *Das Kaiserreich am Abgrund. Die Daily-Telegraph-Affäre und das Hale-Interview von 1908* (Stuttgart, 2002); Kohlrausch, *Der Monarch im Skandal,* 243–63.
37. During Wilhelm's silver jubilee in 1913, the social democratic *Vorwärts* published a collection of the emperor's "Jubilee Preparations," in which the emperor sharply attacked social democracy. *Vorwärts,* 13 June 1913.
38. Compare: Mark Hewitson, "The Kaiserreich in Question: Constitutional Crisis in Germany before the First World War," *The Journal of Modern History* 73 (2001): 725–780; Christoph Schönberger, "Die überholte Parlamentarisierung. Einflussgewinn und fehlende Herrschaftsfähigkeit des Reichstags im sich demokratisierenden Kaiserreich," *Historische Zeitschrift* 272 (2001): 623–666. Above all, a republic in the French mould was rejected. In 1907, August Bebel declared that if he were to choose, he would prefer the English constitutional monarchy over the French republic. See Peter Domann, *Sozialdemokratie und Kaisertum unter Wilhelm II., Die Auseinandersetzung der Partei mit dem monarchistischen System, seinen gesellschafts- und verfassungspolitischen Voraussetzungen* (Frankfurt, 1971), 201.
39. *Berliner Tagblatt,* 22 November 1908.
40. *Augsburger Postzeitung,* 4 November 1908. See also the liberal *Stuttgarter Neues Tagblatt,* 11 November 1908; *Berliner Tagblatt,* 9 November 1908.
41. *Neue Preußische Kreuz-Zeitung,* 7 November 1908.
42. Fehrenbach, *Wandlungen,* 134.
43. Hewitson, The Kaiserreich in question, 770; Fehrenbach, *Wandlungen,* 139.
44. *Germania,* 20 November 1908.
45. On national integration in imperial Germany, see among others Siegfried Weichlein, *Nation und Region. Integrationsprozesse im Bismarckreich* (Düsseldorf, 2004); Werner Blessing, "The cult of monarchy, political loyalty and the Workers' Movement in Imperial Ger-

many," *Journal of Contemporary History* 13 (1978): 357–75; Manfred Hanisch, "Nationalisierung der Dynastien oder Monarchisierung der Nation? Zum Verhältnis von Monarchie und Nation in Deutschland im 19. Jahrhundert," in *Middle Classes, Aristocracy and Monarchy. Patterns of Change and Adaption in the Age of Modern Nationalism,* ed. Adolf Birke and Lothar Kettenacker (Munich, London, and Paris, 1989), 71–93; Wolfgang Hardtwig, *Nationalismus und Bürgerkultur in Deutschland 1500–1914* (Göttingen, 1994).

46. On the relationship between Catholics and the emperor, see Christiane Wolf, "Monarchen als religiöse Repräsentanten der Nation um 1900? Kaiser Wilhelm II., Königin Viktoria und Kaiser Franz Joseph im Vergleich," in *Nation und Religion in Europa. Mehrkonfessionelle Gesellschaften im 19. und 20. Jahrhundert,* ed. Heinz-Gerhard Haupt and Dieter Langewiesche (Frankfurt, 2004), 153–173.
47. Fehrenbach, *Wandlungen,* 135.
48. *Berliner Tagblatt,* 1 April 1913.
49. See, for example, Friedrich Naumann's *Theorien als Versuch der Vereinbarung von Demokratie und Führergedanken,* discussed in Fehrenbach, *Wandlungen,* 200; Hewitson, *The Kaiserreich in question,* 750. While the Conservatives wanted the monarch to act as a bulwark against parliamentary demands, the left liberals emphasized the reforms needed to bolster the "unity of nation and emperor." The left liberals were most concerned with reforming the electoral laws of Prussia, but also with creating ministerial responsibility. *Berliner Tagblatt,* 30 January 1908, 15 June, and 22 June 1913; *Stuttgarter Neues Tagblatt,* 27 January 1908.
50. Fehrenbach, *Wandlungen,* 135.
51. Dieter Langewiesche, *Nation, Nationalismus, Nationalstaat in Deutschland und Europa* (Munich, 2000), 212.
52. Among others, *Neue Preußische Kreuz-Zeitung,* 15 May 1913.
53. Christopher Clark, *Kaiser Wilhelm II* (Harlow, 2000), 49. The idea, apparently accepted even by conservative monarchists, that the emperor must win over loyalty through successful action is reflected in the jubilee article published in *Germania.* The author claims that the love of the people is not something simply inherited by the monarchy, but must be earned. *Germania,* 15 June 1913.
54. On the complex image of Bismarck, see Lothar Machtan, ed., *Bismarck und der deutsche Nationalmythos* (Bremen, 1994); Wolfgang Hardtwig, *Nationalismus und Bürgerkultur in Deutschland 1500–1914* (Göttingen, 1994); Jakob Vogel, "Zwischen protestantischem Herrscherideal und Mittelaltermystik. Wilhelm I. und die 'Mythomotorik' des Deutschen Kaiserreichs," in *'Gott mit uns'. Nation, Religion und Gewalt im 19. und frühen 20. Jahrhundert,* ed. Gerd Krumeich and Hartmut Lehmann (Göttingen, 2000), 213–230; Katharine Lerman, *Bismarck* (Harlow, 2004).
55. There is no space here to examine in detail popular views of the emperor during World War I, but it is clear that critical voices multiplied under the pressure of war. See Clark, *Wilhelm II,* 238–243; also Kohlrausch, *Der Monarch im Skandal,* 305–311.
56. Robert Waissenberger, "Kaiser Franz Josephs Stellung in der Geschichte," in *Kaiser Franz Joseph von Österreich oder Der Verfall eines Prinzips, Sonderausstellung des Historischen Museums der Stadt Wien* (Vienna, 1981), 7–16.
57. Jean-Paul Bled, *Francois-Joseph* (Paris, 1987), 92. On the unpopularity of the emperor in the early years of his reign, see also Georg Christoph Berger Waldenegg, *Mit vereinten Kräften! Zum Verhältnis von Herrschaftspraxis und Systemkonsolidierung am Beispiel der Nationalanleihe von 1854* (Vienna, 2002).
58. See: R.J.W. Evans, *Austria, Hungary, and the Habsburgs. Essays on Central Europe c.1683–1867* (Oxford, 2006), 245–265.
59. Wilhelm Deutschmann, "Das Attentat Johann Libenyis auf Kaiser Franz Joseph" in *Kaiser Franz Joseph von Österreich,* 187–191; András Gerő, *Emperor Francis Joseph. King of the Hungarians* (Boulder, 2001), 77–79.
60. Quoted in Deutschmann, "Das Attentat," 190.

61. Bled, *Francois-Joseph*, 190.
62. See the essay by Hugh Agnew in this volume.
63. On the development of the constitution, see Maren Seliger, "Vom Neoabsolutismus zur konstitutionellen Monarchie," in *Kaiser Franz Joseph*, 73–79.
64. Bled, *Francois-Joseph*, 272. Novotny, *Der Monarch und seine Ratgeber*, 61.
65. On the distinction between constitutional and parliamentary responsibility, see Stefan Malfer, "Der Konstitutionalismus in der Habsburgermonarchie. Siebzig Jahre Verfassungsdiskussion in 'Cisleithanien,'" in Rumpler and Urbanitsch, *Habsburgermonarchie. Bd. VII/1*, 11–237, 23.
66. Ibid., 17, 209. See also Gernot Hasiba, *Das Notverordnungsrecht in Österreich (1848–1917). Notwendigkeit und Mißbrauch eines "staatserhaltenden Instrumentes"* (Vienna, 1985).
67. The emperor energetically and successfully opposed the 1905–1906 efforts by the Hungarian government to divide the armed forces. Kann, "Zur Problematik der Nationalitätenfrage," 136.
68. Cohen, "Neither Absolutism nor Anarchy."
69. *Neue Freie Presse*, 7 May 1898.
70. *Neue Freie Presse*, 7 May 1898; also: the German nationalist *Deutsches Volksblatt*, 2 December 1898; *Arbeiter-Zeitung*, 2 December 1898. See also Bled, *Francois-Joseph*, 92.
71. *Kleine Zeitung*, 2 December 1908; *Wiener Zeitung*, 2 December 1908; *Arbeiter-Zeitung*, 2 December 1908; *Reichspost*, 18 August 1908.
72. See Elgin Drda, *Die Entwicklung der Majestätsbeleidigung in der österreichischen Rechtsgeschichte unter besonderer Berücksichtigung der Ära Franz Josephs* (Vienna, 1992).
73. Sutter and Bruckmüller, "Der Reichsrat," 63.
74. *Berliner Tagblatt*, 17 May 1908.
75. The left liberal and social democratic press of the German Empire emphasized this, and through it implicitly or explicitly criticized Emperor Wilhelm II. In an article titled "Personal Regime," the *Arbeiter-Zeitung* went so far as to claim that the Austrian emperor had totally rescued himself from all political action, in contrast to the personal "interventions" of Wilhelm II. *Arbeiter-Zeitung*, 28 September 1913.
76. *Reichspost*, 14 May 1898.
77. Sutter and Bruckmüller, "Der Reichsrat," 96. The demand for Bohemian state right was an endeavor "to join the Czech-Bohemian lands in some form to the continued existence of the Habsburg Empire." Jiří Koralka and Richard J. Crampton, "Die Tschechen," in Wandruszka, *Habsburgermonarchie Bd.III/1*, 489–521, 504. Franz Joseph was not only Emperor-King of Austria-Hungary, but he ruled over the various crown lands as Archduke of Austria, Duke of Salzburg, etc. The title "Emperor Franz Joseph" reflected the complexity of the state structure, in which Franz Joseph was not only seen as emperor, but as king, archduke and so on. The degree to which these various titles of the emperor affected loyalty to the state as a whole on the local level cannot be considered in this essay.
78. Peter Urbanitsch, "Nationalisierung der Massen," in *Das Zeitalter Kaiser Franz Joseph, 2. Teil. 1880–1916* (Wien, 1987), 119–124, 120; Adam Wandruszka, "Notwendiger 'Völkerverein' oder 'Völkerkerker'?", in Wandruszka, *Habsburgermonarchie Bd. III/1*, XIII–XVIII, XVI; Hans Kohn, "Was the Collapse Inevitable?", *Austrian History Yearbook*, 3, Part 3 (1967): 250–267, here 253.
79. See Jiří Pokorny and Jiří Rak, "Öffentliche Festtage bei den Tschechen," in Brix and Stekl, *Kampf um das Gedächtnis*, 171–189, and the essay by Hugh Agnew in this volume.
80. Brigitte Hamann, *Hitlers Wien. Lehrjahre eines Diktators* (Munich, 1998), 177.
81. Such demonstrations took place, for example, in 1909 in reaction to the rising prices and paralysis in social legislation. Hamann, *Hitlers Wien*, 182. See also Sutter and Bruckmüller, "Der Reichsrat," 100.
82. The Czechs faced pressure from the radical Czech National Socialists, while the Germans were pressured by the Pan-Germans and the German Radicals. Otto Urban, *Die tschechis-*

che Gesellschaft (Vienna, 1994); Lothar Höbelt, "Parteien und Fraktionen im cisleithanischen Reichsrat" in Rumpler and Urbanitsch, eds., Habsburgermonarchie Bd.VII/1, 895–1006.
83. Sutter and Brückmüller, "Der Reichsrat," 97. Also, Höbelt, "Parteien und Fraktionen."
84. Sigfried Nasko, "Franz Joseph (1830–1914)," in Österreich unter Kaiser Franz Joseph, 73–84, here 81.
85. Seliger, Neoabsolutismus, 79; Kann, "Zur Problematik der Nationalitätenfrage," 227. William Jenks, The Austrian Electoral Reform of 1907 (New York, 1974).
86. Arbeiter-Zeitung, 2 December 1908.
87. Quoted in Rudolf Neck, "Zur Innenpolitik unter Franz Joseph I," in Österreich unter Kaiser Franz Joseph, 33–40, here 39.
88. Even in the Social Democratic Party there were national tensions such that in 1911 the Czech group seceded from the party organization. Kann, "Zur Problematik der Nationalitätenfrage," 230.
89. The press often portrayed the general audiences held by Franz Joseph as evidence of his sympathy for the problems and dreams of the population. Grazer Extrablatt, 4 December 1908; Kleine Zeitung, 2 December 1908. In this way, the image of the emperor as the First Bureaucrat who worked tirelessly for the good of his people strengthened the impression of the constitutional character of the state and, on the other hand, the non-partisanship of the emperor, who would not take sides or choose favorites among the many nationalities within his state. Wiener Salonblatt, 5 December 1908; Reichspost, 2 December 1908, Kleine Zeitung, 2 December 1908.
90. During his brief reign as sole Habsburg ruler Joseph II (1780–1790), the son of Maria Theresia, sought to lift the burden of serfdom from the peasantry. It remains unclear as to what degree the Illustriertes Wiener Extrablatt intended to set Franz Joseph in the tradition of Joseph II. The paper emphasized the emotional and personal character of the relationship between the emperor and his people even in Franz Joseph's political actions.
91. Illustriertes Wiener Extrablatt, 1 January 1908.
92. Reichspost, 8 May 1908.
93. Arbeiter-Zeitung, 24 September 1908.
94. Arbeiter-Zeitung, 26 September 1908.
95. Deutsches Volksblatt, 1 January 1908.
96. Reichspost, 2 December 1908; Also: Wiener Zeitung, 13 June 1908; Deutsches Volksblatt 22 May 1908; Neue Freie Presse, 2 December, 1908.
97. Illustriertes Wiener Extrablatt, 18 August 1908. See also Reichspost, 18 August 1898.
98. Neue Freie Presse, 13 June 1908. Steven Beller evaluates the Neue Freie Presse reporting on the procession much more negatively. Steven Beller, "Kraus's Firework. State Consciousness Raising in the 1908 Jubilee Parade in Vienna and the Problem of Austrian Identity," in Staging the Past, ed. Bucur and Wingfield, 46–71.
99. James Shedel, "Emperor, Church, and People. Religious and Dynastic Loyalty during the Golden Jubilee of Franz Joseph," The Catholic Historical Review 76 (1990): 71–92.
100. Illustriertes Wiener Extrablatt, 21 May 1908.
101. Neue Freie Presse, 2 December 1908.
102. See Péter Hanák, "Die Parallelaktion von 1898. Fünfzig Jahre ungarische Revolution und fünfzig Jahre Regierungsjubiläum Franz Josephs," in id., Der Garten und die Werkstatt. Ein kulturgeschichtlicher Vergleich Wien und Budapest um 1900 (Vienna, 1992), 101–115; Katalin Sinko, "Zur Entstehung der staatlichen und nationalen Feiertage in Ungarn 1850–1991," in Der Kampf um das Gedächtnis, ed. Brix and Stekl, 251–271.
103. It is questionable to what extent the Czech refusal to participate amounted to a rejection of the Habsburg Monarchy, but it is clear that the German orientation of the procession, which was controlled by a committee in Vienna, and the cancellation of a Czech theater performance by the city council created a poisoned atmosphere. Compare also Elisabeth Grossegger, Der Kaiser-Huldigungs-Festzug Wien 1908 (Vienna, 1992).

104. Laurence Cole, "Patriotic Celebrations in Late Nineteenth and Early Twentieth Century Tirol," in *Staging the past,* ed. Bucur and Wingfield, 75–111.
105. Unowsky, *Pomp and Politics,* 181.
106. Due to Franz Ferdinand's well known distaste for Hungary and his autocratic tendencies, there was little expectation that he would behave in a non-partisan manner. Günther Kronenbitter, "Haus ohne Macht? Erzherzog Franz Ferdinand (1863–1914) und die Krise der Habsburgermonarchie," in *Der Fürst,* ed. Weber, 169–208. As to what degree Karl could have followed in Franz Joseph's path is difficult to say, since his short time as ruler was overshadowed by World War I.
107. Clark, *Kaiser Wilhelm II,* 116. Clark argues that, since 1890, Wilhelm aligned himself demonstratively with the military and left the responsibility for government to his chancellors, thus furthering the image of a "leader of the nation" outside constitutional constraints. Compare also Jakob Vogel, *Nationen im Gleichschritt. Der Kult der 'Nation in Waffen' in Deutschland und Frankreich, 1871–1914* (Göttingen, 1997).
108. Frank Prochaska, *Royal Bounty: the Making of Welfare Monarchy* (New Haven, 1995), 110.
109. This was demonstrated by the reactions of the German population to the *Daily Telegraph* Affair. Compare the paragraph about the German Empire in this article and Paulmann, *Pomp und Politik,* 173.
110. *Neue Freie Presse,* 14 September 1898. "Nation" and "State" were often employed in the Austro-German press as synonyms.
111. *Neue Freie Presse,* 15 September 1898.
112. *Reichspost,* 13 August 1908. Compare this with Paulmann, *Pomp und Politik.* Interpretations of the success of the monarchy as a political actor in foreign policy were divided according to political party affiliation; however, the significance of the monarch for the prestige of the state was, with the exception of the social democrats, agreed upon by all major parties. On evaluations of the political role of Edward VII in Great Britain, see Keith Robbins, "The Monarch's Concept of Foreign Policy: Victoria and Edward VII," in *An Anglo-German Dialogue,* ed. Adolf Birke, Magnus Brechtken, and Alaric Searle (Munich, 2000), 115–131.
113. Paulmann, *Pomp und Politik,* 409.

AFTERWORD
The Limits of Loyalty

R.J.W. Evans

The dynasty is the oldest theme in Austria's historiography at home and abroad: we need only think of the standard designation of the state, even in its final phase, as the Habsburg Monarchy or (less accurately) Empire. That perception was particularly central to English-language commentators, whether critics or apologists, from Archdeacon Coxe at the beginning of the nineteenth century to Horace Rumbold a hundred years later.[1] Henry Wickham Steed begins his highly influential book of 1913 with firm stress on "Austria" as a "monarchical unity," and on the crown as its "active, driving, sometimes aggressive force." And he concludes: "The power of the Hapsburg dynasty is still the strongest element in the Monarchy—stronger, in the last resort, than the influence of the Austrian Germans, the Austrian Slavs, the Magyars, the Church, or the Jews. Its power is still, to all intents and purposes, absolute."[2]

Such notions have always provided a focus for authors addressing a popular audience, Alan Palmer and Andrew Wheatcroft among the most recent, who employ the dynasty as a vehicle to convey both the structure and the essence of the Monarchy.[3] No less have they informed analytical writing in the biographical mode, from Redlich's classic study of Franz Joseph, presenting its subject as a total devotee of imperial authority and duty, to the recent lives by Bled and Beller.[4] What the aged Friedrich Kleinwaechter long ago persuasively anatomized as the primacy of "dynasticism" over "state-mindedness" in Habsburg governance formed an organizing principle for much writing.[5] Among it has been a conspicuous revival of interest, since the 1980s, in Franz Joseph as personal ruler over the constituent pieces of the Monarchy where he reigned, at least ostensibly, as king.[6] Moreover, from the work of Magris and others we now know much more about how the dynastic bond was reformulated in the literary legacy of Habsburg rule.[7]

Yet, for decades more weight was placed in academic discourse about the last stages of Austrian and Austro-Hungarian history upon "centrifugal" forces, those which tended towards the contemporary and subsequent division of the Monarchy. Such lines of enquiry privileged the triumph of territorial and above all ethnic separateness at the expense of the *Gesammtmonarchie,* the Habsburg state as a whole. Partly, they constituted a more or less explicitly heuristic tool for understanding its eventual dissolution, charting the routes to its dismemberment. Partly too, they reflected the inevitable and enforced limitations of national historiographical schools, the barriers thrown up by language and access to sources, the professional exigencies of different and divergent post-1918 academic environments.

Recently, the balance has begun to change. That was already heralded to some extent by the ambitious and broad-based initiative on the part of the Historical Commission of the Austrian Academy of Sciences from the 1970s onward to publish a multi-volume history of the Habsburg Monarchy from 1848 to its demise, and by more sophisticated approaches to the politics of nationality, such as Gerald Stourzh's powerful analysis of the scope for the resolution of ethnic conflict through the courts and the administration.[8] Pioneering work on two pillars of the monarchical establishment, notably by Megner and Heindl on the bureaucracy, and by Deák and Hajdu on the army, has encouraged further reappraisal.[9] In the last decade or so prominent articles, many of them in the *Austrian History Yearbook* and influenced by larger American debates, have posited the idea of a Habsburg civil society, a community of interest sustained across national boundaries and capable of incorporating the forces of modernization which transformed Europe as a whole over the half-century of Dualism.[10] There is evidently no need for an either/or here; nor for any wholesale denial of received priorities. As John Boyer has put it: "The [Habsburg] state faltered not just because of the nationalities problem, but because of its coupling with reciprocally corrosive processes of politicized administration and anarchized politics."[11]

A further new perspective on the dynastic factor as such has been gained by the extension to Austria of the current vogue for the study of commemorations and monuments.[12] Besides its roots in the search for *lieux de mémoire,* this fruitfully applies to the nineteenth century insights gained from the investigation of court and ceremonial in earlier periods of Habsburg history. How far were such events or memorials manipulated from above? Did propaganda and publicity actually determine mass responses? Redlich wrote of Franz Joseph's "contemptuous rejection of every art, great or small, which might have popularized monarchical activity."[13] Yet the business of personal rule in a representative age and the latter's continuing close association with government made the practice of it unavoidable. Thereby, all manner of synergies evolved between loyalty to the ruler, on the one hand, and to national, regional, class, and other allegiances, on the other. They blend with newer understandings of multiple identity, and also lead to fresh ways of envisaging the interplay of nationalities, as in the earlier sections of Jeremy King's study of Budweis/Budějovice or Urbanitsch's mature reflections on the Habsburg "dynastic myth."[14]

Those are some of the co-ordinates for the present collection, and the contributions deploy good evidence to sustain the thesis that royalism, in the sense of open allegiance to the Habsburgs whether spontaneous or staged, has been underestimated. Each author illustrates this in a different fashion. Thus, *Bruckmüller* demonstrates the ways in which Austrian loyalty and the heritage of particular localities or peoples were blended in school curricula. Though he pays special attention to the wider German context, he indicates the part played by representatives of other nations, as by the part-Czech Anton (or Antonín) Gindely's influential *Lehrbuch der allgemeinen Geschichte*. He explores too how the potent but vague notions of *Heimat* and *Vaterland* (or *Mutterland*) could be construed, often simultaneously, in a narrower or broader way, to embrace one's own province or "Austria" (meaning the Monarchy) as a whole. *Cole*'s analysis of veterans' associations, though concentrating on Italian speaking southern Tyrol, makes the case for the depth of this reservoir of imperial patriotism across most of Cisleithania: expanded after the introduction of conscription, there were over two thousand such organizations after 1900. He also argues for active involvement by the authorities to promote the status of the military ethic within Austrian society. That perhaps made smallest headway among the Czechs; yet *Agnew* documents much spontaneous loyalty among them, alongside the more measured commitment to monarchy evidenced by the long saga of Franz Joseph's proposed Bohemian coronation. He confirms the populist role of the Emperor's official visits to Prague, already investigated by Otto Urban.[15]

The true Habsburg hero for Czechs, at least rural ones, was long Joseph II. *Wingfield* shows how that radically reformist emperor continued to be widely appreciated in 1848 and beyond (even if he remained a bugbear in Hungary, as also, of course, to ultramontanes). His memory was taken up thereafter by the Liberal movement, and by others as far afield as the Ruthenes of eastern Galicia. That raises the issue of rival or complementary claims upon dynastic allegiance, a theme addressed in the next two chapters. *Unowsky*'s instructive juxtaposition of celebrations in 1880 in Galicia makes clear that Franz Joseph's state visit that year trumped the other festivities.[16] His appeal was both transnational and transconfessional, and could embrace most Poles, Ruthenes, and Jews at the same time. In Hungary, however, the scars of his earlier and bitterly resented autocratic regime lingered, and legitimation of Habsburg rule required the aura of Franz Joseph's consort Elisabeth. *Freifeld* makes much of the Queen's appeal (actively and passively) to Magyar sensibilities, even assigning her a "critical role" in the *Ausgleich* negotiations.[17] More strikingly, she draws attention to Sissi's part in the evolution of Hungary's "national" symbols, above all costume. Elsewhere in the country, Franz Joseph could still count on a more personal following, as *Kent* reveals in her lively vignette of his visit to Zagreb in 1895. Croatian identity was historically bound up more than any other in the Monarchy with military-style fidelity, and whereas this rare appearance of the monarch in the South Slav periphery of his realms also excited protests, these were directed against Serbs and Magyars. Our third author on the Hungarian half of the Dual Monarchy,

Rachamimov, addresses the important case of Jewish loyalism, albeit tangentially, mediated through Avigdor Hameiri's writing and recollection. It is worth noting that the chief store of hagiography about Franz Joseph as Hungarian king, published in the year of his death, was a compilation by Adolph Kohut, a prominent Jewish journalist and critic, whose brother and nephew both became rabbis in America.[18]

Finally, *Wolf* ventures some worthwhile comparisons with other contemporary styles of monarchy. She evokes the British model of a harmless non-playing captain and the German one, at once more dynamic and more vulnerable, of the ruler as the leader of the nation. Further and equally diverse examples from the period could have been adduced; yet the more significant feature is a general vogue for monarchy in the later nineteenth century, which could embrace all these local variants. Franz Joseph, in other words, enjoyed the benefit of a surge in loyalism throughout Europe, after the trough of the decades after 1800, when the legitimacy of the institution had been at risk from London to Istanbul, and before the tornadoes unleashed in 1914. This was a veritable Indian summer for royalty, especially for the royal houses of central Europe, which enjoyed a second childhood in the Balkans. As late as 1905, Norway's sturdy, autonomous, and self-reliant separatists, having broken with the Swedish crown, nevertheless voted by almost 80 per cent for a (Danish) monarch of their own.[19]

In such a climate, Franz Joseph came by the turn of the century to enjoy a primacy of respect continent-wide because of his age and his fortitude in the face of the sufferings of his own family. Both those tropes had their place in his public image at home: on the one hand, in the official Austrian campaign to link the old ruler with children and with child welfare;[20] on the other, in his standard "tribal" language of "my peoples" (*meine Völker* or even *Völkerfamilie*), which probably had some purchase with mass audiences, even if he avoided rhetorical effusions on the subject, and despite the fact that the official terminology of *Volksstamm* (and worse still, *néptörzs*) caused pain to those with a more advanced sense of national identity. These were some of the cultic elements in the (self-) presentation of the emperor-king, alongside the flood of petitions to the sovereign, over 30,000 per annum, from all manner of people (although supposedly only from those with some kind of claim to have performed state service),[21] and the ritualized open audiences for three hours twice a week. Historians have studied popular perception of Franz Joseph in some of its manifestations.[22] Whereas certain features of it originated in the quirks of his character—such as his notorious terseness in public utterances and written statements, or his tendency to avoid major ceremonial (only one coronation, and even that took him twenty years to arrange) but unbending formality on lesser occasions—all of them became conscious markers of the Habsburg-loyalist orientation.

*

Yet the chapters in this book have also revealed much about the limits as well as the integrative power of the dynastic bond. *Bruckmüller* notes how Austria's school histories left out awkward memories like the Bohemian revolt of 1618–20. Similar cases could easily be adduced from Hungary too, like the Catholic textbook which passed from the reign of Ferdinand to that of Franz Joseph without mentioning the 1848 revolution at all.[23] There was also a dangerous tendency for the common past to be restricted to the *res gestae* of the Habsburgs themselves, even of the current ruler alone. *Cole* makes clear that loyalism in Tyrol was associated with Catholic and conservative interests, anti-Liberal and anti-Socialist: in other words it was definitely not neutral in local political terms. And loyalism also needed to deliver. *Agnew* argues that the failure of repeated Czech campaigns for the coronation of Franz Joseph as king of Bohemia led to estrangement, with the symbol of the crown being commandeered to support the claim for state right (*státní právo*). The Czechs absented themselves from the whole diamond jubilee procession of 1908 on a trivial pretext—though the fact that the first float depicted Rudolf of Habsburg defeating Ottakar of Bohemia surely played its part.[24] The degree of resultant alienation is hard to measure, but it came to the fore in popular reminiscence and anecdote.[25]

Another liability of dynastic sponsorship appears in *Wingfield's* analysis of the legacy of Joseph II, which was progressively appropriated by German Liberals and then by German nationalists, so that by 1900 it could be used as a weapon *against* the multinational policies espoused by Franz Joseph. That raises wider issues of divergence within the ruling house. The memory of Archduke Johann in Styria or of Archduke József the Palatine of Hungary conveyed patriotic messages which could sit uncomfortably with the priorities of central government. Other provincial tensions are uncovered by *Unowsky* in Galicia, where the Emperor's 1880 visit coincided with competing commemorations of events within or outside the Habsburg tradition. There too enthusiasm for Franz Joseph was in good measure a function of the divisiveness of local politics, and was orchestrated to harmonize with the new Austrian regime of Count Taaffe, which in 1880 had begun to consolidate itself with the backing of Polish conservatives. For Hungary, *Freifeld* suggests features of both divergence and division. Elisabeth's huge reputation there depended substantially on her not being thought Austrian, or perhaps Habsburg at all. And we might anyway wonder whether the cult of the queen really rivaled that of Lajos Kossuth, certainly in terms of the kinds of political commitment it inspired.

Whatever her own reputation during her life and posthumously, Elisabeth knew how fickle crowds could and would be, especially for the Habsburgs in Hungary. Ironically, Franz Joseph enjoyed his greatest popularity there on a visit while still an archduke, in 1847.[26] Then he excited the ardor of his Magyar audience by delivering an address in quite fluent Hungarian. The country's other nationalities, though more inclined to dynastic loyalty precisely as a bargaining counter vis-à-vis the Magyars, could likewise no longer be relied upon. *Kent* suggests that the Croats' historic martial commitment to the Habsburg cause had largely receded by the 1890s in favor of a more conditional allegiance. *Rachamimov* conveys the impression that the young Hameiri's royalism was neither deep nor primary (although he would return to his Hungarian roots later), and that the war constituted a profound break. *Wolf*'s review of some of the pre-1914 evidence makes clear that the rosiest pictures of the dynasty were painted by the Monarchy's Germans, and notes the pressures from dissenting voices, even in the jubilee year of 1908. Besides, she makes a most important broad observation, to which it is worth attaching some concluding thoughts. Wolf remarks that Franz Joseph's popularity depended on "depoliticization," on the perception that he was divorced from politics.

But of course the emperor-king was not, and could not be, divorced from politics. That was quite incompatible with official strategies for maintaining the Monarchy, from autocracy through guided parliamentarism to the enforced introduction of universal manhood suffrage. Survivor dynasties in modern Europe have been those which bent to the power of mass opinion, became showpieces for the harmless kinds of usable tradition. This proved possible for them precisely because they did not, or could not, exercise any real power or rest on sectional interests within (or for that matter beyond) the state. The Habsburgs represent an opposite case: their continued involvement in government was essential for the running of the Monarchy. By the same token they were locked into the fate of that political system. And we should bear in mind Franz Joseph's abhorrence of the very notion of popular sovereignty. In the first weeks of his rule, he colluded in the scheme to strike down the principle as the crux of the clash between Schwarzenberg's regime and the Kremsier assembly. All his subsequent constitutional concessions, from the establishment of the *Reichsrat* to the grant of universal manhood suffrage in Cisleithania, were predicated more or less explicitly on his continued denial of it.[27]

As is well known, Franz Joseph correspondingly preserved (or even enhanced) the prerogative powers of Habsburg rulers. He nominated and dismissed governments, summoned and prorogued parliaments in both halves of his dualist realms. He could use paragraphs 13 or 14 of the 1861 or 1867 Fundamental Laws in Austria, and he could insist on his preliminary sanction of legislation in Hungary. He sustained close control over the Monarchy's joint affairs, i.e., diplomacy and especially the army, helped by the comparative failure of the Cisleithanian and Transleithanian Delegations to exercise any supervisory role. Moreover, he exerted much continuing sway within the Catholic and other churches: the waning of the Concordat of 1855 affected ultramontane rather than regalian rights. Alongside those institutional powers, and more immediately relevant to the kind of research embodied in this book, stood the monarch's associated influence over the ancestral social and cultural pillars of Habsburg authority: the nobles, bureaucrats, officers, and clerics.

The key old-new question now must be how far these ostensibly loyalist cadres resisted the blandishments, if such they were, of the rising national camps: the German and Hungarian ones, as well as those usually reckoned non-dominant and more clearly oppositional within the Habsburg lands. Evidently, the rewards of office still played their part—thus ennoblements for civil and military service (often linked with the award of orders) afforded a binding feature.[28] Equally, Franz Joseph's very explicit and conspicuous choice to identify with an Austrian army establishment gained him credit with much of the soldiery, even as it provoked the fateful clash with Hungary's politicians and much public opinion there. We need more evidence, especially from non-German sources. To take examples from the bureaucracy: how divergent from an Austrian norm were the careers of high-level Magyar officials, or the life stories of small-time Czech ones?[29] And if civil servants became less mobile, because of linguistic boundaries, would they not find themselves more tied to a sectional allegiance? On the whole, it seems plausible that by 1914 these props of the a-national *raison d'être* of the Habsburgs were no longer immune to ethnic attachments, even if they tended still to negotiate them and sometimes sought to make play with immunity from them.[30]

That is also a premise of this volume's introduction, which points to the potential for positive correlations between rising national awareness and dynastic loyalty. As the editors and other contributors show, a heightened sense of identity could certainly take multiple and complementary forms. And yet the resultant supranational resonances would not necessarily be at all the same. In Austria, the dominant idiom of sovereignty remained imperial, but ever since 1804, the Habsburgs had experienced difficulty in defining their empire, in both practical and symbolic terms, and who was to say precisely what fealty to it comprised?[31] Hungarians required a king, but one in their own patriotic image, which meant one without any overt Austrian trappings. Both Franz Joseph's chief jubilees, in 1898 and 1908, showed how remote from each other were the royal conceptions of the two halves of the Monarchy.[32] Elsewhere too, however, models of rulership diverged, *pari passu* with mutual alienation. Bohemian Germans and Czechs might both retain their Habsburg allegiance, but the *Kaisertreue* of the former stood apart from the *Königstreue* of the latter, and rested on two quite different notions of the state. Moreover, the dynasty was frequently reprobated by one group for seeming to favor a rival one.[33]

There is no mention here of the long-time heir to the throne, but the prospect was not an encouraging one, in terms of the dynastic mission. Whereas Franz Ferdinand, had he come to power, would have needed to invoke the same cult of majesty to achieve his ends, he bid fair to alienate many of the neutral and non partisan benefits accrued by his uncle. He would almost inevitably have enhanced the autocratic principle of rule, provoked a clash with the strongest vested interest in the Monarchy, and reinforced those military traditions of the dynasty which, unleavened by the political compromises forced upon Franz Joseph, stretched back through the unbending disciplinarian Albrecht to Archduke Karl.[34] In the event the succession passed to Karl I and IV: a man not just inadequate to the by then wartime situation, but buckling under the weight of the personalized authority so long wielded by his great-uncle. An instance of this was the counter-productivity of the traditional Habsburg resource of receiving petitions; for as these failed to deliver, they delivered a direct blow to the workings of imperial paternalism.[35]

The last finding for our purposes is a very obvious but fundamental one: the dissipation of loyalism in the desperate late autumn of 1918 and its near-absence thereafter. In the aftermath of the collapse and Karl's withdrawal, monarchist groups were very small, even in the Austrian heartlands and even among aristocrats there.[36] Elsewhere, the monarchical function passed relatively smoothly to rival dynasties—Karageorgević and Hohenzollern-Sigmaringen—to a socialist general, to a professor of philosophy, and to an admiral; and whereas Horthy had been close to Franz Joseph, his backing in Hungary came especially from the "free electors," who favored anyone but a Habsburg for the vacant Hungarian throne. The ex-king's attempt in 1921 to re-establish himself on that throne drew on reserves of Catholic and noble support, but it was no mass movement—and Karl had to be protected from the fury of Austrian workers as he crossed back to Switzerland.[37]

There is, finally, a sort of parallel with the earlier great caesura in the history of central European empire—almost exactly 200 years ago—an event in which the Habsburgs were likewise closely involved. The end of the Holy Roman Empire in 1806, like the end of the Monarchy in 1918, was long depicted by detractors as a foregone conclusion. Nowadays, we appreciate better the extent of loyalty to the Old Reich, the *Reichspatriotismus* of its last decades; and we know that the dissolution itself was a traumatic experience for contemporaries.[38] Yet it was the rivalry of Austria and Prussia, a contest promoted by the rulers of both countries, which made that dissolution inevitable, like the subsequent national cuckoos outgrowing their Habsburg nest. In the matter of imperial subversion, the Habsburgs were perpetrators long before they became victims.

Notes

1. William Coxe, *History of the House of Austria, from the Foundation of the Monarchy by Rhodolph of Hapsburgh, to the Death of Leopold the Second, 1218 to 1792* (London, 1807), a work still being reprinted as late as 1905. Horace Rumbold, *The Austrian Court in the Nineteenth Century* (London, 1909).
2. Henry Wickham Steed, *The Hapsburg Monarchy* (London, 1913), 1f., 295.
3. Alan Palmer, *Twilight of the Habsburgs: The Life and Times of Emperor Francis Joseph* (London, 1994); Andrew Wheatcroft, *The Habsburgs: Embodying Empire* (London, 1995).
4. Joseph Redlich, *Kaiser Franz Joseph von Österreich: Eine Biographie* (Berlin, 1928; Eng. trans., London, 1929); Jean-Paul Bled, *François Joseph* (Paris, 1987; Eng. trans., Oxford, 1992); Steven Beller, *Francis Joseph* (London, 1996).
5. Friedrich Kleinwaechter, *Der Untergang der Oesterreichisch-Ungarischen Monarchie* (Leipzig, 1920), 9ff., and passim.
6. András Gerő, *Ferenc József, a magyarok királya* (Budapest, 1988; second edition, 1999), English translation as *Emperor Francis Joseph, King of the Hungarians* (Boulder, Co. 2001); Éva Somogyi, *Ferenc József* (Budapest, 1989); Otto Urban, *František Josef I.* (Prague, 1991; reprint, 1999); Jiří Pernes, *František Josef I. Nikdy nekorunovaný český král* (Prague 2005). This trend was set by the monograph of Stanisław Grodziski, *Franciszek Józef I.* (Wrocław, 1978).

7. Claudio Magris, *Il mito asburgico nella letteratura austriaca moderna* (Turin, 1963; German translation, 1966); L.R.G. Decloedt, *Imago Imperatoris. Franz Joseph I. in der österreichischen Belletristik der Zwischenkriegszeit* (Vienna, 1995).
8. Adam Wandruszka, et al, eds., *Die Habsburgermonarchie, 1848–1918* (Vienna, 1973–). Gerald Stourzh, *Die Gleichberechtigung der Nationalitäten in der Verfassung und Verwaltung Österreichs, 1848–1918* (Vienna, 1985), originally a contribution to *Die Habsburgermonarchie, 1848–1918. Bd.III: Die Völker des Reiches*, ed. A Wandruszka and P. Urbanitsch (2 vols, Vienna, 1980).
9. Karl Megner, *Beamte: Wirtschafts- und sozialgeschichtliche Aspekte des k. k. Beamtentums* (Vienna, 1985); Waltraud Heindl, *Gehorsame Rebellen: Bürokratie und Beamte in Österreich 1780 bis 1848* (Vienna, 1991); István Deák, *Beyond Nationalism: A Social and Political History of the Habsburg Officer Corps, 1848–1918* (New York, 1990); Tibor Hajdu, *Tisztikar és középosztály 1850–1914: Ferenc József magyar tisztjei* (Budapest, 1999).
10. E.g., from Gary B. Cohen, "Neither Absolutism nor Anarchy: New Narratives on Society and Government in Late Imperial Austria," *Austrian History Yearbook* 29 (1998): 37–61, to Ernst Bruckmüller, "Was There a 'Habsburg Society' in Austria-Hungary?," *Austrian History Yearbook* 37 (2006): 1–16.
11. John Boyer, "The Position of Vienna in a General History of Austria," in *Wien um 1900: Aufbruch in die Moderne*, ed. P. Berner et al. (Munich, 1986), 205–220, at 216.
12. Important examples include Alice Freifeld, *Nationalism and the Crowd in Liberal Hungary, 1848–1914* (Washington, DC and Baltimore, 2000); Maria Bucur and Nancy M. Wingfield, eds., *Staging the Past: The Politics of Commemoration in Habsburg Central Europe, 1848 to the Present* (West Lafayette, 2001). The *Austrian History Yearbook* has again been prominent in this area.
13. Redlich, *Francis Joseph*, 536; but at the same time he allows that the monarch "did indubitably possess both popularity and the confidence of his people."
14. Jeremy King, *Budweisers into Czechs and Germans: A Local History of Bohemian Politics, 1848–1948* (Princeton, 2002); Peter Urbanitsch, "Pluralist Myth and Nationalist Realities: the Dynastic Myth of the Habsburg Monarchy—a Futile Exercise in the Creation of Identity?", *Austrian History Yearbook* 35 (2004): 101–141.
15. Urban, *František Josef I.*, 20f., 43, 48, 62, etc.
16. See also his article in *Austrian History Yearbook* 34 (2003): 145–171, and in general Unowsky, *The Pomp and Politics of Patriotism: Imperial Celebrations in Habsburg Austria, 1848–1916* (West Lafayette, 2005). See also Grodziski, *Franciszek Józef I.*, 116–128.
17. Brigitte Hamann, *Elisabeth: Kaiserin wider Willen* (Vienna, 1982), 216–280, passim, confirms this commitment, though the larger political rapprochement was not of Elisabeth's making. Cf. earlier Eduard Wertheimer, *Graf Julius Andrássy: sein Leben und seine Zeit* (3 vols., Stuttgart, 1910–13), i. 270ff.
18. Adolph Kohut, *Kaiser Franz Josef I. als König von Ungarn* (Berlin, 1916).
19. See the bibliography at http://www.nb.no/baser/1905/index.html (accessed 15.10.2006).
20. Maureen Healy, *Vienna and the Fall of the Habsburg Empire: Total War and Everyday Life in World War I* (Cambridge, 2004), 216ff.
21. Ibid., 279ff.
22. Helmuth A. Niederle, *Es war sehr schön, es hat mich sehr gefreut: Kaiser Franz Joseph und seine Untertanen* (Vienna, 1987).
23. Joachim von Puttkamer, *Schulalltag und nationale Integration in Ungarn: Slowaken, Rumänen und Siebenbürger Sachsen in der Auseinandersetzung mit der ungarischen Staatsidee, 1867–1914* (Munich, 2003), 379.
24. Elisabeth Grossegger, *Der Kaiser-Huldigungs-Festzug, Wien 1908* (Vienna, 1992), 163f., considers this only *en passant*.
25. See especially Bedřich Hlaváč, *František Josef I. Život, povaha, doba* (Prague, 1933), 485ff.

26. Kohut, *Kaiser Franz Josef I.*, 21ff.; Dávid Angyal, "Ferenc József ifjúsága," *Századok*, 68 (1934), 391–409, at 407–409; Gerő, *Ferenc József*, 29ff.
27. Cf. *Die Habsburgermonarchie, 1848–1918. Bd.VII: Verfassung und Parlamentarismus*, ed. Peter Urbanitsch and Helmut Rumpler (2 vols., Vienna, 2000), 108f., 120, 137, 600, 622f.
28. See most recently Jan Županič, "Cesty k urozenosti. Nová šlechta v Rakousko-Uhersku," *Český Časopis Historický*, 104 (2006), 269–302.
29. Éva Somogyi, "Vezető magyar tisztviselők a Ballhausplatzon: A Monarchia és/vagy a nemzet szolgálatában?" *Aetas* 16 (2001), 115–139; Pavla Vošahlíková, ed., *Von Amts wegen. K. k. Beamte erzählen* (Vienna, 1998). Also Miloslav Martínek, "Úředníci z moci národní," in *Studie k modernímu dějinám. Sborník prací k 70. narozeninám Vlastislava Laciny*, ed. Josef Harna and Petr Prokš (Prague, 2001), 105–129.
30. Hajdu, *Tisztikar*. Though his work is primarily a social history, Hajdu makes the striking observation (p. 164) that the "enforced supranationality" of Hungarian army officers concealed a "peculiar and anachronistic spiritual Germanness" (*lelki németség*).
31. Cf. R.J.W. Evans, "Císaři bez říše: Habsburkové a *Reichsidee* v 19. století," in *"Per saecula ad tempora nostra" Sborník k 60. narozeninám prof. Jaroslava Pánka*, ed. Jiří Mikulec and Miloslav Polívka (Prague, forthcoming).
32. For 1898, see Péter Hanák, *A kert és a műhely* (Budapest, 1988), 112–129, German translation published as *Der Garten und die Werkstatt. Ein kulturgeschichtlicher Vergleich Wien und Budapest um 1900* (Vienna, 1992), 101–115; for 1908 (in which Hungary played no part), see Grossegger, *Kaiser-Huldigungs-Festzug*.
33. Cf. Somogyi, *Ferenc József*, 240ff. And if Franz Joseph was spared the bitter censure which William II encountered in Germany, we should not overlook the residual powers of the censor, as Gerő, *Ferenc József*, 165ff. suggests for Hungary.
34. There is much incriminating material in Kann, *Erzherzog Franz Ferdinand Studien* (Munich, 1976); on his obsessions, especially in regard to Hungary, see Olivér Eöttevényi, *Ferenc Ferdinánd* (Budapest, 1942, reprint 1991), 184ff., 261ff. For the tradition, see Matthias Stickler, *Erzherzog Albrecht von Österreich: Selbstverständnis und Politik eines konservativen Habsburgers im Zeitalter Kaiser Franz Josephs* (Husum, 1997).
35. For a good analysis of this, see Healy, *Vienna*, 279ff.
36. See, for example, Francis L. Carsten, *The First Austrian Republic, 1918–38* (Aldershot, 1986), 28f.; Peter Broucek, *Karl I. (IV.): Der politische Weg des letzten Herrschers der Donaumonarchie* (Vienna, 1997), 218ff.; Lothar Höbelt, "Nostalgic Agnostics: Austrian Aristocrats and Politics, 1918–38," in *Noble Fascists? European Aristocracies and the Radical Right*, ed. Karina Urbach (Oxford, forthcoming). I am very grateful for pre-publication access to this text.
37. The claims in Aladár Boroviczény, *Der König und sein Reichsverweser* (Munich, 1924), need to be set alongside Georg Fingerlos, "Als die Leute von Bruck a. d. Mur ihren ehemaligen Kaiser, den seligen Karl, töten wollten," *Wiener Zeitschrift zur Geschichte der Neuzeit* 6 (2006): 117–132.
38. Wolfgang Burgdorf, *Reichskonstitution und Nation: Verfassungsreformprojekte für das Heilige Römische Reich Deutscher Nation im politischen Schrifttum von 1648 bis 1806* (Mainz, 1998); id., *Ein Weltbild verliert seine Welt. Der Untergang des Alten Reiches und die Generation 1806* (Munich, 2006).

SELECT BIBLIOGRAPHY

Agnew, Hugh LeCaine. "Ambiguities of Ritual: Dynastic Loyalty, Territorial Patriotism and Nationalism in the Last Three Royal Coronations in Bohemia." *Bohemia* 41 (2000): 3–22.

Anderson, Benedict. *Imagined Communities. Reflections on the Origin and Spread of Nationalism.* London, 1983.

Barkey, Karen, and Mark von Hagen, eds. *After Empire. Multiethnic Societies and Nation-Building. The Soviet Union and the Russian, Ottoman, and Habsburg Empires.* New York, 1997.

Beller, Steven. *Francis Joseph.* London and New York, 1996.

Binder, Harald. *Galizien in Wien. Parteien. Wahlen, Fraktionen und Abgeordnete im Übergang zur Massenpolitik.* Vienna, 2004.

Biondich, Mark. *Stjepan Radić, the Croat Peasant Party, and the Politics of Mass Mobilization, 1904–1928.* Toronto, 2000.

Bled, Jean-Paul. *Franz Joseph,* trans. T. Bridgeman. Oxford, 1987.

Brix, Emil and Hannes Stekl, eds. *Der Kampf um das Gedächtnis. Öffentliche Gedenktage in Mitteleuropa.* Vienna, 1997.

Bruckmüller, Ernst. *Nation Österreich. Kulturelles Bewußtsein und gesellschaftlich-politische Prozesse.* 2nd, expanded ed. Vienna, 1996.

Cohen, Gary B. "Neither Absolutism nor Anarchy: New Narratives on Society and Government in Late Imperial Austria." *Austrian History Yearbook* 29/Pt.1 (1998): 37–61.

Cole, Laurence. *Für Gott, Kaiser und Vaterland. Nationale Identität der deutschsprachigen Bevölkerung Tirols 1860–1914.* Frankfurt a.M.-New York, 2000.

Cornwall, Mark. *The Undermining of Austria-Hungary 1914–18. The Battle for Hearts and Minds.* Basingstoke, 2001.

Deák, István. *Beyond Nationalism. A Social History of the Habsburg Officer Corps.* Oxford, 1990.

Decloedt, Leopold R.G. *Imago Imperatoris. Franz Joseph I. in der österreichischen Belletristik der Zwischenkriegszeit.* Vienna, 1995.

Fischer, Lisa. *Schattenwürfe in die Zukunft. Kaiserin Elisabeth und die Frauen ihrer Zeit.* Vienna, 1998.

Fischer-Galati, Stephen. "Nationalism and Kaisertreue." *Slavic Review* 22 (1963): 31–36.

Freifeld, Alice. *Nationalism and the Crowd in Liberal Hungary, 1848–1914.* Washington, D.C and Baltimore, 2000.

Gerő, András. *Modern Hungarian Society in the Making, The Unfinished Experience.* Budapest, London, New York, 1995.
———. *Francis Joseph, King of the Hungarians.* New York, 2001.
———. *Imagined History: Chapters from Nineteenth and Twentieth Century Hungarian Symbolic Politics.* Boulder, CO, 2007.
Grossegger, Elisabeth. *Der Kaiser-Huldigungs-Festzug Wien 1908.* Vienna, 1992.
Hamann, Brigitte. *Elisabeth: Kasierin wieder Willen.* Vienna, 1982.
Hämmerle, Christa. "Die k. (u.) k. Armee als 'Schule des Volkes'? Zur Geschichte der Allgemeinen Wehrpflicht in der multinationalen Habsburgermonarchie (1866–1914/18)." in *Der Bürger als Soldat. Die Militarisierung europäischer Gesellschaften im langen 19. Jahrhundert: ein internationaler Vergleich,* ed. Christian Jansen. Essen, 2004. 175–198.
Hanák, Péter. *Der Garten und die Werkstatt. Ein kulturgeschichtlicher Vergleich Wien und Budapest um 1900.* Vienna, 1992.
Heer, Friedrich. *Der Kampf um die österreichische Identität.* Vienna, 1981.
Himka, John-Paul. *Religion and Nationality in Western Ukraine: The Greek Catholic Church and the Ruthenian National Movement in Galicia, 1867–1900.* Montreal and Kingston, 1999.
Hobsbawm, Eric J. *Nations and Nationalism Since 1780. Programme, Myth, Reality.* Cambridge, 1990.
Jászi, Oscar. *The Dissolution of the Habsburg Monarchy.* Chicago, 1929.
Judson, Pieter M., and Marsha L. Rozenblit, eds. *Constructing Nationalities in East Central Europe.* New York and Oxford, 2005.
Kann, Robert A. "The Dynasty and the Imperial Idea." *Austrian History Yearbook* 3/I (1967): 11–31.
Krasa-Florian, Selma. *Die Allegorie der Austria. Die Entstehung des Gesamtstaatsgedankens in der österreichisch-ungarischen Monarchie und die bildende Kunst* (Vienna, 2007).
Magris, Claudio. *Il Mito Asburgico nella Letteratura Austriaca Moderna.* Turin, 1963.
Markovits, Andrei S., and Frank E. Sysyn, eds. *Nationbuilding and the Politics of Nationalism. Essays on Austrian Galicia.* Cambridge, MA, 1982.
Möckl, Karl, ed. *Hof und Hofgesellschaft in den deutschen Staaten im 19. und beginnenden 20. Jahrhundert.* Boppard am Rhein, 1990.
Ra'anan, Uri, et al, eds. *State and Nation in Multi-Ethnic Societies. The Break-Up of Multi-National States.* Manchester, 1991.
Rachamimov, Alon. *POWs and the Great War. Captivity on the Eastern Front.* Oxford-New York, 2001.
Rechter, David. *The Jews of Vienna and the First World War.* London and Portland, OR, 2001.
Riesenfellner, Stefan, ed. *Steinernes Bewußtsein I. Die öffentliche Repräsentation staatlicher und nationaler Identität Österreichs in seinen Denkmälern.* Vienna, 1998.
Roshwald, Aviel. *Ethnic Nationalism and the Fall of Empires: Central Europe, Russia and the Middle East.* London, 2001.
Rothenberg, Gunther E. *The Army of Francis Joseph.* West Lafayette, 1976.
Rozenblit, Marsha. *Reconstructing a National Identity: The Jews of Habsburg Austria during World War I.* New York and Oxford, 2001.
Rudolph, Richard, and David Good, eds. *Nationalism and Empire. The Habsburg Empire and the Soviet Union.* New York, 1992.
Schmidl, Erwin A. *Juden in der k.(u.)k. Armee 1788–1918.* Eisenstadt, 1989.

Shedel, James. "Emperor, Church, and People: Religion and Dynastic Loyalty during the Golden Jubilee of Franz Joseph." *Catholic Historical Review* 76 (1990): 71–92.
Sondhaus, Lawrence. *In the Service of the Emperor. Italians in the Austrian Armed Forces 1815–1918.* New York, 1990.
Stourzh, Gerald. "The Multi-National Empire Revisited: Reflections on Late Imperial Austria." *Austrian History Yearbook* 23 (1992): 1–22.
Tanner, Marie. *The Last Descendant of Aeneas: The Habsburgs and the Mythic Image of the Emperor.* New Haven, 1992.
Telesko, Werner. *Geschichtsraum Österreich. Die Habsburger und ihre Geschichte in den bildenden Künsten.* Vienna, 2006.
Unowsky, Daniel. *The Pomp and Politics of Patriotism: Imperial Celebrations in Habsburg Austria, 1848–1916.* West Lafayette, 2005.
Urban, Otto. *Česká společnost, 1848–1918.* Prague, 1982.
———. *František Josef I.* Prague, 1999.
Urbanitsch, Peter. "Pluralist Myth and Nationalist Realities: The Dynastic Myth of the Habsburg Monarchy—a Futile Exercise in the Creation of Identity?" *Austrian History Yearbook* 35 (2004): 101–141.
Wheatcroft, Andrew. *The Habsburgs: Embodying Empire.* London, 1995.
Wingfield, Nancy, and Maria Bucur, eds. *Staging the Past: The Politics of Commemoration in Habsburg Central Europe, 1848 to the Present.* West Lafayette, 2001.
Wingfield, Nancy. *Flag Wars and Stone Saints: How the Bohemian Lands Became Czech.* Cambridge, MA, 2007.
Žolger, Ivan. *Der Hofstaat des Hauses Österreich.* Vienna, 1917.

INDEX

A

absolutism, neoabsolutism, 25, 62, 67–70, 81, 88, 114, 146, 208, 209
Academy of Sciences, Austrian, 24, 224
Adalbert/Vojtěch, 19
Adler, Victor, 211
Ady, Endre, 186, 187
agriculture, 17, 75, 184
Ala, 43
Alps, Alpine provinces, 16, 44, 69
America, 138, 143, 203, 224, 226
Albert, Prince, 146, 202
Albrecht II, 16, 19
Albrecht, Archduke, 38, 50, 229
Alexander II, Tsar, 93
Alexander the Great, 15, 21
anarchists, 154, 155
Andrássy, Count Gyula, 97, 147, 149–151, 155
anticlericalism, 70–72, 81
anti-Semitism, 76, 181, 183, 188–190
Aquileia, 20
Arbeiter-Zeitung, 102, 212
Arco, 43–45, 50
Armenians, 116
army, Habsburg, 2, 5, 13, 22, 36–42, 45–47, 49, 63, 116, 188, 190, 200, 224, 228, 229
    officer corps, 5, 16, 37, 39–49, 89, 181, 188, 191, 228
    veterans. See military veterans
Arnstein, Benedikt David, 63
Aspern, 17
Attila, 16
Auersperg, Prince Carlos, 96
Augarten, 74

Augsburger Postzeitung, 205
Ausgleich (Compromise), 1867. 80, 92, 93, 106, 151, 164, 180, 208, 225
Austria (see also Cisleithania), 1, 3, 4, 12–18, 21, 25, 28, 29, 37, 39, 44, 63, 68–70, 79, 124, 128, 140, 142, 164, 181, 183, 208, 209, 230
Austria, Lower, 11, 38, 67, 76, 105
Austria, Upper, 11, 38, 71, 76
Austro-Prussian War (1866), 38, 91, 92, 144, 148, 149, 208
Avars, 16

B

Babenbergs, 15, 18, 20, 21
Badeni, Count Kasimir, 78, 79, 102
Balkans, 226
Bánffy, Dezső, 155, 171
Battisti, Cesare, 53
Barvins'kyi, Volodymyr, 125, 126, 128, 129
Baudelaire, Charles Pierre, 186
Bavaria, Bavarians, 16, 47, 141, 143, 153, 206
Beethoven, Ludwig van, 17
Belcredi, Count Richard, 91
Bereg, 184
Berlin, 91, 200
Berliner Tagblatt, 200, 209
Beust, Friedrich, 96
Bezzeca, battle of (1866), 47
Bismarck, Otto von, 149, 207
Bjelovar, 172
Bled, 21
Bludenz, 43, 52
Bobeerska-Wasilewska, Felicie, 122
Boer War, 205

Bohemia, Bohemians, 66, 74–78, 87–89, 101, 193
    Czechs in, 71, 81, 92, 93, 96, 98, 99, 101, 104, 106, 107, 200, 210, 229
    Diet, 77, 90, 91, 96, 98, 101, 102
    Germans in, 69, 70, 77–79, 81, 96, 98, 99, 101, 106, 229
    history, 13, 18–20, 25, 63, 64, 67, 93, 227
    Kingdom of, 5, 11, 16, 25, 86–89, 91–93, 96–99, 106, 107, 149, 210
    national issues in, 14, 44, 69, 81, 103, 105, 106
    rebellion 1618–20, 93, 95, 227
    veterans' movement in, 38, 42, 45
Bohemian Museum, 92
Borgo, 43, 44
Bořivoy, Prince, 19
Borkowski, Count Alexander, 121
Bosnia-Herzegovina, 22, 69
bourgeoisie, 43–45, 53, 55, 67, 154
Bozen, 46
Bratislava/Pozsony/Pressburg, 155, 179, 185
    Orthodox *Yeshiva*, 185
Braunau, 71
Břetislav I, 19
Britain, 141, 146, 201–205, 209, 210, 214
    Empire, 199, 202, 203
    monarchism, 200, 201, 207, 209, 214, 226
    socialists, 202, 203
Brünn/Brno, 16, 19, 75, 78, 80
Buda. See Budapest.
Budapest, 92, 139, 141, 142, 147, 150, 151, 153–155, 158, 166, 179, 185, 187–190
    Buda, 16, 139, 143, 145, 148, 149, 151, 153, 156–158
    Buda Castle, 153, 158
    City Park, 150
    Óbuda ship works, 143
    Pest, 143, 145, 148–150, 155–157
    Rabbinical Seminary, 185, 187
    Royal Orpheum, 188
    University of Technology, 157
    Váci Street, 145
Budweis/Budějovice, 72, 224
Bukovina, 39, 79, 129
bureaucracy, 2, 4, 6, 62, 64, 68, 78, 88, 115, 128, 138, 144–146, 165, 166, 200, 224, 228, 229
Byzantium, 28

C

Čas, 102–104, 107
Calvinists, 63, 190
capitalism, capitalists, 62, 181, 203
Carinthia, 17, 20–23, 79
Carniola, 20, 22, 39
Carpathian Mountains, 16, 79, 184, 189, 192, 193
Carpatho-Rus' region, 179, 184, 193
Carst Mountains, 16, 20
Castelfondo, 49
Catholic Center Party (Germany), 206
Cavalese, 49
celebrity monarchy, 138, 139, 141, 146, 150, 158, 163
censorship, 64, 68, 73, 74, 96, 120, 122, 123
Center for Unusual Museums, 141
Chamisso, Adelbert von, 17
Charlemagne, 16, 21
Charles IV, 13, 16, 19, 23
Charles V, 19
Charles, Archduke, 17, 21, 38
Chłędowski, Kazimierz, 118, 121
church-state relations, 50, 62, 63, 67–69, 71–73, 153, 228
Cilli/Celje, 21, 78
Cisleithania, 14, 23, 26, 37, 40, 42, 44, 46, 55, 63, 68–71, 74, 77–81, 93, 95, 103, 115, 117, 118, 120, 124, 181, 208, 209, 225, 228
civil service. See bureaucracy.
Clam-Gallas, Count Christian Philipp, 67
Clam-Martinic, Count Heinrich Jaroslav, 96
clergy, 71, 72
communism, 141, 157
Concordat of 1855. See also church-state relations. 67, 68, 228
Condino, 43
conservatism, conservatives, 13, 24, 50, 51, 68–70, 114–124, 128–133, 155, 169, 170, 202–207, 227
Constance, Lake, 101
Constitution of 1867, 14, 21, 69, 128, 132, 207–210, 213, 228

cooperative movement, 50, 52
Corfu, 142
coronation
    Bohemian, abortive. 87–93, 96,
        98–101, 103–107, 225, 227
    Hungarian, 1867. 92, 93, 105, 106,
        150, 151
Cossacks, 189
costume, folk and national. 13, 73, 75, 130,
    143–145, 158, 163, 172, 225
Counter-Reformation, 101
Cracow, 114–116, 118–123, 128, 130
    Academy of Sciences, 116, 123
    Wawel Castle, 116, 123
Croatia, Croats, 6, 14, 22, 27, 28, 152,
    162–173, 225, 227
Croatian Theater, 163, 164
Croatia-Slavonia, Kingdom of, 163, 164,
    166
Croatian Provincial Government, 169
Crown of St Wenceslas, 92, 93, 95, 97–99,
    106, 107
culture, Austrian, 17, 18, 63
    German, 17, 18, 28, 70, 77, 79, 81,
        99, 183
    Hungarian, 138, 145–147, 150, 182,
        185
    Italian, 50, 54
    Jewish, 182, 183, 185, 192
    national, 12–14, 20, 21, 29
    Polish, 115, 117, 131, 133
    Ruthenian, 124, 125, 131
    Slavic, 21
    Slovenian, 20, 22
Czas, 119, 120, 123, 128, 130, 131
Czech National Socialist Party, 80
Czech National Theater, 92, 93–95, 98, 105
Czech University, Prague, 87, 96
Czechoslovakia. See also Bohemia, Moravia,
    Slovakia, 1, 86, 87, 107, 192, 193
    Communist Party, 87
Czechs, 13, 18, 27, 36, 69, 72, 75, 77,
    79–81, 86–107, 147, 149, 152, 213,
    225, 227, 229
    history, 13, 18–20, 22, 86, 87, 101
    language, 69, 72, 78, 79, 182
    national movement, 64, 86, 92, 93,
        95, 97, 105–107
    progressive movement, 99, 101
    statehood, 5, 91, 92, 96–99, 210

veterans' movement, 42, 44
Częstochowa, 189
Czernowitz, 79

D

Daily Mail, 203
Daily Telegraph Affair, 204–206
Dalmatia, 16, 27, 28, 39
Danube, 16, 18, 19, 138, 143, 156, 157
Deák, Ferenc, 148–150, 152, 153, 155
Debrecen, 145
democratization. See also suffrage, 80, 103,
    200, 211
democrats, 104, 116–118, 121–125,
    128–130, 132, 133
Denmark, 38
Deutscher Schulverein, 69
Deutsches Volksblatt, 212
Deutsches Haus, 78, 79
Deutschmeister regiment, 38
Deutsch-Österreichischer Leseverein, 73
Deutschvölkischer Akademikerverband, 78
Diana, Princess of Wales, 138
diets. See parliament.
Dilo, 124, 125, 127–129
Disraeli, Benjamin, 202, 203
Dobrovský, Josef, 79
Dual Alliance, 1879, 80
dualism, Dual Monarchy, 2, 5, 39, 86, 92,
    93, 97, 140, 142, 147, 149–153, 157,
    163, 166, 169, 171, 173, 180, 182, 191,
    208, 224, 225, 228
Dürer, Albrecht, 17
Dziennik Polski, 120, 123, 128

E

Edward VII, 203, 214
Eger/Cheb, 77
Elisabeth, Empress, 4, 5, 47, 74, 88, 89,
    102, 138–158, 208, 225, 227
Eötvös, József, 151
Eugene of Savoy, Prince, 16, 18, 25, 38,
    168
Eugénie, Empress of France, 146

F

Falk, Max, 150
Fallersleben, Hoffmann von, 17
Ferdinand Karl, Archduke, 48
Ferdinand, Emperor, 91, 98, 99, 227

Ferenczy, Ida, 147, 149
Fernkorn, Anton Dominik, 168
Fiemme, 49
    District Agrarian Consortium, 52
flag, Bavarian, 143
    Croatian, 163, 167
    Hungarian, 163, 167–172
    Serbian, 167
    US, 203
France, 72, 78
    1859 Austrian war against, 38, 201, 208
Francis, Emperor, 17
Frank, Ivan, 167, 168
Frank, Josip, 167
Frank, Vladimir, 167, 168
Frankl, Ludwig August, 16
Franz Ferdinand, Archduke, 48, 105, 229
Franz I, 99, 101
Franz II, 16, 17, 64
Franz Joseph, Emperor, 2–7, 13, 16, 22, 36, 46–49, 51, 63, 68, 77, 79–81, 86–107, 113–118, 120, 122–127, 130–133, 138–140, 143–151, 154, 156, 158, 162–164, 166, 167, 169, 172, 173, 191, 200, 201, 207–215, 223–230
Franz Karl, Archduke, 48
Frederick I, 16
Frederick IV of Tyrol, 16
Fundamental Laws. See Constitution of 1867

G

Galicia, 6, 30, 39, 44, 72, 113–133, 179, 225, 227
    government, 116–118, 120, 122, 123, 128, 132
    peasants, 113, 129
    Poles in, 115–119, 121, 123, 130, 132
Galician School Board, 122
Garda, Lake, 43
Garibaldi, Giuseppe, 47
Gautsch, Baron Paul, 102
Gazeta Lwowska, 116
Gazzetta di Trento, 44
Geneva, Lake, 154
George V, British King 204
German
    culture, 17, 18, 69–73, 79, 183
    history, 17, 28, 30
    language, 15, 18–20, 54, 63, 69, 77, 78, 138, 141, 144, 150, 178, 213
    liberals, 69–72, 76–78, 80, 92, 96–98, 106, 116, 124, 128, 129, 131, 210, 227
    nationalists, 76–81, 105, 106, 227, 228
    nationality, 6, 21, 27, 39, 193, 200, 208, 223
    speakers, 13, 18, 42, 44, 46, 62, 64, 66, 68, 70, 72, 74, 75, 77, 79, 80, 86, 96, 98, 99, 101–104, 116, 144, 145, 209, 228, 229
German Technical University, Brünn/Brno, 75
Germanization, 63, 69, 71, 77–81, 146
Germany, German Reich, 28, 42, 43, 52, 78, 96, 142, 181, 192, 199–201, 204–207, 209, 211, 214
Gindely, Anton, 27, 28, 225
Gladstone, William, 202
Gödöllő, 139, 141, 142, 144, 149, 151
Goethe, Johann Wolfgang von, 17
Görz/Gorica/Gorizia, 21, 43
Gołuchowski, Agenor, 120
Goya, Francisco, 139
Graz, 78
Greek Catholic (Uniate) Church, 72, 114, 116, 124, 125, 127, 128, 130
Greek Orthodox Church, 63
Greeks, ancient, 25
Grillparzer, Franz, 13, 17

H

Habsburg dynasty, 2–7, 13–15, 18, 19, 22–25, 29, 30, 37, 40, 47, 51, 52, 62, 67, 71, 72, 81, 86, 87, 99, 101, 107, 120, 128, 132, 138, 146, 151, 152, 158, 162, 164, 167, 170, 180–182, 199–203, 207, 223–229
Hamieri (Feuerstein), Avigdor, 6, 7, 178–193, 226, 227
Hardie, Keir, 203
Hašek, Jaroslav, 36
Hassidim, 179, 184, 185, 187, 192
Hausner, Otto, 118, 122, 123
Haydn, Joseph, 16, 19
Hebrew, 6, 178, 185–187, 190, 192
Heine, Heinrich, 142, 153, 158
Helfert, Joseph Alexander Freiherr von, 24

Henri, Duke of Orleans, 154
Henry, Duke, 17
Herder, Johann Gottfried, 12
Hermann, 17
Herzl, Theodore, 188
Hofer, Andreas, 17
Hohenelbe/Vrchlabí, 69
Hohenwart, Karl, 96, 97
Hohenzollern dynasty, 7, 200, 230
Holy Roman Empire, 13, 17–19, 24, 28, 43, 230
Horatius Cocles, 17
Hormayr, Johann von, 13
Horthy, Miklós, 157
Hradec Králové/Königgrätz, 91
Humbert, Italian King, 154
Humoristické listy, 99
Hungary, Hungarians, 21, 37, 200, 223
    and Croatia, 163, 164, 167–169, 171, 173
    and fashion, 145
    and the monarchy, 2, 5, 39, 71, 87, 89, 105, 138–158, 207–213, 225, 227–230
    and Prussia, 91, 148, 149
    Ausgleich, 1867, 91–93, 106, 115
    First Republic, 140
    history, 12, 17, 19, 25, 28
    language status, 14, 63, 139, 147, 148
    Legion, 149
    Literary Society, New York, 155
    National Guard, 181
    parliament, 147, 151–153, 212
    Russian occupation, 1849, 143, 207
    schools, 12–14, 18
    State Railway, 163, 167, 170
Huns, 16
Hus, Jan, 19, 101
Hussites, 101

I

Illustrated London Press, 203
Illustriertes Wiener Extrablatt, 212, 213
imperial inspection tours (*Kaiserreisen*), 6, 67, 91, 92, 114–119, 133, 142–147, 162, 183
Independent National Party, Croatia, 164
industry, 17, 62, 74, 77, 99, 184
Innsbruck, 16, 43,
Institute of Austrian Historical Research, 24
insurance, 38, 40, 46
intelligentsia, intellectuals, 138, 142, 152
    bourgeois, 67
    Croatian, 164, 168, 173
    Czech, 79
    Jewish, 192
    Ruthenian, 116, 124, 126, 129, 131, 132
International Anti-Anarchist Conference, 1898. 155
Interpol, 155
Invalids' Fund, 38
Ireland, 204
"Iron Ring" coalition, 69, 97, 98, 115, 117, 129, 131
Israel, 178, 192
Istanbul, 226
Istria, 27
Italian culture, 50, 51, 54
    language and speakers, 5, 20, 22, 28, 29, 37, 42, 43, 47, 53, 54, 148, 213, 225
Italophiles, 53
Italy, 13, 20, 36, 38, 43, 47–50, 89, 146–148, 155, 208, 209

J

Jasygen tribe, 143
Jászi, Oskar, 2, 4, 11, 30, 149, 158, 181
Jelačić, Ban, 168, 169, 171
Jerusalem, 185
Jews, 2, 7, 62, 63, 79, 80, 179–185, 187–190, 192, 193, 223, 225, 226
    Austrian-German, 73, 142
    Carpathian, 184, 193
    Croatian, 164
    Czech, 73, 75
    freedoms for, 6, 63, 152, 182
    Galician, 114, 116, 117, 122, 126–128, 131, 184
    Hassidic, 179, 184, 185, 187, 192
    Hungarian, 142, 150, 182, 184, 185
    in World War I, 187–191
    middle-class, 144
    Orthodox, 63, 116, 182, 184, 185
Johann, Archduke, 227
Jókai, Mór, 148
Joseph II, Emperor, 2, 6, 16, 17, 19, 62–81, 113, 118, 124–130, 225, 227
Josefstadt (Bohemia), 66
Josefswille/Mlatce, 66

Josephinism, 62, 67–71, 76, 81, 128, 130
József, Archduke, of Hungary, 227
jubilee, Emperor Franz Joseph's 50th, 1898, 2, 47, 49, 105, 209, 229
    Emperor Franz Joseph's 60th, 1908, 47, 48, 75, 104, 158, 209, 211–213, 227–229
    Queen Victoria's 60th, 1897, 203
Judaism, orthodox, 63, 116, 182, 184, 185
    reform, 116, 182
Junkers, 211

K

Kachkovs'kyi Society, 127, 129, 132
Karageorgević dynasty, 230
Karl, Archduke, 168, 229, 230
Kaspret, Anton, 27, 28
Kautsky, Karl, 211
Kennedy, Jackie, 138
Khuen-Héderváry, Count Karl, 163–165, 170, 172, 173
Kielmansegg, Count Erich, 105
Klobukowski, Anton, 120
Klosterneuburg, 15
Koerber, Ernst, 102
Körner, Carl Theodore, 17
Kolín, 17, 95, 97
Koruna Česká, 97, 99
Kossuth, Lajos, 143, 148, 149, 151, 152, 155, 156, 227
Kossuthism, 140, 150, 152
Kovals'kyi, Vasyl', 125, 128
Krafft, Johann Peter, 14
Kramář, Karel, 98
Krisvosije, 39
Kroměříž/Kremsier, 88, 228
Krok, Prince, 19
Krpan, Martin, 20
Kršnjavi, Ivo, 167, 172
Kulturkampf, 44, 68
Kun, Béla, 192
Kutná Hora/Kuttenberg, 103

L

La Patria, 44
Ladin, 54
Laibach/Ljubljana, 21
Language Ordinances (Badeni), 78
Latorica river, 184, 185
Ledro Valley, 44, 45

Leibeigenschaft, 63, 64, 75–77
Leitmeritzer Zeitung, 77
Lemberg/L'viv/Lwów, 72, 115–125, 127–128
    Cathedral of St George, 72, 116, 125–127, 131
    City Hall, 121–123
    Hotel Saski, 123
    Old Market Square, 122
    Stauropegion Institute, 125
Leonidas, 17
Leopold I, 15
Leopold II, 62, 64, 71, 92, 99
Leopold III, 15
Leopold, "the Virtuous," 16
Lex Apponyi, 14
Libényi, János, 207
liberalism, liberals, 2, 62, 66, 68–71, 73–76, 80, 115, 123, 142, 149, 202, 206, 213, 225
    and the army, 39, 52, 53
    Czech, 69, 91, 93, 98
    German, 69–72, 76, 77, 80, 81, 96–98, 106, 124, 128, 131, 210, 227
    Hungarian, 149–152, 155, 158
    Italian, 43, 50, 51, 53, 55
    press, 53, 73, 92, 117, 120, 128, 129, 200, 205, 209
liberalization, 67
Libuše, 13, 14, 17, 19, 29
Lincoln, Abraham, 155
Linz, 71
Lipany, 101
Liszt, Franz, 148
Littoral, 20, 39
Lizzana, 45
Lobkowitz, Prince Georg, 98
Lombardy, 43, 44
London, 118, 226
"*Los von Rom*" movement, 79
Luccheni, Luigi, 138, 154
Ludwig II, Bavarian King, 141, 153
Lutherans, 63
Luxemburg dynasty, 19, 25

M

Madeira, 146
Magenta, 89
Magyars. See Hungary,
Malborghetto, 22

Malé, 48
Marburg/Maribor, 21
Maria Louisa, Queen, 139
Maria Theresia, Empress, 16, 19, 25, 62, 64, 75, 148, 155
Marie Valerie, Archduchess, 141, 142, 151
Mariazell, 146
Marmaros, 184
Masaryk, Tomáš Garrigue, 86
Maximilian I, Emperor, 16, 17, 19, 25
Maximilian, Emperor of Mexico, 150
Mayerling, 140
Metternich, Prince Klemens von, 67
middle classes, 45, 53, 91, 144, 164, 171, 205, 212
Mikszáth, Kálmán, 153
Milan, 43
Military service, 39–41, 44, 49, 53, 75, 165, 228
Military veterans, Czech, 42, 51, 90
    Imperial Federation of, 51
    Imperial-Royal Austrian Association of, 41
    Italian-Tyrolean, 5, 37–55, 225
Ministry for Local Defense, 40, 41
Ministry for Religion and Education, 15, 24, 25, 27, 30
Ministry of the Interior, 120, 122
Młocki, Alfred, 118, 120, 123
Mohács, battle of, 16, 19
Moldau/Vltava river, 16, 93, 102
Mongols, 28
Morava river, 16
Moravia, Moravians, 16–19, 63, 64, 67, 68, 72, 75, 78, 88, 91–93, 99, 103
    Compromise, 103
    Diet, 103
    Provincial Museum, 75
Morning Post, 203
Moscophiles, 129, 130
Munkács, 185
Munkácsy, Mihály, 153
Musil, Robert, 7
myths, national, 4, 11–30, 101, 152, 179, 207, 213

N
Nagodba, (agreement Hungary-Croatia), 1868. 164, 171
Napoleon Bonaparte, 22
Napoleonic Wars, 2, 16, 17, 19, 22, 38, 50
Národní listy, 70, 75, 80, 92, 93, 96, 99, 102
Nation, The, 204
National League (Trentino/Italian-Tyrol), 53, 54
National Party, Croatia, 164
nationalism, 1, 2, 7, 14, 40, 113, 181, 186, 199, 200, 204, 210, 215
    Czech, 64, 87, 92, 95, 97, 101, 105, 106, 227
    German, 64, 76–81, 105, 106, 227
    Hungarian, 2, 145, 146, 152, 158, 182
    Italian, 43, 53
    Jewish, 190
    Polish, 113, 118, 121–123, 132, 133
    Ruthenian, 127
    Slavic, 200
    Ukrainian, 113
Nauka, 127, 132
Naumovych, Ivan, 126, 129
Nazis, 87
Neue Freie Presse, 73, 129, 209, 212–214
Newald, Ritter Julius von, 73, 74
New York Times, 155
nobility, 23, 44, 53, 79, 96, 114–117, 130, 132, 154, 164, 228, 230
Norway, 226
Novara, 89

O
Odavidhaza, 184, 187, 192
Odessa, 186, 191, 192
Old Czechs, 93, 98, 106
Olmütz/Olomouc, 19, 68
Omladina trial, 101
Österreichische Illustrierte Zeitung, 41
Otto, 'the Great', 17
Ottokar II Přemysl, 16, 17, 19, 227
Ottomans, 14, 16, 19, 21

P
Palacký, František, 93, 96
Palestine, Mandatory. 180, 187, 192
Paris, 118, 120
parliament
    British, 202, 206, 214
    Croatian. See Sabor.
    Galician. See Sejm.
    Imperial Austrian. See Reichsrat.

provincial, 71, 89, 208
  Tyrolean. See Tyrol, Diet.
Party of Rights, Croatia, 164
patriotism
  Croatian, 170, 171
  Czech, 93, 95, 102, 104
  Habsburg/Austrian, 2–5, 7, 11–13,
    16, 17, 21–24, 26–30, 40–42,
    45–55, 70, 92, 124, 130, 164,
    167, 172, 179, 181, 188–190,
    225, 229, 230
  Hungarian, 7, 152, 156, 179, 181,
    182, 185, 188, 227
  Polish, 118, 121, 123
  Slovenian, 21, 22
peasants, 6, 22, 44, 45, 49, 64, 66, 68, 75,
  76, 79, 190
  Croatian, 22, 163, 166, 168, 170
  Galician, 113, 114, 116, 123–129,
    131, 132
  Hungarian, 139, 143, 145
  Jewish, 184
Pekař, Josef, 87, 102, 106, 107
Pelcl, František Martin, 79
Pest. See Budapest
Pester Lloyd, 150
Piedmont, 1859 Austrian war against, 2, 38,
  146, 201, 208
Plener, Ernst von, 70, 77
Plzeň/Pilsen, 97
Poland, 6, 63, 113, 117, 119, 121–123
  1830 uprising, 6, 113, 118–125,
    130, 132
  1863 uprising, 118, 119, 132
  First Partition of, 63
Poland-Lithuania, 129
police, 73, 114, 116
  and politics, 101, 118–123,
    127–129, 167, 169–171
  censorship, 94, 96, 120
Polish language and speakers, 114–116,
  122, 124, 129, 131, 182
political Catholicism, 44, 50–54, 205, 206,
  227
Popiel, Paweł, 114, 120
Popular Party (Trentino/Italian-Tyrol), 50,
  51, 54
Prague, 16, 19, 20, 28, 70, 86–107, 149
  Academy of Fine Arts, 89
  Bethlehem Square, 101
  Chamber of Commerce and
    Industry, 105
  Charles Bridge, 101
  Charles University, 79, 170
  circle, 183
  ghetto (Judenstadt), 63
  Hradčany, 107
  Jára Cimrman Theater, 87
  Josefstadt/Josefov, 63
  Jubilee Exhibition, 1891, 98–100, 107
  Malostranské náměstí/Kleinseitner
    Ring, 89
  Old Town Square, 93
  Society of Patriotic Friends of the
    Arts, 89
  Society of Sciences, 92
  Wenceslas Square, 103
  Žofín/Sofien Island, 96, 101
Pražský illustrovaný kurýr, 102, 107
Prešeren, France, 20
press freedom, 67, 68
Primislaus/Přemysl, 14, 19
prisoners of war, 191
Prosvita, 125, 132
Protestantism, 62, 63, 68, 74, 79
Prussia, 2, 17, 38, 66, 129, 148, 149, 181,
  206, 230
Przegląd Polski, 116

R

Rabbi (Trentino/Italian-Tyrol), 47
rabbis, 116, 131, 184, 226
Radetzky, Field Marshal, 17, 36, 38, 47, 89
Radetzkymarsch, 36, 47
Radić, Stjepan, 168, 170, 171
Red Cross societies, 53
Reichenberg/Liberec, 38, 67, 78, 99, 103
Reichspost, 209, 212
Reichsrat (Austrian parliament), 20, 50, 51,
  53, 68–70, 75–78, 88, 97, 98, 102, 103,
  115, 117, 124, 125, 128, 131, 200,
  208–211, 214, 228
Reichstag (German parliament), 205, 214
Redlich, Joseph, 223, 224
Redlich, Oswald, 27
republicans, 203, 205
revolutionaries, 67, 68, 118, 119, 123, 143,
  147, 192
revolutions of 1848, 2, 6, 36, 38, 43, 64,
  67, 68, 72–74, 88–91, 114, 115, 119,

139, 142, 145, 147–149, 152, 162, 168, 171, 201, 209, 211, 227
Rezek, Antonín, 102
Richard I "the Lionheart," 16
Rieger, Frantisek Ladislav, 93, 96, 98
Rijeka/Fiume, 168
Rimbaud, Arthur, 186
Risorgimento, 20
ritual, state and court, 2–4, 46, 47, 103, 104, 106, 151, 152, 162, 163, 167, 193, 199, 200, 206
Riva, 43–46, 48, 49
Roma, 184
Roman Catholic Church, 2, 21, 46, 50–53, 66–74, 79, 81, 114–116, 123, 158, 162, 164, 200, 205, 206, 223, 230
Romanians, 79, 152, 184, 200, 212
Romanov dynasty, 3
Romanowicz, Tadeusz, 118, 121–123
Romans, ancient, 25
Romeno, 51, 52, 154
Roth, Joseph, 36, 181, 200
Rovereto, 43, 45, 46, 51
Rudigier, Bishop Franz Joseph, 71
Rudolf I, 15–17, 19, 21, 25, 227
Rudolf IV, 13, 16
Rudolph, Crown Prince, 47, 48, 97, 139, 140, 147, 149, 151–153
Russia, Russians, 28, 93, 124, 129, 170, 179, 180, 191
Russian Poland, 6, 113, 117, 118, 122
Ruthenia, Ruthenians/Rusyns, 72, 79, 113–133, 184, 193, 225
Ruthenian Council, 125, 129
Ruthenian National Institute, 116, 125, 127, 129, 131

S

Sabor, 164, 165, 169
Sadowa, 149
Salzburg, 16, 38
Sava River, 168
Savinja valley, 21
Schiller, Friedrich von, 17
Schmerling, Anton von, 91
Schönerer, Georg Ritter von, 76, 79
schools, 4, 11–30, 47, 69–72, 102, 115, 117, 122, 128, 132, 148, 164, 170, 185, 225, 227
    school reform, 69, 70, 74

Schratt, Katherina, 172
Schubert, Franz, 17
Schwarzenberg, Prince Friedrich von, 90, 207, 228
Schwarzenberg, Prince Karl von, 38
Schwechat, 97
Scitovszky, Prince Primate, 147
Scurelle, 48
Sejm, 114, 116, 118, 121, 125, 128, 131
Serbian Orthodox Church, 167, 168
Serbs, 152, 164, 173, 225
serfdom, 72, 114, 123, 125, 129, 143, 145
Seven Years' War, 66
Severin, 16
sharp-shooters, 53, 54
Sigmund, King of Bohemia, 19
Silesia, 18, 19, 63, 66, 69, 92, 99
Sisak, 170
Slavs, 13, 17, 21–23, 28–30, 69–71, 75, 77, 116, 129, 170, 200, 208, 223, 225
Slawikowitz bei Brünn/Slavíkovice, 67, 75
Slomšek, Martin, 21
Slovakia, Slovaks, 19, 152, 184
Slovenia, Slovenes, 13, 19–22, 27, 30, 78
Slovo, 124, 129
Soběslav I, 19
socialists, socialism, social democrats, 2, 39, 40, 50, 52, 53, 102, 158, 191, 203–206, 211–213, 230
Sokol (Czech gymnastic association), 95
Solferino, 89
Sophia, Archduchess, 147, 149, 207
Sophie, Princess, 145
South Africa, 205
SPD, German Social Democratic Party, 205, 206
Spevec, Franjo, 166, 167, 172
Speyer, 17
Spormaggiore, 45
St. Andrä, 21
St. John of Nepomuk, 101
St. Stephen, 17
St. Cyril, 19, 21, 22
St. Ludmilla, 19
St. Methodius, 19, 21, 22
St. Rupert, 16
St. Wenceslas, 19
Stańczyks, 115, 118–120, 123, 132
Starčević, David, 165
Stephanie, Princess, 48

Stephen, King of Hungary, 21
Styria, 20, 21, 23, 30, 66, 71, 76, 78, 79, 146, 227
Strauss, Johann (the Elder), 36
Stremayr, Karl von, 69
Strossmayer, Bishop Josip Juraj, 168
Stuart-Wortley, Colonel, 205
Stupnicki, Bishop, 124
Sudeten Mountains, 16
suffrage, 104, 115, 132, 152, 158
    universal manhood, 101, 103, 158, 211, 212, 228
Suttner, Bertha von, 40
Svatopluk, Prince, 17, 19
Sweden, 226
Switzerland, 118, 230
Sziget, defence of, 14, 16
szlachta, 115, 117, 118, 122, 130, 131

T

Taaffe, Count Eduard, 69, 97, 98, 101, 115, 117, 120, 124, 129, 132, 227
Tamerlane, 78
Telve, 47
Territet, 154
Terzolas, 47
Themistocles, 21
Thirty Years' War, 17, 20, 93
Thun, Count Franz, 89, 101, 106
Times, The, 203
toleration, religious, 63, 70, 72, 76, 77, 79, 80
    Edict, 1781. 63, 73, 77, 79, 80
Torcegno, 48, 52
Transylvania, 67
Trentino (Italian-Tyrol), 5, 18, 37, 42–55, 225
Trento, 43, 44, 46–49, 51
Trieste, 20, 43
Triple Alliance, 43
Tyrol, 16, 39, 46, 47, 50, 54, 68, 70, 227
    Diet, 50, 51, 71
    German-speaking, 46, 54, 68
    Italian-speaking. See Trentino
    Uprising of 1809, 17, 47

U

Ugocsa, 184
Uhland, Johann Ludwig, 17
Új kelet, 178
Ukraine, 6, 113
Ukrainian language and speakers, 114, 124, 125, 128, 129, 131
Ulrichskirchen, 17
Ungh, 184
USSR, 1, 87
Ústí nad Labem/Aussig, 102

V

Val di Fassa, 54
Val di Sole, 48
Val Fersina, 54
Valsugana, 47, 52
Vatican, 52
Venice, 28, 43
Verein der christlichen Deutschen in der Bukowina, 79
Verein der deutschen Lesehalle zur deutschen Eiche, 69
Verlaine, Paul, 186
Vermiglio, 47
Victoria, Queen, 141, 146, 201–205, 214
Vienna, 4, 5, 13–16, 18–20, 27, 41, 47, 64, 68, 71–75, 79, 88, 92, 96, 98, 103–105, 117, 125, 128, 129, 139, 147, 150, 155, 168, 186, 207, 213
    Academy of Art, 73
    Capuchin Church, 5, 72, 128, 155
    Heeresgeschichtliches Museum, 38
    Heldenplatz, 38
    Herrengasse, 67
    Hofburg, 72, 141
    Josephsplatz, 64, 65, 67
    Leopoldstadt, 74
    Men's Choral Society, 72
    Musikverein, 73
    Operngasse, 73
    Ringstraße, 73, 212
    Schönbrunn Palace, 208
    Schwarzenbergplatz, 73
    stock market crash (1873), 166
    Stubenplatz, 73
    Theater an der Wien, 105
    Turkish/Ottoman sieges of, 14, 16
Vigo di Fassa, 54
Vogelweide, Walther von der, 18
Vysloužilec, 42

W

Wachau, 18
Wallenstein, Albrecht von, 17

Warnsdorf/Varnsdorf, 79
Warsaw, 118, 120
    Belvedere Palace, 118
Warsaw Pact, 1
Wenceslas IV, 19
White Mountain, Battle of, 95, 101
Wiener Allgemeine Zeitung, 128
Wiener Zeitung, 91
Wieniec, 123
Wilhelm I, German Emperor, 28, 206
Wilhelm II, German Emperor, 201, 204–207, 209, 214, 215
Winterhalter, Franz, 140
Wolf, Karl Hermann, 78
women
    dress code in Hungary, 145
    in patriotic politics, 53, 77, 121, 122, 143, 171
    rights for, 142
Woolf, Virginia, 142
Workers' movement, 101, 158, 230
World War I, 40, 55, 62, 78, 140, 156, 157, 178, 181, 184, 187–192, 201, 204

Y

Yiddish, 178, 180, 182, 193
Young Czechs, 69–71, 80, 92, 98, 101–103
Yugoslavia, 1, 30

Z

Zagreb, 27, 162–173, 225
    City Hall, 167
    Frankopan Street, 168
    Gradec (district), 168
    Ilica (street), 167, 168
    Jelačić Square, 167, 168, 171, 173
    Kapitol, 168
    Mesnička Street, 167
    University of, 165–167, 170
    Zrinjevac (street), 167
Zala, György, 157
Zichy, Mihály, 152
Zichy, Nándor, 148
Zionism, 7, 179, 183, 185, 186, 188
Zrinski, Nikola Subić, 170
Zrinyi, Count Miklós, 14, 16, 20
Zweig, Stefan, 12, 181
Zyblikiewicz, Mikołaj, 123

www.ingramcontent.com/pod-product-compliance
Lightning Source LLC
Chambersburg PA
CBHW071228080526
44587CB00013BA/1534